Co–Engineering Applications and Adaptive Business Technologies in Practice:
Enterprise Service Ontologies, Models, and Frameworks

Jay Ramanathan
The Ohio State University, USA

Rajiv Ramnath
The Ohio State University, USA

INFORMATION SCIENCE REFERENCE

Hershey · New York

Director of Editorial Content:	Kristin Klinger
Senior Managing Editor:	Jamie Snavely
Managing Editor:	Jeff Ash
Assistant Managing Editor:	Carole Coulson
Typesetter:	Sean Woznicki
Cover Design:	Lisa Tosheff
Printed at:	Yurchak Printing Inc.

Published in the United States of America by
    Information Science Reference (an imprint of IGI Global)
    701 E. Chocolate Avenue
    Hershey PA 17033
    Tel: 717-533-8845
    Fax: 717-533-8661
    E-mail: cust@igi-global.com
    Web site: http://www.igi-global.com/reference

and in the United Kingdom by
    Information Science Reference (an imprint of IGI Global)
    3 Henrietta Street
    Covent Garden
    London WC2E 8LU
    Tel: 44 20 7240 0856
    Fax: 44 20 7379 0609
    Web site: http://www.eurospanbookstore.com

Library of Congress Cataloging-in-Publication Data

Ramanathan, Jay, 1950-
 Co-engineering applications and adaptive business technologies in practice : enterprise service ontologies, models, and frameworks / by Jay Ramanathan and Rajiv Ramnath.
    p. cm.
 Includes bibliographical references and index.
 Summary: "This book provides knowledge that forms the basis for successful co-engineering of the adaptive complex enterprise for services delivery"-- Provided by publisher.
 ISBN 978-1-60566-276-3 (hardcover) -- ISBN 978-1-60566-277-0 (ebook) 1. Business--Data processing. 2. Business enterprises--Computer networks. 3. Business--Communication systems. 4. Information technology. 5. Management information systems. I. Ramnath, Rajiv, 1960- II. Title. HF5548.2.R27 2009 658'.05--dc22

2008055312

British Cataloguing in Publication Data
A Cataloguing in Publication record for this book is available from the British Library.

All work contributed to this book is new, previously-unpublished material. The views expressed in this book are those of the authors, but not necessarily of the publisher.

Advances in Information Resources Management (AIRM) Series

Editor-in-Chief: Mehdi Khosrow-Pour

ISBN: 1537-3367

Co-Engineering Applications and Adaptive Business Technologies in Practice: Enterprise Service Ontologies, Models, and Frameworks

Edited By: Jay Ramanathan, Ohio State University, USA; Rajiv Ramnath, Ohio State University, USA

Information Science Reference
Copyright 2009
H/C (ISBN: 978-1-60566-276-3)
Pages: 351
Our Price: $165.00

Co-Engineering Applications and Adaptive Business Technologies in Practice: Enterprise Service Ontologies, Models, and Frameworks provides knowledge that forms the basis for successful co-engineering of the adaptive complex enterprise for services delivery. Intended for practicing professionals, advanced students, and academicians, this book enables understanding of the deeper issues and challenges in applying IT to solve business problems.

Best Practices and Conceptual Innovations in Information Resources Management: Utilizing Technologies to Enable Global Progressions

Edited By: Mehdi Khosrow-Pour, Information Resources Management Association, USA

Information Science Reference
Copyright 2008
H/C (ISBN: 978-1-60566-128-5)
Pages: 428
Our Price: $195.00

Best Practices and Conceptual Innovations in Information Resources Management: Utilizing Technologies to Enable Global Progressions provides authoritative insight into emerging developments in information resources management and how these technologies are shaping the way the world does business, creates policies, and advances organizational practices. With chapters delving into pertinent aspects of such disciplines as knowledge management, open source software, systems engineering, project management, and IT governance, this book offers audiences solutions for improved organizational functioning.

Other Books in the Series:

Order Online at ww.igi-global.com or call 717-533-8845 x100 – Mon-Fri 8:30 AM - 5:00 PM (EST) or
Fax 24 Hours a Day 717-533-8661

Table of Contents

Section I:
Adaptive Complex Enterprise Framework: Characterization, Ontology, Principles, Work Products, and Patterns

Chapter I
Characterization of Service Orientation and the Adaptive Complex Enterprise 1

Chapter II
Adaptive Complex Enterprise Framework: Ontology, Modeling,

Chapter III
Governance and Conceptual, Logical and Installed Architecture

Chapter IV

Preface

MOTIVATION

What is the book about? This inter-disciplinary and integrative book combines recent evolutions in enterprise architectures and services to provide a prescriptive framework for the practitioner architect and the needed background for a researcher.

This book covers the:

- *Solution-driven* development and improvement of IT (Information Technology) services for Business Efficiency, Innovation and Agility.

Figure 1. The Adaptive Complex Enterprise framework provides integrated business and technical Co-engineering skills that can be applied to improve changing business processes and complex IT systems.

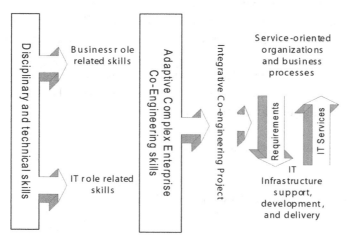

- *Methods* for practicing architects, business analysts, project managers, and software engineers to achieve solution success through creating *Work Products* that reflect a shared understanding of:
  - o Customer requirements
  - o Business goals
  - o Product/service life-cycle
  - o IT Infrastructure support needs
- *Context* for better IT-related decision making through alignment within the complex enterprise.
- *Integrates business and engineering knowledge needed for* practice and research through the Adaptive Complex Enterprise service ontology and framework. This integrated knowledge seeks to give students and professionals conceptual tools for improved practice and a basis for the formalization of experiential learning for further research advancement.

Why is this needed?

Dynamic economic context demands service agility and requires overcoming challenges in the way we:

- Govern complex Business-IT systems and their evolution
- Deal with constant change in underlying business Agents – organizations, processes, and technology components
- Deliver value despite significant business constraints

Motivating Adaptive Complex Enterprise (ACE) Frameworks for

- Adaptive architectures that deploy quickly to allow new behaviors to emerge
- Holistic, interdisciplinary work products that guide effective practice.
- Deeper principles critical to improved analysis, increased re-use, and reduced costs.
- Continued leverage of investments in installed enterprise systems.
- Formal and integrative interdisciplinary knowledge critical to useful academic advancement through leverage of industry practice.

What is the Adaptive Complex Enterprise (ACE)?

- Agents organized by a customer-provider service ontology representing their fine-grained interactions and value contributions (IDC 2007) [a]

- A conceptual framework by which we can continuously improve the value delivered by a complex system of business agents in dynamically changing environments
- A way to integrate the application of interdisciplinary business, systems engineering and IT methods and knowledge

Dynamic Context: Driven by a rapidly changing global environment that includes communications, competition, business growth, and technology innovation, 'services'[b] now account for a pre-dominance of the labor force in most economies. To thrive, the service enterprise must sense, respond, and adapt[c] to external conditions and leverage new opportunities (Haeckel 1999). In addition to addressing externally-driven uncertainty, the service enterprise must also embrace change and variation in interactions within its own organizations and systems that are getting more and more complex. These have been identified as issues to be addressed in the emerging field of *Services Science Management and Engineering*[d].

"Economic conditions like the recent recession are likely to make real-time delivery of products and services all the more attractive. Real-time enterprise technology can enable companies to answer queries instantly, monitor business on a continuous basis for quicker responses to shifting market conditions, and offer new products and services as new data becomes available. Behind the drive towards real-time enterprise is new hardware that gathers more real-world data than ever before, and software technology that eases or eliminates the trade-off between integration and flexibility. The technology is poised to have a tremendous effect on internal corporate operations while at the same time increasing the economy's fluidity--and possibly its turbulence[e]".

These trends severely challenge traditional disconnected business, technology, and architecture frameworks that are designed to manage within simpler and more static and environments. While IT (Information Technology) with SOA (service-oriented architecture concepts and related technologies) is now positioned, it is not yet practically implementable as a tool for the service economy. This requires the development of a new *integrated discipline* for managing complex systems. Such a discipline must enable new tools and methods that are responsive to the external environment, making adaptive behaviors possible. This book is a contribution towards that goal.

Motivating Adaptive Enterprise Frameworks: As companies seek to stay competitive and offer more services through product innovations and variations new processes and information needs arise. These needs are often not met despite the overall investment in enterprise applications (Gartner 2003)[f]. The resulting systems – composed of both organizations and software - are often found to be rigid (Nates

2003)[g]. To succeed we have to think of systems differently – as complex systems of made of a small number of interacting patterns[h].

Services innovation requires emergent architectures frameworks: Service-oriented organizations typically have the dual challenge of embracing complexity due to externally-driven variation while simultaneously managing the evolution of enabling complex IT systems. However, confusing build-versus-buy-versus-adapt options confront the businesses looking to overcome IT limitations. Of these, the buy option is usually pursued first. However, when off-the-shelf applications fall short, service-oriented organizations continue to invest in enterprise-level initiatives and custom integration to improve performance. These investments often fail to deliver the expected value and return. This is due to application challenges such as overlapping application functionality, existing lack of services, and the lack of a practice methodology for developing realistic estimates of costs and risks. It is no wonder that only a small fraction of enterprise projects are on time and on budget. As IT use gets more pervasive within the extended enterprise, these challenges make innovation and adaptation to externally-driven change even tougher. These challenges need to be jointly addressed by the Business and IT organizations. This requires enterprise architectures that can facilitate the emergence of new externally-driven adaptive behaviors.

Creational Versus Operational and Continual Improvement: Traditional Computer Science curriculum has focused primarily on the creational aspects of software and hardware systems. The challenges of enhancing the overall functionality and performance of a deployed system is left primarily unaddressed within the curriculum. With the increasing complexity of deployed systems, there is a need for continual improvement approaches that take a more systemic view and system engineering methods for creative tasks in the context of an operational system.

Holistic, interdisciplinary practice frameworks are required for effective practice. Thousands of relevant books and publications provide an explosion of information - strategies, initiatives, technologies, and practices – all promising to improve the performance of today's Business-IT systems. Five Forces, Balanced Scorecard, Enterprise Architecture frameworks, Customer Relationship Management, Enterprise Resource Management, Supply Chain Integration, Product Data Management, eStrategy, Re-engineering, World Class, Six Sigma, Total Quality Management, Just In Time, Lean, Concurrent Engineering, Enterprise Integration, Workflow Management, Middleware, Web services, Service-Oriented Architectures, Security, and Requirements and Organization Engineering are just a few among the topics covered.

However, this material is very poorly integrated for effective practice (Denning 2003, Armour 2003). Today's knowledge for engineering complex systems is at best descriptive, ad hoc, and pre-scientific[i]. Underlying principles are not abstracted for high-bandwidth communication and effective application by interdisciplinary implementation teams. How can we work locally in technical teams, yet make decisions that further overall business goals? When do we know that the issues we address are adequate and complete? When do we know when we have a truly new idea? How do we asses project impact on organizations and existing systems? How do useful best-practice frameworks relate in a deployment? How can we reduce custom code and reduce maintenance costs? These are just some of the questions that need to be addressed (Computing Curricula 2005).

Re-invention is in Part Due to Failure in Industry and Academic Collaboration. Despite the common elements across projects and businesses, most major IT projects in enterprise integration are often traditionally treated as "one-offs". Further, there is no shared *ontology* and basis for shared principles. The various disciplines involved understand the same enterprise integration concepts in a unique way. For example, the ubiquitous notion of a 'process' means different things to the distinct practicing disciplines of business, systems engineering, and computer science. To illustrate the point, a systems engineer will be concerned with the *behavior* of the process while the computer scientist is more concerned with the *representation* of process behavior.

Consequently, strategies for integration are not only re-invented on a project-by-project basis but left to the particular experiences of the team of practitioners[j]. With some exceptions, much of the needed knowledge is still proprietary and deployed at high costs. To counter the proprietary trends, both end customers and technology and service vendors such as IBM and Hewlett Packard promote open practices and re-use at the more conceptual levels (Herzum 1999).

While the practitioner, analyst, and academic communities have developed useful frameworks over the last few decades they typically have two shortcomings. Either they focus on a very limited *slice of the problem* or the problem is *too abstracted.* In either case research in successful IT practice and deployment is scarce. (See Denning 2003 for a discussion). Within academia green field assumptions also make research less relevant. Thus, unrelated and abstract frameworks lead to a lot of overlapping materials, inefficient communication, and re-invention without the evolution of fundamental underlying concepts.

Deeper Principles are Critical to Increased Re-Use and Reduced Service Costs. Service organizations often focus on *differentiation* as a competitive strategy; on the other hand the business return on IT is tied to increasing *reuse*. Businesses defining their success based on uniqueness are indeed different when examined on the *surface* but often very similar when represented at *deeper* levels (Long & Denning 1995)[k]. In contrast, requirements communicated at the *surface* level generates a remarkably diverse number of IT implementaions. If every IT need is treated as a unique service project, it becomes difficult for technology vendors and IT workers to provide IT supported solutions and systems that are cost effective.

What is the Adaptive Complex Enterprise (ACE)?

ACE is a conceptual view of the complex interactions between services provided by any collection of organizations and systems; and *Co-engineering* is the theory that allows us to analyze, reason about, and improve the ACE performance. The service-interaction-based ontology is also introduced as the basis of the ACE representation (Adaptive Complex Systems 2005). This dynamic structure allows us to create work products that surface performance issues that can be analyzed and Co-engineered.

The ACE framework herein is based on a *service interaction ontology* that provides a *deeper* approach for defining principles that can be taught, practiced, and researched. Leveraging the representational methods of computer science, the analysis techniques of systems engineering, and business decision-making, the ACE framework leads to a shared understanding and increased communication bandwidth for Co-engineering of the Business-IT attributes of complex systems. Requirements and solution cost-benefit tradeoffs can now be discussed at deeper levels. Thus richer dialog can now replace the feeling of helplessness and déjà vu felt by experienced project managers as they face a lack of understanding within each new project team. New tools and methods can be developed. The integrative framework is based both on recent technology advances and conceptual successes of Complexity Theory.

Co-engineering simultaneously engineers the *Business tactics, IT, Operations, and Strategy (BioS)* performance based on established business and systems engineering principles and technology. The *ACE framework,* including both the representation and the Co-engineering theory, builds upon transaction theory to integrate Porter's Model, The Balanced Scorecard, Lean, The Open Group Architecture Framework, Organizational Engineering, IT Infrastructure Library, Component Business Modeling, Business Process Management, Service-Oriented Architecture, and Autonomic Concepts.

The prescriptive performance-centered Co-engineering method integrates these proven and existing best practices at a deep level using precise service-interaction ontology. The result of Co-engineering is a *roadmap* for achieving overall complex system goals and business aspects, like risk management, value creation, return, and payback. Within the organization, business requirements for IT are more clearly defined and deployed to enable business service solutions.

Building upon the core of proven frameworks, Co-engineering also allows us to analyze the ACE Work Products and align performance to the value add desired by the BioS stakeholders. At the same time, it provides a framework to leverage emerging opportunities for managing complex IT systems better with IT itself. Such an *active ACE architecture* advances adaptation by providing a conceptual structure for real-time monitoring of the BioS layers. The alignment across the BioS is achieved by defining global policies for adaptation and providing the context for locally improving autonomous resources.

Using case studies throughout, we show how a small number of ACE framework patterns can be dynamically applied to permit local and lightweight implementations by teams of practitioners. Thus, the ACE framework provides a body of integrated knowledge for high-bandwidth communication and for implementation by inter-disciplinary project teams in a highly distributed fashion.

APPROACH

What is the ACE approach to Knowledge Integration?

- *ACE ontology* is based on the well-studied notion of a customer-provider 'interactions' needed to implement a business transaction using services and related patterns.
- *Captures horizontal and vertical nested interactions to* structure the associations between Business tactics, Business Processes, IT Infrastructure and Strategy.
- *Conceptual architecture and structure* allows measurements and application of Systems Engineering methods that relate IT and Business.
- *Facilitates the application of best practices* through this integrated performance-centered structure.

ACE further leverages the following concepts:

- Complex systems can be represented at ever-deeper levels using and re-using simple patterns that leverage component services.
- Patterns also relate global coordination policies to local business agents responsible for implementing change.
- Integrated framework for measurement leads to predictive and continuous improvement strategies and also improved global policies.
- Leverage technology for componentization and distribution.
- And, technology trends evaluated in the context of priorities and requirements.

Figure 2. ACE framework scope and integrated knowledge

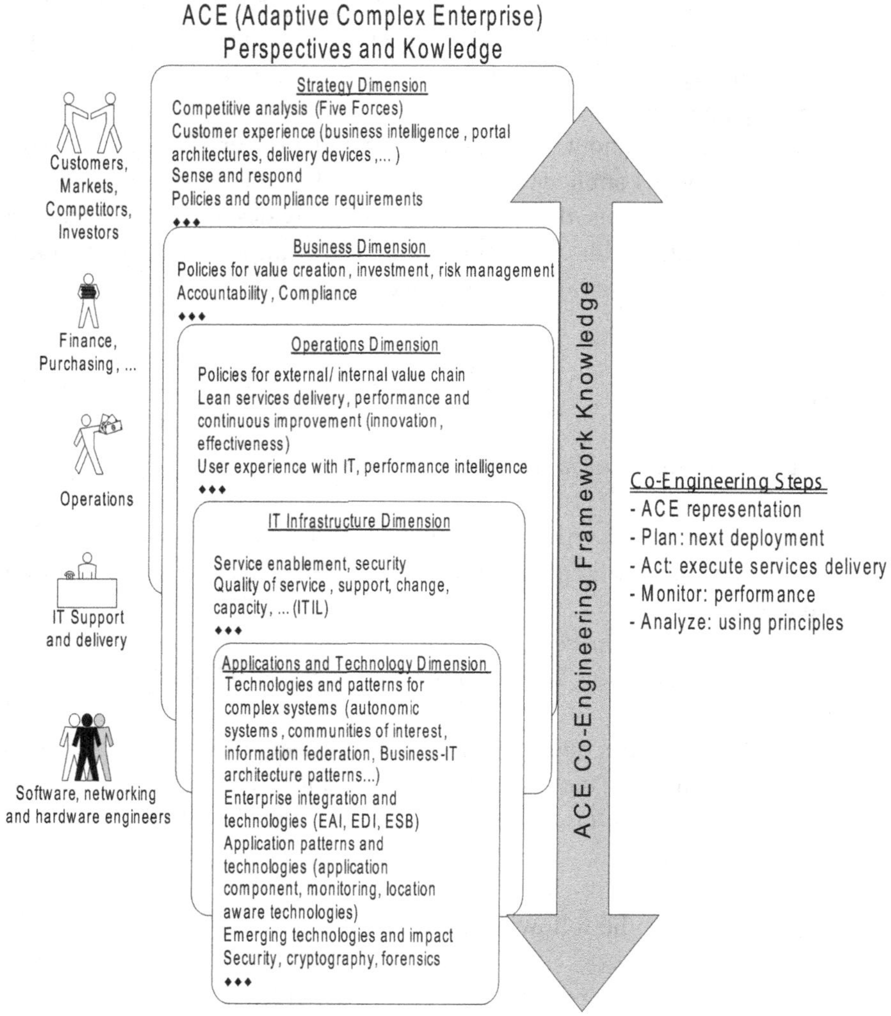

ACE (Adaptive Complex Enterprise)
Perspectives and Kowledge

Strategy Dimension
Competitive analysis (Five Forces)
Customer experience (business intelligence, portal architectures, delivery devices,...)
Sense and respond
Policies and compliance requirements
♦♦♦

Business Dimension
Policies for value creation, investment, risk management
Accountability, Compliance
♦♦♦

Operations Dimension
Policies for external/ internal value chain
Lean services delivery, performance and continuous improvement (innovation, effectiveness)
User experience with IT, performance intelligence
♦♦♦

IT Infrastructure Dimension
Service enablement, security
Quality of service, support, change, capacity, ... (ITIL)
♦♦♦

Applications and Technology Dimension
Technologies and patterns for complex systems (autonomic systems, communities of interest, information federation, Business-IT architecture patterns...)
Enterprise integration and technologies (EAI, EDI, ESB)
Application patterns and technologies (application component, monitoring, location aware technologies)
Emerging technologies and impact
Security, cryptography, forensics
♦♦♦

Customers, Markets, Competitors, Investors

Finance, Purchasing, ...

Operations

IT Support and delivery

Software, networking and hardware engineers

ACE Co-Engineering Framework Knowledge

Co-Engineering Steps
- ACE representation
- Plan: next deployment
- Act: execute services delivery
- Monitor: performance
- Analyze: using principles

Why is ACE effective?

- Provides us with a lens that focuses on dynamic variation and how customer - provider agents provide value when they react.
- Co-engineering refers to 'engineering in context'. Allows us to relate the agent interactions to goals that must improve though prescriptive actions.
- Addresses bounded rationality by permitting improved decisions without requiring detailed modeling of the enterprise.

- Spans Business, Systems Engineering and IT silos of knowledge. The technical and organizational ACE framework complements the business case method with measurement and predictive tools for proactive leverage using IT.

This is a book on service-interaction-based creation of value from business, information flow, operations, and technology performance perspectives. It is not just a book on any single aspect - such as integration, or security or compliance - but on an interaction language for representing and meeting *commitments between all the stakeholder and resource perspectives*. The result is a conceptual ACE representation of an enterprise with performance traceability that allows the Co-engineering of BioS perspectives. Thus the ACE framework allows service-oriented organizations to leverage the speed and dynamic flexibility provided by IT to run the ever more adaptive businesses. (See Christensen 2004 for the need for a more predictive capability and the special issues - Service Orientation 2007 and Services Science 2006 for and excellent background on services).

This book is an *evolutionary* one based on consolidated experiences of hundreds of companies. It is a book for the *successful introduction* of SOA projects into the services organization. And it is a book that describes more than planning for SOA implementation; it provides patterns for strategic planning, execution, and *improvement of business services using specific Work Products*. Finally, it is a book on *in-the-large and in-the-small ACE representation to empower teams* to identify and engineer the Business-IT tradeoffs through good decision making, investments, and implementations.

Thus, this is an integrative, rigorous, yet practical book intended for the advanced student or the practitioner with some real-world experience. It also identifies future research and opportunities for industry–university collaboration that is critical to furthering the discipline of *services science* (Services Science Management and Engineering). To this end, the book is presented in a manner suitable for the practitioner within a services organization and it also has extensive end-notes and annotated references into a vast body of knowledge in three disciplines - Business, Systems Engineering, and Computer Science.

The ACE and Co-engineering framework of this book has evolved over the last two decades of business process solution experience of the authors applying workflow technology to adapt industrial-age enterprise systems to enable new services and business processes. The underlying change-management patterns themselves have been abstracted and validated though projects with over a hundred and fifty different companies and the experiences of even larger communities such as International Standards Organization (e.g. ISO 9000, ISO 20000), Supply Chain Council, Object Management Group, OGC, ITIL, W3C, OASIS, and others.

The main motivation of this book is to provide knowledge that more successfully Co-engineers - anticipates and better predicts - and thus enables an organization to become an Adaptive Complex Enterprise for services delivery.

ACE Knowledge Integration

The approach taken in the ACE Framework is to define a small number of patterns based on the universal and fundamental ontology of customer-provider service transactions. The ontology serves to *unify* a selection of patterns and methods discovered and often re-discovered across the disciplines. (See Alexander 1999 for an overview of patterns).

Componentization: The recent progress in IT technologies, especially in the areas of middleware, workflow execution, and Web services, makes it possible to compose business process enabling solutions by leveraging existing applications (Berners-Lee 2001). There is now also a wealth of experience that allows us to re-use specifications and write adaptors to existing enterprise applications treating them as components within larger systems and business components (Herzum 1999). Vendors such as Hewlett Packard, IBM, and Microsoft and organizations like the OASIS[l], Object Management Group[m], W3C[n], TOGAF[o], and National Institute of Standards and Technologies[p] now represent the experiences of numerous companies in this area.

Complementing the Case Method with Predictive Approaches: Broadly speaking, the widely accepted case method[q] has been used to develop decision-making skills by focusing on the behavior of the business . Here within the business, the IT details are primarily treated as a *black box* (Christensen 1999). The Co-engineering method of this book *complements* the case method by *relating* the business behavior to its internal layers and dimensions - operations, execution, and IT. This treatment of the internal layers as a *white-box* enables teams to explore cause-and-effect relationships and better *predict* the exact areas of maximum system improvement and IT leverage. By reasoning about the internal workings of the Business-IT system, management can now better identify implementation strategies. In summary, for improved business management, the *black-box* case approach identifies the faults of omission. The *white-box* Co-engineering approach discovers faults of commission, pinpointing those parts of the system whose *implementation* is faulty and needs to be adjusted.

ACE can now be Represented at Ever-Deeper Levels Using a Single Pattern Framework: ACE is based on easy-to-learn patterns incorporating uncertainty – dynamically and recursively applied patterns called fractals (Mandelbrot & Freeman 1983)[r] - to elaborate each black box layer with white-box details, repeatedly (CACM 2005). Fractals allow all these internal dimensions to be represented and related more precisely with external events. Thus, macro-level business services and objectives are related to micro-level operating performance targets. The resulting structure now provides cause-and-effect traceability leading to better adaptation.

There is a growing and diverse community that has been applying fractals, and the more general Systems Theory (Skyttner 2005)[s], Complexity Theory (Kiel 1994, Kelly 1998), or Chaos Theory, to characterize and understand the behaviors of complex systems and the manner in which they respond to unexpected demands and changes in their environment. Some examples of these works and initiatives are reported within the Santa Fe Institute[t], the Next Generation Manufacturing (Jordan & Michel 2000, Kiel 1994)[u], and the European Union's Sixth Generation Framework[v]. In general, the exact use of Complexity Theory varies within projects. It has been applied as a model for simulations aimed at understanding growth in biological systems, fluctuations in economic systems, and turbulence in fluids. Complexity Theory also has been used to increase understanding through *analogy* between socio-economic systems and biological systems for greater understanding of socio-economic phenomena[w].

Continual Improvement: Finally, we integrate the concepts underlying Complexity Theory with the pattern in Deming 1982[x] - *plan, do, study, and act* - to locally improve the *service transactions* performed within the ACE at both in-the-large, for example business, and in-the-small; IT, dimensions. The service transaction is itself achieved through the interactions and services of the IT infrastructure made of people, processes, and software applications.

We use examples and case studies to show how the methods and principles can be deployed. By using them along with current technologies we can implement patterns for more flexible cost-effective SOA solutions for the enterprise. We will show how the ACE Co-engineering methods can form the basis for experimentation and science.

Audiences and Learning Objectives

The book is intended for the practicing professional and the advanced student in any of the disciplines of Computer Science, Operations Management, Management Information Systems, Systems Engineering, or Public Policy. Aimed at the advanced or mature student, the book uses an integrative interdisciplinary approach to applying materials from several disciplines to understand and solve concrete business problems using IT and other technologies, as and when applicable (Figure 1).

For practitioners at the executive and senior technical management levels with a background in business, operations, or information technologies, the book provides the precise knowledge necessary to understand and isolate the deeper issues and challenges in applying IT to develop solutions to business problems.

For the advanced senior or graduate student with work experience, the book should be used as part of an integrative program enabling the student to make deep linkages and thus better decisions in the professional world. It is expected that the student will participate in a practicum – such as a two-term *industry-sponsored and industry-relevant project* - applying the methods of the book. Basic project steps and deployment work products are introduced at the end of each chapter to facilitate the learning process.

Solution Architect: We introduce the *solution architect* role as an analyst that has the skills of both the *Business* and *IT systems analyst* to function as an integrator. The business-type benefits from the "white-box" approach followed here in many ways. The Co-engineering method *connects* the *Business analyst* and the IT *systems analyst* with Work Products and tools to negotiate the ACE solution tradeoffs *without* needing very detailed disciplinary knowledge.

Finally, the knowledge presented here benefits IT workers in *technology companies* as well as IT workers working in *companies with internal IT departments*. IT workers in technology companies can deliver products better targeted to the service economy. Similarly, IT workers within internal IT departments can better understand the larger context in which their services have to be delivered. For background, a basic knowledge of business strategy, cost accounting practices, project management, databases, programming, and process/data modeling is assumed. Knowledge of UML and sysML[y] is a requirement and is used to represent enterprise architectures.

Learning Objectives

The student or architect will learn to represent and manage the improvement of complex systems with the following skills:

- Ability to develop conceptual representations and Work Products of Business, IT infrastructure services, Operations, and Strategy and linkages and perform analysis.
- Ability to lead an interdisciplinary team and apply Co-engineering analysis methods to deploy effective and innovative service solutions.
- Ability to apply enterprise architecture concepts to deal with the *conflicting forces* in real-world situations. By articulating tradeoffs and through more complete decision-making, the student will be able to contribute towards successful communication and implementations within the organization.
- Ability to perform gap analysis to identify IT or Business services that have to be created or modified to meet business objectives.
- Ability to identify the role of emerging technology trends in innovation.

- Ability to facilitate decision making through a more thorough articulation of Functional (business) and Non-functional (operational) requirements.
- Ability to implement the governance needed for effective in-the-large and in-the-small program management.
- Ability to apply principles that take into account trade-offs between Business function and IT cost-factors and risks as in any engineering discipline.
- Ability to govern and deploy best practices (like ITIL, Lean, and SOA) more effectively.
- Ability to enable services using technologies (such as Enterprise Services Bus, Enterprise Application Integration, Electronic Data Interchange, J2EE, and architecture patterns).
- Ability to conduct research in the emerging field of services science.

The skills are based on an enterprise framework that brings order and meaning to observations that may otherwise seem chaotic. It explains complexity in a simpler manner by establishing principles. This positions the student to conduct future research in more predictive management techniques and technologies. With this knowledge, the student will be able to play the role of a solution architect within the organization.

Scope and Learning Objects

The scope of topics and relationships is presented in Figure 2. The ACE Co-engineering framework begins by analyzing external influences on the organization. These in turn create Strategy requirements that guide the Business, Operations, and the enabling IT infrastructure of the organization viewed as ACE. The Co-engineering principles help identify evolutionary and revolutionary methods for improvement. The related learning objects[z] are alos as illustrated Figure 2.

Finally, the chapters contain examples of the business-related IT problems solved by the prescriptive Co-engineering steps. They address the real world challenges using rigorous principles. We also include the rationale for why the prescriptive methods work. Typically this will be presented in the form of end notes and references that index into a large body of related knowledge in three disciplines. This background work is presented for academic pursuit and the main flow is not interrupted for the reader with primary interest in practice.

Thus this book is written as a framework and an organized introduction to a vast amount of related interdisciplinary knowledge and underlying concepts that are the basis for Co-engineering complex systems. Many ideas are also presented for additional research. An extensive glossary and templates are provided at the end. We also take advantage of links to Wikipedia and other accessible sources of reasonably factual information. The papers referenced here are selected for historical value and accessibility for the researcher[aa]. Finally, each chapter has suggested readings that form a good background for future chapters.

PREPARING FOR PROJECTS

The instructor is encouraged to identify enterprise architecture projects and project sponsors. Preferred sponsorship would be from the senior management looking to advance the use of IT to improve efficiency or for service innovation.

REFERENCES

Alexander, C. (1999 September/October). The Origins of Pattern Theory: The Future of the Theory, and the Generation of a Living World. *IEEE Software, 16*(5), 71-82.

Armour, P. (2003 September). Closing the Learning Application Gap. *Communications of the ACM, 46*(9), 27-31.

Author, A. (2004). *The Engineer of 2020*. Washington: National Academies Press.

Berners-Lee, T., Handler, J., & Lassila, O. (2001 May). The Semantic Web. *Scientific American*.

Adaptive Complex Systems. (2005 May). *Communications of the ACM*.

Christensen, C., Anthony, S., & Roth, E. (2004) *Seeing What's Next: Using the Theories of Innovation to Predict Industry Change*. Boston: Harvard Business School Press.

Computing Curricula 2005. (n.d.). Retrieved November 23, 2008, from http://www.computer.org/portal/pages/ieeecs/education/cc2001

Deming, W. E. (1982). *Out of the Crisis*. Cambridge: Massachusetts Institute of Technology, Center for Advanced Engineering Study.

Denning, P. J. (2003 November). Great Principles of Computing. *Communications of the ACM, 46*(11), 15-20.

Haeckel, S. (1999). *Adaptive Enterprise*. Boston: Harvard Business School Press.

Hammer, M., & Champy, J. (1993). *Reengineering the Corporation: A Manifesto for Business Revolution*. New York: Harper Business.

Herzum, P., & Sims, O. (2000). *Business Component Factory*. New York: John Wiley.

IBMSSME. (2008). http://www.research.ibm.com/ssme/ Accessed 2008.

Jordan, J., & Michel, F. (2000). *Next Generation Manufacturing*. London: J. Wiley.

Kelly, S., & Allison, M. (1999). *The Complexity Advantage*. New York: McGraw-Hill.

Kiel, L. (1994). *Managing Chaos and Complexity in Government*. San Francisco: Jossey-Bass Publishers.

Long, J. G., & Denning, D. (1995 January) Ultra-Structure: A Design Theory for Complex Systems and Processes. *Communications of the ACM, 38*(1), 103-120.

Mandelbrot, B. (1983). *The Fractal Geometry of Nature*. San Francisco: W.H. Freeman.

Natis, Y. V. (2003). Predicts 2004: Application Integration and Middleware. Gartner Report AV-21-8190, Gartner Research.

Official Introduction to the ITIL Service Lifecycle (Official Introduction). (2007). Stationery Office Books (TSO).

Service Orientation. (2007 November). *IEEE Computer, 40*(11).

Services Science. (2006 July). *Communications of the ACM, 49*(7).

Services Science Management and Engineering. (n.d.). Retrieved November 23, 2008, from http://www.research.ibm.com/ssme/

Shaw, M. (1990 November). Prospects for an Engineering Discipline of Software. *IEEE Software, 7*(6), 15-24.

Skyttner, L. (2006). *General Systems Theory*. City: World Scientific Publishing Company.

ENDNOTES

[a] According to IDC (Filing Information: March 2007, IDC #EMT1P, Volume: 1) Business transaction Management (BTM) is an emerging IT management

concept that can potentially address both IT complexity and business alignment requirements. At its essence, BTM is aimed at detecting and resolving problems at the granular level of interactions between IT elements that form a business transaction (e.g., online stock trade, travel booking).

[b] Some aspects of services: Close interaction between supplier and customer, Nature of knowledge created and exchanged, Simultaneity of production and consumption, Combination of knowledge into useful systems, Exchange as processes and experience points, Exploitation of ICT and transparency (Services Science 2006, p 37).

[c] In Haeckel 1999, the need for service businesses to be externally facing organizations in order to be responsive to changing market requirements is motivated.

[d] This, according to a recent May 2006 Summit, motivates the need for a 'Services Science Management and Engineering'(IBMSSME 2008).

[e] While this is a post Dot Com observation according to the Economist 2002, it well applies to the more recent mortgage crises and future unanticipated events.

[f] Gartner Dataquest (August 2003) forecasts - $536 billion worldwide IT services industry will grow through 2007 to reach $707 billion, with a compound annual growth rate of 5.7 percent. . Financial services providers have learned to bargain with IT services providers but remain dissatisfied with business case development for IT investments.

[g] According to Gartner Research (Natis 2003) industry trend is to replace monolithic, isolated application stovepipes by systems that are partitioned, distributed, integrated and designed-to-be-integrated. A third option of composing systems is being introduced to the more traditional build versus buy decision. However, much research needs to be done in this new arena of coexistence and cooperation of independent components. "Reducing complexity will be imperative to the software industry if it is to avoid massive setbacks and user revolts", according to Natis. The treatment of evolving business requirements, changing software components, and organizations as the Adaptive Complex Enterprise puts forth a framework for reducing the complexity of software engineering, deployment and maintenance. By treating complexity as approached in this book we will contribute towards engineering principles in the design, development and maintenance of complex systems.

[h] Alexander's pattern theories are among those few which have been perceived as so inspiring, or perhaps so fundamental, that they have successfully crossed over and taken root in disciplines for which they were never originally intended for. In this keynotes address, Alexander welcomes the integration of his ideas into the computing profession and hints that he believes it may have a deeper

relevance in this new field than it has thus far been able to acknowledge, perhaps because it has been taken too literally. When computer scientist are introduced to patterns they are often presented chiefly as time saving devices, or little chunks of information that can be written down nicely and referenced as building blocks when new problems are introduced. But do they play a role in a large process and can they truly be generative from a systems building perspective?

[i]   An early paper (Shaw 1990) describes evolution of a typical engineering discipline. In comparison with a typical engineering discipline software engineering is still an art. The evolution of software engineering will require a good coupling between the practice and underlying science.

[j]   Armour 2003 has a good discussion of the devastating effect of this "knowledge gap" on project success. This is also discussed in (Clements, Kazman, Klein 2002).

[k]   Early work (Long and Denning) illustrates differences between deep versus shallow systems. Additionally in the field of artificial intelligence, shallow knowledge is said to be task dependent, additive and brittle. On the other hand deep knowledge is said to be task independent, describes underlying causal relations, and is complete at a certain abstract level.

[l]   OASIS: http://www.oasis-open.org/home/index.php

[m]   OMG - http://www.omg.org/

[n]   W3C http://www.w3.org/

[o]   TOGAF The Open Group Architectural Framework. How does TOGAF help deliver an effective IT architecture? TOGAF represents the world's best practice in IT architecture development: Developed by the members of the Open Group, a not-for-profit body consisting of experienced users and vendors working in combination. Based on Commercial Off-The-Shelf (COTS) open standards. Genuinely vendor-neutral. Does not imply or favor any particular technology or paradigm. Backed by tools and professional services that are similarly independent of specific technology solutions, are practical, and reduce the costs of planning, designing, and implementing architectures based on open systems solutions. Endorsed by a body representing 25% of the world's computing purchasing power. Demonstrated to work in practice by leading user organizations, who have documented their experiences in case studies that are freely available for review ..Available in the public domain (published by the Open Group on it's Web site http://www.opengroup.org)

[p]   NIST – National Institute of Standards and Technologies. Enterprise Integration projects.

[q]   Case method - http://en.wikipedia.org/wiki/Case_method

r   The conceptual ACE *patterns presented here are* based both on recursive Interactions at different scales associated with Complexity Theory as well as the problem solving pattern template approach, forming the basis for re-use and extensibility.

s   International Society for Systems Science: http://isss.org/world/index.php

t   Santa Fe Institute: http://en.wikipedia.org/wiki/Santa_Fe_Institute.

u   In Next Generation Manufacturing: Methods and Techniques (Jordan & Michael 2000) manufacturing consortium projects using Holonics (http://www.cam-i.org/ngms) as part of the Intelligent Manufacturing System is described.

v   European Commission: http://ec.europa.eu/research/index.cfm.

w   Kiel 1994 provides an overview of the concepts of chaos theory and the science of complexity and demonstrates how public administrators can apply these concepts and create a new paradigm of organizational change and transformation of government.

x   Deming is known as the father of quality. Deming stressed the need for Profound Knowledge, consisting of four parts 1) Appreciation of a system: understanding the overall processes involving suppliers, producers, and customers (or recipients) of goods and services, 2) Knowledge of variation: the range and causes of variation in quality, and use of statistical sampling in measurements, 3) Theory of knowledge: the concepts explaining knowledge and the limits of what can be known, and 4) Knowledge of psychology: concepts of human nature. Deming cycle provides a prescriptive process for applying this in the Plan, Do, Study, Act.

y   SysML: http://www.sysmlforum.com/FAQ.htm, expresses systems engineering semantics for requirements management and performance analysis and facilitates automated verification and validation (V&V) and gap analysis. SysML model management constructs support the specification of models, views, and viewpoints and are architecturally aligned with IEEE-Std-1471-2000 (IEEE Recommended Practice for Architectural Description of Software-Intensive Systems).

z   A learning object has been defined in the following ways. An entity, digital or non-digital, that may be used for learning, education or training, web-based interactive chunks of e-learning designed to explain a stand-alone learning objective. More at http://en.wikipedia.org/wiki/Learning_object

aa   And hence we have not included many specialized journal references that address very limited aspects of the solution.

Acknowledgment

We would like to acknowledge the support of our many industry sponsors including City of Columbus, IBM, Nationwide, Ohio Health, OSU Medical Center, McGraw Hill, Motorola, and many others. In addition we would like to thank the various project managers and graduate students, many of whom provided insights or written materials as part of class projects that are incorporated here. In particular we would like to name Joe Bolinger, Krista Dombroviak, Randally Glassgow, Brett Gerke, Vasudha Gupta, Greg Horvath, Farha Mukri, and Kelly Yackovic. The authors would also like to acknowledge the IBM Faculty Grant and the NSF IUCRC grant #0753710 which was fundamentally instrumental in enabling the collaboration with industry and conducting the projects needed to write this book. Finally we would like to thank our families for their support.

Jay Ramanathan and Rajiv Ramnath

Section I
Adaptive Complex Enterprise Framework:
Characterization, Ontology, Principles, Work Products, and Patterns

Chapter I
Characterization of Service Orientation and the Adaptive Complex Enterprise

ABSTRACT

We begin with a characterization of service challenges and a conceptualization of a complex service enterprise as a collection of organizations and sub-organizations. Each organization is in turn in an internal cycle of adaptation characterized by **BioS** - **B***usiness value achieved through an* **I***nformation infrastructure enabled* **O***perations to deliver on* **S***ervice Strategy.* The overview of this conceptualization is illustrated in the Figure 1 and Figure 2. The questions addressed are as follows:

- How can we characterize service enterprises and their challenges?
- What are the challenges of externally-driven services organizations?
- How can we characterize and address the differences from more traditional industrial-age organizations?
- How can we conceptualize a more adaptive performance-driven service enterprise?
- What are the parts of the underlying framework for improvement?

The *car manufacturing enterprise* is used to quickly introduce and illustrate important concepts such as agility, innovation, resilience, effectiveness, sense and

Figure 1 (left): Challenges of the many-to-many interactions across the service layers of the externally-driven enterprise. Figure 2 (right): Adaptive Complex Enterprise conceptualization and the underlying infrastructure of Interacting Agents.

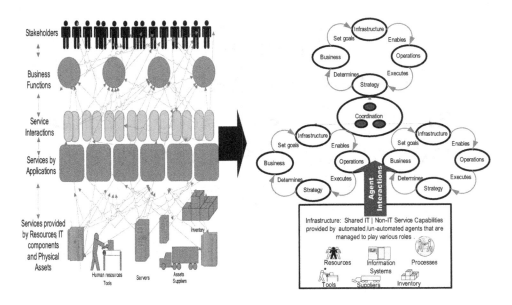

respond, vertical and horizontal alignment. In addition we characterize influences on a complex Business-IT system:

- Service delivery challenges due to Routine and non-Routine services
- Multiple stakeholders
- Chaos due to change, variation, and service layers
- Vertical BioS alignment as well as horizontal customer-provider alignment
- Trends and the Strategic role of IT
- Changing the business versus running the business
- Underlying Enterprise Architectures (EA) and Related Methods

We conclude with the Scope and parts of the Adaptive Complex Enterprise (ACE) framework.

THE SERVICE DELIVERY CHALLENGE

According to the definition accepted by the U.S. Government (Hill 1977): "A service is a change in the condition of a person, or a good belonging to some economic entity, brought about as the result of the activity of some other economic entity, with the approval of the first person or economic entity."

Due to external conditions service requirements between organizations evolve rapidly. Strategically speaking, typical service-oriented *organizations*[a] thus no longer have the luxury of long disjoint planning-followed-by-execution cycles. They must sustain[b] themselves using *sense-and-respond* strategies and quickly adapt to provide value towards *externally-driven goals*[c] (Haeckel 1999). Further, such organizations can also no longer be viewed independent of their enabling IT systems (Kapoor et al. 2005). To illustrate these points, we use the *automotive enterprise* - including car racing, manufacturers and suppliers - to introduce underlying business concepts and vocabulary. These concepts will be used to develop an integrated Business-IT framework for improvement.

Sense-and-Response and Agility: You are at the Indy 500 race car competition. Now imagine trying to win the race with the team or a system – hydraulic, airflow, or fuel –performing at sub-optimal levels. Success will not happen! To win, the driver and the pit crew have to sense-and-respond[d] to the weather and road conditions in real-time, during each lap of the race itself! The driver and the pit crew must work simultaneously and also 'as one' making strategy decisions while assessing the strengths and weaknesses of the competition. Working against time, each member uses precise instrumentation and information to provide expert services and coordinate with others to squeeze every drop of performance[e].

Stakeholders: Today's customers, investors, managers, and workers - stakeholders of an organization - agree that like the challenges of winning at Indy, extreme competition and economic conditions require agility to face externally-driven change (Freeman 1984)[f]. Further, the organization must deliver different types of value to achieve success and this depends on the perspectives of the many different stakeholders. For example, the *value* for racing fans is different from that that of the car maker or the sponsor or the investor. A good strategy requires us to identify and address all goals from the different stakeholder perspectives (Ramnath 2008). See Lynch 1990 for important behavioral insights on achieving goals.

Innovation: Many would also say that the winning high-performance cars at the Indy have also been a source of both design inspiration and product branding for car companies. However, new sources of inspiration also arise around the globe leading to a very competitive climate. Engineering *innovation* needed to meet extreme requirements has lead to the announcement of a new innovation by the CEO of Tata[g]. The recently announced 'Nano' car was designed to replace the motorcycle.

By keeping in mind the safety and mobility needs of the average motorcycle user, the company pioneered technology resulting in the recently announced car, and thus opening up new markets. Innovation and agility are thus often two goals of any organization.

Non-routine and Routine Services/Custom Products: Shifting now to business tactics and operations within the company, car manufacturers (also known as OEMs[h]) struggle to put out new competitive models. They also steadily look for ways to reducing operational costs by out-sourcing more *routine* parts of their operations. At the same they also wish to provide their dealers with more and more flexibility.

Exploring further the specific context for the suppliers of the OEM we illustrate some of the dramatic changes that are occurring in their environment. From a sup-

---

Highlight: An engineer-to-order example illustrating the supplier's operational challenges of handling non-routine requests from multiple OEMs

Events beyond control often govern how a supplier operates in an externally-driven business operation. Take the case of a first-tier engineering and custom manufacturing firm. According to the CEO:

What we need are systems supporting the way people respond to challenges of incoming Requests. Our engineers work in a very dynamic environment. Each engineer works on a task, and discovers the new customer, business, and technical requirements to define the next chunk of work to be undertaken. The engineer often asks other engineers to help with certain sub-deliverables and proceeds to make his or her own commitments. With all these hand-offs we lose program status, visibility, and cost control across projects.

To stay competitive, my business must learn to deal with unpredictable business events and still retain the ability to go after new business. But, I feel I have no visibility into what new business I can take on and how it will impact current operations. I am frustrated by the use of spreadsheets which contain valuable status information!

Within organizations that handle non-routine Requests, managers and workers in diverse professions – health care, telecommunications, aircraft manufacturing, software development, financial services, insurance, banking, and clothing - can all relate to this. The response process for a non-routine Request often takes on a life of its own because Murphy's Law prevails in the real world.

Non-routine Requests: Typically due to new customer requirements, new suppliers, new processes, and new product offerings - involve considerable discovery during the response. The characterization below illustrates the Requirements, Execution and Delivery challenges during the response.

Requirements:

o   The Request requirements are often not fully understood and competition is stiff

o   Designs are provided in a variety of different forms and formats and have to be converted

o   Quotes and time commitments are due even though all the execution plan details are not known

o   Engineers are waiting on responses from other engineers and suppliers on portions of the quote response

o   Quotes are often submitted by using the good old rule of thumb – multiply all estimates by two

o   The resources (including suppliers, capacity, capability, etc.) to handle the Request is not fully known

o   The ability to meet the customer's date may make the difference for winning the business

Execution:

o   The capacity to handle the Request may not be available at the time authorization is received

o   Meeting the committed date is uncertain leading to expediters and that makes the problem worse

o   The processes to implement different Requests vary since variations are discovered along the way

o   Quality is wanting because information is lacking

o   Processes are difficult to enforce across organizations

o   Management has no visibility to help prioritize tasks for improved throughput

o   Information necessary for successful execution is inconsistent and maintained in multiple systems

o   With increasing numbers of internal and external individuals involved, security gets more challenging

o   Execution tracking is difficult because of the information flow gaps due to internal and external suppliers used in the response

Delivery:
- o   Then there are challenges of outbound logistics
- o   Often collection of payment is not triggered in a timely fashion

From the business perspective, the cash-to-cash cycle is unnecessarily extended due to customer disputes and since no one is really sure when all the requirements are met. Overall, the profit margins are also shrinking due to price pressures. It is often not totally clear whether a given job actually made the expected profit or how to fix operational problems.

pler perspective, the demand from any one OEM is unfortunately becoming less predictable. To survive the supplier thus has to be able to service multiple OEMs. That is, the supplier has to become more *service-oriented*, providing engineering and design services to provide components that successfully enable multiple new models for multiple OEMs to be marketed within ever-compressing cycle times.

Hence the supplier has to learn to manage externally-driven change through *agile* practices. This will allow the supplier to deal with different ripples of design changes not only from the OEM but also due to the effects of actions by other suppliers. Imagine the overall complexity of changes due to a new car model design rippling through thousands of suppliers around the globe.

All this requires the typical supplier to think differently. Previously suppliers were used for the manufacturing and distribution of larger quantities of components. Addressing a more predictable demand, they also use established internal processes, resources, applications, and suppliers to optimize costs. Thus, few changes are made when responding to new orders. By and large, available enterprise applications serve most of the underlying requirements well.

Characterization of Non-Routine Requests and Services

However, as these suppliers shift to provide new services dealing with changes to multiple car designs, chaos often results within their engineering organizations. The Highlight example above illustrates the point within the operations of a supplier.

Request: We use the term *Request* here to generally refer to requirements from the customer in a wide range of forms - custom orders, routine orders, service calls, proposal requests, new application requirements, incidents, emergencies, technology changes, defect reports, and even new product/process requirements. *Requests* from the customer require a response. At a high level, requests can be of many types and can also be generally classified as *routine or non-routine.*

Figure 3. Shift from routine requests to non-routine requests drives the complex enterprise to deal with variation through new business and process behaviors.

Service – oriented Enterprise	Non -Routine Request:
	Many Request Types
	Small quantities
	Demand unpredictable
Routine Request:	Quantities not well-determined
Fewer request types	Processes discovered, volatile processes
Demand predictable	Capabilities not fully specified
Quantities determined	Matrix organizations
Processes known	Shared resources, availability of resources not
Capabilities known	predictable
Hierarchical organizations	Knowledge workers (human in the loop for decision
Dedicated resources	making) with flexible capabilities
Data management systems	Information varies with time, more unstructured
Strategies like make-to-stock are viable	information
Production in larger quantities and	Custom servicing
higher throughput rates through	Lean becomes a requirement
automation and routine processing	Automation not always effective

We use Figure 3 to summarize the characteristics of the related business processes. In a continuum of organization types, the 'industrial age' ones are on the left and deal with small numbers of *routine Request* types with known requirements, known demand, and predictable resource needs[i]. These are also referred to *make-sell*[j] organizations since they can anticipate demand to deal with more *routine Requests*, and they have leveraged this to make their processing more efficient.

As mentioned before, such organizations typically also have effective enterprise systems[k] in place to manage the business objects[l] and their underlying data. Within such organizations, IT has often automated specific processes by statically connecting X-to-Y. That is *everything-to-everything* involved in the business – organizations, systems, locations, etc. In today's jargon this often means business-to-customers, business-to-suppliers, business-to-employees, business-to-divisions, and even business-to-products in the field. Until recently, 'connecting' has mainly meant providing data access and point-to-point movement of data between systems and organizations in *pre-determined* ways and, often, at significant costs.

While certain parts organizations of an enterprise can remain in this mode, many others parts are compelled to evolve to the right of the continuum in the face of fierce global competition. These are also referred to *engineer-to-order or mass-customization* (Pine 1993). In this space, since customers have an increasing number of choices, businesses survive by offering increasingly unique services to win the business[m].

Organizations dealing with *non-routine Requests* are often said to be more 'external' or request-driven and opportunistic[n]. In this space every incoming Request is a little different, so anticipating demand (i.e. future Requests and arrival rates) and using captive resources becomes a less viable strategy for efficiency. These businesses must learn to internally deal with variation and volatility. Managing this type of product | process lifecycle is challenging as it also requires managing the *many-to-many* relationships (illustrated in Figure 1) that are varying. The challenge is to manage relationships between services provided by a variety of different human and system resources to meet a variety of stakeholder goals. Management in this space thus requires dealing with the following realities.

Request Variability: Custom responses to Requests (sometimes referred to as mass customization) require an increase of knowledge-based services to understand requirements. There is also a large variety in the types and numbers of incoming Requests. Even though variability has increased in the response, competitive pressures often mean that the ability to respond predictably by the customer's desired date may make the difference between winning and losing the business.

Virtual Strategy: With increasing Request variability, the pre-allocation of specialized or knowledge resources can prove to be very expensive. This leads businesses to explore 'virtual' strategies (Putnik and Cunha 2005). An organization is defined to be 'virtual' if it dynamically links its business goals with the procedures needed to achieve them. To be more specific, Requests for a custom product are satisfied by dynamically assembling the necessary infrastructure services. Examples of these are human resources, information resources, and specialized components from suppliers that meet the requirements. With the advent of the Internet, the virtual organization and collaboration practices are now almost mandatory and with this a stronger case for e-Business and IT-based enterprise integration is emerging.

Knowledge Workers: In many cases, the responses to individual Requests require product | process design and proposal iterations among the knowledge workers. Multiple resources from internal organizations and / or external suppliers as well as information from different applications have to be assembled. These should enable custom services and quantities to be delivered at more competitive costs.

Agents and Adaptive Responses: The responses to non-routine Requests must also enlist the needed services of underlying business *Agents* (i.e. internal /external organizations and workers, primary[o] and secondary processes, IT systems and assets). Since each Agent (or a group of Agents) has a certain collection of skills or capabilities to play different *roles* at specific cost, understanding the service requirements of each Request before assigning tasks for effective processing becomes more important. Finally, given the uncertainty in the arrival of Requests, the *availability* of the Agents also becomes uncertain. In these circumstances 'triage' or dynamic assignment based on business rules becomes important. This is one way in which the responses can adapt.

Viewed another way, most organizations are themselves made up of a mix of *both* traditional *make-and-sell[p]* organizations and *service-oriented sub*-organizations. They have to continuously look for opportunities to make the non-routine more routine. For example, the assembly of quantities of standard configuration laptops is *make-sell* process, whereas the repair of the same laptops is a customized *service*. In an organization which offers both these options, the repair organization might use the assembly services of its sister organization. Dynamic adaptation strategies that allow organizations to mange responses to non-routine Requests and embrace variation to deliver increasing *value*.

Time-variant Information and Decision-Making: A typical non-routine response requires an increasing amount of time-variant information to be synthesized for decision-making. To illustrate this, consider information like a standard component description, a patient's insurance information, or a customer's address. This type of information does not change rapidly and neither does is affect the decision making during the course of the service. For example, the shipping address is not likely to change decision making during a response. In contrast, during custom responses to non-routine Requests, information such as customer-specific design is changed and generated during the process of the response itself. That is, new information is derived based on upstream decisions made during the response to the incoming Request.

Examples of this include a new component design, a new customer's requirements, or a patient's vital signs. When a patient comes into an emergency room, diagnostic procedures result in decisions that in turn derive additional diagnostics and decisions. Similarly, a design change results in other engineering decisions and changes. Thus, the knowledge worker responds not just to facts in a database but also to other decisions made upstream by other knowledge workers. This is achieved by prompting, recording, and flowing these decisions during practice. In addition monitoring and mining this information is also important for the decision-making process and for insights that influence the evolution of future practice. Overall time-variant information is often critical to the quality of downstream tasks - as critical as passing the accumulating collections of documents (Quershi and Keen 2005). The related organizational and technological practices are referred to as an *Enterprise Knowledge Infrastructure or EKI* (Maier 2005).

Business Process Lifecycle and Volatility: We can observe from Figure 1 that each type of service identified on the left relies on other layers. As each particular service evolves, other services also evolve. Consequently, while enabling higher-level organizational improvements to achieve a return on investment, interactions across the layers of the enterprise must be considered. Change in any layer is due to a variety of factors - time-variant information causes processes to be volatile, changes in the business events and the physical world causes a ripple effect in the electronic world, and so on. Thus, each of the layers are impacted both due to changes external to the organization and internal changes from the organizational layers above and below. Thus typical project efforts to improve the features of such systems do not succeed well (Boehm 2000)[q]. One reason is that such systems cannot be locally and easily improved. At the same time few analytic methods exist to identify synergistic requirements in the physical and electronic worlds and achieve effectiveness.

Resilience: From an OEM perspective, the ability to execute business processes reliably is critical. The ability to withstand disruption or discontinuities due to external or internal systemic conditions is called resilience (Hamel & Valikangas 2003). One example is along the supply chain - a single point of failure of a critical component delivery and supplier due to an *external* catastrophic event like a hurricane could be disastrous. An *internal* example of the same is if a enterprise server goes down due to the high volume of website hits resulting from an advertisement campaign. To achieve resilience, the underlying service Agents - suppliers, servers, etc. - have to ensure that potential problems are identified well in advance of the failure and processes are followed for remedial action.

CHARACTERISTICS OF AN ADAPTIVE COMPLEX ENTERPRISE

ACE and BioS Traceability: Here we introduce and define the ***Adaptive Complex Enterprise (or ACE)*** [r] *Framework* as a *conceptual* way to view *any services enterprise.* The term 'complex' is used as in Complexity Theory. By acknowledging the fact that a system is complex we look for simple, recursive patterns for managing more effectively. For example, we will present patterns by which service-oriented

*Figure 4. The BioS chain - Business **sets goals** that determines the Infrastructure that **enables** the Operations which **executes** the services Strategy - that exists for each service within the Adaptive Complex Enterprise.*

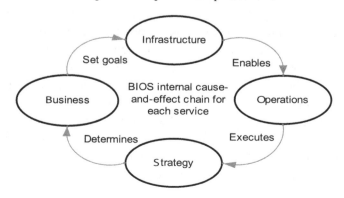

organizations can better deal with non-routine Requests (and of course routine Requests) and underlying variability.

The first repeating pattern of interest is BioS which underlies each of the services delivered by ACE. The BioS dimensions and the acronym arises from the cause-and-effect cycle illustrated in Figure 4: Business sets goals *that determine the* Infrastructure *that* enables *the* Operations *which* executes *the services* Strategy.

This cause-and-effect chain integrates and reflects core contributions of the service layers of Figure 1 and stresses the importance of going beyond financial measures to run a company successfully. More specifically, important thought leaders have stressed:

- Process Improvement *improves* Product Quality *leading to* Customer Satisfaction *resulting in* Business Increase *impacting* Jobs and Economic Growth (Deming 1982). The underlying chain is: O⇨S.
- Infrastructure Learning and Growth *results* in Improved Business Processes *ensuring* Customer Satisfaction *resulting* in Business value to Shareholders (Kaplan 1992). The underlying chain is: I⇨O⇨S⇨B.
- Competitiveness of the service is vital to business sustainability (Porter 1979). The underlying chain is: S⇨B.

Respectively, each stressed the traceability along the cause-and-effect chains as key to improvement, and hence the significance of BioS. Note that in our case we include IT as part of the 'Infrastructure'. The overall benefit of focusing on the BioS of each service is performance-based decision-making and local empowered adaptation contributing value to all *stakeholders* – Business, Infrastructure, Operations[s], and Strategy or BioS stakeholders.

ACE provides the global policies and coordination across the individual BioS cycles (as illustrated in Figure 5 which is a refinement of Figure 4). That is ACE defines and direct how each BioS cycle itself evolves during the service life cycle. This is illustrated in Figure 5 which has two types of arrows between the BioS nodes:

- The inner arrow can cycle determines the tactical value contribution.
- The outer dashed arrow determines the strategic value and continual improvement during the lifecycle of the services taken as a whole.

ACE thus adapts to external variation and, despite volatile business processes, successfully manages BioS *cycles and the lifecycles for each service.* The cycles are accomplished by Agent *Interactions* and the resulting value contributions met from the perspective of the BioS stakeholders.

Figure 5. The BioS value chain for tactical operations is identified by the inner arrows. The continual improvement of BioS during the service life-cycle is illustrated by the outer dashed arrows. These arrows refine those in Figure 4.

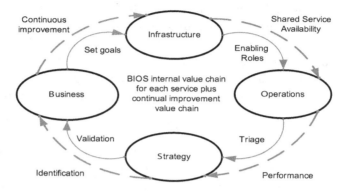

We can now present the complete ACE as having four perspectives or *dimensions* with the continual improvement cycles for *each service*. As a result we have the following eight responsibilities within the organization.

Business: The service value to stakeholders and the costs are together considered and prioritized, relative to other services. The services provided by the business are identified and continuously improved. Related responsibilities are:

1. *Set goals (tactical)* of the service based on actual value delivered, considering all stakeholders.
2. *Continual improvement (Strategic)* actions taken to enhance, create, or retire one or more services to achieve the future to-be state. Set priorities across services.

Infrastructure and information use: Related responsibilities are to manage:

3. *Enabling Roles* consisting of the types of Agents needed and the services they will deliver for *use within the end service*. Artifacts and decision-making services are provided by Agents. This is enabled by IT's management of information for operations. Not only are decisions and process variations recorded, but they are mined for improved performance achievement (Goldberg 1992).
4. *Shared service availability:* Agents that are shared resources are managed for conflicting demands and their use optimized through rules across the many on-going responses that have to be satisfied. Composite shared services that are needed partly in the physical world (e.g. inventory management, assem-

bly, installation) and partly in the electronic world (e.g. inventory and work order management software), are made available in a coordinated fashion for Operations.

Operations: We use the term 'operations' to mean *both the business process design and its execution.* Related responsibilities are:

5. *Request Triage* examines the Requests coming into the organization and classifies the types and requirements and assigns available resources so that their processing becomes more predictable[t].
6. *Interaction metrics:* The end service is delivered as a result of an interaction of Agents that produce the deliverable. Service response metrics to a Request employing other services by shared resources are also recorded. All results of execution including variations and exceptions are reported for future improvement.

Strategy: Related responsibilities are:

7. *Validation:* using metrics to determine the achievement of customer and business performance goals.
8. *Service strategy identification:* defining new services and for these and existing services define the competitive service value and stakeholders goals.

Note the *eight* steps cover both the service business cycle and the continual improvement life cycle. Thus the overall management is based on empowered teams that execute and improve BioS cycles based on overall ACE policies. In addition, metrics are captured in a variety of ways. These metrics are more critical for non-routine services performance than for standard products and routine services since there is so much process variation. Also, new knowledge is constantly create due to the time-variant information and thus knowledge management itself becomes more important as we shall see.

What is the Applicability of ACE? We first note that while ACE framework can derive benefits when automated and used to monitor existing systems; it begins to provide *immediate incremental value even when applied manually.* By looking at an enterprise through the ACE BioS *lens,* we can identify and improve the service-oriented tactics of the organization to better meet primary[u] (and secondary) goals. The tactics can include complex interactions between nested or inter-dependent organizations and can include primary processes, enabling IT departments, or even a supply chain.

The ACE framework provides a conceptual way to manage for effectiveness, innovation, and resilience within the externally-driven enterprise. Before we present this, we will first build on the characterization of ACE given above and present the underlying ontology[v] (see Gruber 1995 for a definition) in the next chapter.

For now we note that the BioS dimensions help us group the organization's stakeholders and their interests in specific service value contributions. We also note how this characterization is fine-grained enough to meet the organizational service goals by using ACE as a tool to:

- Sense new service opportunities by monitoring trends in non-routine Request types[w] that arise in the external environment and respond by assembling routine and, if needed, *non-routine* capabilities *in new ways* to deliver new services.
- Enable *dynamic* Agent Interactions and responses to address Request variation, demand variation, and process variation.
- Enable *autonomous Agents* with accurate information for quick responses, capability improvements, and innovations without the overhead of long planning-and-execution cycles (see Sterrit and Hinchey 2005 for an overview of autonomic computing).
- Systemize the process of identifying Request variations to leverage the dynamic assembly of needed service capability. Thus, the shift is away from long service-development cycles.
- Develop *routine service capabilities* by identifying and optimizing the routine components of the non-routine responses.

We shall show through details and examples in the future chapters the bottom line advantages of having a single ACE representation framework for 'Co-engineering' or simultaneously engineering the multiple BioS perspectives of the complex system.

RELATED BioS TRENDS AND METHODS

Trends Related to the Role of IT

Within the service economy *Information Technology (IT)* itself plays an important infrastructure role. For example it is critical in the delivery of vastly different services ranging from insurance, emergency care, and custom manufactured products. However, it is also true that there has been a devaluing of Information Technology

– a point made in 'IT Doesn't Matter[x]' – due to commoditization and universal availability of technology (Carr et al. 1993).

The belief now is that the future of IT is around innovation and services within the context of environmental trends such as globalization and the removal of 'friction'. Here - "innovation is the transformation of knowledge into products, processes, systems and services with the elements of underlying innovation being 1) knowledge, 2) a skilled work force, and 3) infrastructures[y]".

While IT has been used in every aspect of the organization, its effective use and diffusion takes time. Specifically the more recent drive has been towards Business-IT alignment resulting in the treatment of internal IT organizations as cost centers and the IT outsourcing decisions based primarily on cost. The concept of 'making IT count' evolves IT from 'Running the Business' to 'Changing the Business[z]'. As a first step this requires us to move to the future by measuring the software project's success based on schedule, quality, and cost — the pillars of delivery excellence. This is addressed by best-practices such as ITIL[aa], Six Sigma[ab], centralization and consolidation of IT, standardization, and a focus on governance throughout the lifecycle of the services (Pande et al 2000).

For IT to really matter, it must allow the organization to achieve competitiveness and innovation through information and knowledge flow between business Agents (people, processes, technologies and automated Agents). This requires EA (Enterprise Architecture)techniques which allow us to reason about the roles that IT can play, including the uniform quality of 'products' manufactured anywhere, outsourcing of almost anything, and global movement up Maslow's hierarchy of needs[ac]. These trends have created the need for services that go beyond operational agility to innovation delivering *into the customer's context.*

This implies looking to the future (Figure 6), innovative applications of IT and its resulting value to business must fuel the investments needed to support the evolution to a flexible service–oriented architecture. This in turn requires one to understand business service innovations and how they can leverage technologies like compositional services, mobile computing, location-based computing, and RFIDs, all in today's context of legacy systems. However given the BioS[ad] *complexity*, the journey to a future enabled with *service-oriented architecture (SOA)* and technologies is a long and expensive one. We also know that adding technology does not itself guarantee overall organizational improvement. Existing challenges of disparate systems and organizations have to be also addressed and engineered to provide value to stakeholders.

Business Trends: As mentioned earlier, within service-oriented domains flexibility is imperative and at the same time IT solutions becomes more tightly coupled with the business processes. The overall complexity of IT has also been steadily increasing, and as a result a majority of the IT budget is committed to maintenance

Figure 6. Technology trends

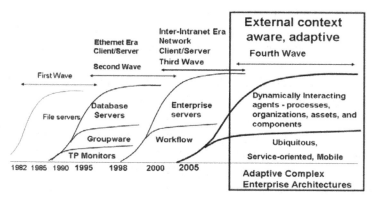

and upgrades, leaving little room for new developments and innovation. At the same time, businesses expect the IT departments to become more accountable and demonstrate value.

Realizing these challenges, EA-based governance is becoming more widely practiced, and is specifically required within federal agencies[ae]. There is now momentum within larger enterprises towards establishing both *EA governance* and *architect roles*. *EA certifications*[af] based on *open* architecture initiatives are also catching on. At the same time project costs are also critical to manage. In this context, service composability and alignment to strategy has the promise of providing flexibility at reasonable costs. For example, as mentioned earlier, the US Federal government[ag] has become a huge proponent, user, and driver of EA to reduce project costs.

Business Process Management (BPM) / Operations Trends: Business Process or Operations Management can now avail of technology to 'enact' processes, guide users, and dynamically link resources to the process. The benefit of enaction ranges from providing simpler role-based access to information, all the way to conducting business processes. Processes – sequences of tasks – can be completed in collaboration with the customers and suppliers. Note that BPM is more than the point-to-point transfer of structured data, e-commerce interactions, or application integration. It includes collaborative business processes execution with Request creation, fulfillment, delivery, status monitoring, and cost accounting closure. The full range of BPM features provides a combination of internal-facing and/or external-facing benefits.

Emerging processes benefit from SOA implementations and developments in web services with the goal of providing self-contained, modular applications that are able to work together without relying on custom-coded connections, because they use open standards. Different web services share a common protocol and so they can communicate with each other. This makes it easy to combine and recombine them to meet the needs of all stakeholders[ah]. Collaborative BPM features with underlying SOA technologies can potentially achieve dramatic improvements even in the face of volatile business processes.

Infrastructure and IT Technology Trends: Hardware, communications and software technology is rapidly evolving allowing us to deploy highly distributed systems (Figure 5). Virtualization is an example of this general trend that shares high-cost computing energy-efficient resources, making these available for many different types of service interactions. Specifically, this applies to the use of abstractions to achieve loose coupling between applications and shared physical assets. Related techniques include 'cloud computing', 'edge computing', 'autonomic computing', and 'grid computing'. The anticipated cost advantage is a simpler and more resilient infrastructure. Another technology trend is computing across software platforms and hardware devices (sensors, actuators, displays, and computational elements) that are embedded seamlessly in the everyday objects of our lives and connected through a continuous network to seamlessly interface the human to machine and machine to machine. Ubiquitous computing has been continuing to mature and such platforms will be soon available.

Newer approaches to software engineering are also gaining traction. Examples are Agile Programming (Cockburn 2001) and Product Line Development. At a high level, Agile approaches implement increments that provide customer perceivable value and the Software Product Line approach plans for reuse though enabling processes. "The asset base includes those artifacts in software development that are most costly to develop from scratch–namely, the requirements, domain models, software architecture, performance models, test cases, and components. All of the assets are designed to be reused and are optimized for use in more than a single system. The reuse with software product lines is comprehensive, planned, and profitable." (SEI 2008). Additionally, mobile computing, RFIDs and sensor networks provide opportunities for increased flexibility and automation for delivering services. Finally, the use of IT to monitor itself is increasing.

Strategy Trends: The environment's force on an organization can be in many forms – competitive, social, economic, technological, etc. Competitiveness and business intelligence gained, for example based on Porter's framework (Porter 1979), has long been a key element of organization strategy. In addition, new trends such as the social impact within a market must be understood by sensing the shifts in individual's interests and life events. Also EA must increasingly consider other impact such as HIPAA[ai], Sarbanes-Oxley[aj] and related security, accountability and audit requirements. And, finally, mergers and acquisitions are getting more and more common. All this requires an enabling strategy based on a system of systems approach.

Having briefly explored the trends from the BioS perspectives, we note that from a user perspective, non-routine Requests force a rethinking of traditional processes. We next examine the resulting trends from this particular 'use' perspective.

Social-Technical Trends and Enterprise Knowledge Infrastructures

Socio-Technical Computing Trends: Some important trends in the way users interact with IT are 'circumstance-based' service delivery and 'communities of practice'. The former requires us to understand the circumstances within which the user uses a particular service so that the delivery is more-and-more tailored. The latter requires us to understand what knowledge is shared by users within the *community of practice* (COP) and help its evolution to benefit the community (Brown 2000). An example of the former is that the 'user wants to travel' and therefore would likely also want the passport service. An example of the latter is a community that is charged to address a merger; or technical design collaboration between engineers within the customer and supplier. These examples are types of user interactions characterized as *socio-technical[ak]*.

The key underlying question is this - after providing the underlying 'boundary-less' infrastructure, in what additional ways can IT help the users [al]? This is the question we ask ourselves as we consider socio-technical interactions (Figure 6). Approaching from the user perspective, how do we ensure that the newer IT tech-nologies are used for business innovation rather than for creating "legacy systems" of the future? To address all this, we first note that existing enterprise systems have evolved well to manage data related to the handling of *routine* Requests. While the *potential* benefits of the technology trends are reduced costs for routine Requests, the greater benefits include support of non-routine Requests, increased business visibility, agility and innovation.

In the context of the trends towards greater service, non-routine Requests, how should businesses leverage technology trends (e.g. SOA), existing enterprise software and better support knowledge workers? For example, how can we enable communities to deal with variation in business transactions characterized by con-tinued negotiation during service delivery, little opportunity for cost amortization, high touch requirements, decisions made on secondary factors – opinion, trust and relationships, and local presence an advantage?

Next we explore in further detail the trend towards more social and collaborative computing that must be supported by integrated back-end IT systems.

EKI (Enterprise Knowledge Infrastructure) Trends: Why there is a need to revisit EA and evolve from our notions of an IT Infrastructure to an Enterprise Knowledge Infrastructure (discussed in Maier et al 2005)? The delivery of a service for a non-routine Request requires enabling the knowledge *workers* with both an underlying organization and IT infrastructure, in new ways (see Figure 6). An example application is the Customer Service Center which requires many interactions and many Agents (both humans and systems) to resolve non-routine incidents as quickly as possible. Socio-technical interactions also result in the EKI or the phenomenon in which local knowledge emerges during practice. A good example again is Customer Support Service Center where insights to known problems with the installed systems reduces the time to handle future incidents. Another example is a learning object[am]. Here the fundamental evolution is to shift from inward looking IT systems and features to user interfaces with a more cognitive basis. However, in practice this knowledge is hard to capture. Support for capture and re-use of knowledge has many known challenges[an] that an ACE must address (Polyani 1958).

ACE EKI-Enabled Communities: Non-routine Requests dealing with variation and requirements need a *case-by-case* treatment and often entail unanticipated processes. Consequently not only are *knowledge* workers heavily involved in the loop, but also customers and suppliers. Underlying information must be accessed from different systems, unanticipated locations, and delivered to the users and beneficiaries. In most cases the information for timely decision making continues to be difficult to access. In addition, new knowledge is often created. The mining of this remains difficult. A well-known example of this requirement in health care is the 'universal patient record' from a business, clinical and practice perspective and that still remains a challenge. Generally speaking, in addition to the *back end* integration challenges, new IT challenges lie in *front end* scenarios where multiple communities must use information in many different ways. Hence we characterize these further.

We suggest a characterization in Figure 6. Here the services-oriented information infrastructure is itself leveraged by a 'front-end' architecture (e.g. portal) that is an ACE EKI[ao]. ACE EKI enables socio-technical interactions, capture of time-varying information, the evolution of practice, and leverages the underlying back-end services. In many organizations portals are emerging as a vehicle for 'front-end' integration architecture enabling the needs of its different internal and external communities of users. That is, by using emerging IT technologies, CMS (Content Management Systems), and network monitoring it is now possible to monitor all Agents and knowledge-enable all Agents. Another example of this is recommender systems.

Before we explore how ACE can become a powerful tool to help us manage and improve service-oriented organizations, we first provide more on the EA background on which it is based. We will then explore what can we take forward and apply to services organizations from a large existing body of useful knowledge.

Background in Enterprise Architecture (EA) and Related Methods

As background we introduce first some key EA terms and best practice frameworks. We also introduce why an ontology critical to achieving high-bandwidth communications between Business-Infrastructure-Operation-Strategy (BioS) stakeholders. See Spyns 2002 for a discussion of ontology versus data modelling.

EA Terminology: The early drivers of EA produced generic Frameworks (such as AMICE 1993 and Zachman 1987[ap]) as well as more technology specialized ones (such as OMG related to the internet) and supply-chain related (SCOR)[aq]. While the field of EA is still in its infancy, recent momentum has lead to some standard and/or widely accepted and EA-related definitions. Related basic terminology is introduced next:

- *Architecture[ar]* is the fundamental organization of a system, embodied in its components, their relationships to each other and the environment, and the principles governing its design and evolution (Shaw 2006).
- *Architecture description* is a formal description of an information system, organized in a way that supports *reasoning about the structural properties of the system*. It defines the components or building blocks that make up the overall information system, and provides a plan from which products can be procured, and systems developed, that will work together to implement the overall system. It thus enables you to manage your overall IT investment in a way that meets the needs of your business. (A detailed architecture example is in Hofmeister 2000).
- *An architecture framework* is a method and tool which can be used for developing a broad range of different solution architectures. It should describe a method for designing an information system in terms of a set of building blocks, and for showing how the building blocks fit together. It should provide a common vocabulary and a basis for analysis (like Clements 2002). It should also include a list of recommended standards and compliant products that can be used to implement the building blocks[as].
- *Architecture views:* There are often several views to the architecture - the *conceptual* view that focuses on "what", the *logical* view that focuses on "how", and the *physical* view that focuses on the mapping to physical systems. Each view can in turn represent specific Agents and their interactions in different ways. The conceptual view is not mapped directly to hardware, but is mapped to functions that the system performs. It is the first place that people will go to find out how the system does what it is supposed to do.

- *Enterprise i*s any collection of organizations that has a common set of goals and/or a single bottom line. In that sense, an enterprise can be a government agency, a whole corporation, a division of a corporation, a single department, a team or a chain of geographically distant organizations linked together by common ownership or purpose.
- *Enterprise modeling* is the process of improving the enterprise performance through the creation of enterprise models. This includes the modeling of both business processes and IT. The result of modeling is a specific *enterprise representation* of the structure, activities, processes, information, resources, people, behavior, goals, and constraints of a business, government, or other enterprises (Naylor 1970, SysML)[at].
- *Enterprise services architecture (ESA):* An architecture which represents enterprise business services separately from the underlying application or component services. The business level services are typically formed from the aggregation of the underlying services.
- *Ontology:* An ontology is an agreement about a shared, formal, explicit, and/ or partial account of a conceptualization of a domain. An ontology typically contains the vocabulary (terms and domain rules), labels, and the definition of the concepts and their relationships for a given domain. Domain rules restrict the semantics of concepts and conceptual relationships that are typically satisfied by all applications that want to use – or "commit to" an interpretation of – an ontology. Some common examples are the library cataloging system or the periodic table. Another approach to this shared, top-down agreement is fostered by Internet features such as 'book marking'. Here individuals or groups create their own organization of labels and concepts (urls and tags). These can be easily passed around achieving some degree of shared understanding. The latter bottom-up approach allows many interpretations and is more flexible. See Gruber 1995 and Senge 1990.
- *Pattern language*[au] is an organized vocabulary of patterns and relationships within a solution. A solution architecture will be made up of many architecture patterns.
- *Pattern* is characterized by:
  - Noticing and naming the common problems in a field of interest
  - Describing the key characteristics of effective solution for meeting some stated goal
  - Helping the designer move from problem to solution in a logical way
  - Allowing for many different paths through the design process
- *Patterns and pattern languages* are formalized decision-making values whose effectiveness becomes obvious with experience but that are difficult to document and pass on to novices. They are also effective tools in structuring

knowledge and understanding of fundamentally complex systems without forcing oversimplification -- including organizing people or groups involved in complex undertakings or revealing how their functions inter-relate as part of the larger whole.

- *Reference implementation:* The prototypical implementation of an architecture or an architecture pattern that illustrates the architecture in operation.
- *Service–Oriented Architecture:* A SOA is a business-oriented application framework that takes enterprise applications and breaks them down into individual *business functions and processes*, called services. An SOA lets you build, deploy and integrate these services in support of business components, leveraging the underlying applications and the computing platforms as appropriate. Service-orientation describes a software architecture that uses loosely-coupled services to support the requirements of business processes and users. Resources on a network in an SOA environment are made available as independent services that can be accessed without knowledge of their underlying platform implementation. These concepts can be applied to business, software and other types of producer/consumer systems.
- *Solution Architecture vs Patterns, Adaptors, Components etc.* Patterns structure the problem solving applied to adaptors, components, packages etc. that are the building blocks used in the developing the solution architecture.

Several standards bodies are now in place to continue to evolve the breadth, the scope and the application of EA knowledge. These bodies serve an important role in maintaining knowledge that can provide a baseline for practice, certifications and research. We start with TOGAF – The Open Group Architecture Foundation – that views itself as a single point of virtual entry and positioning provided to the vast body of related work. Another important source is DODAF. For our purposes of incorporating specific existing works in the ACE framework, we introduce some related important ones next.

TOGAF, ITIL, Component Business Modeling...

TOGAF, initially based on the Zachman framework[av], has evolved to become widely accepted within the Department of Defense[aw]. Its evolution is supported by the "The Open Group" which is the leading vendor-neutral, international consortium for buyers and suppliers of technology. Its mission is to cause the development of a viable global information infrastructure that is ubiquitous, trusted, reliable, and easy-to-use. This is accomplished by providing a single view into service standards that are available for a 'boundaryless enterprise'.

At its core TOGAF includes the vocabulary and processes for the development of an enterprise architecture. The *ADM (Architecture Development Method)* provides the processes by which EA can be created and managed. EA documentation includes[ax]:

- *Business architecture*: Business strategy, governance, organization, and key business processes.
- *Data/information architecture*: Structure of an organization's logical and physical data assets and data management resources.
- *Application (systems) architecture*: Blueprint for the individual application systems to be deployed, their interactions, and their relationships to the core business processes of the organization.
- *Information Technology (IT) architecture*: Infrastructure intended to support the deployment of core, mission-critical applications.
- TOGAF also contains the *Enterprise Continuum* - TRM (Technical Reference Model which provides a model and taxonomy of generic platform services), SIB (Standards Information Base which is a database of open industry standards that can be used to define the particular services and other components of an enterprise-specific architecture), IIIRM (Integrated Information Infrastructure Reference Model, which is based on the TOGAF Foundation Architecture, and is specifically aimed at helping the design of architectures that enable and support the vision of 'Boundaryless Information Flow'). This continuum includes ITIL[ay] supported by the OGC[az]. Whereas TOGAF has architecture development and governance as its primary focus, ITIL focus is on the *installed* IT infrastructure.
- Finally TOGAF has a *Resource Base*. This includes Architecture Board, Compliance, Contracts, Governance, Maturity, Principles, Skills, Patterns (Business, Integration, Application, Runtime etc.), Architecture views, Architecture Building Blocks, Business process Domain Views, Case Studies, etc.

ITIL books with the latest version 3 release provide the only consistent and comprehensive documentation of best practice processes for Service Management, taking a *lifecycle* perspective. This includes 'what services' and 'what service levels' will be provided to the customer by the service provider. The ITIL processes are integrated especially in their use of the underlying representation of the items in the infrastructure. Specifically, the *Configuration Management Database* (CMDB) as an enabling technology helps manage the items in the ICT infrastructure and reduce incident, problem and change management costs. Typical advanced features of which include a) *discovery a* non-intrusive discovery of installed EA items such as a variety of computer systems, network devices, applications, middleware, and databases and a 2) *portal interface* to enable users to create, assign, monitor, notify, act upon and report on change Requests and configuration items leveraging a best practice ITIL process. ITIL also makes the distinction between the business customer and the user[ba]. Especially in version 3, ITIL provides a comprehensive discussion of service management to meet IT strategy goals that enable the business.

The patented *Component Business Model* (CBM) methodology introduced by IBM is a new way of assessing and designing a business at a more conceptual level (Herzum 1999, Cherbakov et al 2005). Business components are the equivalent of interchangeable manufacturing parts but are instead composed of processes, functions, activities, and services, collectively referred to as *capabilities*. Each building block includes the resources (including human resources), activities, and technology needed to produce a service valued by another component, or by an external customer (Ernest 2007).[bb]

Within the enterprise the Customer Service Center (CSC) is the point where the seamless interface to the customer is presented. This is also the point where all the requirements for internal integration and networking arise. The Help Desk Institute (HDI[bc]) is an organization that maintains related best practices.

All of these EA methodologies identified above have been now applied in numerous organizations. This complied body of knowledge represents a very good *background* and the basis for the concepts presented in this book. The reader is thus encouraged to read the related references.

Business-IT alignment and Organizational Challenges: We define *alignment* here to be along both the internal and the external value chain[bd]. The ability to *align* IT services and Business services, especially as the latter sometimes changes dynamically, has itself become critical. Noting again that an externally-driven complex system is turbulent, we need a way to capture the important details of the individual BioS service cycles *explicitly* in order to improve it[be]. This is called the internal Bios alignment. A starting point for this is work that relates operational tactics to the business plan and strategy as illustrated in Figure 7 (Kolber et al 2000)[bf].

In the best of circumstances the EA is explicitly represented, managed, and engineered to meet goal states. However in typical circumstances, the goals and architecture are implicit and in the heads of numerous different people in the organization. A typical consequence of this is a lot of meetings, little effective decision-making, and sometimes even inadvertent undermining of business objectives! Unfortunately, this is even truer when EA efforts are considered to be *overhead*.

So, why revisit EA practice? In a nutshell, most related best practices so far have focused on the processes but not so much on the *representation* of the EA. At a high level, the EA challenge is to manage tactics and the underlying interactions between the business and IT Agents. Often numbering in the thousands these interactions

Figure 7. Evolution of the IT 'back-end' Infrastructure to an Enterprise Knowledge Infrastructure (Cyber Infrastructure) to support frond-end Socio-Technical interactions

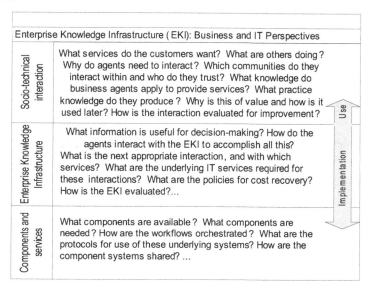

are challenging and means that the BioS alignment has to be very carefully thought out and targeted to improve business. All this also challenges decision-making and alignment of services and their BioS. To address this we need an adequate business-driven 'alignment' framework that allows us to develop the work products which form the basis of analysis and decision making.

Work Products: We need a representation that will derive EA work products for improved governance and deployment. To understand this let us go back to the Indy 500. The Agents (racer, pit-crew members, etc.) come to the race armed with a knowledge of best practices and methods to be applied. However, to win the race this knowledge is applied to an *artifact - the car*. The specific car is analogous to the specific organization's *EA representation* as *work products* or artifacts against which the best practices have to be applied (Figure 8). Stated differently, the best practices are prototypical processes and high-level steps that specify the *"what"* but do not dictate *"how"* an EA should be represented. This ensures that the standard will remain widely applicable. But at the same time, this leaves the underlying methods quite generic and too much interpretation possible.

Conceptual EA work products surface important issues critical to organization governance, achieving consensus, and shared decision-making. It allows the management of interactions within a complex system of Agents and facilitates holistic thinking (for the importance of this see Senge 1990)[bg]. This is especially

Figure 8. Relating actions and goal states while delivering a service

Elements of the Business , Rules, Goals Model

important in the case of non-routine service Requests and externally-driven service organizations, where decision-making is interdisciplinary and driven by dynamically changing needs.

While TOGAF, ITIL, and other related practices are gaining momentum around the world, they do not yet provide a specific ontology for the EA representation. By providing this ontology, we shall see that more prescriptive methods for best practices work products (like the ITIL service catalog) become feasible. Process get more repeatable and principled and analytic methods emerge around precise structures thus facilitating empirical studies.

The conceptual ACE EA work products shared by the organization in order to take actions has many benefits:

- *Strategy related:*
    - o   Agile responses to external conditions and opportunities
    - o   Flexibility for business growth
    - o   Targeted/prioritized innovation within products and processes
    - o   Faster time-to-market
- *Business related:*
    - o   Better return on existing investment
    - o   Reduced risk for future investment
    - o   Faster, simpler and cheaper procurement

Figure 9. Adaptive Complex Enterprise work products and its use in governance and continual improvement processes.

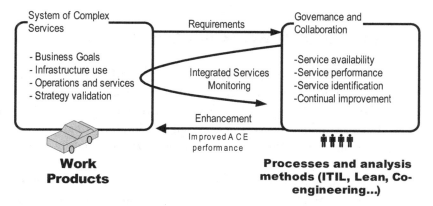

- *Operations related:*
  - Efficiency and Resilience
  - Restructuring of service capabilities and their use to achieve efficient responses
  - Increased standardization, re-use, and modularity
  - Assisted environment for management of a complex system by goals
- *Organization related:*
  - Alignment methods where a few principles can be shared and applied repeatedly for improved decision-making by interdisciplinary BioS teams
  - Incremental, distributed, and concurrent enhancements are effectively managed by small teams
  - Clear definition of roles and responsibilities
  - Faster improvements

The methods and tools to achieve these benefits with the ACE framework are presented in the later chapters of the book.

In summary, using the racing analogy, we note that the organization's EA representation is as important as the tangible manifestation of the race car itself. While the race car team provides services (processes, methods, and tools), these services have to be applied to the physically and tangibly represented race car that reaches the ultimate goal of winning. Much in the same way, the business value is achieved by enterprise solution architects applying services and targeting improvements as guided by the *EA work products and representation*. Thus, achieving a good EA representation for effective decision-making is critical to the application of integrated tools and methods.

ACE FRAMEWORK AND WORK PRODUCTS

ACE is a conceptual representation of the organizations and services of an enterprise. The goals of a conceptual representation is that teams can make critical decisions for continuous improvement without having to understand all the underlying technologies. Further, it supports decision-making highlighting that which must remain fairly constant in the face of change due to environmental, business and technology trends.

Specifically, we focus on the customer-driven delivery and improvement of services enabled by a complex infrastructure of underlying interacting but fairly autonomous *Agents*[bh]. To achieve the desired BioS value we will capture and represent the *interactions* between *customer and provider* Agents. Our focus is also on the services provided by the Agents, rather than the Agents' detailed internal workings. Agents are encouraged to act more *autonomously* within the constraints provided ACE context. That is, decisions for services and improvement can be made locally in adherence to governing policies that meet overall goals[bi]. Thus, the overall complexity of tactics can be reduced due to more adaptive local decision-making.

While the value of EA efforts is *sometimes* challenging to demonstrate, here we introduce prescriptive methods for a more successful analysis, project management, and tools for decision-making. A successful journey requires a representation of service BioS enabling a holistic approach for analysts and managers to decide what, why, when, who, how, and, even whether technology is to be used (Ross 2006)! To enable this ACE fundamentally aligns Business-IT dimensions using a complete framework for practice and research that consists of the part identified in Figure 10. Each of these parts of the framework is discussed next.

BIOS Interaction Ontology: The BioS Interaction ontology allows the sharing and interoperability of knowledge not only across the different processes and best practices but *also across* disciplines and BioS perspectives. While this ontology has significant overlap with those underlying best practices like ITIL, we will introduce somewhat different terms to ensure modeling accuracy when referring to concepts in an unambiguous manner needed for eventual automation.

To understand the problems due to the lack of a shared ontology, consider the ubiquitous word 'activity' and it's various disciplinary interpretations. For a business stakeholder, 'activity' typically refers to an entire organization responding to a Request type. In systems engineering, 'activity' refers to the transformation applied at a work cell. Finally, in computer science, an 'activity' represented in

Figure 10. Parts of the ACE framework

1.	*BioS Interaction ontology* that relates the BioS stakeholders and value expectations of the underlying interactions needed to achieve those values.
2.	*Enterprise modeling notation* that uses the ontology as a basis to represent the represent a group of service organizations in a precise and conceptual way.
3.	*Work product templates, patterns, and principles* that guide the development of standardized work products starting from a representation of a specific organization. These work products guide the implementation.
4.	*Co-engineering methods for analysis prioritization and automation* that use work products needed by practices such as ITIL, TOGAF, LEAN, Six Sigma, RUP[bj], and AGILE to direct actions that make improvements more efficiently.
5.	*Governance, roles and responsibilities for continuous improvement* to implement the above.

UML[bk] diagram refers to either of the above! A deep ontology[bl] will allow us to relate 'activity' from a business perspective to 'activity' at process execution to 'activity' in a software development process.

Thus our goal with the ACE ontology is to detect the performance variation due to non-routine Requests characterized at the right-hand of the continuum in Figure 3. Rather than being internally optimized, the management in service-oriented organizations requires a more dynamic and external facing adaptive method for detecting performance variations and aligning this to business goals.

Enterprise Modeling: A good modeling notation will allow us to surface important characteristics of the organization and enterprise for us to 'see' the problems. The notation introduced here creates a goal-oriented ACE structure that we can analyze and reason about performance. We can use this to see what changes to make to the model that can also be effected into the actual enterprise. Finally, some other starting points are UML and SysML (Friedenthal et al. 2008). A precise model provides a structure to monitor performance so that we can improve in a cycle of continual improvement.

Given the non-routine characteristics and thousands of Agents (resources, processes, IT components, assets, etc.) and services involved in a typical, three phenomenon come into play:

- *Identify and address only the most relevant details:* Any detailed static model of the real world (consisting of process, data, role, and goal models) rapidly becomes obsolete and this does not serve well as the basis for reasoning about adaptation. Given the dynamic characteristics of a complex system it is clear that traditional modeling strategies have to be revisited, but not entirely discarded. For example the models of goals, processes, data, and roles should be able to deal with external variation. We are specifically interested in the impact of revision in one model that causes variations in other models. We must also look for techniques that allow us to enable emergent behaviors. Further, analysis and decision-making should incorporate the ability to predictive behaviors so that corrective actions can be taken before problems occur and on a timely basis. At the same time the models must not dictate too many details that are highly variable and become obsolete rapidly. (See for example Mackenzie 2002, Naylor 1970 for some different analysis methods.)

- *Complexity theory:* We can hope to better understand a complex system if it can be usefully described by a small number of patterns. Complexity theory is leveraged to provide the underpinnings that complex systems are made of a small number of recursively applied patterns. We show that a careful selection and integration of relevant and proven techniques from Business, Systems Engineering, And Computer Science[bm] provides us with the integrative framework for ACE (Adaptive Complex Systems 2005).

- *Bounded rationality:* Individuals can never hope to fully understand the entire complex system[bn] and make the most rational decisions. Acknowledging this, we hope to improve services through collective decision-making based on a characterization of just the essentials and continually collectively improving only those 'critical' aspects of the organization based on performance. Thus, the shared understanding of selective information in balance enables improvement of the complex system. This allows us to better address wicked problems (Churchman 1967). We show how we can address phenomenon in a useful way enabling automation for complex system improvement. We will focus on visibility that will help make high-impact performance decisions. A conceptual representation allows us define and apply analysis tools and methods for decision-making.

Work Product Templates, Patterns, and Principles: Instead of building a 'technology-heavy' and 'business-lite' EA or vice-versa, interdisciplinary teams together own an 'externally' focused or *adaptive* EA representation and work products. The underlying customer-provider interaction ontology is dynamically applicable, provides flexibility, and allows the disciplines to interoperate. The resulting conceptual model reflects overall performance and along with principles and analysis methods aligns *in-the-large* business service perspectives to the *in-the-small* IT and operational service perspectives of the organization.

Co-Engineering Methods for Analysis, Prioritization and Automation: The modeling results in a precise representation and work products surfacing performance trade-offs for decision-making that achieves service BioS goals. The methods and tools for Co-engineering Business-IT take in these work products and identify actions. These methods are identified in the Figure 11 as processes that apply in column 4. These methods allow us to take work products and analyze them or use them for a variety of purposes as discussed next:

- *Monitoring:* As systems evolve, providing stakeholder-value-based information and coordination by leveraging 'back-end' services is not only becoming critical but also increasingly complex. The ACE architecture enables new uses of the IT infrastructure to surface and at the same time allows monitored interactions (who, what, when, why, how long, Requested by, successful delivery etc.) between Agents for both business and technical management. That is, the monitoring includes:
  - o Front-end business intelligence monitoring
  - o Alignment monitoring of interactions to value goals
  - o Back-end resource monitoring

  The monitored information can also be used to update a representation of ACE objects and interactions (as a conceptual view of a CMDB) to facilitate better management of ACE Agents and services. That is, monitored metrics can be aggregated to provide key performance insights into trends, mine intelligence, and make it ultimately possible to create new markets with the existing capabilities, increase flexibility for service combinations, and suggest areas for new IT services and components. Finally, more of the IT infrastructure processes can become automated and IT employees more efficient while providing direct value to the business.
- *Interaction Knowledge:* The ACE modeling concepts apply to interactions within a complex system of Requests and services provided by interacting Agents. Further, new knowledge resulting from the interactions among IT/human Agents enables improved service capabilities and business value. That is, the Agents within the architecture, while autonomous, also interact to create new knowledge. These interactions can be monitored by IT itself to provide the metrics, performance and time variant information to allow the IT infrastructure itself evolve as an Enterprise Knowledge Infrastructure.
- *Lean BPM:* Here our focus is also on looking for ways to improve ACE performance based on technologies like *BPM (Business Process Management)* which can be used to implement L*ean* behaviors[bo] for services. The Request-driven business that has to deal with variation on a case-by-case basis. 'Lean' BPM creates value through processes that systematically minimize all forms of waste at the work or *in-the-small* level. Unlike business re-engineering (Hammer & Champy 1993) and enterprise application integration, which is primarily targeted towards in-the-large processes, BPM is targeted to automating workflow and individual work tasks and decision-making. Thus, it is more analogous to streamlining work processes at the shop floor level. The lean

Figure 11. Scope of the ACE framework – BioS dimensions, services, interactions, roles, and improvement processes.

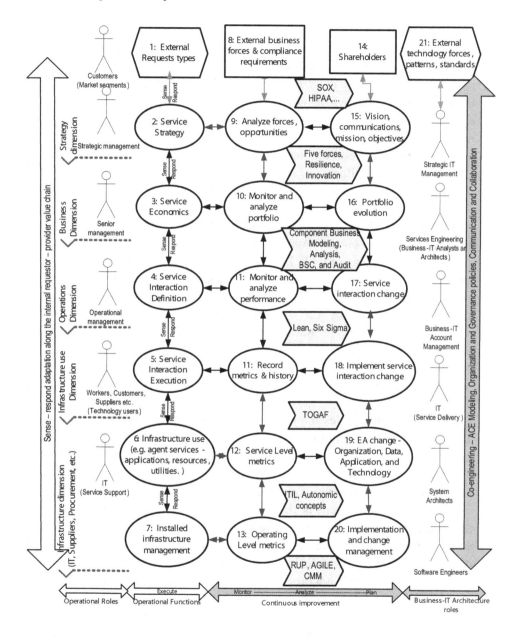

electronic business process uses IT to reduce rework, errors, wasted time, and transit time as well as to improve utilization of resources. The flexibility of IT can also be used in additional ways – the just-in-time assignment of resources to retain maximum flexibility, the shipping of electronic work packages and instructions instantly and globally, and so on. In other words, the flexibility of lean electronic business processes can be put to work to better manage the physical world and resources in order to reduce waste.

The representation of an enterprise is logical, dynamic, flexible and performance-based so that local teams can reason and respond to external events and adapt. The actual changes within ACE are also local and implemented by autonomous Agents that meet global performance objectives. And, from a technology perspective, instead of building environments to be permanent, they are built to change. Using SOA implementations, development cycles become aligned to process behaviors in which silo applications become orchestrated solutions that work together. And rigid point-to-point connections between applications become loosely coupled. All this uses new tools and methods that are emerging to allow the creation of services that can be combined and recombined.

Designed thus, the Lean business unit is flexible enough to efficiently respond to a Request at a time. For example, it can provide dynamic flexibility for service–oriented organizations (Chapter 6). We shall see that such a customer-facing process also successfully integrates all other supporting internal-facing processes and roles within the organization. Business process integration and resulting visibility offers significant opportunity for return as companies transform their business processes by integrating back-end systems (from order entry to supply to demand fulfillment) to create an integrated front-end user experience (be it an internal worker, the customer, or the supplier).

Governance, Roles and Responsibilities for Continuous Improvement: No complex system can change overnight! *ACE* methods for continual improvement target specific areas. With ACE, change can be conceptualized, targeted, and locally implemented. This reduces governance overhead in meetings and discussions. Multiple best practices and principles can be applied to the ACE representation to effect improvements in a consistent way and from all BioS perspectives. BioS perspectives become aligned through enabling specific customer-oriented process behaviors.

To re-emphasize, we define *adaptation* as externally-driven improvement within decreasing time cycles. This requires visibility and a holistic architecture (Shaw 2006) that will *align* IT services and information delivery to the changing information needs of the business processes and organization strategy. To support this,

ACE builds on the ontology as well on existing best practices to provide a logical *dynamic interaction and performance* framework to reason about the 1) short-term improvements, 2) longer-term enhancements for effectiveness and resilience, and 3) points of breakthrough innovation.

The ACE framework itself provides the knowledge for successful governance. The scope the knowledge underlying ACE is thus illustrated in Figure 9 and discussed below:

1.   *ACE Framework Scope:* The full scope of ACE is illustrated in Figure 9 and includes *dimensions* (rows) identifying the BioS stakeholders, associated operational functions, the continuous improvement functions, and associated architecture roles. We introduce and define these further

2.   *Stakeholder roles* in column 1 are vertically ordered by the customer-provider relationships that exist *within the organization.* The starting point – at the top – is the environment where customer Requests originate and strategy is formulated. Each role is the customer for the dimension(s) below and a provider to the dimensions above. The relationships between dimensions, we have also called BioS, make ACE adaptive or externally driven. roles in column 1.

3.   *Functions* in column 2 are associated with stakeholders identified in 2 above. Each function also enables the function in the dimension above.

4.   *Continuous improvement and implementation* functions are identified in columns 3 and 4 and are associated with column 2. Column 3 functions synthesize the metrics and performance to enable the decision-making in column 4.

   a.   Related best practices and methods selected to improve the functions: Five Forces framework and compliance requirements to identify the external requirements that help shape service strategy, the Balanced Score Card (BSC) that relates operational performance indicators to strategy and guides the to-be decision making, the Lean methods to define the to-be efficiencies and the related Service Levels (SLs) and Operating Levels (OLs) to be achieved for this, EKI means of delivery, and finally TOGAF, ITIL, and Autonomic frameworks to ensure the quality of IT service while meeting business needs.

   b.   Architecture roles in column 5 are responsible for adaptation and continuous improvement decisions, and finally the

   c.   Related external Context that drives each of the vertical aspects is indicated at the top of each column.

Thus, ACE integrates a complete suite of best practices and principles for decision-making needed to manage a complex system. These selected best practices (or processes) are well documented and widely accepted standards, in many cases.

However, by their very nature, they are disciplinary and defined to be widely applicable. As mentioned before, they often do not prescribe specific representation methods and leave much to a case-by-case interpretation. To leverage all these identified practices, ACE begins with a performance-centered 'RED ontology' in the next chapter to form the basis of representation and deep engineering methods.

Application of the ACE Framework: In action, the ACE framework produces a representation of the organization's BioS that is both execution and performance focused from a continuous improvement perspective. Teams can apply Co-engineering *processes* both locally and simultaneously across the organization under the guidelines of global policy (such as Lean). The processes are selected here to achieve a continuous improvement cycle through *prescriptive* steps. These are as follows.

BioS Representation: This begins with the as-is *representation* of each interaction and performance alignment to the organization's BioS *dimensions* and *externally defined* competitive objectives. The ACE service-interaction ontology underlying the representation allows us to surface and monitor performance aspects that enable service-providing entities (humans, processes, IT systems, etc.) to effect improvements and embrace local variation while delivering customer services.

'Co-engineering' [bp]: Co-engineering is the performance-based analysis and alignment of the represented BioS layers. The Co-engineering method is based on the following 'co' philosophies:

- *Communication* between Business, IT, Operation and Strategy (BioS) stakeholders using a shared service interaction ontology to align performance to achieve Lean, Resilient, and Innovative behaviors. At the same time the methods succinctly leverage and apply a body of interdisciplinary best practices - Five-Forces, Balanced Scorecard, Sense-Respond, Lean, Quality, and SOA.
- *Collaboration* between the Customer and BioS stakeholders to model, analyze, develop and use service-oriented work products, based on The Open Group Architecture Foundation (TOGAF), ITIL (IT Infrastructure Libraries), and Business Component Model to evolve ACE performance while servicing current operational needs.
- *Continuous Improvement steps* that apply precise *methods* to achieve the to-be ACE. These are the columns of Figure 9 and also form the Deming cycle – *do* the business processes, *monitor* performance, *act* on the needed improvements, *plan* the next deployment. The ACE structure can be monitored by IT itself to inform and implement systems engineering principles and support micro and macro decision making. Continuous improvement is also achieved for

each Agent through a roadmap for overall ACE adaptation to external events based on a performance framework.

- *Concurrent* implementation of local improvements facilitated within autonomous entities based on performance information and precisely stated overall goals and policies of the ACE.
- *Engineering* at both the in-the-large and in-the-small of the enterprise using a small core of patterns and principles that can be taught, re-used, and applied to meet business service solution requirements and constraints.

To recap, the ACE objective it to focus externally on non-routine Requests and service interactions and put in place a performance-centered representation that allows adaptation[bq] through incremental (with the as-is-to-be metrics difference represented as $\triangle$) local engineering. ACE management leverages the representation for Co-engineering. Co-engineering *integrates* proven best practices to provide a *consistent systemic performance-based* approach by which the service-oriented organizations can manage *externally-driven variation*. The holistic enterprise architecture framework also goes beyond the benefits of individual practices by using a shared Business-IT performance ontology to achieve the following business objectives:

1. *Service delivery* improved through Lean methods that treat organizations, processes, enterprise applications and other assets as internal service-providing entities. These also locally manage change and decision-making to deliver capabilities that are adaptive[br] to external events.
2. *Service enablement and innovation* through interdisciplinary problem solving and performance-based governance of the enterprise architecture. The underlying integrated knowledge uses:
    o   Business principles to define the innovative uses of IT to increase competitiveness, value, and define business constraints,
    o   Systems Engineering principles for Lean design and Quality operations, and
    o   Computer Science principles for the application of service-oriented architectures, enterprise modeling, monitoring, and evolution.
3. *Resilience of individual services* through use of IT for performance monitoring and early detection based on Five Forces and Balanced Score Card and that can be used to vertically align the way in which business, operations and IT sense, respond and adapt.

ACE case studies in subsequent chapters illustrate applications.

TASKS RELATED TO PROJECT BACKGROUND

1. Identify an enterprise architecture practice project sponsor and topic. It is advisable to select a project that is main stream and of high value as this will ensure better success. However, it is best that the project is not on a critical path. Some examples include:

    o Innovation of new products and processes that involve IT
    o The improvement of a primary service
    o The improvement of capacity through the better use of organization and technologies
    o Deployment of initiatives like ITIL or SOX

    The deliverable will be a project Road Map and/or a proof of concept deployment.

2. Identify the project sponsor who will be evaluating the project and an architect within the company to work with.

3. Work with the sponsor to collect the *background materials* that will help develop the project charter, scope of work, and a plan for tasks.

4. Begin secondary background research (include best practice and academic research papers) to build up your project team's working knowledge of the domain and challenge problems to be addressed[bs].

5. Get ITIL foundation knowledge (and certification if possible).

THINGS TO THINK ABOUT

1. Identify the types of projects you might encounter in terms of the clarity of the requirements. How do you handle projects where the requirements are not well-defined?

2. Explain the differences between an enterprise architecture, business architecture, software architecture, and hardware architecture. Are there any entities, relationships or commonalities among them? What is the role of architecture in a systems engineering project?

3. Pick an organization you are familiar with and list its essential characteristics, including the environment it operates in. Is it a make-sell organization, a sense-respond organization, or somewhere in between? Use the characteristics identified in Figure 3 to justify your answer. Identify and consider changes in the environmental characteristics would impact the organizations services.

4. Starting with the rightmost column of Figure 11, devise a set of activities you think are essential to managing a service-oriented organization. Then break these activities down into supporting interactions and sub-interactions and

think about the stakeholders, roles at play, and organizational structures required to successfully implement them. Does the ACE interaction framework help you to better communicate or elicit the complex interactions throughout these activities?

5. Identify the processes and roles in ITIL. Compare your answer to the previous question with the service management processes of ITIL which are specific to IT services. Were your answers similar at a high level or quite different? Try to classify the differences in terms of assumptions you made (the kind of service organization you had imagined) or omissions.

6. Read TOGAF and compare and contrast to ACE objectives. How does the ACE architecture support and relate to TOGAF?

7. Discuss the use of the interaction model to facilitate empowerment and its potential as a way to reduce the cycle time.

8. Ubiquitous computing provides an unparalleled platform for interactions to occur. Discuss how understanding these interactions are likely to provide greater capability to sense environmental trends early on.

9. List the ITIL processes and their roles in supporting service delivery or support. Identify one primary Interaction that is critical for each ITIL process. For each process, identify the process roles and use cases for a CMDB (configuration management data base).

10. Compare and contrast model – driven architectures, CMDB, model - driven programming, architecture pattern. You will have to base this on a) current literature search to define terminology and then b) provide thoughtful answers.

11. Research the differences between Industrial and Information age organizations and then a) list five difference between these types of organizations and b) the role of IT in each difference.

12. Research and summarize the features of three different vendor products for each of 1) monitoring complex systems, 2) CRM, 3) product data and configuration management, 4) data mining, and 5) data warehousing.

13. Define Learning Objects, Cyber Infrastructures, Collaboratory, and Enterprise Knowledge Infrastructures. Based on your own research readings, how do they relate?

REFERENCES

AMICE (1993). *CIMOSA: Open Systems Architecture for CIM* (2nd ed.). Berlin: Springer Verlag.

Boehm, B. (2000 September). Project Termination doesn't Equal Project Failure. *IEEE Computer, 33*(9), 94-96.

Brown, A. (2000 January). TI: Transforming Business Structures to Hyborgs. *Employment Relations Today, 26*(4), 5-15.

Adaptive Complex Systems. (2005 May). *Communications of the ACM, 48*(5).

Carr, N. G., Porter, M. E., & Farrell, D. (2003 October). Wringing Real Value from IT (2nd ed.). *Harvard Business Review.*

Clements, P., Kazman, R., & Klein, M. (2002). *Evaluating Software Architectures.* Boston: Addison-Wesley.

Cherbakov L., Galambos G., Harishankar R., Kalyana S., & Rackham G. (2005). Impact of Service Orientation at the Business Level. *IBM Systems Journal, 44*(4) 653-668.

Churchman, C. W. (1967). Wicked Problems. *Management Science, 14*(4), 141-142.

Cockburn, A. (2001). *Agile Software Development.* Addison-Wesley Professional.

Deming, W. (1986). *Out of the Crisis.* Cambridge: Massachusetts Institute of Technology, Center for Advanced Engineering Study.

Eriksson, H., & Penker, M. (2000). *Business Modeling with UML: Business Patterns at Work.* New York: Wiley.

Ernest, M., & Nisavic, J.M. (2007). Adding value to the IT organization with the Component Business Model. *IBM Systems Journal, 46*(3), 387-404.

Freeman, R. E. (1984). *Strategic Management: A Stakeholder Approach.* Boston: Pitman.

Friedenthal, S., Moore, A., & Steiner, R. (2008). *A Practical Guide to SysML: The Systems Modeling Language.* San Diego: Morgan Kaufmann.

Gruber T. (1995). Towards Principles for the Design of Ontologies Used for Knowledge Sharing. *International Journal of Human-Computer Studies, 43*(5/6), 907-928.

Goldberg, D., Nichols, D., Oki, B., & Terry D. (1992 December). Using Collaborative Filtering to Weave an Information Tapestry. *Communications of the ACM, 35*(12), 61-70.

Haeckel, S. (1999). *Adaptive Enterprise: Creating and Leading Sense-And-Respond Organizations.* Boston: Harvard Business School Press.

Hamel, G., & Valikangas L. (2003 September). The Quest for Resilience. *Harvard Business Review.*

Hammer, M., & Champy, J. (1993). *Reengineering the Corporation: A Manifesto for Business Revolution.* New York: Harper Business.

Herzum, P., & Sims, O. (2000). *Business Component Factory: A Comprehensive Overview of Component-Based Development for the Enterprise.* New York: John Wiley.

Hill, T. P. (1977). On goods and services. *Review of Income & Wealth, 23*(4), 315-338.

Hofmeister, C., Nord, R., & Soni, D. (2000). *Applied Software Architecture.* Boston: Addison-Wesley.

Kaplan, R. S., & Norton, D. P. (1992 January/February). The Balanced Scorecard: Measures that Drive Performance. *Harvard Business Review.*

Kapoor S., Bhattacharya K., Buckley S., Chowdhary P., Ettl M., Katircioglu K., et. al. (2005). A Technical Framework for Sense and Respond Business Management. *IBM Systems Journal, 44*(1), 5-24.

Kolber, A.B., Estep, C., Hay, D., Struck, D., Lam, G., Healy, J., et al. (2000). *Organizing Business Plans: The Standard Model for Business Rule Motivation.* The Business Rules Group.

Lynch, D. (1990). *Strategy of the Dolphin.* New York: Ballantine Books.

Mackenzie, D. (2002 February). The Science of Surprise: Can Complexity Theory Help Us Understand the Real Consequences of a Convoluted Event like September 11. *Discover, 23*(2).

Maier, R., Hädrich, T., & Peinl, R. (2005). *Enterprise Knowledge Infrastructures.* Berlin: Springer.

Naylor, T. (1970). Corporate Simulation Models and the Economic Theory of the Firm. In A. Schrieber (Ed.), *Corporate Simulation Models* (pp. 1-35). Seattle: University of Washington Press.

Pande, P., Neuman, R., & Cavanagh, R. (2000). *The Six Sigma Way.* New York: McGraw-Hill.

Pine, B. (1993). *Mass Customization.* Boston: Harvard Business School Press.

Polanyi, M. (1958). *Personal Knowledge: Towards a Post-critical Philosophy.* Chicago: University of Chicago Press.

Porter M. (1979 March/April). How Competitive Forces Shape Strategy. *Harvard Business Review.*

Putnik, G., & Cunha, M. (Ed.) (2005 May). *Virtual Enterprise Integration: Technological and Organizational Perspectives.* IGI Global.

Martin, P., & Tate, K. (1997). *The Project Manager Memory Jogger.* Goal/QPC.

The Open Group: TOGAF ADM and MDA. (2004 May) Retrieved November 23, 2008, from http://www.opengroup.org/architecture/togaf8-doc/arch/.

Quershi, S., & Keen, P. (2005 March). Activating Knowledge through Electronic Collaboration: Vanquishing the Knowledge Paradox. *IEEE Transactions on Professional Communications, 48*(1), 40-54.

Ramnath R., & Ramanathan J. (2008). Integrating Goal Modeling and Execution in Adaptive Complex Enterprises. *In Proceedings of the ACM Symposium of Applied Computing* (pp. 523-539), Fortaleza, Ceara, Brazil: ACM.

Ross, J., Weill, P., & Robertson, D. (2006). *Enterprise Architecture as Strategy.* Boston: Harvard Business School Press.

Saaty, T. (1994 November/December). How to Make a Decision: The Analytic Hierarchy Process. *Interfaces, 24*(6), 19-43.

Schekkerman, J. (2008). EA Good Practices Guide: How to Manage the Enterprise Architecture Practice. Trafford Publishing, Canada. ISBN: 1-4251-5687-8.

SEI (2008). Retrieved December 12, 2008 from http://www.sei.cmu.edu/product-lines/frame_report/

Senge, P. (1990 Fall). The Leader's New Work: Building Learning Organizations. *Sloan Management Review, 32*(1), 7-23.

Shaw, M., & Clements, P., (2006 March/April). The Golden Age of Software Architecture. *IEEE Software, 23*(2), 31-39.

Spyns, P., Meersman, R., & Jarrar, M. (December 2002). Data modeling versus Ontology engineering. *Source, ACM SIGMOD Record archive, 31*(4).

Sterritt, R., & Hinchey, M. (2005 August). Autonomicity: An Antidote for Complexity? *In Computational Systems Bioinformatics Conference: Workshops and Poster Abstracts* (pp. 283-291), IEEE.

SysML. (n.d.). Retrieved November 23, 2008, from http://www.sysmlforum.com/FAQ.htm.

Zachman, J. A. (1987). A Framework for Information System Architecture. *IBM Systems Journal, 26*(3), 276-292.

ENDNOTES

[a]   We use the concept that an enterprise is made up of many organizations - private and public, government and non-government. An organization can be a private business or a public governmental agency. An organization can even be a team or a department. An organization often consists of other organizations. Organization can be a collection of software components!

[b]   Threatened by competition as well as an increasing number of business failures and the economic implosion of the last few years, businesses are managing a wider range of sustainability indicators to better develop and maintain long-term value. Used here in its broadest sense, the term sustainable organization is defined as one whose characteristics are designed to lead to a "desirable future state" for all stakeholders.

[c]   Haeckel suggests that unpredictability requires that the organization must be prepared to assemble its components to meet customer Requests. He also gives many examples of sense-and-respond organization. For example, he points to professional services as an area where this trend was first experienced. He identifies the information architecture of the make-and-sell as one in which each function has its own view of what is going on out there. The focus is on managing the information needed to execute a business plan. In contrast, the sense-and-respond enterprise has its focus on the essential information needed to create a unified view of the environment and key processes. The information is used to support decentralized decision making with focus on what is needed to deliver on a Request. Haeckel's book provides an excellent background for the more technical and IT-oriented approaches of the Adaptive Complex Enterprise architecture.

[d]   The concept of Sense-Respond originates from Haeckel's work in the early nineties concerning organizational models that will help firms lead in the globally competitive environment of today's marketplace. The essence of the term refers to the realization that the product centered focus of industrial age business models is not sustainable in this fiercely competitive landscape. Instead, Sense-Respond argues that business leaders must actively seek out and understand the needs of their customers or potential customers and have the ability, as an organization, to strategically position themselves to meet continuously evolving demands.

e   Note the difference between 'metric' and 'performance'. Metric is a measurement of a system attribute – for example a *time stamp*. In and of itself, it does not tell us much. Performance interprets the metric to describe and predict the desired behavior of the system and is typically synthesized from different metrics. An example metric is the number of *Requests of a type*. We can use this as an indicator of good performance – e.g. increase in service Requests is desirable. Or it can be an indicator of bad performance – e.g. reduction of complaints is desirable.

f   A Stakeholder is a person, or group of persons, that may be affected by the actions or decisions of an organization. The concept of stakeholders is critical to the ACE framework because it lays a foundation for understanding complex systems and interpreting how performance is evaluated. In complex situations decisions often have to be made that address the concerns of a number of stakeholders each of which have their own perceptions about what is and what is not important. This is particularly true for people we call architects or 'C.o-engineers' because they, by their very definition, are concerned with assessing tradeoffs between groups of people that are typically seen as having very different interest, motivations, and priorities. Fortunately, there are a number of decision theories and techniques designed to help make rational decisions in spite of the complexities of situations and the ambiguities of human problem solving techniques. One such technique is the Analytic Hierarchy Process (AHP), which in Saaty 1994 is presented as a method that is both practical to use as a basis for complex multi criterion decision making and caters to the natural processes humans use to make decisions. The AHP first structures a problem by decomposing it into more manageable sub-problems and then synthesizes a solution from a series of simple pair-wise comparisons. Often a decision needs to be made and the decision makers need some assurance that their conclusion was both systematic and consistent with their intentions – the AHP is one such method that a co-engineer can use for both purposes. For a more rigorous discussion on stakeholders - also see Freeman 1984.

g   Tata unveils the Nano, world's cheapest car, http://in.reuters.com/article/businessNews/, Thu Jan 10, 2008 6:13pm IST.

h   OEM stands for Original Equipment Manufacturer.

i   A single enterprise may not be isolated to just one point in this spectrum. Various organizations of the enterprise may be distributed throughout the spectrum depending on the nature or characteristics of the part of the business that they serve.

j   Characterized by SCOR 8.0 Quick Reference Guide, Supply Chain Council, available online at http://www.supply-chain.org/galleries/public-gallery/SCOR_Quick_Reference_Guide_10.23.pdf.

k   Enterprise system is an umbrella term for IT systems that must support large organizations with a high quality of service. Prototypical enterprise systems include Enterprise Resource Planning (ERP), Customer Relationship Management (CRM), Human Resources Management (HRM), Enterprise Document Management (EDM), Enterprise Resources Management (ERM), and Point-of-Sale (POS) applications. We will use the word 'effective' to mean both efficiency and achieving the right goals.

l   A business object is an abstract entity that represents some important artifact or concept in the business domain and encapsulates all the relevant data of that concept. For example, a 'Purchase Order' might be an important notion in the business domain and the corresponding business object representing a 'Purchase Order' would model that business concept in the IT domain. Business objects are distinct from other abstractions in a system because they only deal with essential concepts from the business domain and do not include other peripheral concerns, such as the presentation or user interface or location and access of the data.

m   Service often refers to additional value-added "services" offered in addition to, or on top of, "products." In this sense a "product" may also be a service. For example, a retail vendor may offer a boxed product with online support as the base product and an additional product that offers phone support service in addition to the base product.

n   The importance of catering to non routine Requests is, rather generally, an artifact of globalization and the realization of a buyer's marketplace. For businesses that cannot rely on their brand names or market dominance alone, the capability to quickly respond to unique customer requirements provides a means to remain competitive. (Pine 1993.)

o   A primary process directly satisfies a business need while a secondary process is generally any process with the sole purpose of enabling a primary process.

p   Make-sell organizations are characterized by delivering products or services that are well specified and understood a priori. These kinds of organization will strive to reduce sources of variation to make their operations repeatable, reliable, and generally more efficient under the assumption their products or services will not need to change in the short term. In contrast, a service oriented organization must deal with the unknown requirements and the operational variation that satisfying them may create.

q   Beginning in 1994, the Standish Group beginning publishing a series of *Chaos Reports* which provided widely cited, and dismal, statistics on IT project failure rates and cost overruns. In their 1995 Chaos Report they claimed as many as 31% of projects will be cancelled before completion and roughly 50% of projects will cost twice their initial estimates (http://www.standishgroup.

com/visitor/chaos.htm). Although these reports have been criticized over the years for their questionable research methodology and potentially sensationalized statistics (B. Boehm, Project termination doesn't equal project failure, Computer, Vol 33, 9, September 2000), there is some consensus that as the pace of technology accelerates greater visibility into the external forces and stakeholder needs of IT systems is critical for successful project management and to mitigate the risk of failure in the face of uncertainty.

[r] The 'adaptive' has been used in many contexts. Here we use Adaptive Complex Environment to reflect externally-driven alignment originating from Request events. This is not to be confused with Adaptive Communication Environment (ACE) which is a freely available, open-source object-oriented (OO) framework that implements many core patterns for concurrent communication software.

[s] Here the term 'operations' denotes *both* the business process design and its execution.

[t] For example, satisfying a customer service Request may require the use of multiple physical and electronic resources to produce the deliverable. Although it is simple enough to capture a generic Request though the use of an IT system, the actual response by the organization and all of the required resources may not be known a-priori. Note that both the Request, the executed response, and the deliverable have electronic and physical manifestations that have to be kept consistent and traceable. This element of uncertainty adds a layer of complexity to the overall system.

[u] Similar to the distinction between a primary and a secondary process, a primary goal is one that directly leads to revenue for the business.

[v] Ontology is a specification of a conceptualization, in this case to promote interoperability between Business, Operations, and IT dimensions of a business.

[w] A type is an abstract prototypical specification of something or, roughly, a concept. It's useful to contrast a type with an instance of a type which is a physical embodiment of the type. For example, a human can be though of as a type whereas the particular human, Bob, is an instance of the human type. Note that although one might say the type human is always associated with a name, it is not until an instance of that type exists that a name can be assigned a real value, like Bob.

[x] In his 1993 article, in Harvard Business Review, Carr argues that IT is a commodity today and should not generally be viewed as a source of competitive advantage in organizations. To illustrate his point he draws parallels to major technology revolutions of the past, such as the railroad, and concludes that just like these revolutions provided an early advantage for a small number of

innovators their adoption has become so widespread and affordable that they offer little long term strategic advantages at this point in time.

[y]   Excerpt taken from "Building a New Foundation for Innovation: Results of a Workshop for the National Science Foundation", Rand Corporation, 2002.

[z]   TCS Keynote at SEPE Symposium, TRDDC, 12/13/05 -http://www.tcs.com/.

[aa]   ITIL is a best practice framework consisting of a set of books, and a consistent vocabulary, about various aspects of IT Service Management. ITIL has become popular in practice because of its systematic and integrated discussion of all the pieces that have to be brought together to form a successful service driven IT organization. In this book, we will make reference to Service Measurement and Service Level Management quite frequently which are cornerstone components and key parts of ITILv3's Continual Service Improvement volume.

[ab]   Six Sigma is basically a best practice, developed by Motorola, to systematically reduce defects in a production environment. The title, six sigma, refers to the acceptable variance of the production quality which must constantly be measured and reduced. There are numbers web and text resources that introduce Six Sigma – for a good introduction see Pande, Peter et.al. The Six Sigma Way. New York: McGraw-Hill, 2000.

[ac]   Maslow's hierarchy of needs is a theory about personality and motivation which states that as an individual meets certain needs they progress to focusing their attention on the attainment of other needs further up the hierarchy. Generally these needs progress up the hierarchy from primitive self-centric needs of survival, like the need for food, to social or altruistic centered needs such as respect from their community and a sense of morality. Here, we make an analogy to the hierarchy of needs of an organization, hoping that with proper methods for analysis we can understand the basic needs of the business, satisfy them, and move the focus of the business up the hierarchy where the relationships between the business, it's customers, and the community at large are the primary concern.

[ad]   BioS complexity refers to the difficulty in aligning the long term strategic needs of an enterprise with respect to the daily operations and IT systems. In a live enterprise many of the environmental changes, such as customer expectations and demographics, are first sensed during the day to day operations but must be incorporated into the long term strategy of the enterprise if it is to be truly sustainable. Resource, time, and uncertainty constraints that separate an ideal strategy from an ideal implementation constitute the BioS complexity.

[ae]   The U.S. Government Accountability Office (http://www.gao.gov/) requirements.

af   For example TOGAF and ITIL are a few of the standards bodies offering certification programs around enterprise architecture.

ag   DODAF: http://en.wikipedia.org/wiki/Department_of_Defense_Architecture_Framework.

ah   Stakeholder management is no longer about how the enterprise architecture function "sells" to or "manages" stakeholders but rather about identifying who has real and significant needs that the enterprise architecture approach can help to meet, and how the EA function delivers to those stakeholders.

ai   http://en.wikipedia.org/wiki/Health_Insurance_Portability_and_Accountability_Act.

aj   The Sarbanes-Oxley Act of 2002 introduced standards surrounding financial reporting for public U.S. companies.

ak   Socio-technical refers to situations where people interact with technology for some purpose. Socio-Technical systems rely on both the social structures in place as well as technology components in order to function successfully.

al   TOGAF: http://www.opengroup.org/togaf/

am   A 'learning object' is a resource, usually digital and web-based, that can be used and re-used to support learning. Learning objects offer a new conceptualization of the learning process: rather than the traditional "several hour chunk", they provide smaller, self-contained, re-usable units of learning (wiki).

an   Although factual knowledge is relatively easy for IT systems to represent and process, much human knowledge can not be broken down into concrete, certain, or universally transmittable facts. Michael Polanyi coined the term tacit knowledge in reference to certain kinds of knowledge people retain but have trouble expressing or communicating to others, such as exactly *how* to drive a car. Although one can learn to drive a car it is not quite as simple as memorizing some basic facts from a textbook and then doing it, rather it takes some experience and practice to do it well.

ao   http://en.wikipedia.org/wiki/Enterprise_portal.

ap   Zachman's classic 1987 paper represents a cornerstone in the field of Enterprise Architecture. Drawing a parallel from traditional architecture, in the building sense of the word, he convincingly presents an intuitive conceptual framework for thinking about how Information System Architectures should be planned, designed, and ultimately constructed in an era of increasing complexity. The basis for his argument is that Information Systems can be modeled as a set of views, each one essentially different from one another because each captures the essence of the solution through the eyes of a particular stakeholder, architect, or builder in a manner best suited to their role in the larger context of the enterprise. Together they form a complete model of the Information System but in their separation they provide the essential perspectives for holistically understanding Information Systems and the context they operate in. Above all else, he shows that architecture is relative and more about perspective than it is level of detail.

[aq]   Many of the original enterprise architecture frameworks stemmed from the complexity of Computer Integrated Manufacturing (CIM) efforts in the 1980's. Notable frameworks include the Computer Integrated Manufacturing Open System Architecture (CIMOSA) and the Purdue Enterprise Reference Architecture (PERA). These frameworks were attempts to pull out commonalities from typical CIM efforts and abstract them into a set of relatively simple concepts that could be used as representative building blocks for creating new CIM system architectures. Along with a conceptual framework they also typically included a generic process or methodology, such as PERA's Master Planning Methodology, that an enterprise could follow in order to refine its strategic plan, understand what state they are in, or asses their level of maturity with respect to what state they could reasonably reach. Today, the Zachman Framework and TOGAF are among the most well known EA frameworks and they follow in the spirit of providing a common model, or way to look at various aspects of and enterprise, and some kind development process or method (although how these particular frameworks cater to each is quite different). These are also the basis for well-documented DOD frameworks such as DODAF (http://en.wikipedia.org/wiki/Department_of_Defense_Architecture_Framework). Additionally, today EA is generally seen as being much larger in scope, with a larger focus on human and organizational structures, than it was in some of the more technology centric CIM frameworks. The ultimate goal of EA has always been to provide visibility across all the seemingly disparate aspects of an enterprise, and formalizing the concepts and tools required to make EA systematic, shareable, and repeatable - not to mention comprehendible - is a common goal no single framework has yet achieved.

[ar]   Defined in ANSI/IEEE Std 1471-2000.

[as]   http://www.software.org/.

[at]   Thomas Naylor (Naylor,T. 1970) defines a model as ". . . an attempt to describe the interrelationships among a corporation's financial, marketing, and production activities in terms of a set of mathematical and logical relationships which are programmed into the computer." These interrelationships should (according to Gershefski) represent in detail all aspects of the firm including ". . . the physical operations of the company, the accounting and financial practices followed, and the response to investment in key areas" (Gershefski,G. 1971 : 44). Wikipedia.

[au]   The original concept of a pattern language came from Alexander's 1979 book *The Timeless Way of Building,* and it represents the patterns, building blocks,

or rules of thumb that designers, in any discipline, tend to reuse in their general form as they solve new problems.

av   Zachman's classic 1987 paper represents a cornerstone in the field of Enterprise Architecture. Drawing a parallel from traditional architecture, in the building sense of the word, he convincingly presents an intuitive conceptual framework for thinking about how Information System Architectures should be planned, designed, and ultimately constructed in an era of increasing complexity. The basis for his argument is that Information Systems can be modeled as a set of views, each one essentially different from one another because each captures the essence of the solution through the eyes of a particular stakeholder, architect, or builder in a manner best suited to their role in the larger context of the enterprise. Together they form a complete model of the Information System but in their separation they provide the essential perspectives for holistically understanding Information Systems and the context they operate in. Above all else, he shows that architecture is relative and more about perspective than it is level of detail.

aw   http://en.wikipedia.org/wiki/Department_of_Defense_Architecture_Framework

ax   http://enterprisearchitecture.nih.gov/ is a good example.

ay   Working agreements have been reached between the TOGAF 9 development team and the IT Service Management Forum on key terminology in both the architecture development and service management areas.

az   The U.K's Office of Government Commerce (OGC and formerly CCTA) is the official creator of ITIL. As a governmental institution, ITIL was developed in response to the growth and reliance on IT within governmental agencies and fueled by the realization that inconsistent management those various agencies was unneccesialiy expensive and risky.

ba   The customer is the people generally senior managers, who commission and pay for and own the IT services that are sometimes referred to as the business. Users are people who use the services on a day-to-day basis.

bb   For a more detailed introduction to the strategic Component Business Model and the accompanying Process Reference Model for IT see Ernest's article Adding Value to the IT Organization with the Component Business Model, IBM Systems Journal, Vol. 46, No. 3, 2007. by M. Ernest and J. M. Nisavic.

bc   Help Desk Institute: http://www.thinkhdi.com/.

bd   The supply chain or the *external* value chain has been studied extensively (see for example SCOR). The *internal* value chain includes the organizations contributors of services that result in the value perceivable by the customer.

ᵇᵉ   For examples see the National Institute of Health's Enterprise Architecture (http://enterprisearchitecture.nih.gov/) and The Massachusetts Institute of Technology's Enterprise Architecture Guide (http://web.mit.edu/itag/eag/).

ᵇᶠ   The BRG model shows, conceptually, how individual low-level tactical steps can carried out and quantified in a way that is meaningful to the longer term themes that guide the business (Kolber, A.B., Estep, C., Hay, D., Struck, D., Lam, G., Healy, J., Hall, J., Zachman, J.A., Healy, K., Eulenberg, M., Fishman, N., Ross, R., Moriarty, T., Selkow, W., "Organizing Business Plans: The Standard Model for Business Rule Motivation", The Business Rules Group, 2000).

ᵇᵍ   Problem solving is a fundamental human capability, but it may not be so much of a fundamental organizational ability. Senge argues that successful organizations are those which promote generative, clear, and objective thinking and not those which encourage misdirection and reactive, or event oriented, problem solving. His theme is consistent with the fundamental principles contained in this book and its references – that systems thinking is a necessity for understanding all the complexities of the modern world and that fostering a systemic attitude is a prerequisite for truly collaborative, and successful, endeavors. However, promoting systemic thinking in an organizational setting is itself a process that requires introspection and a clear recognition of the social and behavioral forces that govern it. Although our focus is slightly more technical and prescriptive, we believe that idea's like Senge's are intrinsically a part of the co-engineering process.

ᵇʰ   We use the term *business Agent or Agent* to be a human, a human process, an automated process (e.g. a machine), or a software component.

ᵇⁱ   An autonomous Agent is a system situated in, and part of, an environment, which senses that environment, and acts on it, over time, in pursuit of its own agenda. This agenda evolves from drives (or programmed goals). The Agent acts to change the environment and influences what it senses at a later time. [9, lean paper] Introduce the definition of a system of autonomous Agents.

ᵇʲ   RUP: Rational Unified Process. http://fox.wikis.com/wc.dll?Wiki~RationalU nifiedProcess~SoftwareEng.

ᵇᵏ   The Unified Modeling Language (UML) is a commonly used tool for diagrammatically representing various aspects of a software system or systems. Due to its generic nature it is also useful for many kinds of conceptual modeling activities that do not directly involve software, like organizational structures or business processes.

ᵇˡ   Unfortunately, the term ontology and variations of it such as deep ontology, shallow ontology, and surface ontology have been inconsistently used within many fields of study, and especially within computer science. When we use the term deep ontology we are referring to a specification of concepts that approximately specifies the domain as opposed to a shallow or surface ontology that directly specifies only those fairly standard concepts in the domain. In this spectrum a surface ontology may be too weak for detailed and precise communication while a deep ontology may be too difficult or controversial to construct, since it can only be an approximation. Here we are adopting the position that a deeper set of concepts is needed for the practice of EA.

bm   Enterprise integration today is the ad-hoc result of the disciplines of Business, Systems Engineering, and Computer Science. Each of these disciplines offers mechanisms, principles, and practices. Denning uses the following definitions: *Mechanisms* are basic laws that govern computations, *Principles* are conventions for resolving tradeoffs that are then implemented using the mechanisms, and *Practices* are schemes for applying principles to implemented systems.

bn   Herb Simon created the beginning of the Theory of Bounded Rationality. Essentially, when faced with decision-making within highly complex contexts, the individual may not pick the most rational choice.

bo   An important way of accomplishing the goal of lean is to eliminate wait time (George). In most cases, incoming work waits for servicing by a resource. In a lean process management system, every operation and process becomes flexible so that the actual process transformation step (applied using a resource) for the customer creates a demand (pull) to produce only the amount consumed by that customer Request.

bp   According to Paul Horn, senior vice president of IBM Research … "there is a science underlying services that must be explored. …There are enormous inefficiencies in the global gross domestic product," he continued. "If we take out the inefficiencies with optimization and a whole class of areas, the opportunity is huge." He then offered a challenge to the group. "Services is the biggest piece of the U.S. economy, but there aren't any courses to learn how to be a consultant, nothing teaches about business processes. The academic community could play a significant role in establishing this new practice. There is enormous potential for innovation in services science. Are there things we can do to create an entirely new discipline?" Read more at http://domino. research.ibm.com/comm/www_fs.nsf/pages/index.html.

bq   The shared representation and the continuous improvement cycle relates to IT Services CMM (an approach to improving services proposed by SEI).

br   The term emergent is used to describe behaviors that are not predetermined but are in response to external conditions.

bs   An excellent summary is provided by The Project Manager, Goal QPC.

Chapter II
Adaptive Complex Enterprise Framework:
Ontology, Modeling, Co–Engineering Principles, Work Products

ABSTRACT

The ACE structure for coordination across various services using policies to meet overall goals is presented here. The more detailed depiction of the ACE structure in Figure 1 represents further details than in Figure 2, Chapter I. The structure includes the 1) BioS Stakeholders and Dimension, 2) the goal states of their interest, and 3) Agent Interactions that achieve those goal states. The Goal achievements are aggregated for continual improvement and used in decision-making to fine-tune Interactions. These underlying details are developed based on framework parts presented here. They include 1) Interaction ontology, 2) Modeling notation, 3) Principles for analysis, and 4) Work Products and their use in the continuous improvement. The result is goal-oriented ACE management by objectives at all BioS dimensions as we shall see.

How can we conceptualize the performance of value-producing Interactions within dynamic and changing organizations?

- How do we conceptualize the goals of BioS stakeholders and take actions to ensure value is delivered?

Figure 1. Prototypical ACE structure with vertical dimensions each with stakeholders, actions and goals towards continual improvement of services.

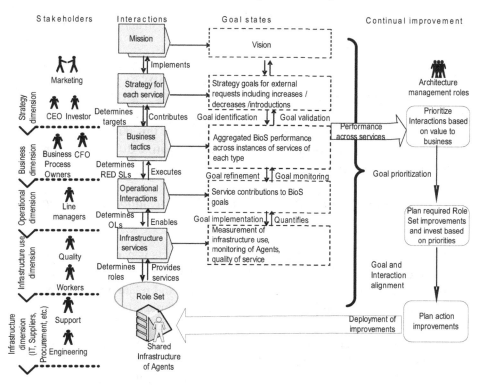

- What is the basic Interaction ontology that defines the points of measurement and service value-add to BioS stakeholders?
- How do we treat shared resources and identify related efficiencies?
- How does it allow us to achieve service planning-to-execution performance traceability?

What modeling notation represents the complex enterprise so that teams can define and visualize important Agent Interactions and their contribution to the organization?

- What is the notation for creating the structure that allows us to view any organization uniformly as Interactions executed by Agents that contribute value to BioS stakeholders (refer to Figure 2, Chapter 1)?
- How does it help us align and improve our achievement of BioS goals?

- How do we use the ACE representation to structure and attain maturity levels?

What principles for analysis can be applied to the ACE structure for concurrent and continuous performance improvement?

- What are the principles that align the BioS perspectives?
- How can we apply business and systems engineering principles for effectiveness?
- How do we develop appropriate representations for this purpose?
- How can we begin to identify, evaluate, and prioritize different options for continuous improvement?

What are the work products resulting from an ACE representation and the application of the principles?

- What range of enterprise architecture work products is needed to contribute to a precise understanding for effective governance of a complex system?
- How do we use the work products to implement and relate best practices for continuous improvement and facilitate more dynamic adaptation strategies?

In the previous chapter we conceptualized ACE as being made up of one or more service BioS that shared some Agents (Figure 2, Chapter I). The BioS nodes in the cycle are in reality *goals* to be achieved and cause-and-effect relationships among the BioS goals. The BioS nodes or dimensions are each made up of additional information such as - stakeholders, Interactions, and goals. To represent all this more easily, we view BioS as a vertical or internal value chain as shown below.

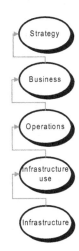

Vertical representation of:

*"**I**nfrastructure and Infrastructure use enables **O**perations to execute **B**usiness tactics that contribute to **S**trategy"*

as an alternate way to look at the associations of the internal value chain. This chain is used vertically, as illustrated in the prototypical ACE structure of Figure 1, and reflects each node of BioS. We separate these as dimensions and can now begin to associate additional stakeholder, Interaction and goal information. Furthermore, acknowledging the importance of users, we introduce an additional Infrastructure dimension that we call Infrastructure use.

Strategy

Business

Operations

Infrastructure use

Infrastructure

ONTOLOGY FOR INTERACTIONS AND BioS PERFORMANCE

Using Agent Interactions to Achieve the BioS Goals within a Complex System: We first conceptualize the performance of on-going value-producing Interactions within the complex system, independent of the actual 'how' details and the states of the underlying associated Agents and artifacts (for related work on value-stream mapping look at Jureta et al 2006). Thus the focus is on articulating the value produced during each Interaction by Agents applied to transform Inputs to Output artifacts to achieve BioS goals[a], over a period of time. To achieve service improvement, the achievement of these goals are assessed and actions are then taken (see related work in Yu & Mylopoulous 1993, Subramanian et al 2003).

The Interaction abstraction introduced next is assembled statically or dynamically into a network of value-producing Interactions. The resulting *ACE structure and representation of a service-oriented organization* has associated performance attributes critical to the various identified BioS stakeholders as illustrated in the pattern of Figure 1 (that is in turn based on Figure 8, Chapter I). With such a structure we can also achieve a basis for applying the Co-engineering methods from related disciplines. It is important to keep in mind that this representation actually models the *execution behavior* of a complex system. This is in contrast to the typical use of modeling approaches for software development which primarily focus on the *creation of the system.*

As mentioned earlier we conceptualize a complex system as an organization of *customer – provider Interactions that contributing BioS value.* We next present this ontology. Following which we introduce the modeling notation that represents the enterprise allowing us to Co-engineer and align BioS Interactions to goals. Related work in enterprise modeling and more formal ontology using OWL[b] is in Fox 2005, Hartung et al. 2008,

RED Interaction and Performance Ontology

Interaction: The basics of an Interaction are introduced in Figure 2 A. Here the Interaction is between Role(s) of the business that are engaged in transforming the Input(s) to the Output(s) artifacts to achieve BioS goals(s)[c]. The term *goal* means a statement of intent whose satisfaction requires a value contributions due to the Interaction. The BioS contribution of an interaction is intuitively like the *performance 'footprint'* of the Interaction.

Service Roles, Agents, and Artifacts: We also use the term *service Role* or often just *Role* to reflect a *prototypical service or skill* provided. The actual services are provided by *assigned Agents.* The Agents play the needed Roles and apply the service to create Output work product(s) starting with Input(s). The Roles might

Figure 2. A: Interaction between input/output artifacts, BioS goals, and roles. B: Illustration of an ACE structure with two interactions during a Pit Stop. C: Illustration of use of the traceability pipe to represent and achieve greater agility during the Pit Stop.

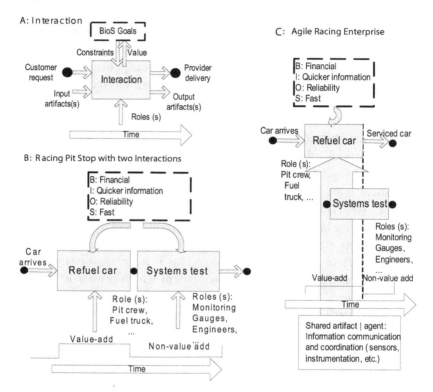

include all types of physical and electronic services to be provided by the Agents that managed within the underlying *infrastructure* of the organization. *Deliverables* are distinguished outputs that are provided to the customer. These can have defects associated with them.

Even Inputs, Outputs, and Deliverables are Agents since the work products can themselves play other Roles. Agents can thus be active or passive components and resources like humans, objects, tools, processes, IT systems[d], and other assets. Thus Agents are defined very generally here. Agents are also ideally viewed here as being autonomous (for ontology research defining autonomous behavior, start with Stojanovic 2004).

Execution of an Interaction: Customers initiate an Interaction by a *Request* event as illustrated by the 'black dot' in Figure 3. During the Interaction, the provider provisions Agents in the *infrastructure^e* and services the Interaction Roles to produces a service *Deliverable*. The completion of an Interaction event is by the provider. The execution is determined as follows:

- An Interaction can proceed as soon as the necessary Roles are assigned Agents that are needed to begin, and
- Inputs needed to proceed become available.

Any time waiting for these two things to happen is considered the *queue time* of that Interaction. Customers and providers can be internal or external to the organization, however internal customers work on behalf of the external one in a traceable fashion by initiating a Request. The provider uses the services of various Roles and Agent resources needed for the execution of the Interaction.

Delayed Binding: Note that the Agents in the infrastructure might not actually be assigned to Roles until the Interaction itself is ready to execute. This is called delayed binding. An Interaction waits only if it cannot proceed. This allows Interactions to execute with as much dynamic (i.e. not explicitly modeled as a precedence relationship) parallelism as possible. The initiator of the Interaction (or a proxy) assigns the initial Roles if defaults are not applicable or available. The Interaction completes with the use of Agents that resource the Roles. Specific time metrics are associated with Agent use. There are also other metrics and these are all reported as actual value contributions to BioS as we shall see.

Service Value-add: Figure 2 B illustrates how the Interaction in A can be used to represent Pit Stop Interactions during a car race. While there are many Interactions during a Pit Stop, we represent only two in this model for simplicity. The Pit Stop representation sequences two Interactions called 'Refuel car' and 'Systems test'. These associate all the artifacts (inputs such as the fuel truck and outputs such as the serviced car), the Roles (the driver, the pit crew, the equipment) to the *business goals*. The Pit Stop representation has a notion of *time* and *value-add*.

It must be emphasized that value-add is always defined from the *customer or request originator's* perspective. Here we can quickly see that the from the customer or strategic perspective (the fans and driver in this case), the systems test does not add value. This Interaction does not directly contribute to the winning strategy goal (it does so only indirectly).

Next in Figure 2 C the improved Agile Pit Stop representation is made up of *parallel* Interactions. Agility here is achieved through improved communication and coordination between the different Roles (pit crew, engineer etc.). The underlying Agents includes sensors, gauges, and other ways of information sharing that allow the engineers to monitor and begin testing as the car is being refueled. Also, in that case, some *non-value-add* time is eliminated. In other word, the communication leverages sophisticated instrumentation providing instantaneous visibility into the most current conditions of the car.

RED Interaction events: In Figure 3 RED steps of the Interaction expands the conceptualization of an Interaction to further include the formal milestone events or hand-off points where BioS value contributions and wait times can be measured. Thus the objective of the RED Interaction structure is to make explicit important transitions from all the perspectives and points of metrics collection. This is achieved as follows:

- *Customer perspective:* A *primary* Interaction begins with the *Request event* (for a particular type of Request) within the end-customer's environment and ends with the related *service deliverable*(s) that adds value to the customer's environment. During the Interaction, there are also many customer Roles (e.g. race car driver, sponsor, etc.) that review and participate as the service progresses.

- *Conceptual RED Interaction and performance perspective:* During the course of the Interaction explicit *transitions between milestone events* (represented as ⇨) occur between the steps- Requirements, Execution, and Delivery (also called R, E, and D or just RED)[f]. The Request is examined and the provider negotiates and understands the service requirements. Then both the customer

Figure 3. Customer-provider service Interaction and RED milestones.

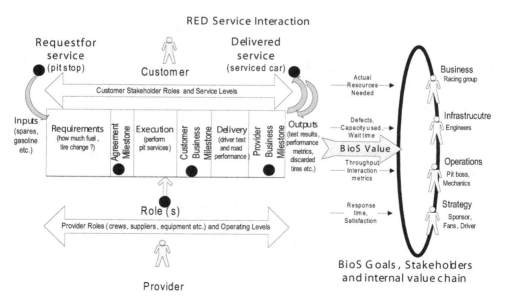

and provider agree to proceed based on a formal/informal proposal or 'agreement milestone'. For example, here the fuel provider would agree on the types of fuel combinations that could potentially be provided, based on weather conditions. Next, transitioning from Requirements to Execution, the provider assigns Agents to the execution Roles to service the Request. The Interaction Roles (e.g. pit crew and fuel truck) together provide the capability to do the necessary set-up, execution, and completion of the service[g]. At the same time the transformations *create value* from the customer's perspective thus completing the next milestone. Simultaneously, feedback to the infrastructure results in future potential to improve the value. Finally the delivery in the customer's environment in the third step results in provider's compensation. In this case this includes compensating for the fueling and system check services.

In general, a service Interaction can be simple as in the case of delivering a product. Or it can be an Interaction like the order fulfillment, or the incident resolution, or even a 'one-of-a-kind' project. In these cases, Interactions often use sub-Interactions that are also initiated with a Request from an internal customer. (Incomplete Interactions and exceptions will be addressed later).

- *Provider perspective:* The transitions between the milestone events are achieved using provider (and sometimes supplier or even customer) services. For each service *Request type* - say complaint type, or standard service type, or design type - handled by the organization, there is a RED service Interaction template with required Roles that will need to be eventually filled by available Agents with certain *capabilities* needed to execute the Interaction (see example in the Highlight later in this chapter).

Highlight: Examples of Interactions

Loan application (requirements) ⇨ Credit and title check (execution) ⇨ Loan approval (delivery)

Patient in for treatment is diagnosed (requirements) ⇨ treatment is delivered (execution) ⇨ payment is collected (delivery)

Purchase requisition (requirements) ⇨ purchase Request (authorizing payment upon execution by vendor) ⇨ receiving report and payment (delivery)

Work order (requirements) ⇨ Work description (execution of actual work) ⇨ Work approval and payment authorization (delivery)

Next a nested interaction example:

Primary interaction: Request for quote (requirements) ⇨ Work order (execution at the shop floor) ⇨ Delivery to customer.

Secondary interaction at the supplier: Bid proposal (requirements clarified) ⇨ Work order (execution upon authorization from customer) ⇨ Delivery for successful customer's work order.

It is also interesting to note that all business related paper and electronic forms used in business embody these interactions. For example a interaction at Amazon.com is:

Request for a book and Credit card payment (requirements) ⇨ Work order to ship book (execution at the warehouse) ⇨ Delivery to customer.

Some interesting points can be made with this particular interaction. A interaction step can involve other sub-interactions – like a credit card authorization. Also, trust is involved – the customer expects to receive the order and makes the payment in advance. Such interactions are supported by the legal system. As a matter of fact, ubiquitous legal support for the customer/provider protocol is even born out by the early recordings of business interactions and commitments in cuneiform tablets of the Hetites in 2000 B.C. where extreme punishment was meted out for a contractual breach.

Interactions are also the very basis of the business language according to the Speech Act Theory (Winograd & Flores 1987), as documented in the SCOR model by the Supply Chain Council with hundreds of industry members, and as captured in enterprise applications.

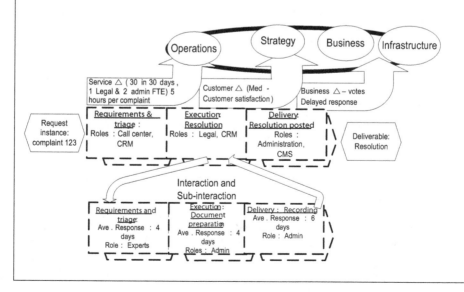

A Primary RED within an organization– a city - is illustrated here. Roles (i.e. Organization, enterprise application) perform the needed services. A secondary Request (sub-RED) to complete delivery is also illustrated. The performance metrics shown are aggregated across instances. They illustrate $\triangle$ contributions to the customer, business, service and capability. The Roles are performed by the underlying infrastructure capabilities.

Note that there can be many Interaction instances of each particular Request type. That is, there can be many on-going races and cars participating in each race. Also it is useful to compare an Interaction with an activity[h] and a pattern of business activity as in ITIL.

RED Interaction Both Separates and Conceptually Relates Customer & Provider Viewpoints: Best practice in collaboration and communications management with the customer dictates that the provider's internal details – such as the operating level details, cost of actual resources, assigned Roles, exceptions, and other implementation details – should be shared with the customer only on a need-to-know basis.

At the same time during the service Interaction customer often needs to be fully involved in much of the technical decision making. This involvement is addressed by the many different customer and provider Roles that are involved during the Interaction. The Role-based access to Interaction details provides the needed information on a need-to-know basis. This is illustrated by the Pit stop Interaction - *the sponsor is typically not interested in the internal provider interaction like the system check.*

Measuring Interaction Contributions to Goals

'A RED Interaction further formalizes the meaning and semantics of an Interaction. It takes a structured view of the Interaction between 1) the customer-provider Role perspectives, 2) the Request and Deliverables perspective, and 3) the infrastructure Roles and resources perspective. this structure can be used to capture and monitor the events 'black dots' of the Interaction in Figure 3. For non-routine Requests typical of a service organization, this allows us to look at an activity in a more *nuanced* fashion and in particular make explicit its contributions to BioS stakeholder goals at these points. The metrics are also captured at the milestones. This is captured more precisely next.

Simultaneous Interaction Value-add to BioS Goals: Any primary or secondary *business-related* Interaction adds some incremental positive or negative value (represented as $\triangle$) *simultaneously* to BioS perspectives. For *each Request type,* the R, E and D the contributions of value are measured at milestones as follows (see Figure 3):

- *Requirements identifying △ needed from Operations*: Upon the arrival of a new Request, its *service requirements* from a customer perspective are identified. This includes technical requirements (such as design, quality, quantity) and business requirements (such as price, lead time etc.). Next requirements from the provider's perspective is identified. This results in identifying the *services and capacity* that must be committed by the *infrastructure* for the next step which is 'Execution'. Some things – say price - is typically shared with the customer as part of the bidding process or agreement.
  The resources also contribute to operational △ measures: throughput and cost. Other things are private - costs are typically not shared. Once the needed investment by the provider is defined, the transition occurs with a formal or informal agreement or *authorization to proceed* to the next step. The infrastructure use estimates during R are as accurate as possible and often refined during E.
- *Execution △ contribution to Strategy*: The execution milestone is completed with the provider's Agents with service capabilities used *to execute* the Roles. These Agents provide the services that *transform* the artifacts (designs, raw materials, components, information, etc.) to create the *delivered service and value to the customer*. The strategy △ is measured as value perceived by the customer (i.e. the increment of 'price' the customer is willing to pay for this step). This could be measured in quantitative or qualitative terms. For example, for a public institution, this value can be captured in relative terms – such as citizen satisfaction - rather than financial terms. The satisfaction measure could be relative as in – 'high', 'medium' or 'low'.
- *Delivery △ contribution and feedback to Business and Infrastructure*: This milestone is reached upon closure at which point the promised quality of service is assured *in the customer's environment*. The actual use of Agents to complete the services and the *quality of the delivered services* is also measured. The infrastructure feedback is often defined as corrective actions, skills training needs, reasons for cost overruns etc. This is the desired improvement or infrastructure △ for future service Interactions. Last but not the least, the resulting *business △* is defined as the value of the Interaction – e.g. contribution to the *margin* (as we shall see later).
  The business △ of an Interaction is also used in competitive analysis. For example, if a Request is processed more cost-effectively within the competition, then it is time to re-asses operations. In the pit stop example, the business closure for the pit crew is compensation for the services.

Note that we will use △ to mean relative increase or decrease in a metric, leaving the actual context to determine the performance specifics. For example, an organization's target Request △ of 50% might represent either that repair Requests *decrease* by 50% or that custom design Requests *increase* by 50%. We will also represent the use of Agents as ‡.

Finally, note that a RED Interaction represents *only the points* at which *commitments* are made between the customer and provider during the execution of their *own respective business processes.* The RED *transition points* and milestones are critical to the measurement of service performance and for continuous improvement. At these transition points the focus is on capturing metrics and *not* on *how* the participating Agents *themselves* are modeled and organized for execution. For example, an Interaction does not dictate how the Agents in organizations report to one another, whether they are internal or external, or whether the process are automated, or the processes and information details employed to complete the Interactions.

Other approaches to the value of service orientation are presented in Cherbakov 2005. Goal-oriented concepts for adding value to business are further discussed in Cameron 2007, Chung 1999, Cunha 2008, Gordijn et al 2006, Lamsweerde et al 1998 and Lamsweerde t al 2001.

Dynamic ACE Structure of Interactions and Sub-Interactions: An ACE structure consists of many *primary* (customer facing) and *secondary* (internal infrastructure related) RED Interactions and sub Interactions that allow us to view the enterprise conceptually – through a performance lens. Examples of primary REDs in an organization include order-to-cash. Secondary interactions enable the primary ones and include procure-to-pay, engineering change, and incident-to-resolution.

A primary RED is typically initiated by filling a *Request form* at a web-site, or an application, or even an email. A Request is also known as an order, a work order, an admittance form, an incident report, ticket etc. Based on the Request type, RED instances can be assembled dynamically (or pre-assembled statically) to form an ACE structure.

At any point during the execution of the R, E, D steps, new Requests can initiate sub-Interactions that complete unanticipated sub-deliverables. Thus a primary Interaction is achieved by internal customers and providers, on behalf of an external customer. For example, when providing a PC installation service unanticipated interactions might include cabling or a non-standard image on the Requested PC.

Finally, the Interaction steps can be in different states of execution - executing with actual resources, waiting on Agents, waiting for other Interactions to complete, and so on. Interaction steps can be scheduled for execution. For example, an agreement on Requirements can be reached and the Execution can take place (iteratively if needed) at a later scheduled time. An Interaction can even be viewed as an Agent for another interactions. Thus the state of an interaction gives us significant insights that can be mined from the metrics.

In addition to the on-going Interactions, the ACE structure has goals of interest to the various BioS stakeholders as illustrated in Figure 1. It also has the various policies for coordination across services that are applied by the ACE architects for continual improvement as shown.

Extensible, Locally-Defined Non-Routine Interactions: New Interactions of different types can also be introduced to an ACE structure at any point – within an existing Interaction or as an independent Interaction. Thus, the simple RED Interaction pattern can be used repeatedly, recursively, and concurrently by different teams to plan and execute the response variations across the enterprise. An interaction is locally defined since the template identifies all its requirements for execution.

A variety of static or dynamic sequencing strategies can be implemented between Interactions, with data artifacts dependency between Interactions and Agent availability being the only real constraint that must be met prior to execution.

RED Commitments, Service Levels, and Events: The real purpose of the Interaction abstraction is to capture metrics and performance. Especially for non-routine Requests, the monitoring is critical from BioS perspectives as it represents commitments between the customer and provider.

The commitment-driven transitions between the RED milestones reflect formal or informal agreements between the customer Roles (e.g. procurement, designer, patient, and insurer) and provider Roles (e.g. customer service, business liaison, engineer and marketing). The typical commitments are:

R⇌E: Customer-provider agreement on the requirements of the deliverable The requirements takes the form of Service Level Objectives, request for proposals or quotes. The provider agrees to provide services in the form of contracts, SLAs[i], or even verbal commitments, and invests in and maintains the infrastructure. The customer agrees to compensate for the services. Some of infrastructure commitments include:

- Capacity of each resource needed
- Cost of each resource
- Risk of successful delivery
- Delivery such as when, where (location) and quality

E⇌D: Provider uses resources to create customer value as agreed to and thus contribute to strategy △.

Metrics from the perspective *of the customer* include:

- Lead time defined as service interaction time
- Service quality and availability
- Price

These are often part of a SLA.

The execution metrics from the provider perspective includes:

- Time for primary and sub Interactions
- Span time (which resources were used and for how long) and wait time for each of the underlying Agents used
- Defects with the deliverable(s)

Here, in order to meet the SLs, secondary agreements with *provider Agents* that perform the services during execution are put into place. These take the form of OLAs[j], OLOs, procurement contracts, verbal instructions, work instructions, job descriptions, and prescribed processes etc.

$D \rightrightarrows$ Closure: Note that at this point we are closing the Interaction by delivering within the customer's environment and context. Here we can identify metrics both for continuous Improvement and the business:

- Value of the deliverable and Interaction closure within the customer's environment resulting value to the business in monetary or relative terms
- Delivered service and process problems identified - deliverable defects detected, wait times, inadequate resource training, etc.)

Noting that most of the metrics identified are based on time duration of associations between Agents and artifacts within an Interaction, we illustrate how we can project these onto different planes in Figure 4.

Infrastructure

To manage the costs of specialized infrastructure resources and increase the utilization, most organizations now share resources across multiple Interactions. For example, knowledge workers, IT database systems, and assets like enterprise systems are often shared. Such resources are known as *shared Agents and resources*. In these organizations, there is also a 'chargeback' question of what costs should be ascribed to which on-going Interactions and Requests types. In addition, these Interactions might each share many resources. To conceptualize all this, we next examine how the infrastructure is shared for Request servicing.

Figure 4. Example of metrics capture based on the standard Interaction ontology

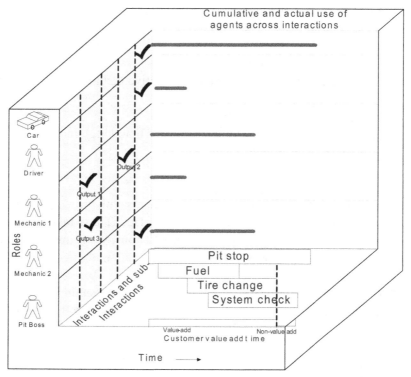

Role set: As introduced below (Figure 6) each Request type has an Interaction template (a kind of project template) that defines its REDs. The template defines the association between specific Interaction steps and also the *Role Set* needed for each of Requirements, Execution, and Delivery. The Roles identify underlying infrastructure services but not the "how." During execution, each RED template instance captures the specific way the provider's Roles addressed local variation with the resources assigned to the Roles, the time taken, why executed, costs, and so on. We define the Role Set as the collection of Roles that are needed, and sometimes required *all together,* to provide the services that produce the R, E, D artifacts.

Role set, Agents, Resources, Components: To understand relationship between these terms and relationships, we note that a particular shared Agent may have the capability to play several service Roles. For example, an expert engineer can play the Role of a 'supervisor' or a 'designer' and meet the respective task descriptions. These Agents also have OL objectives that have to be met for *each* of the Roles that they play. An example OL requirement is 'response time of x hours'. There is also an OL objective for the whole Role set to achieve the Interaction SL. All this

Figure 5. Example of Interaction instance metrics captured and accumulated in the BioS dimensions.

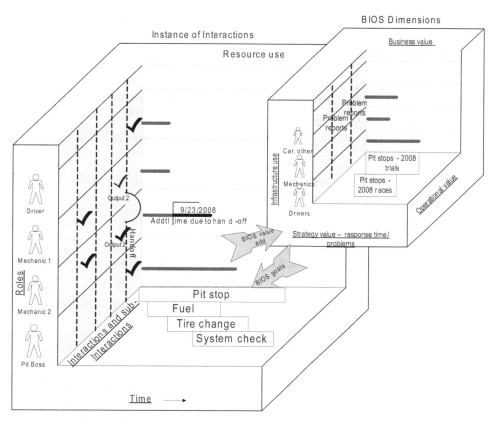

comes at a cost. When we look at an Agent from a cost perspective we will use the term 'resource'. As mentioned previously we use the term Agent in the sense of an 'Agent for transformation achieved through applied services'. In that sense an Agent can be an active or passive software or hardware component, a human, an automated system, or a process.

Planning-to-Execution Traceability in the ACE Structure

Triage and RED Execution Using Shared Resources: The actual assignment of the shared resources to Interaction Roles is often called 'triage' and has the following steps:

Figure 6. Traceability between the Shared resources, the Role Set of shared services, the related RED Interaction type and execution of all its related Requests.

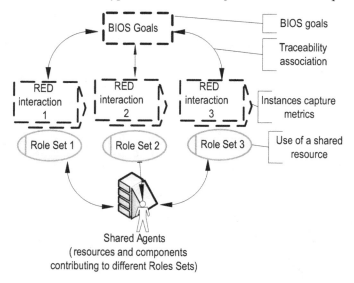

Shared Agents
(resources and components
contributing to different Roles Sets)

- *Logging the Request:* At the point the Request is received, the detailed require-ments are captured and rules applied to classify the Request.
- *Assigning shared Agents:* The type of the Request is *classified* and used to determine the needed Roles. These are then assigned from available infra-structure Agents to perform that Role in execution. Thus for a given Request type (i.e. Design Change RFP) there can be many Interaction instances (i.e. Design Change for Company x, Design Change for Company y,…). Each Interaction instance is assigned specific Agents with the ability to play the designer Role. At that point the Interaction transitions into execution. Finally, sub-Requests can initiate Interactions dynamically to provide sub-deliverables for a parent Request. These are also triaged as needed. Interactions are often dynamically introduced for a variety of reasons – to handle new requirements, exceptions, early notice, etc. Highlight 1 illustrates an incoming complaint resolution Request causing a RED Interaction and a dynamic sub-Interaction to execute within the city government.
- *Dynamic networking and dealing with variation:* The result of triage is that for each non-routine Request type and its RED - Role Set, the binding of re-sources to Roles and the sequencing of the needed sub-Interactions is delayed until more is known about the incoming Requests[k]. this provides a dynamic networking capability that reacts to the exact situation in hand.

The capacity of an agent is impacted when new instances are assigned and queued. An agent's queue time negatively impacts the SL for the RED and the OLO for the entire Role Set. We shall the issue of increasing the capacity to deliver services to meet SLs later in this Chapter. Finally, *Infrastructure use* metrics also allows us to monitor each resource. Since each resource plays many Roles, their RED Interaction metrics allows us to figure out the exact use, the availability and the cost of resources for *that* Interaction.

ACE Structure, BioS Goals and Dimensions: There are many Business, IT, Operations, and Strategy stakeholders and goals – some focused on the tactics and others on longer-term strategy; those concerned about the delivery of a single Request and others ensuring all Requests of a type are delivered efficiently. The term *dimension* is used group all the stakeholders with the similar time and scale perspectives.

Specifically, strategy, business and operational performance is typically viewed in the aggregate or *in-the-large*. The metrics for all Interaction instances is aggregated at the type level – either with a *Request type in the strategy and business dimensions* or with its *Interaction type in the operational dimension* (Figure 5). At the *execution dimension*, the metrics is actually captured at an *instance* level. At execution (typically enabled by IT) the actual value contributions are made *in-the-small*. These are then aggregated *in-the-large*. Metrics are aggregated and synthesized to reflect performance trends that provide input into decision-making for the different stakeholders.

Interactions Performance In-The-Small and In-The-Large: Transactions are the basis for any business (see for example Sampson 2003) - as in order fulfillment - and occur i*n-the-large*. Transactions also occur *in-the-small* when the order fulfillment causes hundreds of data base transactions. Thus they represent how value is added at the level of an IT service, or at the level of the business process, or across the supply chain, or across market segments. Some of Interactions in the organization are *in-the-small* Interactions and others are *in-the-large* and business oriented. Interactions therefore forms a base or canonical concept that relates the enterprise activities *at all scales*.

Here, we use the word 'Interaction' to avoid confusion with many similar words 'task', 'transaction' or 'activity' – like database transaction, business transaction, business activity and so on - and their uses. Using a single term like Interactions allows us to think of the organization as a fractal (Ramanathan 2005). Finally, an Interaction can represent and abstract both *primary* business and revenue generating processes like patient handling, engineering change, etc. and enabling *secondary* processes like IT service support, returns, etc.

Building upon the illustration in Figure 3 where REDs allow us to trace the internal value-chain commitments and resulting simultaneous value-add contribution of an Interaction instance to the Bios stakeholders, we now can see how these contributions can be aggregated to give us the performance from the BioS stakeholder perspectives. That is, Business value of the Infrastructure-based Interaction performance related to Operational cost, and the delivered value contribution to Strategy. The △ RED contributions are aggregated at the Request type as shown by 'Pit Stop trials' and 'Pit Stop races', Figure 5. Thus the ACE structure gives us a conceptual way to view and manage in-the-small and in-the-large Interactions within a single enterprise framework.

Performance Aggregation and Project Management: In a general sense, each RED and sub-RED can be associated with the deliverables and sub-deliverables within a project's work breakdown structure as illustrated in Highlight 1 (see for example Martin & Tate 1997). In addition to representing a project task, the RED template has additional execution semantics that helps us monitor the progress and relate that to both earned value and technical progress (i.e. simultaneous △). Thus, the RED structure goes beyond typical project management to become an Interaction structure with precise semantics that can actually be executed (manually or electronically) to provide a conceptual layer integrating business and infrastructure use. The result is a conceptual performance structure for real-time monitoring and predictive capabilities.

RED risk, early alerts and defects: By monitoring the RED execution we can look for a variety of symptoms. These can be from different BioS perspectives. For example, if a primary interaction does not move from an 'R' to an 'E' state we know that the Requirements agreement was not reached with the customer. This is an indication of proposal and revenue risk. If an Interaction is queued at execution too long, we can also infer that the committed resources are not available. By looking at the defects reported against the deliverable, we begin to look for root causes. For example, was there an adequate assignment of Agents? Another example of the use of metrics for performance is that if an Interaction has moved into execution, then agreement has been achieved and the achievement of business value is will need an investment in resources. When an Interaction moves into execution, we can also provide an early alert to all potential Roles. If defects exist in the delivered service/ product, they could identify the need for training and better tools. And so on.

RED Location and other Contexts: An Interaction can be initiated and executed in a variety of different physical and system contexts. Examples of these include - Location, Organization, Agents, and Other Interactions. An Interaction can also be completed partly in the physical and partly in the electronic world. For example, a claims initiation Interaction might be executed on location but completed with back office applications. An example of many Interactions executed in the context of each other is the global supply chain. For example the portal for a car model design often supports tens of thousands of suppliers around the world that perform

Interactions to complete engineering change needed to build a new prototypes – a non-routine activity. An example of the dynamic interplay between Interactions is studied as the 'bullwhip' effect[l].

In summary, the coordination across the enterprise is based on the fundamental Interaction pattern, first introduced in the field of economics[m] to explain the behavior of markets. The Interaction concept is refined here to represent the internal value-chain of complex organizations reacting to external trends. We call this a RED service Interaction. Specifically a RED (Requirements ⇨ Execution ⇨ Deliver) service Interaction and its value-add contributions to the BioS dimensions and stakeholders forms the basic ACE ontology for performance traceability. Using this we will also draw upon the insights of a growing and diverse community that has been applying fractals (recursive structures based on the more general Complexity or Chaos Theory) that allow us to characterize and understand the behaviors of complex systems and the manner in which they respond to unexpected demands and changes in their environment[n]. We will show later that the characterization ACE itself is based on a small number of patterns. We will also look at the ways to monitor interaction events and gain additional knowledge.

MODELING: ACTIONS, STATES, AND BIOS STAKEHOLDERS

The starting point for an ACE structure in Figure 1 is the modeling notation in Figure 7 and the concepts introduced below[o]. The reader is encouraged to refer to both figures.

Goal States

We begin with an *organization* that is made up of dimensions. Each dimension groups the stakeholder Roles, their desired goal states and required Interactions to achieve those states. More formally, a goal state is a prescriptive statement of intent whose satisfaction in general requires certain Interaction metrics to be achieved through Agents. As illustrated in Figure 1 the BioS goals also collectively ensure the enabling agent services are available across Request types and at the right cost to meet the external customer requirements. The different dimensional perspectives ensure all aspects of each single Interaction are addressed. These BioS perspectives are given next starting from business:

- *Business goals* refine external facing goals to ensure that business value is created by an optimal infrastructure capable of addressing different types of

Figure 7. Modeling notation with Actions, States, and Roles.

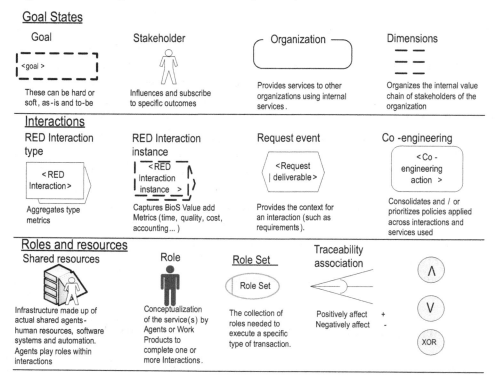

Requests and their Interaction requirements. This defines business value and priorities and used this to define budget allocations and investments.

- *Infrastructure-use goals* typically validate that all the workers that complete primary Interactions and sub-Interactions contribute value as efficiently as possible. Typical metrics that can be captured at the RED points include:
- *Business–related:* As primary Interaction value delivered for the services used.
- *Infrastructure–use-related:* As actual service and resource costs.
- *Operations-related:* As throughput, service failure incidents, knowledge used for execution, and suggestions for improvement. These are often referred to as non-functional aspects of the system in software engineering.
- *Strategy–related:* As time to respond and requirements met in customers' environment.
- *Operational goals* implement the specific provisioning for individual Interactions of a Request type to ensure that it meets business and strategy goals.

- *Strategy goals* are identified based on *customer* service needs and trends, new opportunities, and the competitive environment.

As illustrated in Figure 1, the goal states influence each other. This is discussed next.

Dimensions - in-the-large to in-the-small: Recall that Interactions on the left of Figure 1 achieve certain goal states identified on the right. That is, the execution of the mission achieves the vision state, strategy is a component of the mission, tactics implements the mission, and operations executes the business tactics achieving the goal states on the right. The Interactions (also actions on the left) elaborate the in-the-small operational Interactions, infrastructure services used by these Interactions, and shared Agents providing these services needed for the in-the-large business tactics. Interactions within the organization execute the tactics, and services are consumed during the Interaction. On the right we see how in-the-small metrics achieved due to actions contribute to the organization's vision.

The BioS *dimensions* structure the *Stakeholders, Roles and Responsibilities* that deal with the in-the-large actions and the equally important in-the-small Interactions within the organization. Some of the Roles within a dimension complete actions that achieve immediate performance objectives, others focus on long-term performance. The engineer Roles are typically responsible for longer-term infrastructure improvements, whereas the line workers Roles deal with processing of Requests. A worker is more immediately focused and on a single Request. When these types of Roles complete actions, they contribute to the performance goals in-the-large. Figure 8 gives examples of the different types of goals and perspectives.

Within a dimension the stakeholder goals have similar scale of interest in terms of individual Requests or groups of Requests. For example, the investor-stakeholder is interested more in the *volume* of Requests handled in-the-large, whereas the line management-stakeholder is interested more in ensuring the quality of deliverable for *each* Request in the small. The dimensions thus structure according to the *scale* of the goals of interest and the *stakeholder Roles*. Note that we can have additional dimensions and even nested dimensions.

Internal Sense and Respond Value Chain: Referring to the arrows between the dimensions of Figure 1, we also note that each dimension identifies the goals and stakeholders or internal customers[p] that form the target context within which the nested provider dimensions must perform. This is especially true for a service organization that must remain adaptive to the external influences. The responsibilities along the *secondary customer–provider* value chain are as follows:

- *Strategy dimension responsibilities:* These Roles interact with the different customers and market segments[q]. They are also one of the stakeholders of the

Figure 8. Examples of different goals from different shot-term and long-term BioS perspectives.

Tactical goals	Strategic goals	
Business and financial tactics	Strategic value	
Increase revenue	On-time delivery	Customer demand and loyalty
Increase margins	Customer service	Customer satisfaction
Operational tactics	Operational strategy	
Increase throughput	Intellectual capital	Product/process innovation
Product/process quality	Time to market	Knowledge management
Reduction of waste	Empolyee skills	Time spent with customers
Cost of resources		
IT Infrastructure tactics	IT Infrastructure strategy	
Support and delivery	Information needs	
Security and compliance	Knowledge re-use	
Disaster recovery	Product/process innovation	
Service quality	New technology opportunities	

organization's nested *business dimension*. A major management responsibility is to identify the external forces and longer-term trends, using Porter's competitive analysis framework as outlined in the next section, and convert it to immediate service performance targets for the nested dimensions as Figure 7 shows. These Roles must also define *Request types* to be handled and the competitiveness requirements with respect to each of the different *Request types and their market segments*. Based on this the CEO^r and business development Roles must articulate the goals that improve the organization's current Request performance. This requires performance information *aggregated* for all instances of that Request type. The time-frame is determined by the market and competition.

- *Business dimension responsibilities:* These Roles manage the financial performance of the organization, and sub-organizations like departments, by considering the aggregated business value contribution due to each Request type. The Roles here 1) allocate budgets to achieve the RED Interaction and SL requirements, 2) measure financial effectiveness, and 3) make investment decisions based on priorities. They are responsible for the *business dimension* of the organization and are the stakeholders of *operations or the business process* dimension on which they exert certain constraints. The time frame of interest is based on the financial planning cycles.

- *Operation dimension responsibilities:* These Roles manage service effectiveness and throughput. They manage the 1) performance of RED Interaction instances of a Request type to meet SLs, 2) Lean agent provisioning to provide services, 3) meet OLs, and 4) deliver the desired service to the customer. The primary Roles here include line managers. These Roles are in turn the stakeholders of the next nested *execution or infrastructure use dimension*. Their time frame for response is determined by the average cycle time of the Request. (For background start with Lean Enterprise Institute, Womack & Jones 2008).

- *Infrastructure-use dimension responsibilities:* These Roles provide services and deliverables to the customer. The execution *simultaneously* adds business and technical value to the other BioS dimensions when completed. The primary Role here is the worker applying the transformation service as needed for the specific Request *instance*. The primary stakeholders are the end customer as well as the operations dimension. The time frame is immediate. Actual metrics are captured.
- *Infrastructures resources:* These are the shared resources that get assigned to play Roles at a certain cost. The objective is to enable the efficiency of Interactions and the resources are often valued based on the Interactions that they support. Thus the primary stakeholder is the operation dimension.

In summary, each provider dimension in the internal value chain performs to meet the goals of its customer dimensions and stakeholders as we see in the middle column of Figure 7. A good starting point for management roles and responsibilities is in Drucker 1975.

Primary and secondary organizations and value-chain: We may wish to represent details of many related organizations in a single ACE structure using the organization symbol. There are often many value chains of interest to be represented. An example of a primary organization and its value chain of customer facing RED Interactions in operations is 'Sales→Claims'. Here after the Sales Interaction completes, the Claims Interactions can occur. Such a value chain also has typically has secondary organizations such as IT, human resources, internal | external suppliers etc. The sole objective of the secondary organization such as IT is to meet the performance goals of the primary organization.

Within a function, the BioS dimensions identifies the internal value chain and goals and takes actions to meet states. When many organization are involved we may not always represent their internal value chains separately. this is in order to keep our structures as simple as possible.

Interactions

To-be goals states are achieved by continuous improvement actions that implement the tactics as shown in. The Interactions are specialized as follows:

1. *Request event:* A Request is initiated in the strategy dimension – that is, by the customer. The Request details the customer's context and requirements. Characterizing the different Requests types is critical so that the appropriate provisioning can drive the organization's response. For example a high-level characterization of Requests could be:
    o   Routine Requests
    o   Non-routine Requests needing special processing
    o   Non-routine Requests further characterized as seasonal variation, emergency and so on
2. *RED Interaction Type definition:* For each Request type, this object is planning to meet the RED milestones using Roles that apply to inputs to produce outputs. At the same time these Roles contribute value to the different dimensions.
3. *RED Interaction Instance:* The execution of the Interaction is achieved by assigning the actual resources to its Roles. Note that all Actions - Requests or Interactions - have associated quantitative or qualitative metrics.
4. *Co-engineering:* The Co-engineering action applies policies *across all types of other Interactions* based on the performance of RED Interactions and Request Types. The performance contribution to the goals of each of the dimensions of the organization is evaluated and optimized by applying certain policies. The policies combine priorities and actual performance to determine next target priorities for improving future Interactions and, thus, goals.

Roles and Resources

Complexity in service organization arises in part due to the need to manage high-cost shared resources in the face of uncertain demand. To address this, the ACE notation also identifies shared resources and Roles they play in different Role *Sets* of Interactions. In the previous chapter we have shown the delayed binding relationship between Interactions, Roles, and resources, achieved through the conceptualization of a Role Set.

An example of a Role Set is - document sharing site *plus* permitted title Agents that provide 'home title check' services. Without the Agents, the Interaction cannot successfully complete. Another is - Yahoo Groups *plus* the knowledge workers that work on a proposal. A final more challenging example is - level 2 support groups *plus* CRM software *plus* ERP services for status check *plus* tooling and human resources needed to manufacture a custom component. Note that the related terms Agents, Roles and resources are used here frequently, leaving the context to determine the exact meaning.

Thus the Role Set concept is a composition of all of the required physical and electronic Roles that are all needed to provide services to complete a particular

RED Interaction type. For example, many different organizations and applications provide the cluster of Roles and services - or the Role Set - to complete 'claims'.

Role Sets also provide the needed resources to execute all the Interactions of a given type. This concept is quite similar to a physical work-center which is organized to provide the needed tools and Agents for transformations. We can think of the Role Set as an *eWorkcenter* (or an electronic work center).

Some specific aspects of the logical ACE structure and conceptualization are:

- The Roles can be dynamically bound, if needed, to available Agents at any point before needed within the Interaction execution. Thus a Role is simply a placeholder that allows us to delay the association between a service requirement and Agents with the needed capabilities. Thus, the 'virtual' enterprise concept can be implemented.
- Since a resource is shared, the operating level requirements imposed through the Roles in different Role Sets are different.
- Since a shared infrastructure agent can fill Roles in many different Role Sets, available capacity can be more fully utilized if conflicting demand can be managed.

Traceability and monitoring: From the prototypical *ACE structure* in Figure 1, we can see different associations between the dimensions and between the Interactions and goal states. We generalize all the cause-and-effect *propagation* along the underlying associations between actions and states to the single abstraction we call *traceability*. Traceability is a two-way association; each node senses and posts information for other nodes as needed and based on underlying rules. The traceability relationships can show a positive or negative contribution to the goal.

Complete traceability is achieved across dimensions and between individual BioS goals, actions and Roles. Some related points:

- Performance traceability between individual Interaction metrics in-the-small and aggregated in-the-large performance related to *hard goals*.
- A hard goal is implemented by one or more Interactions, each of which might in turn use many other different services provided by different types of Agents.
- Finally, there are many traceability chains of interest along which alignment can occur. For example, related to IT use: "IT Resource $\triangle$ ↔ Service execution $\triangle$". Another example is of course: "Requests $\triangle$ ↔ Operations $\triangle$ ↔ Business $\triangle$ ↔ Strategy $\triangle$". This is the traceability needed for the balanced scorecard[s]. Traceability leads to information needed to populate such frameworks and dashboards.

We will next see how traceability - the propagation of Interaction metrics-based attribute values along the chains of actions and goals help monitor service consumption and achievement of business goals. This also provides a basis for analysis and Co-engineering of an ACE model representing a specific enterprise. Finally, the EA team is responsible for improvements through BioS alignment.

Interactions and BioS Goal Alignment

A challenge in Co-engineering a complex system is the range of goals - some tactical, others longer-term and strategic; some hard and others soft and qualitative - that have to be met. Some of these goals are often overlapping and at other times conflicting from the perspective of different stakeholders. For example, in a sense-and-respond organization, the long-term strategic goal of improving customer satisfaction may require operational and technology investments to adapt to the environment and new opportunities. But at the same time the tactical investments and operations must also meet the short-term goals and Interactions for improving margins. Seemingly conflicting goals have to be identified and addressed through Interactions that can satisfy them to some degree. Thus, the EA team needs a way to maximize the partial degrees to which goals can be met[i].

Co-engineering requires optimization of short-term and long-term goals with respect many factors - current status, the potential to improve, relative value of the Request type, costs, and criticality from the perspective of stakeholders. To aid in the decision-making leading to maximal value for stakeholders' over time, the EA team needs performance-based methods to reconcile goal states desired by the stakeholders with actions and Interactions that make it possible to achieve those states. More generally speaking, strategic goals are usually met by Co-engineering actions applied to other on-going actions[t]. Such actions are by the EA team.

Co-engineering actions and methods require an understanding of the different types and attributes of goals.

Hard and soft goals: Different types of goals exist. Some goals are qualitative or *soft*. Soft goals are based on more qualitative attributes of interest to the stakeholders. For example *'increasing* trust' is not precisely measurable. We can however ascribe a relative-high or a relative-low value to 'trust'. Hard goals are quantitatively measurable and prescriptive. For example 'increase revenue by x%'. Hard goals can contribute to other hard or soft goals.

Traceable actions and goals: Our focus here, as illustrated in Figure 1, is on actions and hard goals that are *traceable* through the BioS framework. That is, to represent and Co-engineer and align the organization's BioS goals, we must also consider following six *continuous improvement actions and states*:

- *Goal identification* for primary *Request types* with goals set by the strategy stakeholders[u],
- *Goal refinement* using *RED Interactions* required by Request types to achieve business goals,
- *Goal implementation* through *Interaction* execution using *Agent Services*,
- *Goal monitoring and audit* of each Interaction's contribution to BioS goals,
- *Goal validation* based on the aggregated performance contribution of an Interaction type to strategy,
- *Goal prioritization* across *Request types* and their contribution to business value,
- *Goal and Interaction alignment* through to-be Co-engineering across dimensions and targeting new services, service enhancements, or improving the underlying infrastructure services.

In general we shall say that hard *traceable goals* are based on Request type performance that can be aggregated from individual Interaction instance metrics. The prototypical ACE structure of Figure 7 thus incorporates the goals of the service lifecycle.

Service improvement cycle: Stated another way, an organization ensures that the primary Interactions deliver value by setting goals and ensuring secondary Interactions (within the Infrastructure) provide effective enabling services. Often this takes the form of allocating appropriate budgets for infrastructure services and capacity as well as human resources that contribute operational goals that in turn contribute strategic value. Thus the BioS stakeholders each have their own goals for service improvement that are targeted through the next round of *to-be* budgets and investments.

ACE Maturity Levels

The benefit of ACE modeling is to create a traceable structure for continuous improvement that can act as a transformation tool reflecting the SEI maturity model[v].

As the maturity of the organization improves, its capability to comprehend and respond to variation improves. The ACE framework supports this improvement in five distinct stages by enabling increasingly adaptive and automated enterprise management principles and processes[w]:

- *Level 1 – Ad-hoc analysis and problem solving:* At this stage the organization's processes for enterprise architecture and its performance are usually ad-hoc. The organization does not provide an environment for enterprise modeling and problem solving. In spite of this ad-hoc, chaotic environment, maturity level 1 organizations often produce services that work however their efficiency is below par. They frequently exceed the budget and schedule. They rely on individuals rather than on teams. Consequently, such organizations tend to work in a crisis mode.

- *Level 2 – Repeatable:* ACE representations are used as a general qualitative enterprise framework for communication and architecture governance in critical parts of the organization. With an ACE representation in place, the decision-making is documented as a first step towards shared, solution-oriented, communications. The minimum process discipline is in place to target Interactions for improvements, investments, manage resources, and improve the success on projects. The decision making processes are explainable.
- *Level 3 – Defined:* ACE governance structure is in place for integrated in-the-small and in-the-large alignment and management. The architecture governance processes are in place to define goals and collect Interaction metrics that are traceable to goals. The organization's ACE representation is used for Service and Role catalog definition, Role assignments, organizational engineering, and improvement over time. Governance is also in place to establish alignment across the organization and dimensions and the processes at level 3 are applied consistently. Consistent communication, assessment, and tradeoffs form the foundation for decision making.
- *Level 4 – Quantitatively Managed:* Organizations at this level set hard (and soft) goals for both primary and secondary Interactions. Organizations also clearly define their services and begin to invest to decouple their services for increased reuse. ACE structure-based performance monitoring guides improvement actions to set SLs and OLs. ACE governance Co-engineers primary and secondary Interactions and underlying Roles and resources to improve OL performance to meet SLs. Those responsible for Roles Sets are empowered to make local improvements as much as possible. At maturity level 4 there is predictability of performance.
- *Level 5 – Adaptive:* Continually improving service performance is achieved at both in-the-small and in-the-large. That is, incremental and innovative organizational and technological improvements with respect to the long- and short-term goals are happening across the organization in a concurrent, decoupled fashion. Quantitative improvement goals are established and met rapidly through articulated policies for in-the-large and in-the-small alignment. This enables local adaptations that are defined and executed autonomously and automated when possible. Traceability of as-is and to-be goals and actions empowers the organizations' resources to conduct measurable improvement activities locally. These can eventually reflect changing goals. Thus the organization has the ability to rapidly adapt to external changes. At maturity

level 5, services feedback are concerned with addressing common causes of service variation and changing the service to improve service performance and to achieve verifiable alignment with goals.

In summary, the ACE representation provides a structure to manage both effectiveness and innovation within the externally-driven enterprise. The framework can be applied widely to reason about Interactions across:

- Organization's primary processes (e.g. those that contribute directly to revenue)
- Related infrastructure and secondary processes (e.g. those that enable primary processes - like IT or procurement)
- Complex organizations made up of many nested or inter-dependent organizations and their processes (e.g. a primary process and its enabling IT department, also treated like a business)

While ACE can derive significant benefits when implemented at maturity levels 4 and 5, it begins to provide immediate value even when applied manually at level 3 as we shall see with an example next. For a background on capacity, start with Nolan 1973.

Sharing IT Capacity

We next illustrate how an ACE representation can help institute enterprise-wide planning and communications relating the goals and tactics for the IT organization as a separate operational unit and a shared infrastructure.

The Business Challenge: The enterprise faces organizational and application challenges in the attempt to better manage expensive Enterprise System capacity that is shared. As with most other enterprise-wide initiatives, the improvement of the maturity of capacity management is a difficult problem. Different primary business processes and goals within the different operating organizations makes it difficult to:

- Connect past business process capacity usage with future capacity needs
- Provide visibility into available capacity, especially for on-demand and unpredictable events such as business fluctuations, emergencies, or unforeseen events
- Charge accurately for capacity use

There are tactical and strategic imperatives to address the enterprise capacity management challenge.

Tactical goals:

- Ensuring current and future quality of IT services
- Better sharing of IT services as a way of optimizing operational costs
- Business-IT alignment through activity-based costing and chargeback

Strategic Goals:

- More effective enterprise-wide operations through visibility and traceability - improving capacity management maturity through enabling EA governance processes will also improve other enterprise functions such as development of new services, customer service, business accountability, and auditing. Traceability is more than trending of a particular set of dependent variables – it relates trends and dependencies across value chains thus helping the organization mature.
- Innovation of new business services through composition and use of service-oriented architectures requires traceability to underlying IT services and their quality to ensure robustness.

Problem Analysis: The challenge of managing the capacity of high-cost enterprise system resources is due to the many different applications and organizations that are serviced by these shared resources. The goals of sub-organizations within an enterprise tend to be internally-focused and are often not visible across the entire enterprise. Compartmentalization of planning can result in operational units implementing conflicting goals. For example, without capacity plans that are consolidated at the enterprise level, the timely and cost-effective reaction to increased capacity needs is difficult to implement.

Best practice: Within most enterprises, enterprise mainframe capacity is expensive[x] and also directly affects the quality of primary services. Existing best practices suggests that capacity management aspects be included in the forefront of business and operations planning, and be informed from business scenarios. To accomplish this and establish a unified enterprise-wide plan, it is useful to understand what Capacity Management is, and what it is not. Capacity management can be described through related vantage points[y]:

- *Business service capacity:* referring to the demand a given business domain can satisfy as identified by its market segment or demographic. This is the potential of the business.

Figure 9. ACE structure for communication traceability for capacity management.

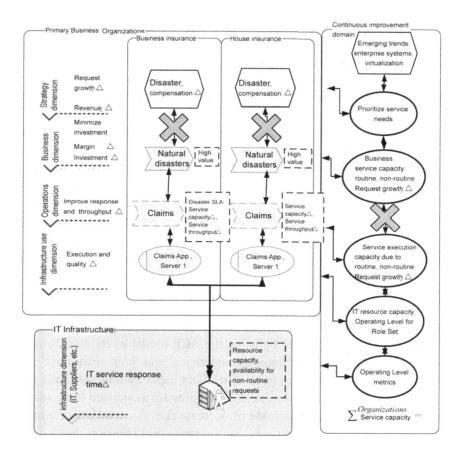

- *Service execution capacity:* supports business service capacity and referring to the demand a particular service can sustain. This is the current service as delivered to the customer.
- *IT resource capacity:* referring to the demand that a given resource can sustain in support of some level of Service Capacity. This is the application and underlying IT capacity.

ACE Modeling: We next show the application of the ACE notation to represent the enterprise-wide system capacity management and related organizational engineering. Each organization within the enterprise may have its own understanding of non-routine Requests handled and periods of vulnerability when specific events might result in demand fluctuation. This is illustrated in Figure 9 and expanded further below:

- *Modeling of a Primary Organizations:* An enterprise consists of several organizations as illustrated. Here we have two primary organizations - business and house insurance, a continuous improvement organization, and an IT organization that provides enterprise system capacity and related insurance applications. Key aspects of the organizations illustrated also include services that are aligned along the internal value-chain.
- *Certain organizations are associated or shared.* Organization are also dependent on other organizations as indicated. For example, IT supports the increase, decrease, retirement, and creation of the service execution capacity to respond to fluctuations in business service Requests of the primary organizations. Hence the IT infrastructure is itself a business organization and is shared. Capacity management is not locally determined but is driven by different primary business organizations that are external to the IT organization.
- *Continual Improvement Organization:* Captures and consolidates the changes in Request type goals and Interactions across other organizations for the purpose of improvement - in this case managing capacity at optimal costs.

Using Traceability to Identify Communication Disconnects: The traceability for capacity management is achieved by using the ACE model as follows. Non-routine Request types – in this case 'business insurance' and 'home insurance' – are identified to capture the strategic goals that affect capacity and may take place within an organization or line of business. Attributes are associated to capture the performance target in terms of increase or decrease (i.e. $\triangle$), creation, or elimination of an organization or Request type. In the strategy dimension the $\triangle$ values capture what happens during a disaster. That is, the additional targeted number of Requests to be handled. Next the business dimension determines the value of these Request types as 'high' and defines the goals that govern operations, say increase margin by 3%. In the next dimension, the service level, the needed claims service capacity and so on is identified for the expected number of service Interactions. Next the ACE structure is used to propagate goals and the capacity needed for meeting those goals. The needed information (i.e. target, capacity $\triangle$ s) must be summed and communicated along different dimensions. Next the values must be consolidated to define business service goals, service capacity needed, and finally the IT resource capacity as shown.

Achieving Level 3: The ACE model identifies points (illustrated by 'Xs' in the figure) where information is needed but the existing disconnects (missing traceability) make it difficult to improve capacity management. More generally, based on the complete ACE model, we can now propagate △ (as-is/to-be goals) information for services along traceability associations within each organization and sum it across business organizations to get the overall impact to SLs that IT is to meet.

However, as the model illustrates, in this case the attributes needed to develop SLs for IT services are broken! Using the model disconnects can be traced back to the lack of service strategy knowledge, in this particular example. ACE governance must therefore be established to ensure that proper information is collected and propagated. That is the target numbers related to business capacity illustrated by the 'X's' in Figure 9 are a source of missing traceability and information to be provided by the organizations. Note also that the 'X' now pin-points the root causes of the disconnect that was identified at a high level and the dimensions that are responsible for providing it.

Also, the information identified helps capacity planners prepare for 'non-routine' Requests triggered by disaster events. During such events, there is interference between business organizations and increased needs for capacity that would not normally exist. In such cases, the traceability information needed along the business improvement organization and the BioS value chain is:

Business constraints and investment (\$) ↔ IT resources (i.e. Σ capacity used for routine and non-routine Requests types) ↔ Operational service execution capacity metrics (Requests processed and quality) ↔ Strategy (non-routine, routine Requests growth)

The true value of addressing capacity management in this systematic way is to institutionalize the culture of disciplined communication for enterprise-wide agility. Consistent communication, trade-off assessment, and decision making is made possible across a broader scope of the organization. Finally, if the IT dimension knew the potential capacity spikes more accurately, they can have local strategies to address them. The example illustrates how to improve services by:

- Improved communications and accountability between Agents interacting to complete actions that meet goals
- Defined and clear Roles and responsibilities
- Improved local ability to adapt services to changing conditions

BUSINESS AND SYSTEMS CO-ENGINEERING PRINCIPLES

The ACE modeling notation previously presented focuses on representing associations between actions and goal states. To enable improvement we must also define principles by which we can look at different represented associations and ascribe as-is and to-be attributes. We next present these principles that can be used to analyze the associations in an ACE structure. (Other approaches are described in Ernest & Nisavic 2007, Jordan & Michel 2000, Kapoor et al. 2005)

Relating Strategy to the External Forces

Competing for Requests: The strategy of each service or group of services provided by the organization depends critically on the ability to *attract* the desired Requests from the external environment. This must be accomplished successfully in an environment in which there are also many different forces. These forces are due to economic pressures, competition, disruptive technologies, disasters, and so on. To identify these forces, Porter 2008[z] provides the 'Competitive of Five Forces' framework that shapes each industry and market. This well-applied framework helps identify and analyze the intensity of competition to the attractiveness of a service in a market segment[aa]. As illustrated in Figure 10, Requests for a service arise in the customer's environment but the organization's ability to *compete* for the service depends on the competitive forces. These forces originate within the context of related market segments. They five forces are defined as the:

- Bargaining power of *suppliers and customers*
- New *entrants and the substitutes* for a service
- *Rivalry* within similar companies vying for the Requests

Figure 10. Porter's competitive forces model

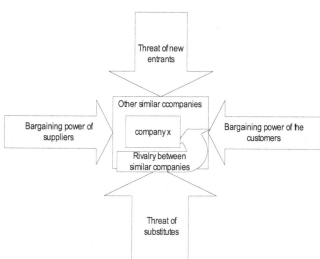

By understanding these forces, we can better define the organization's strategy for providing a competitive service. That is, we can use Porter's model for competitive analysis to identify the goals in the context and environment in which the Request type itself can be defined, attracted, serviced, and satisfaction determined. Once the Request is received the organization must also respond in an efficient fashion by meeting other goals as we shall see later.

A common example of a service-driven organization is the hospital. Applying the competitive model we note that suppliers, customers and rivalries form weak forces. That is, in this case, Requests from patients are not dampened by these forces and the hospital services continue to be in demand. An example of a substitute is a specialized clinic (e.g. for plastic surgery). However, this has not yet emerged an immediate threat for most hospitals. As a result most hospitals today do not face many competitive forces and competing for patients is not yet a big issue. However, longer term, there is a real threat might be due to competitive global medical services and high cost of local medical care.[ab]

The more recent theory of innovation in Christensen 2004 suggests that we can seek new opportunities to service by looking at the customer's circumstances in which the Request arise. For example, returning to the hospital, not only are the numbers of different types of Requests significant, but also the *cause* for the Request is significant. Understanding these can lead to new areas of circumstance-based innovation – home care, telemedicine and preventative medicine. The fluctuations in Requests also have important implications to providing more competitive care and improving the underlying infrastructure if response and quality is to be maintained in a cost-effective fashion. A recent example of such innovation is a product that helps organize the environment for the elderly.

From a strategic goal-setting perspective, organizations must also focus on the origin of emerging relevant Requests to identify new opportunity. Thus the highlighted Co-engineering Principle 1 allows us to use Request types and metrics to establish more prescriptive strategy goals. Also note that all sources of variation and competitive threats are also attributable to external Requests.

Relating Forces to BioS Goals

The external forces impact the strategy goals and in-turn this impacts the provider's internal value-chain. Therefore we must look not only at the external impact due to forces but also the internal Interactions impacted by these forces. Our motivation is to ensure each Request type and its Interactions producing the delivered service is as *competitive* as possible.

The underlying business concept is illustrated in Figure 11. For example, as the provider responds to Requests for re-furbishing laptops for a company, each

Co-engineering Principle 1: Relating external Requests and Strategy Goals

The organization's strategy determines goals associated with Request types. The method for defining goals is 1) identify common requirements and characteristics originating from the customers' environment, and 2) apply five forces to determine the externally-driven targets for non-routine Request types. For example, prescribe the number of Requests per time period, response times, and deliverable quality.

Customers
(Market segments)

Strategic management

Strategy dimension

Requests types

On-time delivery
Service quality

Figure 11. The value-add due to the primary activities or Interaction value chain, the infrastructure costs, and margin

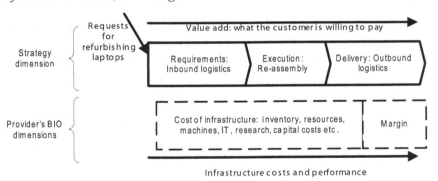

primary or Interaction in the strategy dimension adds a certain value from the customer's view that the customer is willing to pay for. From the provider's organization perspective this value-add was attained through the costs incurred within the infrastructure. Thus from the total yield due to the Request type, we subtract the cost of infrastructure to obtain the provider's service margin. This allows us to define the next principle.

Specifically, each primary RED Interaction completed by the provider represents benefits to the customer provided at a price. The provider of the service also incurs certain costs. These are due to the cost of services provided by the organization's *infrastructure*. The infrastructure includes many types of capabilities – such as

Co-engineering Principle 2: Relating Strategy to Business Goals

Request Margin = the Total Yield- all Infrastructure costs. Here the yield includes what the customers paid for organization's services and infrastructure costs that includes what was used for that Request type, in a given period of time (including the cost of capital).Hard business goals are thus quantified by the target RED margin, the cost of the infrastructure used, and the price of each Interaction within the customer facing value-add chain.

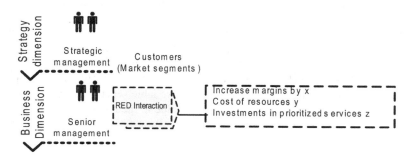

other organizations (finance, human resources, procurement, product research and development), IT (software, communications, and networks), processes (supply chain, design, and development), warehouses, facilities, and assets. That is, the provider's organization represents investments in the supporting infrastructure and transformation capabilities called secondary activities by Porter (the lower box in Figure 11). To increase the margin, the infrastructure must be as effective as possible. These relationships are made precise by Co-engineering principle 2.

Here our focus is on looking at the performance for each Request type and thus on *service-based costing* that generalizes the concepts of activity based costing[ac]. Based on the Principle 2, we can now begin to understand how the organization better *ensures* its survival by managing underlying traceability to improve margin and effectiveness. Alternative ways of looking at principle 2 are given in Co-engineering principle 3.

Relating Infrastructure and Infrastructure-Use Dimensions and Goals

The importance of *infrastructure use* is critical within a service-oriented institution since not only will the processing for different Request types vary widely, but often Requests of a single given type also vary widely. Consequently the use of the

Co-engineering Principle 3: Relating the Roles and Interactions to Business, Infrastructure, Operation and Strategy Goals

The business value contribution can be relative or precise and tied to the margin due to a Request type. The value can be increased by increasing the yield due to additional Requests or by reducing infrastructure costs needed for processing. That is, the derivations from principle 2 that relate BioS are as follows:

1. Increasing Requests can increase yield (with traceability: $\triangle$ Requests of a type, in a period $\rightarrow$ $\triangle$ Interaction yield).
2. Improving infrastructure effectiveness can increase throughput and quality, and consequently yield (with traceability: $\triangle$ infrastructure costs and service quality $\rightarrow$ $\triangle$ customer satisfaction $\rightarrow$ $\triangle$ Interaction yield). This is also the basic principle underlying Norton and Kaplan's Balanced Scorecard. In other words, a well-managed shared infrastructure not only provides reliable service for improving the primary Interactions but also increases the value to the business.

Each service Interaction's $\triangle$ contribution to the business, the operational, and strategy goals due to infrastructure use is measured at the RED milestones.

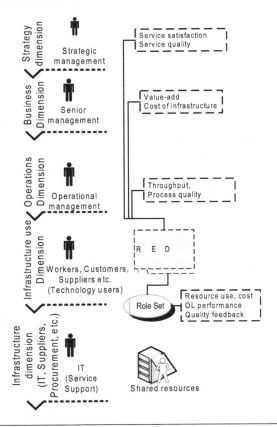

Co-engineering Principle 4: Relating Strategy to Lean Processing and Infrastructure Goals

The infrastructure used for each Request is determined by the Role Set of the RED Interaction. Furthermore, the Lean goal is achieved by1) systematically eliminating wait times at the RED points that contribute $\triangle$ value to BioS, 2) maximizing resources applied directly in support of requirements as perceived by the customer. Both are achieved as follows:

1. The wait time and actual use of resources (e.g. full time equivalents, CPU time, storage) used for an Interaction execution is measured at the RED milestones. That is, for each Request type:
   ⇢ Business $\triangle$:Interactions' contribution to value and yield.
   ⇢ Infrastructure use $\triangle$: agent costs and times used to complete Interaction. Also span time, queue time, etc. can be measured.
   ⇢ Operations $\triangle$: Requests completed in a period of time (i.e. throughput = number of Requests per time period).
   ⇢ Strategy $\triangle$: customer satisfaction with the services (typically this is either qualitative based on a questionnaire or quantitative based on defects etc.)
   These BioS measurements at the RED milestones allow us to determine each Interaction's simultaneous value-add and reduce the wait times at these points. This was also illustrated in the previous highlight.
2. Since all the RED Interactions are initiated directly or indirectly by the customer, the delayed assignment of resources to the Roles Set is Lean.

---

underlying infrastructure varies widely. This also affect the cost of the infrastructure attributable to the Request type for chargeback and more effective use of the infrastructure to achieve overall efficiencies.

To illustrate the point, consider different civil service complaints or emergency Requests. Each of these within the City administration will have dramatically different responses. This also makes the availability of underlying resources hard to determine and poses challenges during execution. In most cases, incoming work waits for servicing by a resource. Work queue measurements such as span time, wait time at the RED milestones provide the basis to reduce wait time and improve throughput. This is achieved, as we shall see, by taking a Lean approach to Interaction sequencing and execution.

In traditional Systems Engineering an operational strategy is to reduce resource wastage using *Lean*. In its essence Lean requires that the only resources applied are those required for the customer's Request to add customer-perceivable value. This is achieved by the elimination of wasted time (work waiting to be processed, resources with too little work, etc.). The general underlying Co-principle 4 is given above and explored further.

Lean RED Interaction and enabling Role Sets: The Interactions' Roles Set allows us to delay the assignment of a particular infrastructure capability or resource until the arrival of a customer Request. With this, the infrastructure becomes *on demand* (assignment based on an incoming Request) and *Lean* (see Womack and Jones 2003) by achieving the following flexibility:

- Dynamic allocation of resources to Roles based on their time availability.
- Internal resources can be better applied to higher-value Interactions.
- Easier outsourcing of Interactions if the skill is not core to the business and does not have to be maintained in-house. This leads to the idea of 'virtual organizations':
  - *Virtual organization:* Increasingly, even the smallest organization or capability must stay competitive and demonstrate bottom-line efficiency and value to the core business. Otherwise, efficiency considerations may require work to be outsourced. Supplier organizations often enable businesses to reduce costs. The trend is to retain only those resources within the business unit that are part of the core competency of the business[ad].
- Predictable Interaction response times. An Interaction takes *time-* during *Requirements* (for activities such as triage, negotiation, coordination, routing, set-up, etc.) and *Delivery* (for activities such as quality check, transportation, etc.) in addition to *Execution time* (for value added due to the Request). In addition, sub-Interactions are used to complete the primary Interaction. The time available to meet demand with sub-Interactions can be understood using the concept of *TAKT time,* in the context of obtaining a lean operation, or by considering Amdahl's Law.
- *TAKT:* In systems engineering terminology *TAKT time* is defined to be the total (maximum) amount of time available to perform processing for a given demand based on direct value to the customer. TAKT = time avail / demand for the primary Interaction. Dependent sub-Interactions have TAKT time allocated based on the time available for the primary Interaction and service. Some ways to achieve and improve TAKT time include:
  - Reduced dependency between Interactions so that Interactions can execute concurrently.
  - Increase automation - self routing – if a particular service is needed in a step, the resource is automatically alerted. For example, if a machine needs repair, it routes itself to the hardware specialist.
  - Self managed infrastructure – if a particular resource has capacity available, posting it to allow for better capacity utilization across Interactions.

Figure 12. Time available for Interaction and sub-Interactions to process 20 laptops based on direct value to the customer

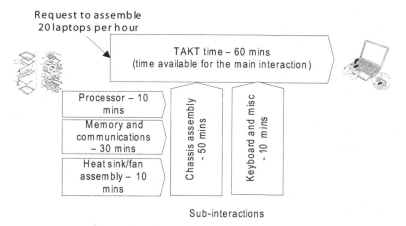

Sub-interactions

o   *Amdahl's Law*[ae]:Also well known within Computer Science, Amdahl's law is used to find the maximum expected overall improvement, or speed-up, of a system when only some part of that system can be improved. In reality, Amdahl's law is a generalization of intuitive law of diminishing returns and by using it one can ensure that, when given a choice to improve some parts of the system, the part that has the most performance impact is chosen.

The Co-engineering[af] Principle 5 arms us to look for the opportunities for maximize organization performance using IT.

ACE WORK PRODUCTS

ACE Structure-Based Work Products: Using the principles in the previous sections, as identified in Figure 13, we will next derive the ACE structure-based work products that will provide us with a basis for analysis and the EA actions for continual improvement. The *ACE structure* relates Goals, Actions, and Infrastructure providing the context for the following work products:

A.   *Request strategy catalog consisting of Request types, deliverables, and strategy goals:* These identify the business customer facing items in a service catalog (using ITIL terminology) and goals.

Co-engineering Principle 5: Efficiency of an Interaction.

Interaction efficiency = value-adding time RED / total lead-time RED. Hard goals for infrastructure improvement are derived from this principle. This principle can be implemented by IT in many ways. The related concepts for increasing efficiency are identified below:

⇢ Reducing dependency between Interaction executions to maximize concurrency. Eliminating wait time for sub-Interactions and design Interactions with minimal dependency (i.e. an Interaction waits for another Interaction only if it needs specific inputs from it).

⇢ Delayed binding of Roles to the infrastructure Agents so that the Agents can be shared. Allow resources to be flexibly assigned to Roles to reduce queue time.

⇢ Bracketing the execution with a step for requirements that is as complete as possible to reduce discovery in the execution step; and a delivery step that provides feedback for improvement.

⇢ Lowering infrastructure costs and retaining flexibility for outsourcing of Roles, on an Interaction basis.

⇢ Allowing discovered Interactions to be processed in routine and automated ways if possible.

⇢ Eliminating Interactions through new technology or consolidation.

⇢ Sharing of high cost resources allow a service to contribute to the yield of many Interactions.

B. *Request Priorities and Project Portfolio:* This define the relative value of each Request type to the business which is the basis for focusing improvement resources to achieve to-be service levels. The gaps between the to-be and as-is along with the relative value of fixing the Interactions and underlying Agents forms the project portfolio. The project portfolio consolidates across Interactions based on the costs, value, and scope of Agent improvements.

C. *RED, Roles sets, and SLs:* for each Request type, the as-is/to-be Interaction service levels, the RED metrics, and the Role Sets and Roles needed to achieve the service.

D. *Request Triage* rules for incoming Request classification and resource assignment.

E. *Roles and OLs:* A catalog of Roles and OLs needed across all REDs.

F. Agents *and Skills:* These define what is available to fill Roles as resources.

These work products are needed to execute strategy are the responsibility of different stakeholders and Co-engineering actions as follows.

Figure 13. ACE structure and Context for EA operations (1-7), Work Products (A-F), and the Co-engineering actions (8-14)

Portfolio of Projects: IT projects n3eeded for continual improvement are increasingly managed like a financial portfolio. However, software project portfolios have some differences. Because the result of investment is changes to the IT infrastructure that cannot be undone, we cannot change our mind easily about the amount spent on a project. Also an IT projects is successful only if the whole Role Set for an Interaction is considered when planning for improvement. That is, usually the resources in a Role Set cannot be improved in isolation for us to see the Interaction improve. Whereas the assets of financial portfolios are liquid and therefore can be assessed or re-assessed at any point in time, the opportunities for new projects are often limited and projects that have already been initiated cannot be abandoned without the loss of the sunk costs (i.e., there is little or no recovery/salvage value of a half-complete IT project). At the same time some of the aspects of management are applicable to virtually any kind of portfolio. An applicable concept is *risk tolerance* of an investor defined as how much risk is acceptable for a given return. Traditional techniques use historical variance as a measure of risk. However, portfolios of assets like one-of-a-kind IT projects don't usually have insights like "historical variance" for a new piece of software. The investment is therefore expressed in general terms like "chance of an ROI less than cost of capital" or "chance of losing more than half of the investment" or "payback time". In the next chapter we explore more quantitative ways of analyzing architectural options.

All this increases the importance of a precise representation of the ACE structure and work products. This representation gives us the basis for further analysis as we shall see. The Highlight below summarizes our discussions this for into prescriptive steps to develop the ACE work products for an organization.

Highlight: Prescriptive EA Roles, Work Products and Co-engineering Actions

⇨*Identify the organizations (major departments, teams, etc.) and relationships that will take part in strategic planning and on-going improvement.*

⇨*Identify EA members that will interview organizations and sub-organizations to get their as-is. The Bios template for this is given in Appendix I. EA members use this for the to-be development (refer to* Figure 13*). 1-8 identify the stakeholder Roles and context, 9-14 identify the EA Work Products and Co-engineering discussed below.*

⇨*Strategic Planning:*

Work Product A: Request Strategy Catalog. set goals for each Request type.

→*Create | enhance the business catalog of routine and non-routine Request types. Define strategy goals for each Request type.*

→*Identify Request goals to address competitive forces in related market segments. Thus for each Request type define the customer/market objectives for each Request type as △ improvement goals (e.g. increase the number of development projects per month by 10%) to address the forces. Identify any external goals related to risk, disaster, compliance, security threats, disruptive technologies, etc.*

→*Using business intelligence capture sources and types of Request variation.*

→*Analyze forces to compete successfully by applying Co-engineering Principles 1 and 5.*

→*Use Co-engineering Principles 5 to identify Request and Infrastructure innovation opportunities.*

Work Product B: Request Priorities and Project Portfolio. Manage the project portfolio prioritized based on the Requests that provide higher value to the business.

→*Set Business goals and priorities to maximize the Request type improvements based on value-add to the business. Use Co-engineering Principle 2 to maximize the business contribution of infrastructure. That is, service a maximum number of Requests while also satisfying individual customers.*

→ *Establish business-oriented goals for each primary Request type.*

→*Prioritize across Request types based both on market opportunities, value to the organization, and ability to be competitive in the future.*

→*Validate business value achievements of Request types by monitoring the total as-is value. Each Request type's contribution is by aggregating value achieved through execution and across all its RED instances.*

→*Identify opportunities for improving Interactions. Especially for high-volume high value Interactions this can identify automation opportunities for improved performance.*

→*Define the to-be goals of each Request type.*

→*Define the underlying project portfolio to achieve these improvement goals for high-value Request types.*

→*Provide the resources for investment and improvement.*

⇨*Execution of Strategy*

(Note, the prioritization of Request types leads to the Financial Management in the business dimension and to execution strategy with service design, service transition, and service operation.)

Work Product C: REDs, Role sets, and SLs. Ensure technical and business performance.

→*For each Request type, Define RED goals like throughput, response time that are traceable to business value creation and strategy goals.*

→*Apply Co-engineering Principle 2 to achieve Request type goals through RED Interaction plans and execution.*

→*For each Request type associate RED Interaction details such as Role Sets, SLs, and the metrics to be collected at the RED milestones. This relates the technical work done by the Roles to the metrics collected.*

→*Identify deliverable types and list all the component deliverables and services that make up the final, customer ready, deliverable types.*

→*Identify any know sub-Interactions that might be dynamically needed (or statically determined).*

→*Apply Co-engineering Principle 4 to look across Interactions and optimize.*

Work Product D: Request Triage Rules. Identify the Triage rules execution that start with the incoming Request and identify requirements to assign initial resources to the Roles Set of that RED. Record Metrics and History.

→*Requirements-based triage execution to classify the initial characteristics of each incoming Request. Also set priorities for execution of the Request.*

→ *These rules classify Request types using attributes based on the customer priorities, types of Roles required, deliverable types produced, and difficulty. Use additional attributes to reflect the unique processing needs of the Request – like customizations and custom processes. Non-routine Requests can also include internal product/process improvement, corrective actions, technology evolution, and so on to create a useful and fine-grained classification.*

→*Execute with assigned Agents. Log and address any discovery by dynamically invoking sub-Interactions to complete sub-Requests. (If all the sub-Interactions are known prior to execution then we can leverage a static process flow.).*

→*For each Interaction type also maintain aggregated SL metrics (time to commit, cycle time, cash-to-cash, etc.) and BioS traceability. See figure for examples. Measure and monitor at the RED transitions. Determine SL metrics delivered by the Roles Set.*

→*Reduce variation in processing by 1) identifying new Request types or by re-organizing existing Request types and 2) create | enhance RED templates to streamline the triaging and processing of that type.*

→*Use Co-engineering principle 3 and the traceability chain to diagnose points of inadequate improvement.*

Work Product E: Roles and OLs. Create a Roles and Resources catalog with OLs.

→ *This identifies all the Roles sets that a Role participates in and the needed OL for each Role set. This view of resources allows us to determine overall capacity and improvement needed to meet the OL for each RED. Note that a Role in turn may have sub-roles and this must be recorded.*

→ *Identify Roles that need to be improved based on performance measures and quality of deliverables.*

Work Product F: Agents and Capacities. Measure OL of each agent/resource assigned to each Role set

→ *Measure the Agents use and individual OL needed to deliver satisfaction within the customer's environment.*

→ *Initiate Requests of type 'Feedback or Corrective Action' identifying opportunities for improvement.*

→ *Use feedback to improve infrastructure Roles, Resources, and operating level metrics.*

To proceed with a quick example, we note that an organization handles many Request types with its Infrastructure. These Requests are organized and their definitions form the Request Strategy Catalog (work product A). The Highlight below provides an example of the range of Request types within a supplier organization.

Highlight: Request Catalog Overview

Increased service orientation is critical for the survival of many suppliers. The service catalog for a tier 1 automotive supplier that provides parts to many OEMs (Honda, Ford, etc.) can contain over hundreds of Request types. Often these Request types arise due to new business opportunities. Such organizations also benefit greatly from having rigorous engineering change management practices. At the heart of an effective change management practice is the careful definition of Request types and service catalog.
Routine Requests:

- *Change delivery address, Change quantity. Deliverable type: modified order.*
- *Regularly scheduled maintenance. Deliverable type: machine quality assurance results updated.*
- *Packaging change. Deliverable type: Change of encasing color, etc.*

Non-routine Requests:

- *Product design change. Deliverable type: modified design and approvals.*
- *Process design change. Deliverable type: modified tooling with approvals.*
- *Internally generated corrective actions. Deliverable type: change implemented and quality assurance results updated.*
- *Modify work instructions. Deliverable type: modified instructions and quality assurance updated*

> • *New technology requirement. Deliverable type: Impact to strategy and invest-ment.*
>
> *As this example illustrates, in a service organization our focus and energies should shift to understanding the Request types – the source of variation – and leave the pro-cesses to be flexible to accommodate this.*

The Request Strategy Catalog is based on future intelligence (for example in terms of customer preferences and new opportunities). The Role of marketing in defining and achieving these goals is often most critical to growth. It is also one of the most challenging – involving a lot of 'art and gut'. All the same, the resulting Interaction representation and prioritization allows the rest of the organization to adapt to changes and become more responsive in terms of new services and in-novations as illustrated next.

Examples of RED Interaction entry and work product C are in Figure 14 with goals. Here we show the BioS for two Request Types - 'New Design' and 'Packaging change' - using shared resources within the Infrastructure of a first tier supplier. (We assume for simplicity that there is only one primary RED for each Request type, as shown.) These two Interactions are supported by the underlying infrastructure as illustrated in grey. The example also illustrates the current BioS performance and the goals which are specifically indicated in parenthesis. That is, the 'New design component' has a current volume of 10 per month, the target goal is indicated as (40). This target is based on competitive analysis (e.g. the competitor's does 40 Requests per month).

The use of BioS traceability for business decision-making using the two example Request types and the aggregated performance is illustrative. In the example, the competition's R value-add is 40% suggesting that *New designs within Engineering change* provides significant value add to the customer. In other words, the organi-zation is losing to the competitor with greater product options and custom service. This is also seen by the low percentage of customer approvals (35%) for incoming Requests going to execution. That is, while the RED value-add in the business dimension identifies the target activity that is not competitive; it is usually only a symptom of problems elsewhere, in this case within the operating dimension. Given this, the hypothesis of the IT team was that a document and workflow management system to hold product-drawing changes and manage configurations would allow more design productivity thus improving the number of approved designs and also the span time. And, that the resulting increase in revenue would help justify the project costs (darkly shaded area) and amount to invest.

Figure 14. RED Interaction work product C. Two primary Interactions – 'new design' and 'change Request' are illustrated along with the Roles sets for R,E,D and the OLs using the shared infrastructure.

Strategy	New design component = 10 (40)		
Business	R: Engineering change	E: Manufacturing	D: Delivery
	value add = 20% (40%)	value add = 70% (50%)	value add = 10%
	Priority = 10 (3)	Cash-to-cash = 60 (60) days	Revenue = 15% increase
Operations SL	%Approved = 35% (65%)	Throughput = 10 (40) per month	Response time = (30)15 days
Strategy	Change request packaging = 30 (40)		
Business	R: Engineering change	E: Manufacturing	D: Delivery
	value add = 20% (40%)	value add = 70% (50%)	value add = 10%
	Priority = 11 (11)	Cash-to-cash = 60 (60) days	Margin = 15% (15%)
Operations SL	%Approved = 65% (65%)	Throughput = 30 (40) per month	Response time = 15 days
Infrastrucutre use	15 (15) FTE	100(100) FTE	2(3) FTE
Role Set OL	CRM software, Sales, Engineers	MRP, Suppliers, parts, shop floor	Logistics
> Engineering Agent OLA	Design Span = 10 (2) days	Span = 10 (10)	Span = 2 (2)
	Queue time = 3 days (1)	Queue time = 1 (1)	Queue time = 1 (1)
	Engineering design span from 10=>2 days, Project costs. - Time 3 months for installation and data conversion - Cost of software. - Cost of training and process design		

As can be seen below, the traceability chain underlying the Interactions allows us to surface issues in the larger context. For example, what value-add contribution happened before and after the specific R, E, or D execution? What happened to all Requests of this type, and why? The resulting insight allows us to Co-engineer across dimensions to achieve the desired improvements. In the example the traceability chain[ag] for competitive adaptation to be managed by the ACE governance is:

⇨ *Increase Requests of a given type (engineering changes)*
⇨ *Improve simultaneous value-add by (execution dimension)*
> ⇨ *Increase the business value add at the close of Interaction s (increase success rate of proposals that respond to the Requests).*
> ⇨ *Improve process value-add and reduce infrastructure resources used (reduce queue time).*
> ⇨ *Improve the product value add (better assignments of resources to Requests)*
⇨ *Increase Request throughput (operating dimension)*
⇨ *Increase business value-add due to Request type (business dimension)*
⇨ *Customer satisfaction (new business)*

Starting from the beginning of the chain, one main question was how could demand for product variations be increased? Without performance metrics, it is not as clear how to go about this. By examining the performance of Request types in the operating dimension we have greater insight. We see that most of the current Requests are for a change in the packaging of the product. Packaging change Requests are from current customers and therefore do not reflect an improvement in the number of new customers. Thus it becomes evident that to improve the relative value-add of New design R, there is a need to increase product variations and to improve R's engineering throughput.

CO-ENGINEERING

As enterprises get complex, adding investment and technology does *not* automatically guarantee services will improve. The performance of such complex systems is best improved by creating and maximizing the value that meets the goals of the stakeholders[ah]. To accomplish this we are interested in services of all the Agents, both humans and non-humans, and their performance contribution to the goals of the stakeholders.

Co-engineering represents the simultaneous engineering of such an organization, from the perspective of each BioS dimension, to achieve desired results. Co-engineering methods and principles introduced in this chapter are based on the ACE performance structure introduced in Figure 1. The fine-grain monitoring of service Interactions and their simultaneous $\triangle$ to BioS provides immediate visibility within service-oriented organizations that must deal with uncertainty, changing requirements, and goals. This is especially true because within such environments resources are shared and execution status is hard to obtain. For example, the availability of resources becomes harder to predict as they work on many ad-hoc Requests that result from requirements discovery. As a result, the ability to meet the customer-promised dates becomes harder and satisfaction is negatively impacted.

Plan-Execute-Monitor-Analyze Quality Cycle: RED is a single conceptual structure for *service planning and service execution.* As we have shown *planning* consists of defining the Request type strategy and business value, *execution* consists of RED Interaction execution with appropriate resources, *monitoring* consists of metrics collection, and *analysis* consists of using work products to identify performance-to-goal analysis, prioritization and decision-making. RED Interactions allow us to relate and 'trace' the precise infrastructure service used, to customer benefits, to business and infrastructure capability. This is in terms of $\triangle$ contributions to stakeholder *dimensions* within the customer and provider organizations.

An important aspect is feedback to improve future infrastructure capabilities for future value-add. This value is created in a variety of ways – corrective Requests that require a fix to the infrastructure, more accurate status, history of successful application of knowledge, etc. Consistent with most quality initiatives (e.g. Six Sigma), the feedback to 'fix' the quality problems with the infrastructure is key to improvement[ai].

RED Interactions also represent commitments as points of measurement that enable focus on continuous improvement from the perspective of all the BioS dimensions. These include both business and technical Roles. With real-time visibility (e.g. Request status, progress on deliverable, resources applied, availability of resources, quality, earned value[aj]) of these transition points ACE can target $\triangle$ improvements for maximum impact. (Unfortunately even with today's systems, this traceability is difficult to obtain, as we shall see later). In addition, there are often new insights gained during execution – ideas for better work instructions and performance improvement suggestions. These can provide requirements for improved training, knowledge consolidation and delivery. For example, a worker may identify a better way to process a Request or reduce errors. These become important sources for internal process innovation.

Standards For Composability, Replacement, etc. of Services: Services capabilities provided by the shared infrastructure have to be composed quickly as needed to provide the primary services. If a capability is not available, suppliers may be asked to provide it. This requires a standardized description of each service. This is needed not only for human Agents but also for all others – machines, processes, software etc. For example, for software services this includes the standardized use Web services. We will also cover this in future sections.

In summary, the ACE ontology allows an organization to sense external Requests from its environment and respond competitively by embracing variation with its underlying infrastructure. The Interactions not only deliver services but, as we shall see, they also use visibility to accomplish business and cost objectives by steadily eliminating variation to achieve efficiencies. Finally we will see how this contributes to insights needed for innovation.

TASKS FOR DEVELOPING THE ACE STRUCTURE AND WORK PRODUCT

1. Begin the requirements gathering effort. Perform primary research for your project by meeting with the sponsor organization's project members and collecting as-is information related to all the organization dimensions including:

- o *Business* – How are they implementing those goals? Is the organization divided up in some way based on function, location, or other concerns? Who sets and evaluates operational goals? How do they relate to strategic goals?
- o *IT* – What purpose do the IT systems serve? Are there redundancies or opportunities as a result of the IT organization?
- o *Operations and Processes* – What processes enable their primary functions? How are these processes evaluated? Are their similarities across operations?
- o *Strategy* – What are the organization's overall goals? Who sets and evaluates those goals?
- o Any other related information you feel is important (see the appendix for an interview template that might prove to be of use).

2. Begin a draft enterprise architecture using the ACE modeling notation. Be sure to include relevant stakeholders at each dimension, Roles, and Interactions. After discussion within the team, work with your sponsor to identify missing elements and reinforce your understanding of the enterprise architecture.
3. Work with your project sponsor to develop a project charter.
4. With the ACE Structure as context, begin the development of EA work products that capture the aspects to become part of your project.

THINGS TO THINK ABOUT

1. How does ACE Interaction modeling differ from process, data, role, and goal modeling? What are the similarities? How does this relate to UML?
2. Imagine you are managing a team project in a work environment. Can project management be thought of as completing Interactions? If so, why might it help you as the project manager?
3. How does ACE Interaction Modeling relate to 1) business process modeling, 2) workflow modeling, and 3) to project planning?
4. Define and identify the differences between the primary Interactions| secondary Interactions | sub-Interactions, value chain | supply chain | internal value chain. Identify the cause and effect relationships within each group.
5. Traditional system modeling techniques are hyper-rational and focus analysis on the most efficient way to build an enterprise IT system based on current needs. Yet, the most efficient way to build a system may not be the best if it ignores variation due to external constraints(political or resource). Systems approaches often ignore political or budget timelines and therefore render projects susceptible to interruption. By including these timelines and prioritizations during decision-making, using mechanisms like triage, the development of

RED enabled systems potentially becomes increasingly modular so that they could be built within a cycle instead of across disruptive cycle breaks. Give examples illustrating this phenomenon.

6. How do Goals interact, what is the nature of hard Goals, traceable Goals and soft Goals, and how do multiple Goals and Interactions relate?

7. What is the difference between a Request Catalog and a Project Portfolio?

8. The ACE approach represents not only models for delivering services but also the very processes by which these models evolve. Thus it provides the representational ability to model change itself. As a result, the software based on this representation will also be adaptable. The resulting ACE architecture will use successful patterns of Interactions from previous Requests to enable workers to quickly respond to non-routine Requests for which no existing response procedures exist. Agree or disagree. Justify you answer.

9. How does the ACE model leverage the continuous infrastructure provided by the Internet to enable effective dynamic responses across boundaries (i.e. coordinate across the boundaries of departments, as well as within them).

10. Read about the IT Services CMM and compare it with the ACE maturity model. What is the difference between CMM and CMMI? Why are maturity models important and what purpose do they serve in an enterprise architecture project?

11. Within a service–oriented organization, traditional process modeling is viewed now as Interactions and transformation services completed by capabilities. Give the underlying rationale.

12. How does Interaction modeling relate to data, process, and organizational modeling?

13. Review the Unified Modeling Language, a standard notation for representing aspects of software intensive systems. Could the ACE notation be done in UML (think about the important concepts in the ACE ontology)?

14. Execution of Interactions can be policy based. Give some examples and then think about why an enterprise model might be useful for creating policy

15. Read about common project management practices and terminology (or see exercise 7). Compare the relationship between an ACE representation and a project plan.

16. How can ACE be used to identify areas of high project risk?

17. Explain how you could apply strategic thinking to curriculum development and knowledge creation. Can a strategic framework like Porter's Model help? How would you develop the controls and feedback mechanisms to ensure that your strategy was both implemented correctly and succeeding?

18. Exercise based on the *Project Management Memory Jogger* (ISBN 1576810011):

- o   Apply ACE modeling to reflect the method in Project Management at a glance (page 10) and Generic Life Cycle stages (19). Reflect the important project management concepts (pgs 11-12). Use your model to answer the following questions.
- o   What are the two most important project metrics associated with your model?
- o   What happens to your model if new sub-deliverables are discovered? How does it impact the metrics?
- o   How will the Interaction structure change if a new subproject were introduced? Specifically discuss the impact to the project metrics.
- o   Give an example that illustrates the benefit of including Interaction modeling to data and process modeling.
- o   Sometimes an Interaction maybe closed (aborted etc.) without executing R, E, or D. Give an illustrative example. What are the effects of this on the project metrics? Also identify other metrics and insights that can be obtained in this case.

REFERENCES

Cameron, B. G. (2007). *Value Network Modeling:A Quantitative Method For Comparing Benefit Across Exploration Architectures*. Thesis, Department of Aeronautics and Astronautics and the EngineeringSystems Division, Massachusetts Institute of Technology.

Cherbakov, L., Galambos, G., Harishankar, R., Kalyana S., & Rackham, G. (2005). Impact of Service Orientation atthe Business Level. *IBM Systems Journal, 44*(4) 653-668.

Chung, L., Nixon, B. A., Yu, E., & Mylopoulos, J. (1999). *Non-Functional Requirements in Software Engineering*. Boston: Kluwer Academic.

Cunha, M. M, Cortes, B. C, & Putnik, G. D. (Ed.)(2006). *Adaptive Technologies and Business Integration - Social, Managerial and Organizational Dimensions*. IGI Global.

Christensen, C., Anthony, S., & Roth, E. (2004) *Seeing What's Next: Using the Theories of Innovation to Predict Industry Change*. Boston: Harvard Business School Press.

Drucker, P. F. (1975). *Management: Tasks, Responsibilities and Practices*. New York: Harper & Row.

Ernest, M., & Nisavic, J. M. (2007). Adding value to the IT organization with the Component Business Model. *IBM Systems Journal, 46*(3), 387-404.

Fox, M. S., Barbuceanu, M., Gruninger, M., & Lin, J. An Organization Ontology for Enterprise Modelling. In M. Prietula, K. Carley, & L. Gasser (Eds.), *Simulating Organizations: Computational Models of Institutions and Groups* (pp. 131-152), Menlo Park, CA: AAAI/MIT Press.

Gordijn, J., Yu, E., & Raadt, B. (2006 May/June). e-Service Design Using i* and e3value Modeling. *IEEE Software, 23*(3), 26-33.

Hartung, R., Ramanathan, J., & Bolinger, J. (2008 September). Ontology for Enterprise Modeling.In *Knowledge-Based Intelligent Information and Engineering Systems* (pp. 799-87). Zagreb, Croatia: Springer Berlin / Heidelberg.

IEEE Std 1320.1-1998. (1998). *IEEE Standard for Functional Modeling Language— Syntax and Semantics for IDEF0*. New York: IEEE Computer Society.

Jordan, J., & Michel, F. (2000). *Next Generation Manufacturing: Methods and Techniques*. London: J. Wiley.

Jureta, I. J., Faulkner, S., & Schobbens, P. (2006 September). Justifying Goal Models. In *Proceedings of the 14th IEEE international Requirements Engineering Conference* (pp. 116-125). Washington, DC: IEEE Computer Society.

Kaplan, R. S., & Norton, D. P. (2004). *Strategy Maps: Converting Intangible Assets into Tangible Outcomes*. Cambridge, MA: Harvard Business School Publishing Corporation.

Kaplan, R. S., & Norton, D. P. (1996). *The Balanced Scorecard*. Boston, MA: Harvard Business School Press.

Kaplan, R. S., & Anderson, S. R. (2004 November). Time-Driven Activity-Based Costing. *Harvard Business Review, 82*(11), 131-138.

Kapoor, S., Bhattacharya, K., Buckley, S., Chowdhary, P., Ettl, M., Katircioglu, K., et. al. (2005). A Technical Framework for Sense and Respond Business Management. *IBM Systems Journal, 44*(1), 5-24.

Kazman, R., Barbacci, M., Klein, M., Carrière, J. S., Woods, S. G. (1999 May). Experience with Performing Architecture Tradeoff Analysis. In *Proceedings of the 21st International Conference on Software engineering* (pp. 54-63), Los Angeles, CA: ACM.

Keyte, B., & Locher, D. (1994). *The Complete Lean Enterprise: Value Stream Mapping for Administrative and Office Processes*. New York, NY: Productivity Press.

Lamsweerde, A. v. L., & Willemet, L. (1998 December). Inferring Declarative Requirements Specifications from Operational Scenarios. *IEEE Transactions on Software Engineering, 24*(12), 1089-1114.

Lamsweerde, A. v. L. (2001 August). Goal-Oriented Requirements Engineering: A Guided Tour. In *Proceedings of the Fifth IEEE International Symposium on Requirements Engineering* (pp.249-262), Toronto, Canada: IEEE Computer Society.

Lamsweerde, A. v. L. (2008). Requirements Engineering: From Craft to Discipline. *SIGSOFT FSE-16,* Atlanta, Georgia, USA. ACM 978-1-59593-995-1.

Lean Enterprise Institute.(n.d.). Retrieved November 23, 2008, from http://www. lean.org

Martin, P., & Tate, K. (1997). *The Project Manager Memory Jogger.* Goal/QPC.

Nolan, R. L. (1973 July). Managing the Computer Resource: A Stage Hypothesis. *Communications of the ACM, 16*(7), 399-405.

Porter, M. E. (January 2008). The Five Competitive Forces That Shape Strategy. *Harvard Business Review.*

Ramanathan, J. (2005 May). Fractal Architecture for the Adaptive Complex Enterprise. *Communications of the ACM, 48*(5), 51-57.

Sampson, G. (2003 November). The myth of diminishing firms. *Communications of the ACM, 46*(11), 25-28.

Sondhi, R. (1999). *Total Strategy.* Airworthy Publications International Ltd.

Stojanovic, L., Schneider, J., Maedche, A., Libischer, S., Studer, R., Lumpp, Th., et. al. (2004 July). The Role of Ontologies in autonomic Computing Systems. *IBM Systems Journal, 43*(3), 598-616.

Subramanian, N., Chung, L., & Song Y. (2006). An NFR-Based Framework for Establishing Traceability between Enterprise Architectures and System Architectures. In *Proceedings of the Seventh ACIS International Conference on Software Engineering, Artificial Intelligence, Networking, and Parallel/Distributed Computing* (pp. 21-28), Washington DC: IEEE Computer Society.

Winograd, T., & Flores, F. (1987). *Understanding Computers and Cognition: A New Foundation for Design.* United States: Addison-Wesley Pub Co.

Womack, J., & Jones, D. (2003). *Lean Thinking: Banish Waste and Create Wealth in Your Corporation.* New York: Free Press.

Yu, E., & Mylopoulos, J. (1993 December). An Actor Dependency Model of Organizational Work: With Application to Business Process Reengineering. In *Proceedings of the Conference on Organizational Computing Systems* (pp. 258-268), Milpitas, California: ACM.

ENDNOTES

[a] I* and e3value network modeling are two approaches to that can be used to examine the design of a service-oriented enterprise. The aim of both techniques is to allow decision makers to explore the design space of a service-based opportunity from an early stage, before significant development begins, in order to elicit and bring out the objectives, who will be involved, why they will be involved, and ultimately which objectives can be met. From this perspective, the i* technique helps a designer frame a reasonability realistic picture of all the actors that will cooperate and how their decisions to carry out various cooperative tasks will globally affect the system to be designed. e3's complementary approach helps to quantify the notion of system value, in economic terms, so that designers can estimate if their solution is likely to be successful or not if it is eventually implemented.

More specifically, "I* is based on a goal model that is basically an annotated AND/OR graph showing how higher-level goals are satisfied by lower-level ones (goal refinement) and, conversely, how lower-level goals contribute to the satisfaction of higher-level ones (goal abstraction). The top goals are the highest-level ones still in the system scope whereas the bottom goals are assignable requirements or expectations (Lamsweerde, A.v.L. 2008). " We use this type of goal model as a starting point and integrate the Interactions that need to occur to achieve the goals of a specific stakeholder.

[b] OWL: Accessed December 12, 2008. http://www.w3.org/TR/owl-features/

[c] [IDEF0] http://www.idef.com/idef0.html.

[d] Through examination of IT enabled companies, Nolan presents a preliminary theory describing how organizational management evolves in response to the employment of computer based resources. His stage theory suggests that organizations go through four phases, or milestones of evolution, and at each stage the management strategies mature as the role of technology within the organization becomes better understood and aligned with its values and business goals. The stages loosely progress from initial periods of technology introduction, acquisition, and general uncontrolled excitement to the final stage where technology is seen as a resource that must be managed and controlled with respect to business users, their goals, and the efficency of the overall

business. The final stage which he calls user and service orientation is still very consistent with the focus on service orientation today and highlights why it is such as valid realization for management.

[e]   An infrastructure consists of the basic structures which are required for further development. For example, computers, staff, and electricity are basic infrastructure components any IT enabled business will require.

[f]   These milestones are similar to the transition points of the negotiation cycle first introduced in Winograd, T. and Flores, F. Understanding Computers and Cognition - A New Foundation for Design, Addison Wesley Publishing Inc, Reading, USA. (1987).

[g]   We use the term deliverable to refer to this final service.

[h]   Here we are using the term activity with respect to an IDEF0 activity which can be thought of as a function with inputs and outputs, may be subject to controls (constraints), and may use mechanisms (resources) in addition to the inputs it consumes. At the same time we use the notion of activity to reflect *activity-based* costing. This simple concept associates the cost of doing an activity with the activity itself. Time-Driven Activity-Based costing is a technique Kaplan 2004 introduces as a practical method for doing activity based costing, without getting into excessive detail, by focusing on resource cost per unit of time and time it takes to complete each step in a customer facing activity (rather than trying to directly estimate how a given resource spends it time). This focus very much mirrors the ACE methodology that has been discussed in this book and once again underscores the importance of looking at systems engineering problems from the viewpoint of the environment – that is to understand the relationship between the business customer and the organizational response.

[i]   A service level agreement, as defined in ITIL, is a formal negotiated document that defines the service being offered to the customer. These agreements should concentrate on quantitative service measures when possible, so compliance can be objectively assessed, but qualitative service definitions are often necessary. Service level objectives define the goals to be achieved.

[j]   An operating level agreement, as defined in ITIL, is an internal document that defines the relationship between different functional areas within an organization. Generally, operating level agreements detail what various sub-units, or contractors, of the service providing organization must do In order to meet their customer's service level agreements. Underpinning documents formalize the contracts with suppliers. Operating level objectives define the goals to be achieve.

[k]   There are many issues like Interactions that do not complete and internally generated Requests, which are covered in the appendix.

l   http://en.wikipedia.org/wiki/Bullwhip_effect

m   Coase, R. The nature of the firm. *Economica n.s. 4* (Nov. 1937), 386–405..

n   The exact use of Complexity Theory varies in projects. It has been applied as a model for simulations aimed at understanding growth in biological systems, fluctuations in economic systems, and turbulence in fluids. Complexity Theory also has been used to increase understanding through analogy between socio-economic systems and biological systems for greater understanding of the former. Kelly, S.; and Allison. M. A. (1998). The Complexity Advantage. New York, NY: McGraw Hill.

o   Event driven Process Chains" (EPC) have been introduced by Keller, N ttgens and Scheer and they have become a de facto industry standard in German speaking countries. For users of Microsoft Office products, EPC shapes are being shipped with the diagramming tool Visio. A pure Visio-based creation of business processes using Visio's EPC shapes is a great bargain and very easy to use. For use in larger projects, some basic functions of professional modelling tools are needed. Especially important is the ability to show a distinction between model objects and how they are shown in drawings, navigation tools, export / import interfaces and reports. Traditional Visio shapes have no rules and they can be connected without regard of EPC methodology rules. Interfaces and reports require the syntactical correctness offered by SemTalk.

p   Recall the word 'customer' can refer to either internal or external customers or both as determined by the context.

q   Here *market segments* are understood as groups of similar service-providing organizations.

r   CEO – Chief Executive Officer; CTO – Chief Technology Officer; CIO – Chief Information Officer; CXO – executive level Role.

s   The Balanced Scorecard may have been brought about for a different reason than Zachman's Framework but their principles are surprisingly similar. Kaplan and Norton 1994 and 2004 presents the Balanced Scorecard as a solution to the myopic and excessive business performance measures that had been popularized throughout the industrial age and remain in employment today. They argue that to achieve a true gauge of performance it's more important to consider the major perspectives of the business, relative to one another, than it is to build performance models from any one perspective to a great level of detail. In the Balanced Scorecard they present four such facets of the business, each designed to asses the goals of a particular set of individuals that interact with the business and each in relation to the others. As a result overall performance is not artificially coerced into a measure that can only be understood from a particular viewpoint, but rather is visible through a set of lenses that more accurately represents the concerns and values of the business.

Kaplan R. S. and Norton D. P. (1992) "The Balanced Scorecard: Measures that Drive Performance", *Harvard Business Review,* Jan – Feb pp. 71-80.

[t] Note the categorization of the goals is related to the Balanced Scorecard.

[u] There are a number of well known goal oriented analysis techniques that can help system designers elicit, understand, and evaluate the needs and measures of success of stakeholders. One particularly useful approach is the i* model of strategic dependencies which pinpoints how stakeholders and Roles depend on one another in a complex organizational setting. What is the reference?

[v] http://www.sei.cmu.edu/cmmi/general/index.html

[w] These levels are based on IBM's definition of an autonomic maturity model in which software intensive systems and organizations progress through five levels: Basic → Managed → Predictive → Adaptive → Autonomic. This progression is intended to lead the organization from a baseline level through states where processes become defined, standardized, repeatable, and predictable to states where the organization's processes and IT systems are capable of responding to environmental change in a safe, sound, and responsive fashion in accordance with the organizational goals. Richard Murch. Autonomic Computing. Prentice Hall, 2004.

[x] Especially in view of current trend to migrate to mainframes.

[y] Ogc, Ogc. Itil Lifecycle Publication Suite. London: TSO, 2007, http://www.best-management-ractice.com/gempdf/itSMF_An_Introductory_Overview_of_ITIL_V3.pdf

[z] Porter's model of competitive forces showcases five major aspects of an industry that businesses should take into account when crafting a viable strategy for growth or survival. Like much of the material that is present in this book and its selected references, the model reiterates the importance of using multiple frames of reference for the purposes of making a decision that is not biased by one particular facet of the organization. Porter's competitive forces do this at the strategic level by pointing out the sources of vulnerability and opportunity in an industry with respect to the ever changing landscape of the global marketplace. The success of a strategist, just like an architect, depends on this ability to analyze a plan of action from many seemingly unrelated, but often very interrelated, points of view.

[aa] While many other strategic frameworks exist (see http://www.12manage.com/ for a comprehensive list), our goal here is to begin with Strategy forces to create an integrative framework that includes Business and IT operations. And with that in mind, Porter's provides an excellent starting point.

[ab] A growing number of Americans are taking that path, traveling to countries like Thailand, Costa Rica and Malaysia for cosmetic, orthopedic and heart surgeries and other medical and dental treatments that cost 20 to 80 percent

less than at home. Jennifer Alsever, *New York Times*. Published: October 15, 2006.

ac   In general activity based costing means that all costs an organization incurs are mapped backed to the activities used to create the end product or services (the deliverable). Although the principle is very straightforward it is not quite so easy to implement in a real organization.

ad   Malone, Michael. The Virtual Corporation. New York: Harper Business, 1993.

ae   Formally, Amdahl's Law is: $S = \dfrac{1}{\sum\limits_{k=0}^{n}\left(\dfrac{Pk}{Sk}\right)}$

Where S is the total speedup (or slowdown), each Pk is a percentage, each Sk is a speedup (the improvement), and n is the number of n is the number of changes to be made to the system (including any unchanged portion). For example, if there is a 2 part process and the first part consumes 40% of the time and the second part 60% of the time and part 1 can be speed up by a factor of 2: $S = \dfrac{1}{\left(\dfrac{.4}{2}\right)+\left(\dfrac{.6}{1}\right)} = 1.25$ meaning the total system runs 25% faster.

ag   Thus, at this point we observe that with the use of the Interaction traceability we have prescriptive steps that satisfy ITILv3. *Service Strategy* defined for each Request type based on the identification of market opportunities for which services could be developed in order to meet a requirement on the part of internal or external customers. The output is a strategy for the design, implementation, maintenance and continual improvement of the service. Continual improvement is viewed here as an organizational capability and a strategic asset. *Continual Service Improvement* focuses on the ability to improve the quality of the services that the IT organization delivers to the business. A key aspect of this is Service Reporting, Service Measurement and Service Level Management. This is supported by the RED Interaction performance.

ah   The Kano Model is a well known is a well known characterization of the drivers of customer satisfaction and is best thought of as means to asses how a customer will perceive some aspect, or feature, of a product or design. As such, it can be a useful tool for discussion with perspective customers or making tradeoffs when constraints prevent all aspects of a solution from being fully developed. Kano's model characterizes product features into five distinct classes: attractive, one-dimensional, must-be, indifferent, and reverse. For example, must-be product features are those which will lead to great customer dissatisfaction if they are not properly implemented in the product, but provide relatively little satisfaction if they are done well – in other words they are taken for granted.

On the contrary, attractive features may not lead to any dissatisfaction if they are not found in the product, but may contribute a remarkable increase in satisfaction if they are included – in other words they may be somewhat novelty. By understanding how individual aspect of a product will impact the perceived quality, or the customer's satisfaction, a provider can make better decisions and align them to the current strategy. Note Kano's model is used as a basis in a number of other quality oriented frameworks such as Quality Function Deployment (QFD).

[ai]   Quality initiatives, like Six Sigma, stress the importance of reducing defects by systematically re-examining operational processes on a continual basis with repeatable and scientifically sound analysis. In general, the goal of continuous analysis is to consistently recognize, isolate, and remove the sources of variation.

[aj]   Earned value is a measure of the amount of work accomplished for something and is usually independent of time.

Chapter III
Governance and Conceptual, Logical and Installed Architecture Alignment Using Work Products and Workflow

ABSTRACT

Governance and related alignment methods for the management of complex systems are introduced here to facilitate and better decision making. The goal here is to increase re-use and agility. We also show how EA governance can leverage technologies like middleware and workflow to enable service evolution. The methods and work products of the previous Chapter 2 along with the following EA layers guide continual service improvement.

What is the ACE EA governance?

- How is the organization established?
- What are the goals and benefits of EA governance?
- What are the different roles and responsibilities of the EA team?

How does the Conceptual ACE structure guide the EA team to make enhancements to the Logical and Installed architecture layers?

Figure 1. Lifecycle approach to Solution and Architecture management

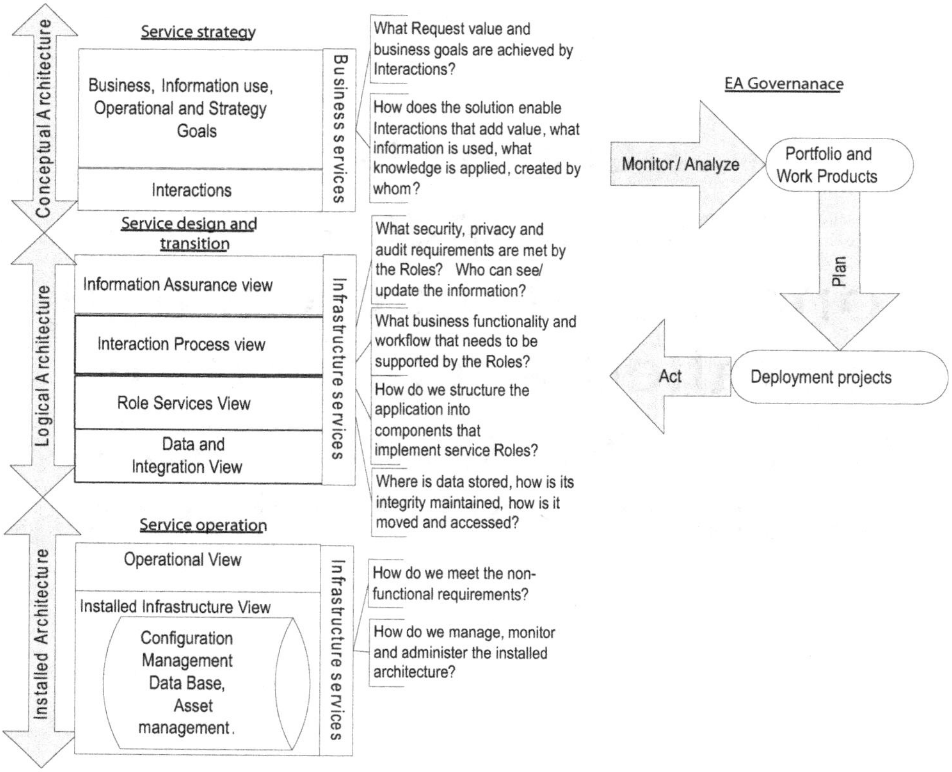

- What is the service life-cycle and how does this use the architecture layers for service improvement?
- How does the conceptual architecture relate to the logical and the installed physical layers?
- What types of work products are needed to enable the entire service life-cycle?
- How is the conceptual layer used to determine governance Roles and responsibilities?
- How does EA governance facilitate continual improvement?
- What types of business and operational information is needed for engineers and architects to analyze and improve the Interaction performance?
- What is missing?

How do workflow management, standards, emerging technologies, and patterns assist with service life-cycle management?

- How do we better bridge conceptual, logical layers and installed architecture with workflow management?
- How can Workflow Management and related technologies assist in increasing more conceptual organization of services?
- What standards and technologies are relevant to complex architectures?
- What are the tradeoffs?

EA GOVERNANCE

The ACE structure and work products guide the decision making by the ACE governance team. This team is made up from the CIO (Chief Information Officer), Chief Technology Officer (CTO), Architects, Software Engineers, System and Business Analysts, Application and System experts, Procurement, Finance, Human Resources, Project Managers, and operational members drawn from Line Managers and other workers. With quite a few members involved, it is useful to establish an EA organization with program roles and responsibilities as follows.

Establishing the EA Organization and Program

The EA organization has an important performance improvement Role within the service-oriented complex of primary and enabling services. In order to be successful the EA organization requires some critical dependencies met:

- *Executive support and sponsorship:* the CIO and IT senior management must understand and support the enterprise architecture program. CIO executive support and sponsorship does not imply automatic approval of all EA recommendations. Each EA recommendation will be reviewed by the appropriate governance body and judged on its own merits, as well as its contribution to the overall EA Roadmap.
- *Program Approvals:* This is for the EA *Program Charter* and associated EA *Program Plan* and EA Roles and Responsibilities document by the CIO[a].
- *Identification and allocation of appropriate resources for the EA Program.* The EA organization implements a program that is resourced separately from the other organizations to achieve the benefits of systemic thinking and achieve overall efficiencies. As we shall see below, many of the resources are from

the domain and responsible for aligning 'in-the-small' with the 'in-the-large' business details.

- *Objectives:* The EA program management objectives include the following:
  - ○ Document the EA process, policies, and procedures
  - ○ Communicate the EA benefits
  - ○ Augment, as necessary, personnel with in-depth expertise to support the EA program
  - ○ Include part-time virtual team participation, co-opting of staff and acquisition of full-time resources on a project-by-project need basis
  - ○ Install the necessary tools required to perform and report on the EA program
  - ○ Identify the company strategies and objectives as the base for the architecture
  - ○ Define the architecture principles which will guide EA direction
- *Goals:* The Goal of EA governance is to develop, continually refine, and deploy a *strategy-driven* future state design. This is achieved by enhancing the current services in a variety of ways. As illustrated in Figure 1 the service life-cycle[b] consists of:
  - ○ *Service strategy* for Request types and portfolio management defined using the *conceptual architecture layer.* This includes the as-is and to-be.
  - ○ *Service design* for to-be enhancements to the *logical and installed architecture layers,* focusing on the activities that implement strategy. The design work products include all aspects of the proposed service, as well as the processes intended to support it. Key areas are Availability Management, Capacity Management, Continuity Management and Security Management.
  - ○ *Service transition* into the *logical and installed architecture layers* focusing on the implementation using the output of the service design activities to create a production service or modification of an existing service. There is overlap between Service Transition and Service Operation. Key areas are Change Management, Release Management, Configuration Management and Service Knowledge Management.
  - ○ *Service operation* addresses all aspects of the *installed infrastructure* use (hardware and software) and includes handling incidents, access, and so on. The focus is on the activities required to operate the services and maintain their functionality as defined in the Service Levels expected by the customers. Key areas are Incident Management, Problem Management and Request Fulfillment. Another process is Event Management which is concerned with normal and exception condition events. Events

have been defined into three categories: Informational events -- which are logged, Warning events -- also called alerts, where an event exceeds a specified threshold, and Critical events -- which typically will lead to the generation of Incidents.

o   *Continual service improvement* the layers of the architecture on the left provide a representation and context for service enhancements and related decision making on the right of Figure 1, in addition to supporting current operations.

- *EA Objectives:* The ACE EA organization uses the work products to represent the primary and secondary services to achieve continual improvement through management of their life cycles. More specifically the work products are used to:

    o   Create an EA Roadmap of the recommendations for moving from current state to the future state

    o   Identify opportunities to leverage existing solutions/components/approaches and/or other low-hanging-fruit opportunities throughout all EA Interactions

    o   Integrate the EA process into IT management and governance processes

    o   Define/refine the policies for *chargeback* (measuring costs and charging the customer organizations for the service delivered)

    o   Develop business processes to guide information, technology, and application future-state design

    o   Define/refine work products, patterns, and technologies

    o   Perform a gap analysis comparing current IT systems with the future state EA, including IT technology standards

    o   Define/refine the information management and content environment

    o   Define/refine the information technology standards and overall direction

    o   Define/refine the project portfolio and component reuse strategy

ACE Governance Roles

The EA governance roles and responsibilities are given in Figure 2[c] along with the use of ACE methods for governance. Specifically, EA governance aligns conceptual-to-logical-to-installed layers of the architecture (as illustrated in Figure 1) to:

- 'Monitor' operations and BioS performance either manually or in an automated fashion.
- 'Analyze and plan' the enhancements of ACE.
- 'Act' through implemented changes in the logical and installed architectures and work products.

Figure 2. ACE Governance Roles and Responsibilities (based on TOGAF).

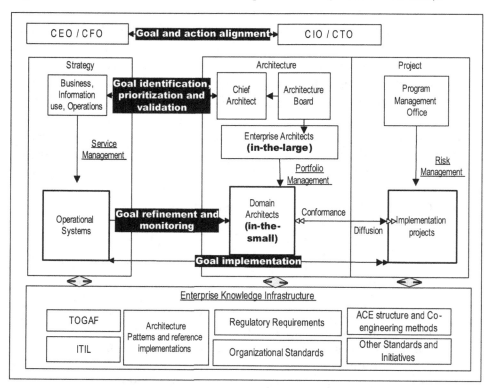

The governance roles and responsibilities for this alignment are as follows.

Role of Enterprise Architects: All the architects have expert level knowledge of the BioS alignment methods. An important aspect of their Role is *in-the-large* alignment including:

- Monitor current BioS performance for Request types and validate strategy
- Define / Refine BioS goals for each Request type and set priorities across Request types, work with business
- Work collaboratively with in-the-small architects to align goals with actions
- Create a portfolio of projects prioritized for investment to maximize goals

Role of Domain Architects: Define *in-the-small* management needed for each Interaction:

- Monitor current performance and traceability to BioS goals

- Define / Refine to-be performance to align Role OLs to meet Interaction SLs
- Responsibility for specific Interaction goals and their achievement though managing the Role sets
- Innovate to achieve goals (for example, identify opportunities to 'package' services for reuse and reduced costs)

Role of Program and Project Managers: Implement goals through solutions and project actions needed for improving Interaction performance.

To summarize, the in-the-large governance processes ensure that 1) the work products are created and reviewed with in-the-small expertise and 2) the work products are reviewed and prioritized within the in-the-large context. It is important to emphasize the symbiotic nature of the in-the-large, in-the-small, and program management Roles and these Roles fundamentally complement each other.

Enterprise Knowledge Infrastructure: The governance is informed by a variety of methods, patterns, standards and other tools that acts as the enterprise knowledge infrastructure (or Enterprise Continuum as defined by TOGAF). We will cover ways in which we can create knowledge about the installed systems in a later chapter.

Conceptual, Logical, Installed Work Products for Service Life Cycle Management

The EA and Project management Roles are responsible for developing the work products, implementing the projects, and managing the portfolio as shown in Figure 2. These work products are used to accomplish the goals identified above. For this, it is essential that the EA be represented in a manner that facilitates good decision making. Therefore we revisit the conceptual ACE structure and *work products* of the previous section and put it in the larger context of the logical and operational layers. This is to ensure that the EA governance has the complete set of work products to 1) *adequately* represent the architecture, evolving services and relationships, and operations, and 2) govern effectively throughout the service life cycle. To accomplish this first we identify the contents of a complete collection of Conceptual, Logical, and Physical work products in the rest of this subsection starting with the Figure 3.

Conceptual | Logical | Installed Work Products Aligned using the ACE Structure: The ACE structure allows us to identify and develop all the architecture work products needed for governance. The complete scope of work product is illustrated in Figure 3 - the 'what work product', 'how implemented', 'where applied/implemented', 'who is the customer(s)', 'when used', and 'why relevant' perspectives are illustrated. Note that the organization and technology trends like globalization,

Figure 3. Work products and views for service strategy

Work product Based on ACE strucutre	What	How	Where	Who	When	Why	Continual improvement
A: Request strategy.	Strategy goals (Conceptual, in-the-large)	Interactions value network.	Delivery goals.	Market | Customers.	Request events and business cycles.	To meet Strategy goals.	Goal identification and validation.
B: Request priorities & Project portfolio.	Business goals (Conceptual, in-the-large)	Investment in Agents, chargeback.	Interactions.	Stakeholders.	Roles executed by agents/ resources.	Direct resources to meet goals.	Goal refinement and prioritization.
C: REDs, Role sets, & SLs .	Information use goals (Logical, in-the-large)	How do the Roles sets deliver using applications and resources?	Interaction location.	RED milestones and value add.	Interaction events.	To meet SLs.	Goal implementation.
D: Request Triage Rules.	Technology use goals (Logical, in-the-small)	Triage rules applied for effective assignments.	Information flow to meet Interaction needs.	Which Roles are authorized for which resources.	When and how long are the Roles resourced.	Maximize value due to shared resources.	Goal implementation.
E: Roles & OLs.	Operational view (Installed, in-the-small)	Agents | components availability for execution, non-funhctionals.	System architecture - hardware and software components relationships.	Resources performing Roles,	Timing and sequencing.	To meet OLs with shared resources.	Goal monitoring and audit.
F: Agents, capacity, associations, and skills.	Installed infrastructure view (Installed, in-the-small)	Capacity of Agents and components (e.g. CIs in CMDB) .	Physical architecture.	Solution configuration items and security.	Communication facilities and availability.	Processes for enhancement and change.	Goal implementation.

consolidation and virtualization, affect the 'where'. Also the rows *form an internal customer-provider chain* as mentioned previously in Chapter 2. That is each row facilitates the goals of the row above as in a sense-and-respond system.

In the Figure 3 all the needed service enterprise work products and details for effective governance are summarized starting with the well-known Zachman-based (Zachman 1987) matrix. We have added the continual improvement column on the right. The entries of the column 'What' in Figure 3 are in terms of the ACE structure based work products introduced in Chapter 2. The remaining columns indicate the content of the work product. They are now assembled into a more complete and precise picture with conceptual, logical, and installed layers as in Figure 1.

It is important to note that the starting point for this matrix is the ACE structure that relates all the work products together. We next explore the contents of the individual layers further.

Conceptual architecture work products (What should the services delivered do for business and strategy?): This layer describes the organization, the Interactions and its Request goals. The objective of the related work products is, as we have shown, is to Co-engineer complex systems based on goals (as shown in the previous Chapter 2). It identifies Interactions in order to surface all the contributing factors that impact the 'what' for service strategy, service performance, underlying Agent costs, service value, and impact to goals.

Logical architecture work products (How are the systems in the IT infrastructure used?): This next layer below conceptual in Figure 1 looks at IT as an infrastructure from both the *in-the-large business perspective and its alignment to in-the-small operational perspective.* From an underlying IT technology perspective these are also the business priorities work products that define the IT value-add from the customers' perspective and then sets SL goals. The IT Agents that provide services are business application components (HR, financial, human resources etc.), software and architecture components (data bases, web servers etc.), physical infrastructure, and human resources. Combined they provide services that fulfill Interaction Role set requirements (Figure 3). Whereas the conceptual rows above describe the business view as perceived by the people performing business Roles, the logical architecture rows below describe the use of components that provide the information and enabling services. Finally, the lower technology layers describes how components address the information needs identified in the previous rows.

TOGAF refers to the software and hardware combinations as building blocks. *Solution building blocks* (also known as SBB[d]) play functional Roles in Interactions to achieve Interaction SLs. Also, the SBBs use *architecture building blocks or* ABBs. The ABBs are actual technology-aware components in the IT infrastructure layer. These building blocks are composed to meet the OL requirements in turn needed to meet the SL requirements identified in the layers above.

We use the term *'component'* to refer to a software or hardware system that provides services. We will also use the term *'Agent'* to refer to a building block since 1) we envision an evolution towards more autonomic[e] building blocks with properties like self-monitoring and self-healing, and 2) human resources that also provide services that enable solutions and Roles and thus are part of the 'building block'. Solution Roles and Components (SBBs), Technology Roles and Components (ABBs), and their relationships constitute a view of the logical enterprise architecture.

Installed architecture work products (How are the systems in the IT infrastructure implemented and installed?): Moving to the final layer at the left of Figure 1, we note the term 'installed architecture' from an IT perspective refers to operational | functional and non-functional behavior, the constituent configuration items, and the underlying hardware software infrastructure. As illustrated in Figure 3, this includes the exact description of the how the components in the logical view are constituted by configuration items and their relationships within configurations as installed in a specific operating environment. The CMDB is also a work product that consists of the configuration items and relationships installed in the particular site.

The example of Figure 4 draws from eGovernment which has significant service-oriented goals and is also illustrative of the typical service-oriented enterprise components. It includes logical components (SBBs and ABBs) that deliver to different stakeholders. It is interesting to note that as our attention shifts to the Roles and Communities (made of Roles), we once again encounter significant complexity in the use of the underlying architecture. We will address this in later sections. We

Figure 4. High-level example of solution architecture components and relationships that provide services for Roles to execute Interactions

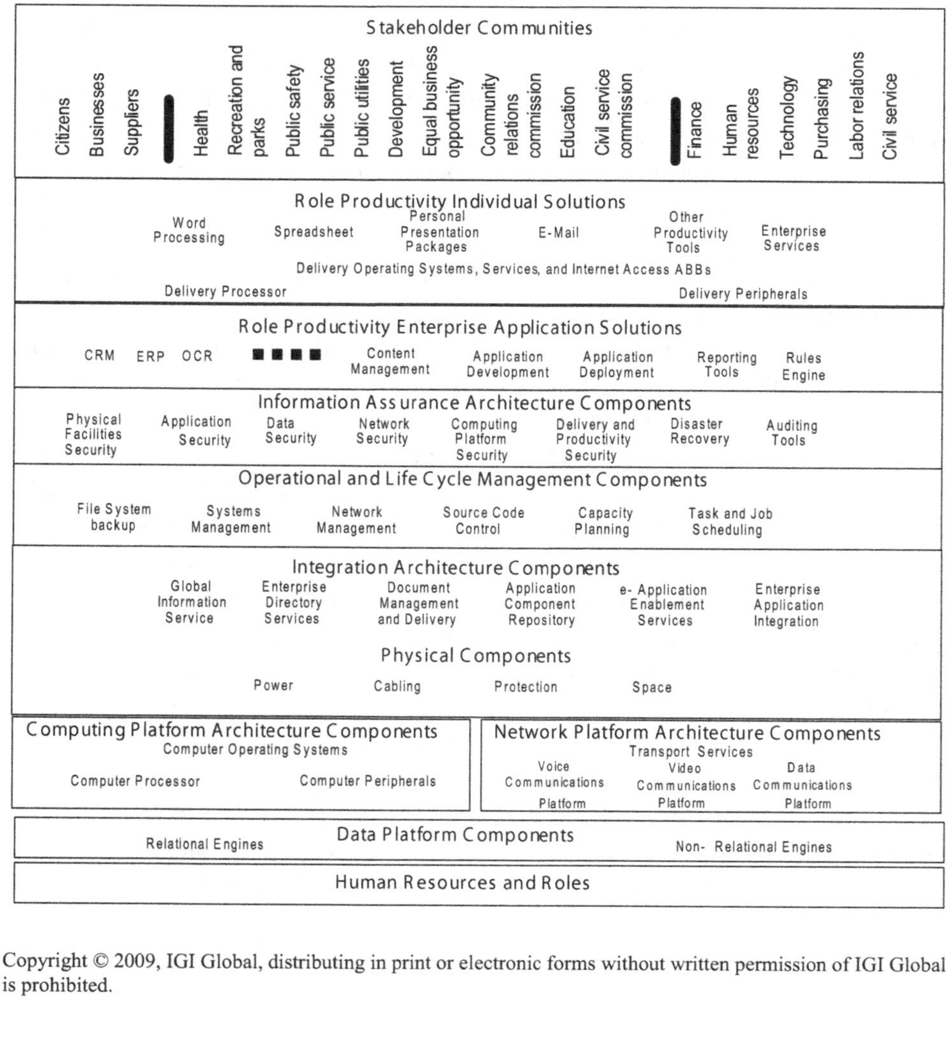

will also show how the ACE structure is used by the EA team for governance and decision making.

To conclude, the EA governance requires work products that reflect the layers and relationships of the EA architecture on the left of in Figure 1 to facilitate the continual improvement process on the right of the figure. Using this to guide decision-making, the EA governance Roles take actions illustrated at a high level on the right of Figure 1. Before proceeding, some points are worth re-iterating. It is important to note that all the enterprise architecture work products must be visited from both continual improvement and service life-cycle perspectives[f]. That is, in addition to the creational aspects, the work products should also focus on service Interaction monitoring critical for decisions related to service enhancement and retirement.

Complete Enterprise Architecture Template for Work Products

In this chapter we have thus far identified the work products for documenting the entire enterprise architecture[g]. In subsequent chapters we show in greater detail how the work products are developed and used. To recap, the enterprise architecture work products consists of the 1) conceptual Interaction layer and work products for performance analysis, and 2) logical and physical components implementing the conceptual layer. As also noted before, each of the dimensions is the customer of the services provided by the nested dimension and, consequently, the work products of each dimension are often determine the goals and objectives implemented by the nested dimension.

The enterprise architecture work products template presented below captures BioS goals, Interactions, Functional, Non-functional, information needed for analysis, improvement, and decision-making throughout the lifecycle of the service. In addition to more standardized methods for developing work products (Ambler 2005, Ben 2003, Domges 1998, Dumas et al, Hoffman 2001, Schwaber 2004), there is also now a large body of work on architecture patterns (Erl 2005, Fowler 2005), analysis (Clements 2002), and related standards (WFMC 2008) to draw upon and capture knowledge related to specific implementations. We build upon this body of work to define next an integrated template with guiding questions (details are in the Appendix) to capture specifics of the conceptual, logical and physical work products. Importantly, the template provides questions and guidelines to address change and evolution.

EA Service Life-Cycle Documentation Template

Conceptual:

What Business, Information use, Operational, and Strategic functional, and non-functional requirements drive the decisions related to a service Interaction change?

Strategy goals: Work Product A: Request strategy. The customer situations in which the Request type is motivated, what is the fundamental business reason and competitive strategy.

Example: A real world business example demonstrating the existence of the problem and a need for the Request type.

Problem: The problem the Interaction solution addresses.

Business goals and analysis: Work Product B: Request priorities, Project portfolio analysis including an analysis of why the problem is solved. The fundamental solution principle underlying the Interaction support for the Request type. What major infrastructure service Roles are impacted by new or changed Interactions? What are the issues, alternatives, assumptions, risks, costs, value add, schedule implications, decisions, and justification? Underlying licensing, maintenance, and upgrade issues.

Logical:

Consequences: Work Product C: REDs, Role sets, & SLs documenting the business and operational performance benefits of providing the Interaction solution and any potential liabilities.

Structure: Work Product D: Request Triage Rules. High-level process flow or package diagrams. A detailed specification of the functional and structural aspects

Operational IT:

IT goals and dynamics: Work Product E: Roles and OLs. Use cases. Typical scenarios describing the runtime behavior of the Interaction from the business-user perspective.

Logical system view: Work Product F: Agents, capacity, associations, and skills. The components involved including libraries, application programs, databases, etc. This includes not only where the services provided, but also where they are used. Package diagrams with the architecture and solution components that have been approved (and with exceptions documented). How are the impacted technology components affected in their on-going Roles and capacity utilization within service Interactions? Did any vendor products or packages impact the architectural decisions and have these external constraints been documented?

Data and Integration view: The messaging that takes place in order to send or receive information through a common interfaces. (Bus, data source, etc...) (Sequence diagrams).

Security view: A) Authentication, authorization services B) Detect, resist, mitigate C) Logging.

Deployment view: This is how the packaged code will be deployed, a mapping from the logical view to the physical view. (Deployment packages). How are the changes reflected in the CMDB, chargeback accounting, and Customer Service Center? Are all the ITIL process requirements for change management, support, and availability identified and resolved? What is the feedback and experience after deployment, especially in the case of new services?

Physical view: Aspects of deployment such as servers, routers, workstations, firewalls.

Concurrency view: When a complex system is deployed onto computational resources, this view is needed to reason about the communication and sharing of data later in the Service Level analysis. (State chart diagrams).

Scalability and Performance view: Availability analysis, capacity.

Configuration Management view: Configuration management, backup and recovery procedures.

System Management view: Administration, backup, and recovery.

Related information:

Experience: Potential enhancements in the current system. The capture of decisions and tradeoffs related to the above models. This includes the costs, value, performance.

Related Best Practice, Standards, Technologies and References: Corporate standards and other information in the enterprise architecture continuum.

USING TECHNOLOGIES, STANDARDS, AND METHODS FOR SERVICE EVOLUTION

Organizations moving to deliver end-to-end services or new services often find that their current architecture cannot effectively adapt to facilitate underlying processes. While enabling enterprise integration and work flow technology has significant promise for assembling and delivering boundary-crossing services, the scale and scope of customization requirements often leads to poor technology deployment and project performance. We illustrate this using an example and introduce some of the important technologies, standards, and methods to address this challenge. And, towards the end of the chapter an architecture options framework to match innovation opportunities with stakeholder value to ensure business success is presented.

Figure 5. Service Progression - Increasing Scope of Services, Role of BPM and project complexity

External facing						
Organization-to-organization	Informational website : Company information , catalog , pricing ,...	Access to a single : system Create a request	Customer service management : end-to-end, status	eCommerce eMarket New products and services	Participation in the value chains Enable new markets and processes	Frictionless collaboration across enterprise boundaries
Internal facing						
Organization-to-stakeholders	Information and Training	Global access to collaboration sites	Efficient HR and internal processes	IT infrastructure services and processes	Effective fulfillment across the supply chain	Virtual organization , supply chains and resource efficiency
Features						
	Information access	Collaboration	BPM across multiple systems , Data Warehousing	Business intelligence mining	Business activity monitoring and real-time decision -making	

a   **b**   **c**

Service progression ⇨increasing difficulty , multiple systems and boundary-spanning processes

What is the typical service progression?

- How does the insertion of a workflow component into a complex system increase its adaptability?
- When is an organization ready to introduce a technology like workflow automation to improve services?
- How can workflow be effectively introduced given the current investments in enterprise systems as well as legacy processes and systems that are in place?
- What are the types of standards? Tradeoffs?
- What are the elements of the total cost of ownership?

How can EA governance plan ahead and justify enterprise architecture investments?

- How can we identify the value of architecture to increase the chances of project success through options for future innovation?
- How can we design adaptability into the systems so that it can provide greater value to stakeholders over a longer period of time?

For *routine* services and end-to-end business processes, there are enabling enterprise data repositories and with embedded BPM. While these can potentially provide a range of features needed for *non-routine* service delivery, successful deployment projects for *non-routine* services are challenging. Even though strides have been made in technologies a clear business return is more the exception. We use a specific business example to analyze some of the underlying organizational and technology reasons and suggest steps for ensuring success.

Typical Services Progression: As the EA team seeks to help organizations make their services more relevant it places many significant requirements on information flow. The concept of circumstance-based innovation best describes the trend towards services that relate to the customers' needs and the context of those needs (Christensen 2004). An example illustrating the IT aspect of these trends is an enterprise using its ERP capability to provide the customers with the service of managing their own replenishment.

Putting this in a specific organization's context we note that the typical evolution of eBusiness is from the left to right and with critical points as illustrated in Figure 6. As the organization progresses from specific local access features to external and internal BPM integration (from '*a*' to 'critical point *b*' in the Figure 5) the lack of underlying re-useable services becomes a hindrance.

Some reasons include multiple sources of information relating to the customer, or Roles and access privileges, or order information. Often a shared common business vocabulary is missing, thus requiring extensive data translations. The challenges can together have a negative effect on organizations embarking on enterprise integration projects to facilitate seamless BPM and collaboration.

This also makes it difficult for the organization to leverage IT to achieve competitive innovation at 'c' and beyond. Most enterprises reach the critical point 'b' without the architectural 'service options' in place. This means that a huge amount of custom code had been created over time making it almost impossible to move further along the progression, due to exorbitant infrastructure and replacement costs. Because of this, the goal of close to real-time monitoring and decision-making with the right information is also very difficult for the stakeholders to achieve.

The Business Challenge

The problem, generally stated is how can the EA team ensure that systems provide value through their ability to fulfill stakeholder needs and wants? These needs evolve over time and may diverge from the installed system. A system's value may diminish over time because stakeholder wants and technology needs evolve and maintenance costs increase. As a result systems have to be updated at substantial cost and disruption that may not be affordable. This relegates organizations to business as usual through necessity, but not through choice. We begin by understanding the evolution of non-routine services within a typical externally-driven organization. We use a major telecommunications company to base our examples.

Strategy dimension: The TelCo's engineering organization supports sophisticated products and services. Each installation is thus a non-routine request. An example of a service is wiring a national chain for daily sales and other communications. Specifically, multiple telecommunications products are installed in a variety of configurations that take into consideration the unique features of the specific customer site. An installation project – that can last from days to months – gets awarded based on preliminary engineering and competitive bidding. In an increasingly competitive climate, the *strategic goal* was to increase the level of customer satisfaction to retain customers and get repeat business. Customer self-service and monitoring websites were expected to help increase market presence. The expectation was that dramatically improved *customer satisfaction and process efficiency* would accomplish the strategic goals.

Business dimension: The *business goal*s were improvement of Order-to-Cash cycle by 40%, the monitoring of bid status, and response time by 40%. Given the small margins in the business, any technology expense had to be very carefully justified. By installing the BPM architecture, the company expected to position itself for customer self-service and future business process models. It was expected that the first installed system would pay for the customization costs in about a year, with the second BPM project (that made use of the now available BPM infrastructure) to justify the full license costs.

Operational dimension: The TelCo sales and engagement organization had external-facing product catalogs, internal websites accessing customer emails with request information and so on. The departmental 'silo' websites had been justified overtime to improve worker productivity and were justified and implemented within the department's budget. Also, the many existing home-grown solutions avoided the software license costs - but increased the custom coding and hence increased maintenance and migration costs in the longer run. At the same time, the organization was at point 'a' in the Service Progression of Figure 6.

The challenge scenario that operations was trying to address is summarized here. In general terms, there are a couple of hundred of active requests and a dozen small design and engineering teams distributed across the country. On a typical day TelCo's Account Team (AT) handles a large variety of different request types each with different pricing strategies and underlying contracts. Incoming requests are reviewed to determine whether or not it is for additional or standard services (as defined in the customer-TelCo contract). Based on the review, the request will follow different paths: standard services or additional services. (This is later referred to as request conversion.) The typical response process involves multiple organizations that require *time variant* information before producing their own outputs. Technical Services (TS) works with solution experts to provide a technical assessment (additional services) or a network engineering review (standard services) of the request. The AT works with the customer and TS to complete order entry forms (as required) after network engineering review. These forms are submitted to the customer for

Figure 6. Agents in TelCo.

Roles	Typical Products and other Resources
Tracking of status, customer response, log of customer Interactions	Excel™
Database applications for order entry, tracking	Access™, Oracle™, DB2™ (IBM mainframe database)
Project documents and templates.	File servers and document management systems.
Electronic Mail	MS Exchange™ (Corp), MS Outlook ™
Enterprise Customer Management (CRM)	Seibel™
Project Management	Microsoft Project 98/2000™
Order entry and asset management applications Engineering and deployment	Several Mainframe Applications Twenty five engineers working on proposals, seventy five in installation

approval and requirements signoff. Each of the organizations has individual sets of forms and information requirements that must be filled and passed on. As each functional organization, completes their documentation, all the proposal specific information is captured in a standard form to develop pricing based on the contract's standard pricing elements. The final proposal is submitted. Post award, the workers need to interact with additional systems, like the order entry system and the asset management system, in order to execute on the now-accepted proposal.

IT dimension: Project information (tied to the proposal planning and execution of each request) is typically stored in different systems as shown.

TelCo organization anticipated an ongoing evolution of the business process that the IT architecture was expected to support. Process tuning and change to existing processes after implementation had to be possible. The bids process receives its input from separate processes and must eventually be capable of providing output to other, installation-focused processes.

Traceability between BioS dimensions: The key challenges underlying the scenario above are next analyzed. The Balance Scorecard (Kaplan 1992) helps identify the *cause and effect* relationships that affect business performance. The traceability chain to be managed can be summarized as: *IT enabled engineering workflow processes, features, and costs* ⇨ *decrease service response time* ⇨ *increase operational efficiencies* ⇨ *improved customer satisfaction* ⇨ *increased average revenue per employee and faster order-to-cash cycle.*

Figure 7 shows how the business performance is related to IT features and uses specific traceability to build a business case for a BPM architecture. The leftmost column reflects these BioS goal attributes of interest. The table also goes further in the next two columns and correlates the business dimension to the operational

Figure 7. Traceable Performance Monitoring

Business and Strategy Performance Goals	⇐ Related Operational Interaction goals	⇐ Benefits of IT enabled BPM
Improve customer satisfaction (Qualitative)	Reduce time-to-bid (By 40%) Successful on-site tests, on-time (To 90%) Customer self-care and Role-based access to all project information (Qualitative)	Reduce queue time through better routing to available knowledge resources - just-in-time resource assignment Re-use of knowledge to reduce span time Collaboration (routing, handoffs and tracking) with the customer on Requests (Orders) and on site-specific project tasks during installation Web access enabling customers and workers distributed globally Alerts monitoring by account team. Single point of access from the web - as the process progresses, project information is in CRM, document systems as well as (legacy) order entry systems need to be integrated – demand based delivery of information
Accelerate order-to-cash process (Up 40%)	Projects should not lose money on proposals (95%) More effective tracking of project for timely billing 100% on time	Improved pricing through collaboration with internal and external providers Process triggers each invoice on completion of activity
Increase average revenue per user (Up 20%)	Putting out more winning proposals in less time (70% hit) Reduce time to deploy new services (By 20%)	Reduce queue time while improving collaboration with all internal and external providers and account team On-line guidance
Increase operational efficiencies and capacity	Increase throughput From 200 on-going responses to 300 in 60 days Reduce re-work and eliminate inefficiencies due to poor information Reported quality incidents down (By 20%) HIPAA and other compliance audit (100%) Re-use of time-variant information FTE 100	Process context pulls the information delivered to worker Single point of access Decision capture and re-use Ability to insert sub-processes onto meet the needs to the request

and BPM benefits to resource effectiveness in completing Interactions. By empowering each worker with the ability to institute lean practices[xx] as identified in the rightmost column, the immediate impact of BPM is on operational performance with net impact on the business goals. This traceability is articulated in the table below. This will be used later for a more direct analysis of the benefits of the BPM architecture.

The rightmost column provides a business reason to proceed with a lean approach that reduced wasted time and resources. We next introduce related background in technologies and standards that the EA organization must look into.

BACKGROUND AND BEST PRACTICES

Business Process Management (BPM) technology: Workflow technology treats the business process or just 'process' as a collection of tasks that have to be completed. Each task can have attachments or 'locators' used by the workflow engine to obtain and deliver information from the underlying applications to the resource. This uses other middleware technologies. When a task is completed, the next electronic task is delivered to the user/Agent/resource queue. Thus, much like the material movement systems, the workflow engine delivers information on demand to the user. Specifically, 'information access services' can allow programmatic access to browse, get, and update objects from an application or 'post a request' for the application. (For related experience refer to Ramanathan 1996, Ramanathan 1999, Ray 2006)

The enaction and completion of a task can be by a human Agent interacting with the task or by automated Agents that provide Role services. Resources can include internal workers, suppliers, customers, and automated Agents (applications managing machines, schedules, and so on). The resources can be further grouped into management hierarchies or into Roles that they can play and the task can be dynamically customized to present information views based on the Role. A resource can execute tasks anywhere in the world.

BPM business rules guide users using task routing features[h] thus coordinating multiple Agent resources involved in an end-to-end process. Tasks also assist in invoking the underlying Agent services – for example running applications, accessing data, and handling exceptions - based on the process state. Sub-processes can be dynamically invoked. The BPM engine *enacts* the underlying process model and synchronizes the behavior of Agents. Thus the potential here is a direct cause and effect between the process model improvement and the business performance improvement. We next provide an overview of BPM as it relates to automating the ACE Interactions.

Conceptual-to-Logical Mapping: One of the major benefits of workflow technology is that we can model the flow of work within an organization at a conceptual level. The underlying engine interprets the model and executes the underlying application component services. Thus mapping the conceptual layer to the logical layer. This is illustrated by the RED Interaction 'pattern' workflow in Figure 8.

The function provided by such processes can vary widely. Examples at the micro-level include the control of the services of a complex application. Here the process flow is used to orchestrate the execution of fine-grained services that implement a user-facing high-level service (using for example BPEL[i]). Another example is the support of the business or operations. As this macro level each process task is completed by human services as well as application services. Also note the completion of a task causes the transition of an underlying business object (e.g. an order) from one

Figure 8. Use of work flow and standards to manage complex systems conceptually

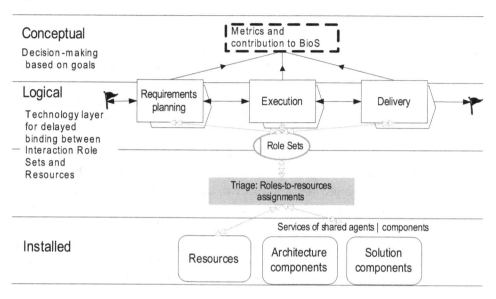

state to the next. In both these examples, the workflow acts fundamentally to provide the context for the use of a collection of services provided by the Role set.

In general, there are many different types of processes that all aim to reduce the complexity of interacting with complex systems by matching different socio-technical needs. For example at one end of the spectrum we have micro-level processes reflecting the state of a data object or work instructions that apply to a physical or electronic object. More macro-level processes include coordination processes that sequence tasks within teams, primary customer facing and secondary internal providing services, inter-departmental processes reflecting the end-to-end services needed by the customer, and supply-chain processes. (For discussions on different types of workflows see Jorgensen 2001, Holowczak 2003, Ramanathan 1996, Ramanathan & Beswick 2000, Ramanathan & Ramnath 2004, Seth 1997, Sriram 2002, Wil van der 2004, and Zhang 2006)

Challenges with Interaction type workflows: In the macro examples, the workflow engines act as the 'controller'. As such, the rules associated with the workflow become exceedingly complex as the rules end up setting up parameters to invoke other components in the Role sets, diagnosing the results of underlying services, triaging the next assignments, and so on. More generally, as the use of BPM technology evolves to meet socio-technical patterns, we note that the proper application of the technology to achieve maintainability, adaptability and so on also gets exceedingly complex.

One approach to reducing the complexity is to localize and hide the complexity as Agents that service Roles. Each Agent has its own internal processes for using resources and delivering on requests for multiple Interactions and OLs.

There is also a need to provide context information for the Agents. This is achieved by the 'Interaction' workflow illustrated in Figure 5. This type of Agent orchestration can be implemented using standards (like BPEL). Thus at the macro level, the BPM primarily implements Interactions between Agents, rather than implementing the details that can be addressed by Agents. In other words, workflow can orchestrate Interactions to provide the context for the use of autonomous Agents and to act as a conceptual performance monitoring engine as we discuss next.

Interactions between Autonomous Agents: An Agent assigned to participate in an Interaction is provided the needs through the request. This context is communicated in the form of directives to the Agents during triage. The rules result in the queuing of requests assigned to an identified Agent(s). As illustrated in the figure, each Interaction explicitly abstracts out the desired performance SL and uses the Role set and assigned Agents with their respective OLs to achieve that performance. It acts to meet RED performance goals (along with other Agents in the Roles set) and effects changes through the deliverables. The result of the Agents' actions is a change in its environment as illustrated in Figure 9.

The underlying principle in the Roles of the Interaction workflow and the Agent is the separation of concerns as in the architectural pattern - Model-View-Controller. 'Here to reduce the complexity of applications, it is useful to separate data (model) and user interface (view) concerns, so that changes to the user interface will not affect data handling, and that the data can be reorganized without changing the user interface. The model-view-controller solves this problem by decoupling data access and business logic from data presentation and user Interaction, by introducing an intermediate component: the controller (Gamma et al.).' In a similar way the Interaction structure acts as a controller leading to an explicit decoupling of Agents and their internal logic that provide different data access from the process, presentation, Role and security services.

Interaction metrics are gathered by the workflow engine rules. The rules can also advance and monitor the milestones, guide the assignment of available Agents to Roles, provide early alerts if the span time of R, E, or D is too long, monitor things like the cash-to-cash cycle from the start of E to the close of D, monitor unsuccessful bids that don't progress beyond R, keep a history of content used in highly successful bids, record defects and so on. Thus by abstracting Interactions from other detailed models, performance monitoring can be at a conceptual Interaction level. Finally, the dynamic Interaction structure unifies planning, guidance,

Figure 9. Relationship between the Interactions and use of Agent Services.

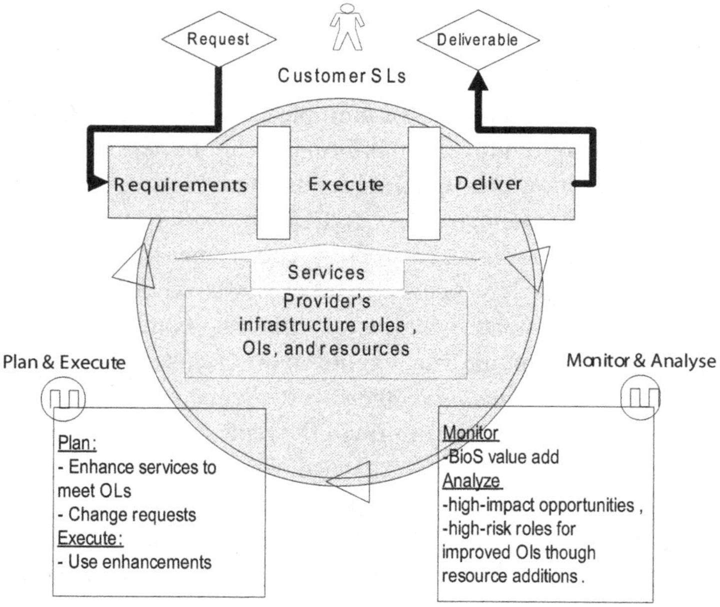

execution, and monitoring by providing the performance context for both initiating individual Agent execution and monitoring of the results. (See Kephart 2003, Kephart 2005).

EKI: The request is also the 'sensor', the deliverable is also the 'effector'. Intuitively we can mine Requests for information and sense the needs of the environment. We can also effect changes in the environment through the deliverable. Further as process-based decisions are made, this time-variant information can be captured as history. Each worker/resource applies transformations to incoming objects and makes decisions that create outputs. For example, an order, design, work instructions, quality documents, corrective actions, and the numerous physical components are related and further attributes like which resource worked on this, why, what were the key decisions and so on must be recorded for downstream tasks. That is, the outputs of the processes are traceable to the original information objects and the tasks record the history of the transformations. This time-variant process audit can be used to better guide workers. It can also be used for compliance. It can thus be seen that the dynamic BPM layer can provide valuable knowledge for the evolution of practice within an organization. A starting point is provided in Puustjarvi 2006.

Business infrastructure and security: As the process engine interprets the process model, it queues process tasks for assigned Roles and resources. Once a task is queued for execution, only the authorized resource can access the task. Access rights are determined by looking up the 'directory services'. As an example, consider the current situation where each enterprise application provides user and password administration services. When BPM spans systems and organizations, not only does the user end up having to log into multiple application systems, but also needs to log into the networks. A single sign-on with knowledge of Roles and authorizations becomes critical. Often organizations go to a system of record (such as the human resource management system) to populate the directory services for sign on.

On demand and Lean BPM: Each task with its Role set (e.g. engineer, order entry system, design tool) can be thought of as a *work center*. It is the electronic analogy of the physical work center but with certain advantages. An electronic work center can be accessed from anywhere and sent anywhere. The work center itself can be dynamically routed (re-assigned to) an in-house resource, an offshore resource, or even be sent to field Agents with mobile devices or directly to a piece of equipment. Note that the tasks and underlying rules 'pull' objects from the enterprise applications to where they are needed in the process. Thus, as tasks are completed they cause the request-driven flow of information to where and when needed.

Two points can now be made about lean task execution 1) the electronic objects are obtained from the company's information sources and queued for the resources and 2) the resources work on each task as required for the customer request. The task becomes the process context in which requisite information must be delivered to complete that transformation. The process context pulls the information that must be delivered to the resources so that appropriate decisions can be derived from the information and recorded. This derived information then becomes the input required for the next process context(s) so that worker can benefit from the most recent time-variant information. The electronic process-driven information flow thus directly contributes to the value add of the physical transformation tasks and thus the process.

Note that while the information is pulled on demand, the process itself is not Lean. For it to be on demand, the process should only execute those tasks that are needed for the particular Request. That is the process itself should be *discovered* based on the needs of the non-routine request. That is static process flows do not support Lean.

Workflow Challenges: However, the process rules associated with workflow tasks are difficult to implement. For example, to be useful, a considerable amount of knowledge is often associated with each task. Assignment rules must help select the most effective and available resources at a given point. Time variant information must be managed for subsequent transformations by other workers and is published for future tasks. The result of completing each task must be posted and accumulated to get a consolidated business view across all workflow instances. Finally, as Agents/systems get more service-oriented and the processes get more

Figure 10. Different types of associations between Process, Data and Resources

Socio-technical aspect of Interaction pattern	Technology example(s)	Interaction scope	Customization and costs
1. Asynchronous point-to-point	Email, access to web-sites	Entire organization	Email clients, servers. Low customization, off-the-shelf
2. Asynchronous, broadcast	Point-to-point exchange of data with clean-up and consistency as in data warehousing (using middleware and messaging technologies)	Entire organization	High customization of underlying Agent services, data translations
3. Asynchronous, publish and subscribe	Sites for sharing data and documents	Team	Email clients, servers. Low customization, off-the-shelf
4. Synchronous, ad-hoc, interactive	Collaborative tools such as net meeting, access to data	Entire organization	Desktop tools and servers Low customization, off-the-shelf
5. Synchronous, static process, data use, application use, resource use, interactive	Process for service delivery and monitoring, typical enterprise system (access to single system as in above figure)	Process Agents	Client-server (two-tier architecture); sometimes client/middleware/server (three-tier), enterprise integration framework typically requiring customization of underlying services
6. Synchronous, static process, data use, application use, resource use, interactive, underlying ontology for sharing	End-to-end routine service delivery and monitoring, across multiple enterprise systems and organizations (BPM in above figure)	Many processes and Agents	Any client/ standard middleware/ any server (using Web-services, n-tier and loosely coupled architecture), BPM framework, High customization of underlying Agent services
7. Combination Ad-hoc/ Synchronous, non-routine virtual process, delayed binding of data use, resource use, and sub-process use	End-to-end non-routine service delivery and monitoring (discovered BPM)	Many processes and Agents	Clients and Web-services, loosely coupled architecture High customization of underlying Agent services, binding at runtime
8. Asynchronous Interactions between Agents for non-routine events - delayed binding of process, data use, resource use	End-to-end non-routine service delivery and monitoring using Sharepoint™, Teamspace™ with event monitoring	Many processes and Agents, delayed binding of processes and resources. Multiple devices and Agents coordinating.	High, customization of underlying Agent services

dynamic, a variety of security issues also arise. Based on the Roles - customer, provider and other stakeholders – each user has different visibility into the system. Other 'business rule services' must provide the goals to be achieved by the tasks and aggregate the simultaneous value-add to BioS dimensions.

Collaboration tools: While BPM can be viewed as a tool that sequences (synchronizes) tasks performed by different Roles, at the other end of the spectrum we have tools that are asynchronous. Email, conferencing tools, project sites and web 2.0 are examples that have also dramatically improved task-related communications. And, these technologies are also easier to deploy because little customization is needed. Collaboration tools and approaches are also important for product design. These types of environments have been explored at length by (Sriram 2002).

To better understand when the expenses for BPM are justified based on value to the business, we next look at some of the socio-technical aspects of these technologies and the related trade-offs.

Socio-Technical Aspects and Trade-offs: A variety of different socio-technical collaboration patterns have been identified over the last decade. Workflow characterizations as 'ad-hoc' and 'production' processes have existed for a while, providing initial insight into work patterns(Puustjarvi 2006). Meanwhile, within systems engineering a distinction has typically been made between job instructions within a work center and the process representations depicting the flow between work centers. By understanding such distinctions and socio–technical patterns, we can better match the needed technology, customization, and costs.

The table highlights different patterns and related costs. As the table indicates the customization and costs of deployment increase dramatically as we progress down the table (and towards point 'c' in Figure 5).

Standards: For complex architecture to be adaptable we must ensure that the conceptual, logical, and installed architecture layers and Interactions can all evolve at different times and independently. That each component can evolve independently of the others and having minimum of impact on the others[j]. Further within the installed architecture, the layers illustrated in the interoperability stack (Figure 11) must also all be implemented correctly. The greatest challenges remain at the top of this stack where the meanings of the business objects being communicated are critical. The lower layers are easier to implement as they focus on the syntax of the messages and not on how the message is interpreted. In other words, XML[k] for example, appears in almost every layer in this stack since different standards groups have adopted XML.

XML is a markup language that can be used to tag collections of data with labels. As part of a standardization activity, communities can agree on the names for these labels. This helps interoperability. However, the major interoperability problem remains since different Agents have different understandings of the mean-

Figure 11. Interoperability stack and some standards

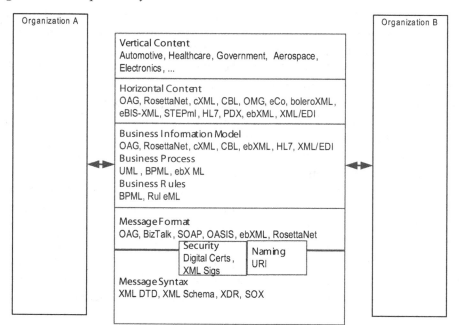

ing of these names. XML standardizes syntax but it does not capture or standardize semantics. The meaning of the data has to be understood in the same manner by both organizations. For example, during mergers and acquisitions, problems arise when moving data from one system or organization to another. Consequently, the process of achieving interoperability remains a highly manual process, with computers executing only the most basic steps in this process. An example of work in such semantics is by the OASIS 2008. Using business process web services to orchestrate services is being addressed by BPEL4WS (Gordijn 2006, Norton & Pedrinaaci 2006, Zhile 2006). Dealing with this type of limitation of computers is also the focus of projects at the National Institute of Standards and technology[1]: the Automated Methods for Integrating Systems (AMIS) project, the B2B (Business-to-business).

Initiatives: In addition to interoperability between systems and organizations, many initiatives are involved in aligning BioS vertically. From a service lifecycle and stakeholder perspective many standards and initiatives make it easier to integrate organizations with better information flow. Figure 12 provides a sampling of some of the applicable methods organizing the vertical content identified in the figure above.

Figure 12. Some of the standards and initiatives that apply within an organization

Dimension	Examples/types	Applicable Standards bodies and other Initiatives[m]
Strategy	External compliance and regulatory requirements	SOX, HIPA, ANSI HSSP Homeland Security Standards Panel, Safety, Environmental Standards Compliance, ...
Business	Accounting and audit practices	International Accounting Standards Board (IASB) and Information Systems Audit and Control Association (ISACA) are examples. In particular Control Objectives for Information and related Technology (COBIT) is a set of best practices (framework) for information technology (IT) management created by the Information Systems Audit and Control Association (ISACA). ANSI-X9F Data and Financial Information Security, ...
Operations (Business Process Management)	Business processes, Manufacturing processes, Chemical processes, IT intensive business processes, Service processes.	Lean[n], Resilience, Total Quality, Six Sigma, and SCOR[o].... The components of the BPM technology are defined in a standardized manner by organizations such as the Workflow Management Coalition[p], OMG[q],...
Infrastructure: Enterprise applications and interoperability	Customer and order management Product data and configuration management Resourcee panning and supply chain management Project management Enterprise document management	ISO 10303 (ISO, 1994), a set of standards for the exchange of product model data. ASC X12 (also known as ANSI ASC X12) is the U.S. national standards body for the development and maintenance of Electronic Data Interchange (EDI) standards. The Federal Enterprise Architecture (FEA) is an initiative of the US Office of Management and Budget that aims to comply with the Clinger-Cohen Act and provide a common methodology for information technology (IT) acquisition in the United States federal government. TOGAF - The ANSI/IEEE Standard 1471-2000 specification of architecture (of software-intensive systems) may be stated as: "the fundamental organization of a system, embodied in its components, their relationships to each other and the environment, and the principles governing its design and evolution."
Infrastrucutre: Individual productivity tools	Desktop tools, analysis, design tools	De facto standards such as MicroSoft Office.
Infrastructure – middleware, workflow, Web Services, enterprise application integration and exchange standards	CMS – content management systems Enterprise Frameworks (e.g. SAP's NetWeaver), Data base management (IBM, Oracle), Enterprise service bus (brokers like MQ Serices, TiBCO, BEA Systems), EDW (Informatica, Oracle, DB2)	OMG - Object Management Group. OASIS- Organization for the Advancement of Structured Information Systems Consortium. W3C - World Wide Web. WS*[r] ISO/IEC 9126-1[s] The fundamental objective of this standard is to address some of the well known human biases that can adversely effect the delivery and perception of a software development project. These biases include changing priorities after the start of a project or not having any clear definitions of "success".

continued on the following page

Figure 12. (continued)

Infrastructure – IT management and monitoring	Configuration Management Data Base Capacity Management	ITIL version 3 - A configuration management database (CMDB) is a repository of information related to all the components of an information system. Although repositories similar to CMDBs have been used by IT departments for many years, the term CMDB stems from ITIL. In the ITIL context, a CMDB represents the authorized configuration of the significant components of the IT environment. A CMDB helps an organization understand the relationships between these components and track their configuration. (wikipedia). Computer Measurement Group (CMG), is a worldwide non-profit organization of data processing professionals whose work involves measuring and managing the performance of computing systems. In this context, *performance* is understood to mean the *response time* of software applications of interest, and the overall *capacity* (or *throughput*) characteristics of the system, or of some part of the system.
Infrastructure development	Application development Security implementation	IEEE Software Engineering Body of Knowledge (SWEBOK). IEEE 1600.1 Standard Upper Ontology (SUO) Working Group. IEEE P1700 Information Assurance Standard. Information System Security Assurance Architecture. IETF-SEC Security Area (IP Security Protocol, S/MIME, PKI Using X.509). INCITS CS1.1 Role-Based Access Control (RBAC). INCITS TC V2 Information Technology Access Interfaces.

TelCo Business Case

Return on Investment: Continuing with the pilot project challenges at the TelCo, we note that rows 1-6 of the Figure 10 do not match the socio-technical needs of the organization. With so much of discovered processing during engineering services and so many Roles involved in generating time-variant information, there was a need for visibility to manage customer expectations. This required the workflow-driven process technology layer. Thus this enterprise integration project falls to the lower end of the table requiring customization of four or five systems from the perspective of multiple organizations.

Cost factors: The Figure 13 illustrates the ACE structure with the primary Interactions for Design as well as the associated Role sets. In addition, as with any typical enterprise integration project, the needed project resources consisted of about five business process analysts representing their organizations, five IT Roles with skills ranging from project management, software engineering, data base management, middleware and systems, five operational Roles from the departments, application use experts, etc. In addition the typical time scale for such an integration project becomes twelve to twenty four months. The typical software costs (workflow server and user licenses) plus the service costs are incurred at the outset of the pilot phase. The service costs include creating application services to update information in applications. Let us estimate this to be a half a million dollars. In addition, when

Figure 13. Interactions and Shared Agents in the TelCo Infrastructure

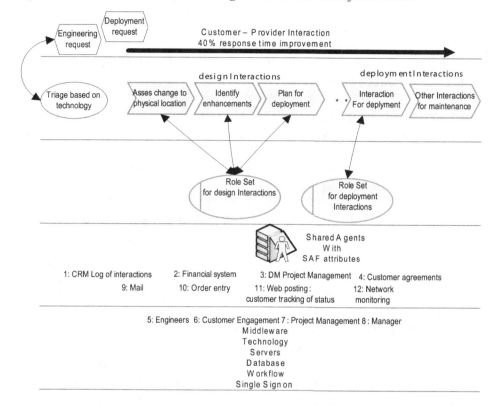

production users come on-line, costs are also incurred due to loss of worker productivity (typical reasons are data migration and initialization costs). Finally, the system must be in production for a period of time to begin a contribution to worker productivity, operational value, customer value and business value.

All this is challenging and cause for concern for many reasons. Firstly, for small numbers of users, it is difficult to show a business return. For a larger numbers of users, it is more straightforward to show a return for both the business and the vendors involved. In general an integration project aimed at about ten or twenty engineering users often *fails to show a return*; whereas a project with a couple of hundred users or more shows a better return.

Typically, most engineering business units that deal with *non-routine* services do not have large numbers of users that all require the identical process integration solution. Hence, the poor effectiveness of integration projects and high cost of ownership (i.e. though the life-cycle of the software) make it harder to realize benefits in exactly those non-routine service Roles that need to be enabled as a high priority.

This type of situation leads to important questions often faced by the EA group:

*   How can we meet the workflow requirements of smaller groups of users and show an overall benefit to the business?
*   How do you justify the investment in architectural products, like workflow, that are not directly seen by the business users?

We next present a method to quantify and improve this type of decision-making by understanding and analyzing the related costs and value to the stakeholders. The concepts of IT-enabled adaptation build on earlier work in Ramanathan & Ramnath 2006 and George 2002. Other approaches to related decision making are introduced in Walter & Sharon 1986, Fisher et al 2005).

Framework for Investment and Exercise of Architecture Options

By anticipating the service progression in Figure 6, a company can better justify architectural investments early on and more easily recover the investment over several enterprise integration projects. To see this we next present an analytic method to justify a suitably diverse portfolio of IT projects for services and applications to support critical business Interactions.

Defining Architecture Options: The value of a system and its Agents depends on how well it satisfies the stakeholders' expectations. However, as time progresses, the value desired by the stakeholders also often increases as their expectations increase. If each Agent as well as the entire system is static, it will not be able to cater to the increase in the desired value by the stakeholders. As a result, the value of the overall system will diminishes over time. The system may need to be replaced or changed to provide the added value which involves considerable effort and cost.

On the other hand, if the system and its Agents were designed to be changeable and adaptable in the first place, the value-add could have been provided by incremental modifications or upgrades to the system. This has motivated the design of systems to be more robust and adaptable by using the idea of architecture options.

An *architecture option* is a quantitative means of implementing optimal degree of design flexibility in a system to maximize its lifetime value to its stakeholders. It is similar to the notion of a stock option. It justifies the early architectural investments of a company which can lead to greater benefits and cost recovery over a period of time (Engel & Tyson 2006).

For example, when is workflow technology investment a good architecture option? Inserting a workflow component as a conceptual management layer into the system often involves considerable costs and effort. However, insertion of workflows can also be viewed as an architecture option which provides the stakeholder with long-term advantages of greater productivity and performance traceability. The later is a side benefit that might provide additional BioS value to justify costs.

Option Value (OV): The option value of an Agent is defined as *the relative ability of that Agent to provide value to one or more Interactions*. This can be measured in terms of an increase in throughput contribution and *consequent increment in business value*. To understand this let us consider two Agents - a design tool and a CRM - and the Interactions for Design and Deployment as in Figure 13 .

The CRM order management is not critical in the Role set to improve the throughput of the 'design Interactions' of Figure 13. However, it is more critical during 'deployment Interactions' in terms of increasing the throughput. This is because CRM is more significant in enabling deployment Interactions and managing related time-variant information thus improving the productivity of a larger Role set (i.e. with more assigned resources) resulting in a greater overall throughput gain and resulting value increase to business. Thus CRM in this way of looking at things has a larger option value than a design tool.

Let us now consider a design tool that is more critical to 'design Interactions' with a smaller Role set. When viewed in throughput terms of the 'design Interaction' alone, the design tool has a smaller overall value contribution. However increasing 'design Interactions' also means an increase in 'deployment Interactions'. The latter would not be possible without an increase in 'design Interactions'. The 'deployment Interactions' cannot be increased without the 'design Interactions'. Thus when viewed in terms of the workflow needed to increase the value of the 'deployment Interactions', a design tool has more value. Recall this was also illustrated in the supplier example of Chapter 2.4.

Thus, from a service portfolio perspective, different Agents – design tool, CRM - have different *relative option values* based on the Interactions that they contribute to both near term and long term. The sum of the relative option values of each of the Agents is set out of 100.

System Adaptability Factor (SAF): In order to address the issue of designing an adaptable system of Agents, a metric called System Adaptability Factor (SAF) is first defined. This composite metric quantifies the inherent flexibility of an Agent to contribute to different Role sets by relating it to the non-functional factors and metrics. The diagram in Figure 14 lists the factors and metrics (and sub metrics) based on the ISO/IEC 9126-1 standard. Each metric factor is measured on a [0,1] percent scale. The SAF is defined as the weighted average over all the adaptability metrics:

$$SAF = w_F F + w_R R + w_U U + w_E E + w_M M + w_P P + w_{Av} Av + w_{As} As + w_{Ad} Ad$$

where w_F, w_R, w_U, w_E, w_M, w_P, w_{Av}, w_{As} and w_{Ad} are the weights of each of the system adaptability metrics also illustrated in Figure 14.

Calculating SAF of Architecture: Consider a system with multiple Agents. The expected economic value contributed by each Agent is distributed and related positively to the function of option value OV_n multiplied by its corresponding SAF_n adaptability factors and negatively to the expected costs associated with implementing the interfaces between the Agents and between the Agents and the Interaction. Thus, the value of Agent X_j is given by:

$$X_j = \sqrt{\sum (OV_n * SAF_n)^2} - \sum (\text{Interaction interfacing costs})$$

The economic option value is thus adjusted by the cost of interfacing to the Interactions that the Agent participates in. The value of the entire system is the sum of the values of each of the Agents.

We will now use this framework to illustrate how we can arrive at a value of an architecture:

- The interfacing cost between any two Agents is '1' for implementation, plus an additional '1' for any license cost incurred.
- The Role set is defined to be the composition of individual Agent services. These composition costs are '1' if the Agent(s) is used within an implemented interface.

Figure 14. System Adaptability Factors of each Agent based on ISO/IEC 9126-1 standard components

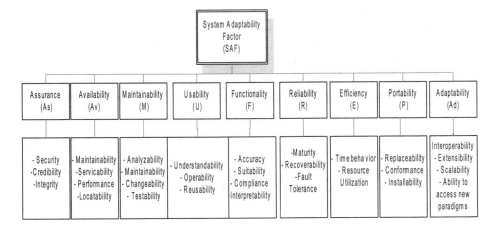

- Workflow implements multiple Roles Sets (i.e. composes the same Agent services in different ways) and reduces the cost of composition and integration. Thus, the cost of the first Role set using workflow is '1' for integration with each Agent and '1' for the license. From that point out, integration cost is '½' for *each* new Role set that this Agent participates in and the license cost is '1' for each new Agent.

For our example, consider the Agents CRM, DM, Mail (or M), and Engineer (or E). The architecture options approach allows us to compare the value of the system before and after the addition of workflow component as an architecture option. By considering the architecture with and without workflow we can show the case with workflow has higher option value.

System Adaptability Factor for TelCo: Let CRM, DM, M, and E be the Agents. The following table has initial OV and SAF values for the Agents along the diagonal. It uses an Interaction-*based* value assignment for the OV each Agent as indicated. That is, the OV of an Agent is determined by the total contribution it is estimated to make to the improved throughput due to all the Role sets of all the Interactions it participates in. On the other hand, the SAF is determined by the actual inherent factors of the Agent. For example the Agent might not be 'reliable'. Hence the value for this factor will be low. For example if 'E' has created many defects, 'E' has a lower 'reliability' factor.

Agent	CRM	DM	M	E	Role sets for design
CRM	OV : 20 SAF: 0.3	2	0		1
DM		OV: 30 SAF: 0.2	1		1
M	2		OV: 30 SAF : 0.4		1
E	2	2	2	OV : 30 SAF : 0.3	1

Both the 'Role sets' column and the intersection of 'Agents' also indicates the integration costs between the pair of Agents – from a service provider Agent to the service customer Agent - as they participate in a Role set. For example, this could be due to the need to keep data consistent or maintaining an association. In the TelCo case of email, there were implementation costs due to the fact that customer requests came in through emails and these had to be maintained in the CRM Agent through a service. For simplicity we assign a cost of '1' for an implementation resource and a cost of '1' for a new license. These assignments are for a standard time period. The last column indicates the integration costs within the Role set and the workflow execution environment.

Thus the value of each Agent within the overall system is given as:

$$X_{CRM} = \sqrt{\sum} (20 * 0.3)^2 - \sum (2+1) = 3$$
$$X_{DM} = \sqrt{\sum} (30 * 0.2)^2 - \sum (1+1) = 4$$
$$X_{M} = \sqrt{\sum} (30 * 0.4)^2 - \sum (2+1) = 9$$
$$X_{E} = \sqrt{\sum} (30 * 0.3)^2 - \sum (2+2+2+1) = 2$$

and, the Adaptability Value of the System Architecture is given by:

$$V_1 = X_{CRM} + X_{DM} + X_{M} + X_{E} = 3+ 4+ 9+ 2 = 18$$

In general, once the Agents support each other and the Role sets for the initial Interactions, the value of the system diminishes over a period of time since the stakeholder expectations increase. In this case the Agents needed to provide *additional* value through Role sets that support *additional* 'maintenance Interactions'. For example, once the initial *design Interactions* are supported within the current deployment, the value of the system actually depreciates after a while because now the stakeholders want the additional *deployment and maintenance Interactions* supported.

More generally, this means that if you have Agents and granular Roles grouped into more Role sets, it is better than Agents grouped into one or two Role sets. This backs intuition that with fine grain Agent Roles we are building more modularity in the system. And, since modularity itself can be thought of as an architecture option, it is evident that inserting the workflow architecture can raise the option value of the system. The underlying principle is actually based on the mathematical identity that 'the square root of sum of squares of numbers is less than the sum of square roots of the numbers'. However, there is one interesting aspect – the argument would be valid only on the assumption that the values of the interface between the components remains the same irrespective of whether they are grouped in one Role set or different Role sets; or, even if it varies, it still keeps the value in the second case greater than in the first.

Telco Pilot Project Staffing and Sizing

Defining Project Charter: Reverting to the case, the Telco pilot scope was to improve the design Interactions creating business value by submitting more winning proposals. To do this we begin with collecting Interaction information, filling in the RED Interaction template (Appendix 1). This knowledge acquisition process allows us to identify and bound all the primary Interactions and its sub-Interactions that have to be improved to achieve value to the organization. Based on this initial analysis the following decisions were arrived at:

- The scope of the pilot would be limited to the improvement of just two primary Interactions and the 'triaging' of incoming requests and the Role assignments for the primary 'design' Interaction'. Depending on the request classification, one or more of a variety of different primary design Interactions (e.g. new design, changing of installed routers, etc.) were involved. The time for this process itself was several days and thus its improvement would be useful.
- *Cost – benefit analysis:* For the identified Interactions, the contributions of any improvements to the BioS goals can be now defined.
- *Business goals:* The costs factors included license costs and Agent integration costs. The methodology in the previous section illustrates how to justify the technology costs base on architecture options to be exercised for additional interactions at a later time. The benefits included increased value to the business because of increased throughput in terms of # of bids during a time period.
- *Infrastructure use goals:* Approximately twenty five engineers improve their response time by half and this benefit would be demonstrated by the pilot.
- *Operational goals:* The time for triage can be significantly reduced. The Role sets even for this bounded project were diverse since there were different Requests types. No surprise here as this was the cause for the delayed times and therefore the cause of poor response times.
- *Strategy goals:* The value to improving these Interactions was that the customer would at least know the responsible engineer and assignment status.

CONCLUSION AND RESEARCH

Businesses that have "silo" applications and wait to think in architectural terms (till point c) have waited too long. Not only because of previously sunk costs, but also due to data duplication that negatively impacts worker productivity and dramatically increases the service cost of any future integration project. While the migration of existing applications to use new infrastructure services is always challenging, waiting makes these costs go even higher.

EA Decision-making: Investments in infrastructure and a more adaptive architecture are recovered across multiple applications of the technology. Investments for providing shared IT Infrastructure services should get ascribed to the business progression of the enterprise starting at point 'a', Figure 6. We suggest that the ACE conceptual structure provides a way to link architecture options to business value. Further research needs to be done in this area. For example, can we show that the architecture options increase not only due to reuse but also due to increased transparency and reduced risk.

In order for architectural components like workflow to offer adequate return on investment to business it must provide flexible yet auditable collaboration through an interface that mirrors the socio-technical requirements. For many potential areas of application, processes and models must be easily adaptable to handle an organization's non-routine Requests for many different Interactions. An Interaction based workflow engine with client side service integration is the first step towards these goals.

The ACE structure also provides an EA planning tool to help create the project charter, the plan and the scope. Specifically the typical units of improvement are an Interaction or a Role. The resulting value increase forms the portfolio with priorities and costs. When used in this manner for deploying changes to the logical and installed IT services, ACE encompasses operational execution needed for the management of the service life cycle. Its value is in ensuring that the decision-making is business goal driven. It is an example of a strategy-driven *SOA* approach that aligns conceptual architecture, logical architecture, and installed architecture details.

Project management: At a conceptual level, an ACE representation and its Interactions provide the high-level project plan needed for service delivery. It can thus be used for planning service projects in addition to providing a framework for Interaction monitoring that we discuss next.

Interaction monitoring and management by goals: The electronic representation of the ACE structure provides a structure for Interaction performance monitoring in real-time. It guides the instrumentation of resources and services within ACE itself. This facilitates management by goals since the achievement of defined BioS goals is now easily visible. This use of IT for ACE management not only supports a reflective practice within the organization, it also supports real-time monitoring and continuous improvement in accelerated timeframes.

There are distinct primary objectives for improvement – *effectiveness, resilience, and innovation.* Effectiveness is directly related to the Lean use of resources to improve margins, resilience is the concept applied to identifying and addressing business risks, and innovation is tied to new Interaction opportunities. Examples of using the EA work products for these applications are in subsequent chapters.

TASKS FOR DEVELOPING WORK PRODUCTS A-F

1. Refine the ACE structure. Identify the forces and develop the strategy for your selected project.
    o   Develop the Five Forces Model for that organization by doing research on the industry and provide supporting data. For example, who are potential competitors and dominant players?
    o   Develop the enterprise architecture Request Strategy work product and analysis of tradeoffs that serves as input to portfolio.
    o   Perform a technology survey and analysis as it relates to your project.
    o   Asses the readiness of the organization for a change. At this point, you may not know enough to propose changes but you should be able to identify potential barriers or opportunities for change within the organization. Your assessment should consider characteristics of the organization's structure as well as the scope of your project within the organization. Use the assessment to develop points of measurement, management, documentation, and training requirements that will facilitate an eventual change. (Appendix provides an assessment that determines an organization's readiness for service-orientation).
2. Present the results - charter, scope, and goals - to the sponsor and get authorization to proceed.
3. Create a detailed project plan. One of your initial tasks in the project plan should be to start assembling the ACE work products. It will take time to gather enough information and develop the understanding required to complete them so be sure to allow for multiple review sessions of the work products.
4. Using the Five Forces Model you have just developed, revisit the enterprise architecture model you have built and see if it lends any additional insight. Discuss your Five Forces Model with your sponsor and, if there are differences in opinion, try to find out why using supportive evidence where possible. It may help to get insight from more than one person. For example, if your sponsor is an operational manager see if you can have a discussion with his or her boss – if your sponsor is an executive see if you can have a discussion with someone involved in the day to day operations. Although Porter's Model is about strategy it's important to understand how that strategy is understood in all dimensions of the organization.

THINGS TO THINK ABOUT

1. How does the ACE structure relate to the EA template (see details in the Appendix)?

2. The EA template identifies all architecture documents that are eventually produced. Discuss how can we develop an *architecture life-cycle management environment* to increase 1) access to the right information throughout the service life-cycle with semantic querying technologies, 2) re-use, and 3) identify emergence of new service use patterns so that they can be fully leveraged.

3. Identify and contrast the Socio-technical Interaction patterns within an 'industrial' age and an 'information' age within the organization.

4. How does this impact the alignment between the conceptual architecture and the logical and physical layers? How does the ACE structure help? What are the advantages in terms of monitoring the ACE structure?

5. How can the EA template be applied to support semantic querying (reference Berners Lee et al 2001) and support an Enterprise Knowledge Infrastructure?

6. When implementing workflows with delayed binding between process, resource, and application, what are some of the challenges and the limitations in capturing metrics? What technologies are available to overcome these challenges? What are the organizational challenges in capturing the time each Agent is used in an Interaction?

7. Apply the architecture option methodology to more components and graph results. Comment on the trends. How can this methodology be developed further to monitor and better manage installed architectures?

8. In general, the ACE framework of RED Interactions helps the enterprise architecture life-cycle management by creating work products that represent the Business-IT system. Used in conjunction with TOGAF and ITIL it provides a prescriptive performance based framework for prioritization. TOGAF for example provides a complementary process for framework application called the Architecture Development Method. How does an ACE structure help the method? Finally, the monitoring of ACE is not unlike the use of the Configuration Management Data Base (i.e. CMDB as introduced in ISO 20000) to manage and monitor the installed IT infrastructure. Again how does the ACE model help? Comment, providing detailed examples.

9. Read Porter's Five Forces model and the Norton and Kaplan's Balanced Score Card and relate to Interaction analysis and traceability.

10. In your opinion, how does a service-oriented Interaction differ from an industrial-age Interaction? In what other ways is this distinction important? How can understanding this distinction help better with service management?

11. Discuss and critique the modeling notation for ACE by showing how traceability facilitates the implementation of any one of the following standards or initiatives - ISO, Six Sigma, Malcolm Baldridge, SOX, etc. Look up the websites for a description. Discuss why ISO standards etc. are agnostic to the 'how'. Give a for example.

12. What is the Role of workflow in ACE Co-engineering?

13. Refer to the Service Science 2006 and Service Orientation 2007 papers and suggest ACE research areas and practical applications?

14. How can data mining techniques apply to the Request, Interaction and Role instances?

15. In what way does workflow provide a technology for lean operations?

16. Describe at a high level vendor products and features in each of the following categories - workflow, collaboration products, frameworks for interoperability, data warehousing, and tools for enterprise modeling. discuss their roles and what is missing.

REFERENCES

Ambler, S., Nalbone, J., & Vizdos, M. (February 2005). *The Enterprise Unified Process: Extending the Rational Unified Process.* Publisher Pearson PTR.

Avner, E., & Browning, T. R. (2006). *Designing Systems for Adaptability by Means of Architecture Options.* INCOSE 16th Annual International Symposium Proceedings.

Bass, L., et.al. (2003). *Software architecture in practice.* Boston: Addison-Wesley.

Berners-Lee, T., Hendler, J., & Lassila, O. (May 2001). Scientific American: The Semantic Web.

Christensen, C., Anthony, S., & Roth, E. (2004). *Seeing What's Next: Using the Theories of Innovation to Predict Industry Change.* Boston: Harvard Business School Press.

Clements, K. K. (2002). *Evaluating Software Architectures.* SEI Series in Software Engineering. Addison Wesley.

Domges, R., & Pohl, K. (December 1998). Adapting Traceability to Project-SP. *Communications of the ACM, 41*(12).

Dumas, M., Reichert, M., & Shan, M-C. (Eds.) (September 2008). *Business Process Management. 6th International Conference, BPM 2008*, Milan, Italy, Book Series Lecture Notes in Computer Science Publisher Springer Berlin / Heidelberg Copyright 2008, ISBN 978-3-540-85757-0.

Erl, T. (2005). *Service-Oriented Architecture.* Upper Saddle River: Prentice Hall Professional Technical Reference.

Fisher, A., Fournier, F., Gilat, D., Rackham, G., Razinkov, N., & Wasserkrug, S. (2007). *Calculating the Business Importance of Entities in a Service-Oriented Enterprise.* IBM Research Laboratory in Haifa, Israel. IBM Global Services, NY, USA

Fowler, M. (2005). *Patterns in Enterprise Software.* http://www.martinfowler.com/articles/enterprisePatterns.html (accessed August 18, 2006).

Gamma, E., Helm, R., Johnson R., & Vlissides, J. (1995). *Design Patterns, Elements of Reuseable Object Oriented Software.* New York, NY: Addison Wesley.

Gordijn, J., Yu, E., & Van der Raadt, B. (June 2006). e-Service Design Using i* and e3value Modeling. *IEEE Software, 23*(3), 26-33.

Hofmann, H. F., & Franz, L. (August 2001). Requirements Engineering as a Success Factor in Software Projects. IEEE SOFTWARE.

Holowczak, R. D., Soon, A. C., Artigas, F., & Atlurit, V. (2003). Customized Geospatial Workflows for E-Government Services. *Proceedings of the IEEE/WIC International Conference on Web Intelligence, IEEE.*

Jorgensen, H. D. (2001). *Interaction as a framework for flexible workflow modeling Workflow Systems.* GROUP'01: International Conference on Supporting Group Work (pp. 32-41).

Kaplan, R. S., & Norton, D. P. (1992). *The Balanced Scorecard - Measures that Drive Performance.* January HBR.

Kephart, J. O. (2005). *Research Challenges of Autonomic computing.* IBM Research Report.

Kephart, J. O., & Chess, D. M. (2003). The Vision of Autonomic Computing. *IEEE Computer, 36(*1), 41-50.

Maximilien, E. M., & Singh, M. P. (2004). Toward Autonomic Web Services Trust and Selection, ICSOC'04, November 15–19, New York, New York, USA. Copyright 2004 ACM 1-58113-871-7/04/0011.

Nord, W. R., & Tucker, S. (October 1986). *Implementing Routine and Radical Innovations.* Publisher: Lexington Books ISBN-10: 0669095656.

Norton, B., & Pedrinaci, C. (2006). *3-Level Service Composition and Cashew: A Model for Orchestration and Choreography in Semantic Web Services.* Book Series Lecture Notes in Computer Science, Publisher Springer Berlin / Heidelberg ISSN 0302-9743 (Print) 1611-3349 (Online) Volume 4277.

OASIS. (2008). http://www.oasis-open.org/home/index.php

Puustjarvi, J. (July 2006). *Integrating Learning Objects to Business Processes Advanced Learning Technologies, Sixth International Conference, 5*(7), 618 - 622.

Ramanathan, J. (1996). Support for Workflow Process Collaboration. M. B. Waldron & K. J. Waldron (Eds.), *Mechanical Design: Theory and Methodology.* Berlin: Springer-Verlag.

Ramanathan, J. (1996, November). Workflow and Business Process Management in the Virtual Enterprise. *SME Autofact Proceedings.*

Ramanathan, J. (1999*). Enterprise Integration with NIIIP Protocols, SME, ASME Autofact Proceedings.*

Ramanathan, J., & Beswick, R. (2000). Imperative: Why Process-based Architecture is Essential for Successful Supply-Chain Participation. *EAI Journal.*

Ramanathan, J., & Ramnath, R. (2004). *IT Architecture and the Case for Lean eBusiness Process Management.* Knowledge Supply and Information Logistics in Enterprises and Networked Organizations. Fraunhofer-Institute for Software and Systems Engineering ISST.

Ramanathan, J., & Ramnath, R. (2006). Co-engineering Business, Information Use, and Operations Systems for IT-enabled Adaptation. *In Adaptive Technologies and Business Integration: Social, Managerial and Organizational Dimensions.* Hershey, PA: IGI Global.

Ray, S. R., & Jones A. T. (2006). Manufacturing interoperability. *J Intelligent Manufacturing 17*, 681–688, DOI 10.1007/s10845-006-0037-x.

Schwaber, K. (March 2004). *Agile Project Management with Scrum.* Publisher: Microsoft Press # ISBN-10: 073561993X. ISBN-13: 978-0735619937.

Service Orientation (2007 November). *IEEE Computer, 40*(11).

Services Science (2006 July). *Communications of the ACM, 49*(7).

Sheth, A. (1997). From contemporary workflow process automation to adaptive and dynamic work activity coordination and collaboration. *8th International Workshop on Database and Expert Systems Applications (DEXA '97).*

Sriram, R. D. (2002). Distributed & Integrated Collaborative Engineering Design. Sarven Publishers Glenwood MD 21738. isbn 0-99725064-0-3.

van der Aalst, W., & van Hee, K. (March 2004). *Workflow Management: Models, Methods, and Systems (Cooperative Information Systems),* Paperback: 384 pages, Publisher: The MIT Press ISBN-10: 0262720469, ISBN-13: 978-0262720465.

WFMC. (2008). http://www.wfmc.org/

Workflow Simulation for Operational Decision Support Using Design, Historic and State Information. Book Series *Lecture Notes in Computer Science*. Springer Berlin Heidelberg, ISSN 0302-9743 (Print) 1611-3349 (Online), Volume 5240.

Zachman J. A. (1987). A Framework for Information System Architecture. *IBM Systems Journal, 26*(3), 276-292.

Zhang, L. (Dec. 2006). *Research on Workflow Patterns based on Petri nets, Robotics, Automation and Mechatronics,* IEEE Conference on Publication Date: ISBN: 1-4244-0025-2. 2006-12-04.

Zou, Z., & Duan, Z. (2006). *Building Business Processes or Assembling Service Components: Reuse Services with BPEL4WS and SCA European Conference on Web Services (ECOWS'06)* (pp. 138-147).

ENDNOTES

[a] For a quick reference and introduction to some of these terms, use *Project Management Memory Jogger* (ISBN 1576810011).

[b] Wiki. Refer to ITIL v3 for further details.

[c] These are based on TOGAF.

[d] Solution Building Blocks (SBBs) relate to the Solutions Continuum (*The Solutions Continuum*), and may be either procured or developed. SBBs: Define what products and components will implement the functionality, Define the implementation, Fulfill business requirements, Are product or vendor-aware. Architecture Building Blocks (ABBs) relate to the Architecture Continuum

(*The Architecture Continuum*), and are defined or selected as a result of the application of the ADM. ABBs: Define what functionality will be implemented, Capture business and technical requirements, Are technology aware, Direct and guide the development of SBBs. More available on TOGAF 8.1.1 http://www.opengroup.org/architecture/togaf8-doc/arch/toc.html.

[e]   Define an autonomic component

[f]   "A key change to the latest ITIL version 3 has been a repositioning of the framework from the previous emphasis on process lifecycle and alignment of IT to "the business", to the management of the lifecycle of the services provided by IT, and the importance of creating business value rather than just the execution of processes."

[g]   Some examples of enterprise work products are in websites (*FEA, NIH amd MIT websites*).

[h]   A quick definition of tasks, processes etc…from wfmc. See WFMC for standard definitions.

[i]   WS-BPEL provides a language for the specification of Executable and Abstract business processes. http://en.wikipedia.org/wiki/Business_Process_Execution_Language.

[j]   Early efforts to architect more Open Systems resulted in CIMOSA [AMICE, 1993]. Later efforts focused on 'message' content standards. For example, ISO 10303 (ISO, 1994), which is a set of standards for the exchange of product model data. One of the more widely adopted component, ISO 10303–203 (ISO, 1994b), is estimated to be saving the transportation equipment-manufacturing community a significant amount in mitigation and avoidance costs.

[k]   XML: the eXtensible Markup Language (http://www. w3.org/XML/.

[l]   NIST – National Institute of Standards and Technologies. Enterprise Integration projects. http://www.nist.gov/.

[m]   http://en.wikipedia.org/wiki/Standards_organization#International_Standards_Organizations provides a good overview of global standards efforts.

[n]   http://en.wikipedia.org/wiki/INCOSE provides current research papers.

[o]   http://www.supply-chain.org/cs/root/home.

[p]   The Workflow Management Coalition (WfMC) is a standards body that caters to business process management (BPM) related standards and interoperability among compliant vendor solutions. Their latest handbook (2007 BPM & Workflow Handbook) details the current trends and case studies relating to BPM and more technical details are publicly available in their standards documents (available on-line at http://www.wfmc.org/standards/framework.htm)..

[q]   OMG: http://www.bpmn.org/ with a good summary in http://en.wikipedia.org/wiki/BPMN.

[r]   There is a large body of standards surrounding web services and interoperability collectively known as the WS-* standards. These standards span a wide variety of concerns from basic service discovery, definition, and orchestration languages to additional aspects such as policy enforcement and reliability guarantees. Most of the current standards are not under the control of a single standards body but organizations like WS-I (Web Services Interoperability) are working to define vendor neutral collections that can be used by any organization. For a thorough discussion of web services and their larger Role in technology enabled service oriented architectures see Erl's Service Oriented Architecture (SOA): Concepts, Technology, and Design (Erl 2005).

[s]   Lean Institute - http://en.wikipedia.org/wiki/ISO_9126.

Chapter IV
EA Knowledge for ACE Deployment

ABSTRACT

The knowledge infrastructure for enterprise architecture presented here has a taxonomy of useful patterns and pattern applications illustrated in Figure 1. The applications help deploy EKI and enable operations as illustrated herein.

What architecture patterns inform the EA team?

- What are the patterns for enabling Interaction goals with existing enterprise systems?
- What are the logical patterns enabling enterprise integration?
- How are underlying enterprise systems and tools enlisted within these patterns?

As emphasized previously, since the organization progresses towards more comprehensive or customer circumstance-based services, it becomes necessary to support many new types of Requests. From the business perspective, the underlying enterprise interoperability problem is typically stated as a requirement to produce an improved business result from services implemented in software tools. These include communication endpoints by which the systems can be considered to be components that will interact with each other and thereby form a new, integrated service capable of performing new functions. In turn, each system that contributes

Figure 1. Taxonomy of Enterprise Architecture Patterns

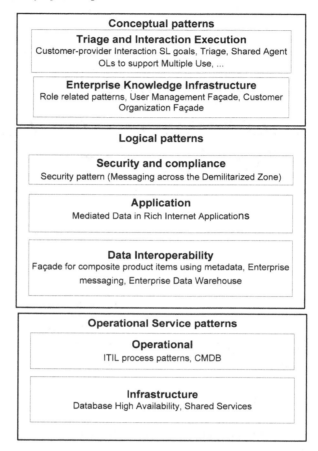

information or functionality is often required to expose new services. Thus, the trend is toward exposing more-and-more functionality from existing applications and using interoperability to *compose* these functions in different and new ways.

Related work in Software Product Line 2008 is relevant as the goal here is also to create a base of reusable knowledge. According to this Software Engineering Institute site:

A Software Product Line (SPL) is a set of software-intensive systems that share a common, managed set of features satisfying the specific needs of a particular market segment or mission and that are developed from a common set of core assets in a prescribed way. Product line adoption involves moving from some form of developing software-intensive systems with a single-system mentality to developing them as a software product line. A software product line is a set of software-intensive systems sharing a common, managed set of features that satisfy the specific needs of a particular market segment or mission and that are developed from a common set of core assets in a prescribed way. The adoption objective is to:

- *Have a core asset base, supportive processes, and organizational structures*
- *Develop products from that asset base in a way that achieves business goals*
- *Institute mechanisms to improve and extend the software product line adoption effort as long as it makes sense.*

Here we also show how pattern applications can contribute to the SPL methods by describing the software architecture in a standard way that highlights the:

- Business context
- Externally visible properties of components and how they contribute to the business context
- Software components and structural and dynamic relationships among them
- Role of integration and deployment methods

Knowledge EA Governance: To briefly review, an Enterprise Knowledge Infrastructure (EKI) is for improved service delivery and related information about the communities and stakeholders. Here we show how to use architecture patterns and pattern applications to form the knowledge base with which new service options can be implemented for increased enterprise systems and business adaptability (as discussed in the previous chapter). The EA team can use this EKI to increase its maturity and performance as follows:

- Identify the market drivers for new services and their impact to the functional and non-functional architecture attributes and their future *states*. For example, several services might require more flexible ways of managing customer communities as a way of delivering custom services and this identifies significant re-use potential.
- Maintain a catalog of pattern applications and reference implementations as practice knowledge. Identify common functional and non-functional requirements that in turn can be reused to develop new services more rapidly.
- Challenge the new requirements and underlying patterns with use cases and proof of concept projects that will make them viable for greater re-use. For example, several projects might be developing 'facades' and 'mediators' as a way to progress to architectures that provide services that are composable. Make these robust.

- Identify redundant investments and opportunities for reuse through architecture standardization across the corporation, based on frequency of occurrence.

Motivated by these goals, here we will cover the taxonomy of EA patterns and applications illustrated in Figure 1. These applications and the underlying patterns (Adams et al, Alexander 1979, Fowler 2003, Fowler 2005, Gartner 2005, Gamma et al 1995) illustrate how different organizations are modifying existing enterprise systems to deliver new services. The top-to-bottom summary is as follows:

- *Conceptual patterns:* These patterns provide ways to apply enterprise systems to enable new Interactions and performance. Examples include aligning Customer-Provider RED Interactions to SL goals, Triage or virtualization, Shared resource OLs to enable multi-use. In addition they collect time-variant information that can lead to monitoring and mining of organizational knowledge. Overall these patterns treat the underlying IT infrastructure from a user perspective and make it easier to deliver new services by addressing the users' interaction patterns and the domain details. Examples of underlying knowledge issues addressed include deployment of the Interaction ontology using related patterns and user perspectives.
- *Logical patterns:* The logical patterns identify the component services needed to implement security and compliance, use of application frameworks for display-rich and multi-tier applications, data warehousing and mediation.
- *Operational patterns:* The operational patterns are processes for installed architecture monitoring and improvement. Some of these are on ITIL and include management for reliability and high availability, and monitoring.

The EA template given in the previous Chapter 3 is used here for documentation but, in the interest of space, only the aspects that lead to useful illustrations are expanded.

CONCEPTUAL PATTERNS

Triage and Interaction Execution with Enterprise Systems

The *following three* related patterns allow us to *deploy* an ACE structure within enterprise systems to 1) improve Interaction performance based on traceability, 2) use a conceptual architecture to support virtualization and more effective management of resources, and 3) provide requirements for configuring enterprise system frameworks and development efforts. The relationship between the three patterns is in Figure 2.

Pattern: RED Interaction

Associates a customer service Request type with 1) provider Interaction(s) and identifies Requirements resourced by Operations and Agents, 2) Execution BioS value created for the Customer while Delivering Business value and providing Infrastructure feedback.

Conceptual

Strategy goals: Due to the variation in the custom and non-routine Requests, the related processing is highly variable causing the business to struggle with achieving

Figure 2. A view of the ACE structure with Interactions illustrating Triage, RED Milestones, Role sets, and Shared Agents

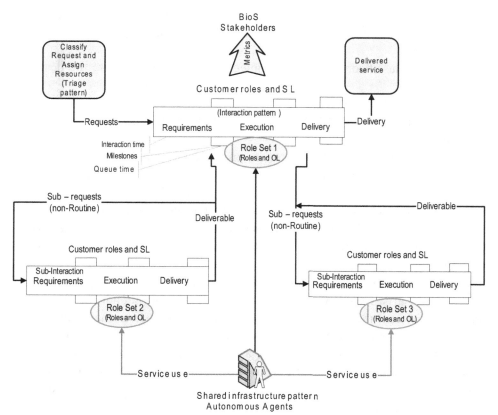

customer goals in a predictable way. Delivery involves unavoidable requirements discovery and knowledge that makes static processes obsolete during execution. Thus process and resource usage varies widely making management difficult. The organization would like to provide non-routine services more effectively through efficient and effective use of resources. The business would like to retain flexibility to take on new service opportunities while at the same time achieving performance critical to all BioS goals. Organization would also like to identify new service opportunities. Any solution would require working with enterprise systems that manage request information.

Example: Within the hospital emergency room, patients are questioned to identify the initial Request and assign the first Interaction or type of tests and medical service to be completed. During the Interaction, additional Requests might get defined. Typical visits to the emergency room require considerable waiting.

Problem: The organization must move from static processes to dynamically discovered processes to accommodate variation. How can we represent and enable Request variation, process variation, and variation in the use of shared resources? At the same time, despite the dynamic environment, how can we successfully apply principles, tools and methods for performance improvement?

Operational goals and analysis: The ACE structure is used configure enterprise system behavior with the following execution characteristics:

- Requests classified, triaged and routed to Agents that execute the desired REDs.
- Each RED uses underlying Role set services.
- Customer–Provider 'RED' Interactions metrics of value-add reported to BioS stakeholders.
- Each infrastructure Agent – human, process, application, data, and asset - contributes its services to multiple Role sets.

The RED milestones measure Interaction performance between the customer who Requests the service, and the provider of the services. The RED milestones also provide a process abstraction of the behavior, metrics, and value goals achieved by using underlying Agents.

We can manage the organization servicing non-routine Requests by noting that the complexity arises due to the number of things happening but not due to a large number of different things happening. Each organization has a small number of primary Interactions. Each of those in turn might have a small number of potential secondary Interactions. For example, as the organization scales its operations in the market, thousands of RED instances might exist which in and of itself is not complex. The complexity arises due to the increasing associations introduced amidst the Agents. These are not well tracked by our enterprise systems. Reduction of management complexity begins by recognizing that only a small number of patterns exist. Thus, the focus here is on Interactions and milestone contributions to customer strategy, business, operations, and infrastructure stakeholder performance goals.

Consequences: The ability to 1) decompose a 'fuzzy' service into granular increments based on well-defined Requests, 2) the dynamic determination and assignment of resources (shared, external, specialized, etc.) to achieve the Interaction goals, 3) the continuous improvement of service value to achieve stakeholder goals and associated KPIs[a], 4) the ability to more precisely define Request, Role set and Resource catalogs with SLs and the needed OLs within the provider, 5) the identification of requirements for the configuration of enterprise system systems and frameworks[b], 6) the ability for real-time project monitoring where there is discovery, and 7) the sensing of new Request circumstances contributing to business intelligence regarding new opportunities.

Structure: The RED Interaction provides a universal abstraction of a customer-provide process with a focus on performance. This abstraction is agnostic to the details of the process, resources, and data variation. The Roles identify underlying infrastructure services but not the 'how' details (such as work instructions or process details, how data is represented, Agent reporting structure, etc.). The resources can be dynamically assigned based on their availability. The Roles can also be statically assigned for routine Interactions.

RED accomplishes this through the principle of delayed binding - applied twice – between the incoming customer Request to the provider RED, and the between the RED-Role set to Resources.

RED Interactions within the organization are dynamically (or statically) assembled into a virtual execution structure with Requests, Interactions, Role sets, and Resources associated to goals that are achieved upon Interaction execution. The primary RED Interactions are the main nodes with the potential sub-Interactions as the child nodes. Primary RED Interactions complete a service or part of a service whose value is directly perceptible by the external customer or an internal customer who acts on behalf of the external one. Sub-Interactions are used by the primary ones but only *as needed* for non-routine Requests. Note: that there might be different associations such as data flow or time sequencing between Interactions. Thus the REDs can be assembled dynamically to provide the customer-provided engagement visibility to the stakeholders to facilitate real-time decision making. ACE structures can also contain nested organizations as we shall see later. We call this the ACE structure (Figure 2).

IT goals and dynamics: A RED Interaction is typically initiated by filling a Request form. The initiation can be due to an event in the customer's environment

– like a need for replenishment or service. The Request contains essential details like the origination information, quantity, requirements, etc. More traditionally, a Request is also known as order, work ticket, admittance form, incident report, and the like.

When received, a Request is logged, routed, or assigned, to a specific Interaction's Role set during triage (see pattern discussed next) based on the Request's type. From that point on, all the Request metrics are captured. The execution of the Interaction occurs with the Agents in the provider's infrastructure playing Roles for the Interaction's Role set as we shall see. RED types can be assembled dynamically to form a structure. That is at any point during the execution of the R, E, D, sub-Requests can initiate and associate sub-Interaction s that complete unanticipated sub-deliverables. In other words, a primary Interaction is achieved by internal customers, on behalf of an external one. When the service is delivered the Request form is completed to record the Interaction (or Interactions) – often with a signature – and accounting closure occurs.

The end-user goals are to complete the Interaction milestones. In turn this simultaneously measures $\triangle$ from multiple stakeholder perspectives (see details in Chapter 2):

- Business $\triangle$
- Infrastructure improvement $\triangle$
- Operations $\triangle$
- Strategy and customer $\triangle$

Related Information

Known Uses: The pattern is applicable to one-of-a-kind service projects (Memory Jogger 200?), customer service centers, custom engineering services, emergency, IT services, and maintenance processes.

Related Patterns: Triage and Broker patterns are used to implement dynamic assignment and virtualization.

Similar Patterns: The Request-Deliverable pair is also referred to as a business object. While the milestone steps are similar to the SCOR pattern[c], we have generalized SCOR's "Request-Plan| Resource| Make| Deliver" in two ways. RED applies both *internally* across the service layers of the organization and across the *external* supply chain. Also, we treat the resourcing as an assignment of Agents within the RED steps.

Experience: This pattern applies to a range of Enterprise System configuration projects, service project management, and process management. This has also been applied to applied to lean analysis, chargeback, portfolio development and CRM configuration as documented in future Chapters.

Related Best Practice, Standards, Technologies and References: Covered in future Chapters.

Pattern Application: Triage (or Request Broker)

Dynamic Brokering of Request-to-REDs and Role set-to-Resources to meet SLs.

Conceptual

Strategy goals: Non-routine Requests each require different processing and infrastructure resources for creating the deliverable. The expensive underlying resources are also often shared across Requests and not dedicated to a particular type. Thus, there is need to characterize the known and unknown requirements of incoming Requests so that the resources can be most effectively assigned for the next increment of processing. Finally, there must be a single customer-facing interface for the status of Requests and the management of underlying capacity.

Example: A custom service-oriented organization like the emergency room has a large variation in incoming Requests. Most incoming Requests also have associated service requirements that are not fully understood until they are examined by the knowledge workers (like doctors). The Triage nurse applies rules to ensure that the Request is correctly classified and based on this proper services can be applied by health care provides that are available.

Problem: Effective use of resources given Request variation.

Operational goals and analysis: From the BioS stakeholder perspectives we need rules for 1) the most effective assignment policy across Request types for resources to meet SL goals, 2) define the SLs and ensure the SLs performance by dynamic Agent assignment rules and options for meeting OLs, and 3) identify new Request variations as this reflects new customer opportunities, or opportunities for improving efficiency. Rules Broker between 1) the Requests and the REDs and 2) the assignment of resources to the RED Role set by logging and classifying Requests.

Consequences: Triage rules provide *dynamic and knowledge-based* routing for the just-in-time assignment of resources. Since all Requests and sub Requests are customer driven, triage implements *Lean*. Just as the work centers on the factory floor are organized for the Lean routing and transformations, the virtual ACE structure is organized for Lean execution through triage. Finally, triage builds resilience capability through the alternate assignment of resources. That is, while the ACE structure specifies the potential Interactions, the execution of an Interaction can be re-assigned dynamically to achieve resilience (assuming adequate capacity can be obtained). Triage supports an on-going dynamically evolving process while at the same time retaining traceability.

Structure: Figure 2.

IT goals and dynamics: Triage rules support the following use cases:

- *Logging* of Requests.
- *Classification of the customer requirements*: For each Request common initial classification rules are applied. A typical initial classification is *routine* (i.e. low-to-medium priority, standard quantity, reasonable desired date) or *non-routine* (i.e. new requirements, high priority as determined by the customer and also the provider). Additional classifications are also applied (see highlight in x). The classification results in the proper association with correct RED and its Role set and the selection of effective and available resources for the specific Interaction (s). This is also often referred to as workflow 'routing'.
- *Characterization of needed Interaction (s):* Identify the RED Interaction (s) to be executed using the ACE structure.
- *Assignment of Execution Resources:* Here the actual Agents within the infrastructure are identified based on availability and capability and assigned the task of performing the service Role within the Interaction.
- *Execution metrics:* Recording details such as Interaction metrics, resources assigned, and status.

Rules for Role assignment and routing are initially applied by Customer Service Center Agents, but later by the different specialist Agents executing Interactions. For the *non-routine* Interactions that are identified at triage, the R, E, D sub-Interactions[d] (to handle *discovered* customer requirements in-between Interactions) are also triaged. (For the *routine* Requests, the Interactions apply in a known order and form a static workflow.) The goals of triaging are to ensure that queue time is minimized.

Related Information

Known Uses: Triage is applicable to CSC, value-based program management, and resilient supply chain management. Today's enterprise systems can be configured to implement the triage pattern. See Chapter 7 on Lean implemented within a CSC. Management to generate greater value from high cost resources.

Related patterns: RED Interaction, Shared Infrastructure.

Similar patterns: Broker pattern. Implemented within enterprise systems for routing requests.

Experience: Need more accurate monitoring of resource availability. In general, within the organization, there are many ad-hoc demands on the resource. This makes it very hard to determine the availability of a knowledge resource. Thus the time reporting should be at a fine enough granularity so that the availability of a resource can be determined. See chapters in Part III of this book.

Related Best Practice, Standards, Technologies and References: ITIL goes into rules that need to be applied at the CSC. The ACE structure provides a way of discovering those rules. The related applications / technologies include CRM, Self-help.

Pattern: Shared Infrastructure

Meets RED Service-Level requirements using Operating-Level requirements and Agents shared across multiple Role sets.

Conceptual

Context goals: Increase the use of shared resources within Interactions and at the same time achieve predictable response and lower costs.

Example: To complete the services for an emergency patient, there is often a need for composite mixed-mode services such as equipment, technicians, doctors, nurses to be *all available* (synchronized) before treatment can start. In the application of high-cost of resources (knowledge workers, enterprise applications, servers, tools, etc.) that are shared and not dedicated to individual Interactions, SLs are highly unpredictable.

Problem: Consider the challenge that when multiple shared Agents are needed, they all have to be synchronized to ensure that they can complete the Interactions and meet the RED SL. Also while the needed service Roles for an Interaction are known, the actual time of use is event-based and triggered by the arrival of an external Request and hence not predictable. This makes the availability of shared Agents more uncertain. Maximize the availability and use of shared Agents through management of their capacity and without requiring dedicated Agents.

Operational goals and analysis: The fundamental solution principle underlying the pattern is again the delayed binding concept - *Role set*. This is introduced as a composition or collection of required *Roles and OLs* that are needed to provide services to complete a RED Interaction type. There is a Role set for each RED Interaction. The union of the Role sets form the Role Catalog supported by the provider's infrastructure.

Triage provides delayed binding between the Role set and Agents provided by the underlying infrastructure needed for any RED's *execution*. That is, when a Request is queued by triage for a particular Interaction, the Roles needed by the Request is dynamically assigned based on the *availability* of the underlying Agents. Note: in actuality, the Roles can be bound - assigned Agents to act as resources - either statically or dynamically. Through the assignment, Agents provide services in a composition that will result in the service deliverable of the Role set as a whole.

The individual Agent might perform different Roles for different Role sets. However, the Role set allows us to relate the OLs of the composite services both to the SL performance of the Interaction and to the individual Agent OL services in the composition. Example metrics captured are:

- *RED SL* (customer perspective): Average response time, satisfaction, queue times.
- *Role set OL* (operational perspective): Throughput, wait time (i.e. non-value added time spent in specific queues), defects.
- *Agent OL* (shared infrastructure use perspective): Resource times used, defects.

The Request-RED-Role set-Agent associations implement the *virtual* service organization in several ways:

- Shared Role definitions specify responsibility and a clear interface so that, without necessarily loosing autonomy, Agents can perform to meet multiple Role set OLs and meet multiple RED SLs.
- Available infrastructure capacity - i.e. lightly loaded agents - can be used more efficiently for processing Request variation because of the delayed binding between the Role sets and Agents.
- The dynamic routing of the Request to the RED (that is like a work center) and the allocation of Agents (resources) generalize the familiar concept of process flow along the factory floor. But, there are also some differences from the traditional factory floor. The RED Roles can be dynamically assigned to available Agents at any point upto just before execution. Thus a Role is simply a placeholder that allows us to *delay the association* between a service requirement and an Agent.

Consequences: The dynamic assignment requires project management practices to be in place to determine the availability of a resource. See the chargeback methods in Chapter 7. Also some differences between the physical and electronic worlds have to be understood when we apply the ACE patterns to the specific enterprise. As an example, consider that while physical routing and travel takes time, it is instantaneous within software systems. Thus, electronic workflows already present in existing enterprise software do not have the overhead of travel time. Queue time, however, is there and indicative of waste in both worlds! Synchronizing services to minimize wait time is therefore critical to performance improvement. The physical services synchronized have to be synchronized with the electronic flow of Requests. Often this can be done though technology, for example the downloading to mobile devices or easily accessible terminals, reduces wasted wait and travel time. The chapters in the remaining part of this book provide the examples applying these ACE patterns.

The delivery of services is managed from the following two perspectives:

- *Customer perspective* in which multiple Agents provide services that must cooperatively meet the performance requirements of REDs and customer SLs.
- *Provider infrastructure perspective* in which each Agent has the maximum flexibility to negotiate and meet its own OL constraints imposed by multiple REDs and act in an autonomous fashion. This will minimize the coordination overhead.

By separating the two, we provide a way to effectively coordinate and manage the many-to-many associations between the REDs and their infrastructure Agents used for services, without requiring these *associations to be pre-determined.* The result is an implementation of virtualization, at any levels, providing flexibility in the use of resources.

Structure: Figure 2.

IT goals and dynamics: Typical scenarios describing the runtime behavior of the pattern from the business-user perspective.

Role OL definition: Roles are associated to multiple REDs and their SLs (that can also be thought of as the goals of the Interaction). The OL for the Role is determined by taking the union of the needs across the RED SLs.

Agent OL definition: An Agent might satisfy the multiple OLs requirements of each different Role set it participates in. The Roles comprise the total 'job description' for the Agent. For example, a human resource can be an 'installer' in one Role set or an 'assembler' in another. In this application the resource needs to have both skills.

Infrastructure capacity definition: For each Role shared across Role sets, identify and sum the associated Agent service time and other skills needed for the Role sets to meet the RED SLs. This allows us to identify how much total infrastructure capacity is needed and used.

Capacity and availability: Based on the Agent reporting and at any time, the availability of a particular Role is determined.

Performance reporting and traceability: The *cause-and-effect* at execution along the chain – Request, the Role set assignments, RED performance achieved, the Agent performance, and defects are determined. By aggregating this RED performance we now have the performance *for each Request type.*

Agent reporting: Every Agent has visibility into the other Roles and reports time spent on each Role. An Agent plays perhaps multiple Roles in different Role sets based on its *capabilities* thus time in each Role is recorded.

Related Information

Known Uses: The Role definitions are used in Triage at the CSC to determine which are the most cost effective resources to assign an incoming Request to.

  Related patterns: RED Interaction, Triage.

  Similar patterns: Lean methods.

  Experience: As mentioned before, need more accurate monitoring of resource availability.

  Related Best Practice, Standards, Technologies and References: ITIL goes into rules that need to be applied at the CSC. The ACE structure provides a way of discovering those rules. The related applications / technologies include CRM, Self-help.

ENTERPRISE KNOWLEDGE INFRASTRUCTURE

This subsection uses a range of EKI architecture-level pattern applications as they appear in order to illustrate the trend and need for flexibility in the way applications are used by different communities of users. That is, as services get numerous, more and more 'customer' intelligence is need to achieve the quality and ease of service delivery. The goal is to tailor the services to the role and circumstances of the user. The examples service delivery here include the customization of information and media provided to the user, the management of communities of users, and facades to provide simple interfaces to access based on rights information.

Pattern Application: Dynamic Authorization Decorator for Role-Based Access to Enterprise Information Services

Based on users' sign-on using Internet directory services generate dynamic filters (such as an *SQL where clause*) to provide users with restricted views of the enterprise information (EI), authorized based on their different roles.

Conceptual

Strategy goals: Providing wider access to enterprise information services is generally beneficial to the organization and creates a business advantage but can potentially increase the burden of privacy and security administration. We call these systems Enterprise Information Services (EIS). Examples of EIS include Enterprise Data Warehousing, Enterprise Document Management, and Content Management System (CMS). Particularly with these types of EIS, there is also a need to comply with HIPAA[e] and ensure access control based on user's roles within the organization and the individual's need for privacy. Most organizations have a single sign on component (SSO, see Web Single Sign on 2008) which typically maintains users' password but does not support the many new EIS needs due to self-serve and service of specialized communities that are constantly arising.

Examples: A person in a sales role in one region should not be able to access sales data from another region. However, a person in a manager role in one region should be able to access sales data from another region. Parents coming to the city website want information only on children's health but senior citizens want other views of the same sources of information. And, in an emergency situation security personnel can access certain restricted information, based on policy.

Problem: Different customers and providers have different rights authorizing them to different views of objects, records and fields based on their roles. Thus, additional role-based access processing is needed above the standard password information maintained in directory services.

Operational goals and analysis: The access to these multiple applications and information is through a single Information viewing Portal to a centralized server. This provides access to a range of user and role information such as security profiles, preferences, configuration, entitlements, rights, and personalization information. The fundamental solution principle is to delay the binding of the user role to the actual query that constructs the correct view. The actual binding is done at execution, when the user's role is determined. The security information is based on a directory (such as LDAP). The query customization is used to provide object item/record and field level access control. Fine grain field-level access control now made possible due to role management.

Logical

Consequences: EIS access is implemented on a need to know basis thus supporting different roles, communities, and organization structures. This also minimizes the administration of number of account/password pairs and improves overall ease of use.

Structure: A high-level diagram is given in Figure 3. The user and access control information for the organization is maintained in the Internet directory (using LDAP) is imported and enhanced in the EIS to manage users and groups that they belong to based on their role. When the user logs on, in addition to controlling the access (using LDAP information), the users role is determined by the EIS component. Any query is dynamically modified based on the roles of the user. The entitlements are determined by that component. The users' query - often 'canned' based on the underlying model used by the EIS - is modified dynamically.

Operational IT

IT goals and dynamics: Typical scenarios describing the runtime behavior of the pattern from the business-user perspective include:

- Portal business user roles: Access to authorized information based on role, group membership and security.
- Corporate Administrator: Single point of administration of users.
- Portal administrator: Administers users, groups, roles and entitlements.

Logical System and Data Integration view: Figure 3. Users are imported/exported to/from a centralized SSO to feed an EIS repository or the Entitlements system

Figure 3. Component Interactions illustrating the replication of users' sign-on data and its enhancement to determine the dynamic customization of incoming query and particular view of data.

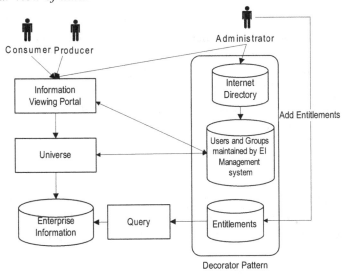

for further application-level user management. The integration of various security domains: Enterprise Identity Management, Application & Database is required and needs to be implemented.

Related Information

Known Uses: Support flexible access of data based on simple role or community membership. More complex access determined by participation in one or more roles or communities and policy.

Experience: Pattern replaces the data base management system's late binding of a where clause. The shortcoming is that users also needed database accounts and therefore could bypass the business metadata layer of the reporting tool and go directly to the database. This allows unregulated queries. Additionally, user has to manage both a reporting tool and a database account, which expired at different frequencies. This leads to user frustration.

Related Best Practice, Standards, Technologies and References: Data Warehouse implementation practices by vendors such as IBM™, Informatica™, Oracle™ [f].

Pattern Application: Community Views of Taxonomy

Process for creating views of a standard underlying taxonomy of content (services and products) to simplify navigation and increase currency.

Conceptual

Strategy goals: Enterprise Portals and similar EIS support communities of customers and other stakeholders requiring views of products and services based on their roles. These views should be easy to create and deploy especially as the underlying taxonomy of products and services changes.

Examples: A taxonomy of city services needs to be viewed from the view points of different communities or individuals. Example of communities includes senior citizen's health and children's health, each interested in two different views of the underlying health services taxonomy. Another example is based on professors that need to find quickly and accurately relevant course materials from a publisher. Different disciplines view the same materials differently.

Problem: A single taxonomy for organizing information is not specific to the circumstances and needs of different communities interested in underlying information. Furthermore, as content is updated, the viewing requirements of the base taxonomy also change. However, adding these views is not an efficient process for content editors. On-line services should not be interrupted.

Logical

Consequences: Communities see relevant information views without long lead times for refresh. System management complexity.

Solution goals and analysis The taxonomy update and view creation processes and roles are supported while at the same time, the updated taxonomy and views are published without significant interruption of services.

Structure: Figure 4 illustrates how the tool provides the business user role features to add announcements, custom hierarchies, and views for specific communities of users.

Figure 4. Process for creating custom community views

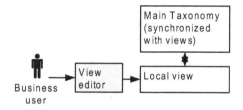

Figure 5. Editing of custom user view - Logical view.

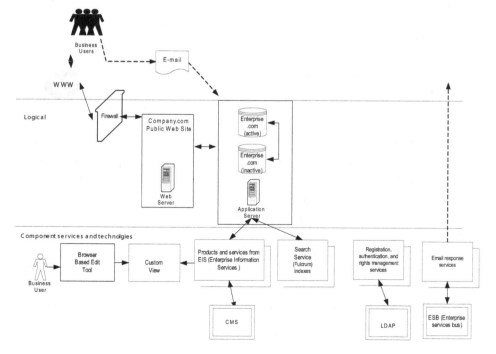

Operational IT

IT goals and dynamics: Provides user- and community-based views of Taxonomy.

Logical view: Figure 5 gives an overview of the components and functions involved. The off-line version is used for updates and view creation.

Data and Integration view: Underlying enterprise application publish to CMS, which acts as a staging area for business users to create custom views. Finally, the information is published to the offline database of organization's portal. On a scheduled basis the off-line view becomes the on-line view.

Deployment view: The *Web Server* has all of the graphics, java scripts, style sheets, and some other files residing in separate subdirectories on the site server. The *Application Server* has all of the JSPs, Java class, property and other processing files are located in the web archive (war) file on the production server. There is a web archive file for each of the subdirectories.

Security view: Business users are validated through the Role Management before being allowed to create or edit custom catalogs.

Scalability and performance view: Minimum lead time achieved by maintaining two versions of the taxonomy.

System Management: The standard taxonomy data is stored and cannot be changed by business users through the CMS.

Related Information

Known Uses: Portals that provide self service features for different communities of users and with a rich collection of services.

Other applicable Best Practice, Standards, Technologies and References: Further information related to facets and taxonomies (Lambe 2007).

Pattern Application: User Management Facade

Managing user accounts usually depends on multiple backend application systems. Interacting with these systems adds complexity that is hidden by a façade to the client.

Conceptual

Strategy goals: Customers would like features to use and re-use content based on their digital rights.

Example: Users within a community have rights to modify and use content based on the role.

Figure 6. User Management Façade - Conceptual view (top) and Logical view (bottom) for Soap Implementation

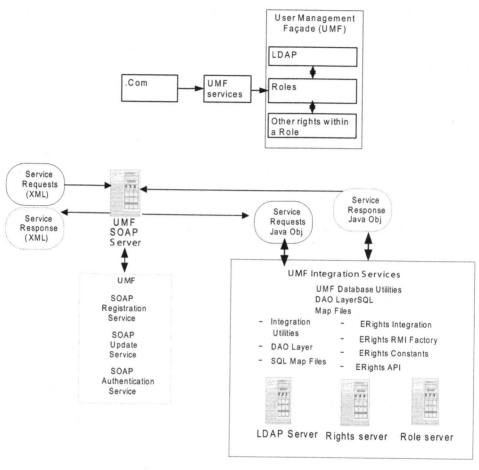

Problem: Hide multiple backend systems and present a coherent standard interface to allow user related information management.

Operational goals and analysis: Create a single point of service Interaction between the internal and external systems.

Logical

Consequences: Allows the backend services for user management to be enhanced/ changed with minimum impact to current services.

Structure: Figure 6.

Operational IT

IT goals and dynamics: Accepts SOAP messages to retrieve the rights based on the role of a user.

Logical view: SOAP Server communicates with UMF (at some unknown physical location) which interfaces with the following: UMF Database, Role Server, Rights Server, and LDAP Server.

Data and Integration view: UMF integration application creates a java object. Then the SOAP client converts the java object to XML. Finally, the UMF SOAP Server converts the XML to a java object.

Deployment view: One application server and one database server.

Security view: Application validates the user entries before sending the object to the SOAP client. SOAP client validates converted XML against the appropriate schema. XML returned to .COM application is validated against the appropriate schema.

Physical view: Different application and data base servers.

Concurrency view: Synchronous action of sending user management information request and receiving a response. Some actions like user registration are accompanied by an email confirmation, which is asynchronous.

Related Information

Similar Patterns: Web Single Sign[1] and Single Sign-On[2]

Related Patterns: J2EE patterns for DAO (Data Access Object discussed in Alur 2003).

Other applicable Best Practice, Standards, Technologies and References: SOAP is a protocol specification for XML messaged over the Internet. The standards are maintained by W3C XML Protocol Working Group.

Pattern Application: Managed Community Framework (CF) Façade

Provides a Community Framework (CF) for managing different relationships using community models with roles, associations between individuals, and specific individual details. The CF instances can are managed using customer provided data or data from other sources. The CF can be used for secure access to custom services (by role, project, file type, etc.). The location of an individual in a specific instance of CF can be used to dynamically customize other services (e.g. for content creation, review, use, assessment, and viewing). It is also used for reporting addressing privacy and trust. Duplications and consistency in this data is addressed.

Conceptual

Strategy goals: Service-orientation to provide more custom services requires rich models of the customer organization to address all types of service delivery commitments between all the consumer and provider roles. This must also address privacy, trust, and security.

Examples: Service providers deliver custom services appropriate to the particular user and where they are located in the hierarchy. An example is a state, regions, school districts, schools, classes, teachers, and students. Another example of a hierarchy is state, counties, cities, neighborhood associations, and citizens.

Problem: Custom delivery features often require highly sophisticated models of customer organizations. This is generally true of combination physical and electronic services because there are many customer roles that have to be satisfied by different components of the service. An example is the student health assessment and the delivery of the data to the parent, school, city, and state. Enterprise applications provide some of these services but require unnecessary duplication and complexity as they manage customer information.

Operational goals and analysis: The CF represents a single consistent view that can be used for different purposes along with different applications services. Each CF has a *master framework* that is a meta model comprised of the totality of nodes and node relationships needed to fulfill all needed process-specific framework views (non-master frameworks). Examples framework instances include enrollment frameworks, reporting frameworks, test administration frameworks, data collection locations frameworks, etc. Many applications can use the CF. Because CF services can be used by any application, the actual administration can also be through off-the-shelf products. The fundamental solution principle underlying the pattern is to support any customer organization with rich attributes and avoid duplication of this service.

Logical

Consequences: A single consistent view of the customer organization for the delivery of all services. It is important to note, that in many cases the community data might duplicate information maintained in enterprise systems.

Structure: CF establishes the nodes and relationships of each community (e.g. organization of students). Additionally hierarchies represent actual node instances for each framework node (for example instances such as individual schools, individual students) according to the relationships defined in the corresponding framework. Some attributes may have inheritance relationships between lower/higher levels nodes within one or more frameworks. For example a state may establish curricular standards to be applied statewide, while a specific district may impose additional standards. This could have corresponding implications for assessment content, analytics processes, and reporting views.

The CF also serves to maintain a single image of the customer service status though a variety of attributes like assigned providers, administration status, data retrieval status following test administration, production workflow status, etc. The services delivered can be aggregated through a rich variety of reports while ensuring that only authorized roles can view the reports.

Hierarchical relationships within the CF may be linked to specific attributes, for example a student may be linked to a Health nurse, to a Math teacher for purposes of administering a Math test, and to a Science teacher for purposes of administering a Science test. A community relations member maybe related to a particular town hall meeting.

Operational IT

IT goals and dynamics: Typical Use cases describing the use of the pattern follows:

- Actor: *Customer management roles* (such as district, administrators, teachers)
  - o View authorized information only, this may be limited to data defined below one of more specific nodes in the master framework or one or more of the non-master frameworks.
  - o View organizations' collaboration (i.e. tests, assessments) results as reports and aggregated reports.
- Actor: *Individuals*
  - o Complete forms, instruments, etc., view individual reports
- Actor: *Provider*
  - o Create content
  - o Delivery and retrieval of materials and reports
- Actor: *Coordinator*
  - o Administer assessments per schedule to complex organizational hierarchies based on customer data.
- View reports

Logical system view: A CF façade is implemented using an application server and content management system as shown. CF manages its own data in the data base management system. The management and runtime interface is a JSP/Java applica-

Figure 7. The components and Interactions involved in delivering customized application services using Community Framework.

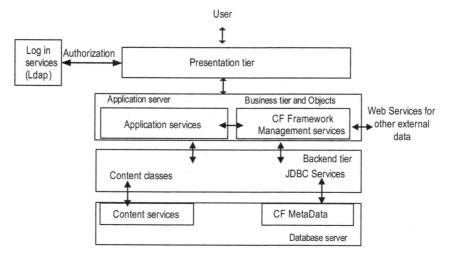

tion. The backend is implemented using the Apache web server and an application server. The components related to CF illustrated in Figure 7 interact as follows:

- Login services authorize the user and the user' role is determined based on the CF hierarchy. This role determines other application services provided.
- CF and the applications services are implemented as JSP/Java applications implemented on Application Server providing provide client access to the data access applications at the server side.
- The access layer to the CF models uses JDBC.
- Other applications, such as the testing administration application use this façade to obtain provide customized services.

Data and Integration view: The CF model is maintained in the database and accessed through a JDBC interface at the server side as shown. The CF component also obtains data from external applications using Web Services.

Security view: The Login services are based on LDAP for basic access. Additional content authorization (for reports etc.) is enhanced based on roles is using the CF.

Related Information

Related Patterns: Single sign on façade for existing sources of user and password information. CF needs the sub-pattern *framework import* to obtain customer information from other sources Customer databases etc. Thus this requires interoperability and synchronization of CF hierarchies with enterprise systems (provided though a enterprise service bus) and use of data from customer-provided files. Both of these are addressed.

Similar Patterns: Other examples of the use of the pattern include ED role model and authorization, and role-based sign-on and rights management in many enterprise applications.

Experience: All customer facing applications requiring a customer organization model with user roles determining the delivery of services. Build versus buy decision based on need for flexibility to address future trend in customer-centered requirements. Vendor customer framework products have been evaluated and found to require significant customization.

LOGICAL PATTERNS

This section presents a common security, application, and data interoperability patterns. The next section generalizes to a framework for thinking about security Interactions in a systematic way.

Pattern Application: Messaging Across the eDMZ

How to layer middleware services in order to pull messages from the eDMZ into backend systems for near real-time performance.

Conceptual

Strategy goals: Restrict access to backend systems to protect stakeholder data, privacy and reduce risk.

Example: Security breach.

Problem: Messages cannot be pushed to the backend system since external application must have no knowledge of internal systems.

Operational goals and analysis: Allow backend system process to pull messages from the message Broker bus on the eDMZ.

Logical

Consequences: Added message delivery delay to the backend systems which is minimized by having the backend system pull data every few milliseconds.

Structure: Figure 8.

IT goals and dynamics: Backend system only receives messages upon request; therefore it does not weaken existing security barriers.

Operational IT

Logical and Data and Integration view: Figure 8 shows the logical separation of components between the eDMZ and backend systems. It also highlights the message bus and the major components on the bus that allow for seamless data integration.

Concurrency view: Figure 7 shows the two concurrent processes used in sending messages across the eDMZ. The first process places messages on the adapter while the second process pulls these messages to the backend systems.

Security view: Backend system only receives messages upon request; therefore it does not weaken existing security barriers.

Figure 8. Messaging Across the eDMZ - shows how the message Broker spans the eDMZ and backend systems

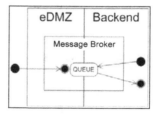

Figure 9. Messaging across the eDMZ - Logical view

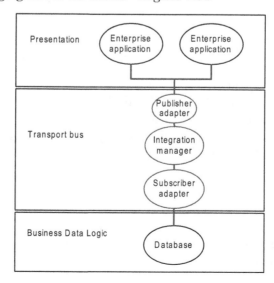

Potential Security Problems

Potential Errors	Possible Reasons	Solution Strategy
Data base source adapter fails	System Failure	Check the adapter log file and take corrective action
Data base connection lost	Database or Network Failure	Certified Messaging will prevent the loss of messages. If the request/reply adapter is used for lookup purpose, make sure that the IM (Integration Manager) engine is correctly started after the database is brought up and request/reply adapter is restarted.
Data casting error within IM	Table structure change.	Check if table structure has changed. Modify class if necessary.
Other IM error	Unknown.	Identify and correct.
IM engine and or server fails.	System failure	Certified Messaging will prevent the loss of messages. But check the IM log files (engine and server logs) for the errors and take appropriate action.
Target adapter fails.	System failure	Certified Messaging will prevent the loss of messages. But check the adapter log file for the errors and take appropriate action.
Data is not inserted into the staging table	Message format is not matching with the staging table format	Check the staging table structure to make sure that there is no truncation issue or data type mismatch. Check the adapter exception table for the error Interaction, and correct the definition of the staging table accordingly
Database operation failure	System failure	Certified Messaging will prevent the loss of messages.
Messages are not confirmed.	Incorrect CM or Session Names. Or Subscriber is down	Check the configuration for Pre-Registered and Known Listeners, or re-start subscriber

Scalability and Performance Analysis: No definitive numbers available, because of the dependency on the hardware.

Availability Analysis: Availability dependent on subscribing adapter on.

Conformance To Corporate Standards And Guidelines: eDMZ Guidelines Supported.

Related Information

Known Uses: Security.

Similar Patterns: Proxy Pattern (http://en.wikipedia.org/wiki/Proxy_pattern), Reverse Proxy (http://www.modsecurity.org/archive/ReverseProxy-book-1.pdf), Message Channel (http://www.enterpriseintegrationpatterns.com/MessageChannel.html)

Variant Patterns: Batch and hierarchical replication.

Experience and Metrics: Experience has shown not to send messages into the bus that are larger than 1mb in size. After the first 6 months 7000 orders processed.

Pattern Application: Mediated Data in Rich Internet Applications

Rich Internet Applications can offer a better user experience than traditional desktop application software or request and reply style web applications by putting the responsiveness and visual appeal of desktop applications in a web accessible package. However, these benefits from the perspective of the user come at the cost of increased complexity in the data management protocols that drive Rich Applications.

Conceptual

Strategy goals: From a strategic perspective, the distinguishing aspect of a Rich Application over a traditional one is its ability to entice, attract, and engage the consumer community.

Example: A company hopes to stimulate interest and increase awareness of a new brand they will be launching. As a part of the overall strategy they develop a Rich Application to attract potential customer and engage the online community.

Problem: Engaging features have the potential to attract new customers but they incur investments. However there is an underlying performance penalty and a learning curve. How can we optimize this investment across multiple projects?

Operational goals and analysis: Abstract and consolidate the primary complexity of Rich Applications, the data management, in a Data Mediator.

Logical

Consequences: The Data Mediator encapsulates all the management operations and removes Rich Application's dependency on knowledge of the underlying communication protocols and full data lifecycle within the context of participating enterprise backend systems.

From a business perspective the use of a Data Mediator may have little payback if the application is very specific or will have very limited use of any other enterprise systems (in which application it is still useful as a software design pattern). If the application may be interacting with a number of additional enterprise systems or data sources, or parts of the mediator have a potential to be shared then the pattern can provide significant business value by promoting reuse and mitigating the risk of change.

Structure: A client side mediator handles remote communication tasks in order to keep the client's data model consistent with any remote data models, or other colleagues which are involved in the application's data management lifecycle. Colleagues may include additional enterprise applications, other clients, or any other remote party.

Operational IT

IT goals and dynamics: Typical improvement in performance and usability experience.

Logical view: This is best understood in terms of the classical mediator pattern. The client side mediator (Figure 10) takes on the responsibility of collaborating with the remote colleagues in order to prevent the client application from having to know about their existence. The data mediator may provide any number of data related services to the Rich Application. Those services must allow the application to access and update *what* data it is interested in. *How*, *where*, and *when* aspects are not exposed to the application and become the responsibility of the mediator.

Data and Integration view: The data mediator(s) act as messaging channels through which the application accesses data and can be integrated with the collaborative colleagues. From a technical standpoint this weak coupling between the Rich Application and its data and integration requirements are where the primary benefits are realized.

Security view: If security is a concern this pattern may be a good candidate. If the security protocols are sufficiently complex, for instance they involve collaboration between a large number of distributed parties or there are multiple types

Figure 10. Client side mediator

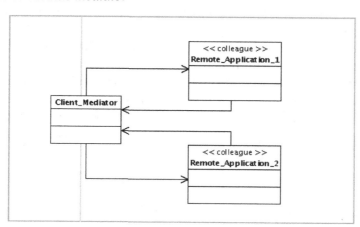

of data related security profiles in the application, then a data mediator may be useful for handling these details. For general security concerns the data mediator is unlikely to help

Deployment view: The mediator is a single logical component that is deployed with the Rich Application. The mediator itself may be implemented in any number of ways and can be further componentized depending on the complexity of the application.

Concurrency view: When a complex system is deployed onto one or more computational resources, this view is needed to reason about the communication and sharing of data later in the Service Level analysis section that follows. (State chart diagrams)

Scalability and Performance Analysis: If the application must scale and perform well, which is common in Rich Applications, a data mediator is very relevant. The data mediator can make use of other design patterns and strategies to adapt to scalability needs. Since these strategies can become complex and may need to be swapped out to handle new scenarios or infrastructure changes, a mediator is a good way to consolidate these concerns.

Related Information

Known Uses: This pattern is often found when existing desktop applications are moved into a web environment. In these situations the expectation of users, in terms of aesthetics, responsiveness, and the like, is already established and complex data management routines are required to retain them in a web environment. The data mediator can use efficient strategies, such as application check pointing, delayed communications, pre-fetching, or proxied communication to suit the needs of the application.

Experience and Metrics: The loose coupling the pattern introduces can become very valuable when the supporting infrastructure or backing data source changes or evolves over the lifetime of the application. In these cases only the mediator needs to be changed in order to support the new requirements of the application in its operating environment. This pattern may not be appropriate if the application's data needs are very simple or straightforward, in which application the additional mediator component may become a bottleneck and add unnecessary complexity. More on this pattern is available in Keen et al 2005 and Manouvrier 2008.

These next five example pattern applications illustrate back-end interoperability.

Pattern Application: Enterprise Messaging With Brokered Communication

Within an enterprise there are often many IT systems or data stores scattered throughout the infrastructure that rely on each other for operations. In this context, data often needs to be synchronized between a logical *owner* system and multiple *satellite* systems within a given timeframe and potentially with other quality guarantees, such as reliability or security. A Brokered communication infrastructure is a general pattern for achieving this style of inter-application connectivity where the Broker takes on the role of a mailman and ensures each application can send and receive messages with a strategy that's suitable for their role in the enterprise.

Conceptual

Strategy goals: To get an accurate business status, an enterprise needs to consolidate data from multiple applications.

Example: A company has a single point of entry for all new customer data, but that data is also must be available for reads and updates to a collection of satellite systems. Many of the applications use different communication formats and have various requirements on how the synchronization must be done. For instance, they have a catalog mailing system that should be consistent with all their customer data but it only needs to be put in a totally consistent state once every few months, or an application used by sales needs to be updated on a near real time basis.

Problem: From a business standpoint the need to integrate heterogeneous applications that have been developed as the business has grown is difficult to avoid. It is not time and cost effective to build integration solutions for each new scenario as the business continues to grow and evolve under new opportunities.

Operational goals and analysis: A Broker centralizes the role of application integration and provides flexibility to meet the requirements of new integration scenarios. Since this pattern is so common, technology vendors offer a number of mature, highly configurable, solutions that can fulfill this need with reduced custom development. There are many specializations of the general Broker pattern which build upon it to cater to particular scenarios and a number of additional patterns that work very well to complement it. Among these specialized styles are Message Queues and Publish/Subscribe channels and common complementary patterns including the Process Manager, Message Splitters, and Content Aggregators (Hohpe 2006)[g].

Logical

Consequences: The Broker gives the enterprise a common infrastructure for application integration and the flexibility to meet new demands quickly. If there are only a couple applications that must communicate or there are have very special communication requirements then directly connecting them may be more appropriate. The standardized approach minimizes the need to retain expert knowledge for custom built integration solutions and increases the likelihood that the solution can be reused in new situations. One of the largest benefits of Brokered communication comes from their standardization since packaged solutions can often be configured to meet the needs of the various enterprise applications. If the business has specialized needs, such as very strict real time communication requirements, a Brokered solution may or many not be applicable.

Structure: The basic structure of a Broker is identical to the structure of mediated data communication. Instead of applications communicating directly to one another, they forward all communication to a Broker, or set of Brokers, that determine when, where, and how to deliver the message and any responses. The basic structure is known by a number of names, like Hub and Spoke communication, and is characterized by the introduction of the Broker, or hub, which provides connections to all the applications.

Operational IT

IT goals and dynamics: Support for scenarios describing the need for information and acceptable time delay from the business-user perspective.

Logical view: The logical representation of the Broker can be seen below and also illustrates why it is commonly referred to as a hub and spoke model. A Brokers plays the role of a coordinator, or mediator, to individual applications. The Broker will offer specific services to each application when it is specialized for a particular situation, for example by providing topic-based channels or named message queues.

Data and Integration view: Since a Broker offers a set of communication services that client application may use, adapters are often required so the client can pass a message to the Broker. These adapters are often built on top of or into the client applications but they may also be part of the Broker and offered as a transformation service.

Security view: Supports authentication, authorization, directory services, logging.

Figure 11. Broker and client applications

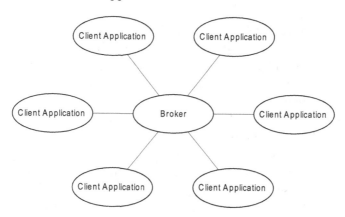

Deployment view: The broken pattern does not require a particular means of deployment, although it's typical for the Broker to be a dedicated server, or cluster of servers, with networked connectivity to all the clients.

Concurrency view: Message Brokers are typically asynchronous in the sense that client applications send a message and then continue on with their work. However in general, the Broker can also provide synchronous messaging between applications but it is often a much less efficient strategy for the most common application integration scenarios.

Scalability and Performance view: Brokered communication decouples each application from the manner in which messages are exchanged. Typically the Broker components can be scaled, by adding additional, hardware without any complications to the individual applications. Once again, in extreme situations it's possible for the Broker to act as a bottle neck. For example, if one application must send a huge amount of data to another application, say every few months, the Broker may become a bottleneck for the entire operation during that period. In these cases a Brokered solution may not be appropriate. Brokers can essentially serve as staging areas for applications that go down from time to time by storing messages that can not be delivered.

System Management view: The Broker offers a central point of management and monitoring inter-application communication which can be useful for many management activities including capacity planning, maintaining audit trails, and dealing with faulty data.

Related Information

Conformance To Corporate Standards and Guidelines: The standardized approach means that integration is treated uniformly across all applications. If there are standardized policies and procedures for dealing with situations like faulty data, availability, or infrastructure use, it can be monitored, controlled, and dealt with uniformly by the Brokered architecture.

Similar patterns: The Broker pattern can be found in any Message-Oriented-Middleware, or MOM, solutions. Typically, they provide a number of options that specialize the Broker pattern, such as publish/subscribe (or topic-based) communication and reliable messaging (which emulates point-to-point style communication by informing the sending application when it's message has been consumed). More on available Brokers at http://en.wikipedia.org/wiki/Message_Broker. Also refer to Hohpe 2003.

Pattern Application: Façade for Composite Items and Their Variations

The façade to access composite items that are managed using item meta-data that extends the CMS to include additional data managed in the database management system. The implementation uses a content management system's interface classes (IC), JDBC interface to the database management system, and the components deployed on an application server.

Conceptual

Strategy goals: Ability to manage complex items with features that are not provided by any one vendor.

Example: A single complex content item (for example many items with many different associations) with many associated service attributes has to be managed efficiently from the customers' perspective.

Problem: Competitive portal features often require highly customized versions of service content items. Vendor products and metadata does not provide enough flexibility and has to be expanded. The underlying metadata needs customization of vendor products.

Logical

Structure: Specific requests formulated based on user Interaction and the item metadata are filled and the value object returned from the underlying data bases, without needing to know the implementation details. The *item data* illustrated in figure 2 above uses the infrastructure in the figure 3 below.

Operational goals and analysis: The item façade abstracts metadata and provides seamless access to composite item objects managed across a CMS and Database. Thus objects are stored across multiple repositories and accessed from clients.

Operational IT

IT goals and dynamics: Typical scenarios describing the runtime behavior of the pattern from the business-user perspective include:

- *Actor:* User or Application
- Accesses and update to composite content item
- Search logical database of composite items, seamlessly

Logical and Data Integration view: An Item is a document/content (in the form of XML or other format) in EDM supplemented with additional metadata to enhance the possible reuse or other analysis that could be performed to improve the future test design process. The item information is also linked to other frameworks maintained in database tables.

The middle-tier and backend tier components and façade are in the figure below. The façade promotes looser *coupling* between the EDM applications, the JDBC applications, and the metadata. Only the JDBC interface has detailed knowledge of the EDM and Oracle application classes. Requests from the business objects and application facades are sent to the DAO which in turn sends messages to the backend façade which passes them on to any other classes that need to be informed at the server side.

The backend tier contains services that are accessible to clients and the middle tier only, through the Application Server. Application Server protects these data repositories by restricting direct access by end users.

Applications in the backend tier are EDM and Data Base Management applications that are based on a shared meta-data of the composite item objects in the Data Base. With connection pools and caching, Application Server uses back-end resources efficiently and improves application response. For example, a JDBC connection pool is defined in the Application Server. This opens a predefined number of database connections. Once opened, database connections are shared by all Applications—using DAOs—that need database access. The expensive overhead associated with establishing a connection is incurred only once for each connection in the pool, instead of once per client request. Application Server monitors database connections, refreshing them as needed and ensuring reliable database services for applications.

Finally, EDM provides a set of Java classes and interfaces, called IC or Interface Classes, that provides an object-oriented application programming interface (API) for accessing EDM functionality. These APIs are used by the façade to retrieve portions of the object in EDM and in Oracle so the value of the object requested can be returned.

Security view: The pattern relies on other application login services to provide authentication, authorization, etc. and not on EDM .

Scalability and Performance views: If you store the Meta data into an Item XML and store it into EDM, then querying the Meta data becomes difficult (for example the use of query for relational table join) and quite slow. However, storing into the database the item meta-data and into EDM the item XML, takes an acceptable amount of time. Storing the records for an item into Oracle is extremely fast. The main reason for doing this way is the effective use of meta-data for analysis.

Related Information

Similar Patterns: Pattern for creating taxonomies that allow viewing of content in multiple ways.

Pattern Application: Loosely-Coupled Source-to-Target Data Movement using Metadata

Data movement between data stores using a loosely-coupled approach building on a metadata layer to achieve a consolidated Data Warehouse (or DW). The metadata layer of abstract source and target objects separates conceptual and transformation logic from the underlying implementations and/or changes to the physical sources of data.

Conceptual

Strategy goals: To get an accurate business status, an enterprise needs to consolidate data from multiple applications.

Examples: A single consistent accurate target image of information created by multiple sources is desired. This information can be created by business applications, application performance monitoring tools, system performance monitoring tools and so on. It can be mined to provide knowledge to a variety of different communities of users.

Problem: Data integration is typically implemented via some bus architecture with custom-coded adaptors (or façades) that deal directly with the application-specific APIs (SQL scripts, methods, data structures etc.) and physical data stores (specific tables and locations). Data movement logic is often hardwired within the 'last mile' logic related to quality and recovery or ignored completely. This creates a brittle point-to-point coupling between source and target data store adaptors and a legacy data integration application that limits re-use of the data management and integration adaptor objects.

With numerous heterogeneous sources and targets, there is a need for a standardized effective method for staging, translation, error handling, and management functions to increase programmer productivity, data quality, and reduce case-by-case implementations.

Operational goals and analysis: Metadata, often stored in different source repositories, is used as a resource to:

- Abstract source and target data stores to create unified integrated metadata across systems. Specifically, metadata is defined as the shared representation of data across systems. (See Figure 12)
- Use the metadata to define abstract objects and scripts (façades).
- Use these abstractions to achieve transformations and to manage data flow between systems.

Figure 12. Development of a shared metadata representation and metadata-based transformation logic for data movement (Informatica™)

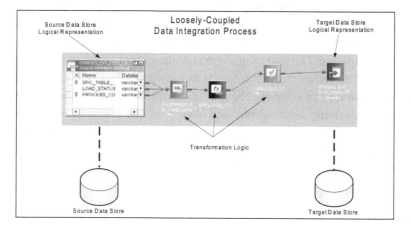

Figure 13. ETL development tools for mapping source to target metadata (Informatica™)

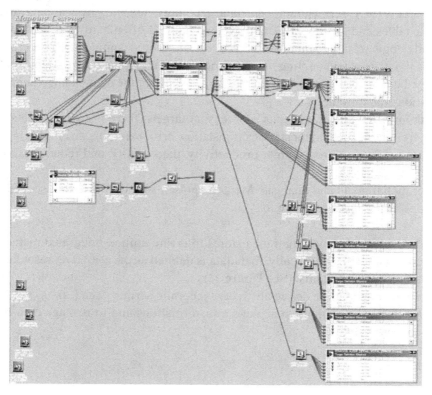

The principle used here is:

- **Source and target metadata:** Physical data stores and application-specific APIs' are abstracted and properly represented as logical constructs (i.e. all the order details rather than just order shipping are treated in a logical way).
- **Loose-coupling:** The mapping logic and movement logic uses the metadata-based facades rather than direct calls to the sources and targets.
- **Object re-use:** Not only are the metadata objects used as 'facades,' thus allowing underlying applications and data stores to be switched out without changing the mapping and movement logic, these objects are also searchable and their relationships are traceable.

Logical

Consequences: Different business definitions, data types, attribute names for the same attribute and other anomalies are overcome by properly maintaining metadata for these attributes in the centralized repository. Metadata can be used to map the underlying data up to and between source and target objects. The use of metadata plays a vital role in explaining about how, why, where data can be found, retrieved, stored, and used efficiently in information stewardship. For example the metadata allows business rules to be identified to clean source data and move it to a single consistent view of data (e.g. the DW view). Additional logical relationships can be established between other metadata and used for a variety of purposes, such as to ensure quality and completeness of data. Finally, the metadata is also be also used for recording the history of the movement of data.

While vendors provide standard tools, service level considerations typically require a closer examination of implementation standards.

Finally, abstracting the metadata and providing ETL tools to monitor end-to-end movement of data yields effective 'last mile' support.

Structure: The functional and structural aspects of the pattern reference implementation are as follows. Extract Transform Load (ETL) tool is used to assist the process of developing 'facades' and transformations using the metadata abstraction. The reference implementation uses Informatics' ETL tools (see figure above).

With the ETL tool, a logical representation of source and target data stores can be created. These are stored and manipulated in the ETL tool's metadata repository. The metadata repository can be searched for impact analysis when a source or target definition changes. This achieves loose-coupling by using logical representations of the data objects rather than implementation-oriented representations.

Data Integration developers can check the repository for available logical objects when creating a new data integration programs (known as an ETL mapping).

IT goals and dynamics: Use cases:

- *Architect:* Manages metadata tables for source and target objects, operational tables for monitor/load processes, error records, and re-start processes.
- *Owner:* Source and target application administrators examine failed records determined against the metadata and correct errors.
- *Knowledge users:* Accesses consistent, correct data, and audit reports.

Logical view: ETL development tools (as in Figure 12 and Figure 13) manage the metadata repository and provide for editing at a logical level. All the metadata information about source, target, transformations, mapping, workflows, sessions etc., is stored. During the ETL process, when mapping source and target systems, it is the metadata that is actually mapped in order to achieve the loose coupling. Metadata can also be manipulated, queried and retrieved with the help of wizards provided by metadata capturing tools. Finally, transformation rules can be associated with the mappings illustrated in Figure 13.

Operational IT

Data and Integration view: The overall logical flow of data (see Figure 14) helps identify the points at which metadata is used to extract, transform, load, and perform other related functions:

- Extract data from applications (like ERP) and send this data into the staging warehouse area (DW Staging) so that the validations (non-functional checks, business rules, and transformations) against the metadata can be applied without impacting the source performance.
- Validation checks are performed at staging and written to temporary staging tables.
- The temporary staging tables are read and loaded into the operational tables (DW operational data store) and from there is moved to the data warehouse (DW) tables (See Figure 14).

Figure 14. Staging areas where validations are performed using the underlying metadata and transformations

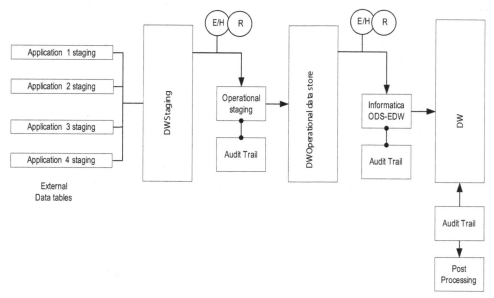

Scalability and performance view: The requirement for the outlined DW reference implementation is that the ETL processes run nightly and load approximately 1.5 – 2 million rows. The specific load will run concurrently with other dimension tables in DW. The performance expectation for the entire procedure is 10 to 30 minutes. Since several data cleanup functions are performed using the metadata and during the movement of data, it is the experience that several optimizations are of particular importance:

- Eliminate duplicate lookup processing. Since lookups are resource intensive, perform all related operations (e.g. lookup plus capture target values plus perform validation check) at the same time if possible.
- Cache Sizes for lookups need be set appropriately. Caching the look up table (using suggested formulas) may have to be evaluated against direct update for large volumes.
- Consider Flat File temporary storage. Reading and writing to a flat file is much faster than to relational sources.
- Leverage Partitioning when possible. For example different threads can move data in parallel. These can be partitioned based on key ranges.

Physical view: The following configuration for staging is a typical example - 20 dual-core Sun CPUs, 80GB RAM; and 10g Database.

Related Information

Similar Patterns: References to patterns that solve similar problems include Broker messaging, EDI, FTP.

Experience: Comparing methods that use meta data:

- Bulk Data Movement: Extract Transform Load is a methodology designed for data store-to-data store movement & heavy transformations. It eliminates the overhead of Relational-to-XML and XML-to-Relational conversions (which can be computationally expensive) and has end-to-end visibility due to the provided metadata toolset.
- Electronic Data Interchange: A well known approach that also has tools for end-to-end movement, quality, and monitoring of data moved in standardized, though proprietary, formats.
- Other approaches that do not use metadata can be compared for source-to-target data movement. For example:
- Messaging Patterns: Messaging based on Publish/Subscribe, Asynchronous, loosely-coupled approaches, or SOAP/XML/Web Services are often very

poor for batch-oriented, or bulk, data movement. In addition, they typically are not accompanied by the metadata tools intended to provide the end-to-end visibility. This may require extensive custom code for comparable "last mile" assurance. Flat File/FTP is a simple approach that should only be used when other approaches do not suffice or are not possible. In this application the lack of integrated assurance and controls makes the process a "blind handoff" of data.

• Reference: Bontempo & Zageglow 1998.

Pattern Application: Error Detection Using Logical Transaction-Based Metadata

Business level error detection and logging based on data quality analysis rules implemented using the logical transactions and relationships captured in metadata.

Conceptual

Strategy goals: To get an accurate business status, an enterprise needs to consolidate data from multiple applications.

Example: Improve quality of logical transaction information from a customer perspective.

Problem: The quality of business-level transactional data is hard to maintain because the source data is often distributed across tables and applications which make it difficult to relate and keep consistent. For example, a sale transaction is initiated in the database, when a customer order is entered in the ERP. From there on, the order will traverse through various statuses like Booked, Hold, Shipped, Backordered, Closed, Invoiced etc. before its life cycle ends. An order can have many order lines and each can be in various statuses mentioned above. Hence, there could be the associated data scattered throughout different physical tables – for example, Order line details, Order pricing details, Order hold details, Order shipping details, Invoices corresponding to closed lines.

Operational goals and analysis: The data for an object (say an order) may reside in various physical database tables, but all these data together is a part of a complete *sales* Interaction (transaction) and hence will constitute a logical record. Therefore, the business validation and error handling process will verify each *logical Interaction record* for completeness and correctness before it is marked eligible for loading to the Operational Data Store (ODS). In other words, ODS is populated with *logical* records rather than *physical* records. The solution relies on the concept of the logical Interaction. While loading data from staging to ODS, data is validated based on business conditions. ETL is used to establish logical relationships in metadata and use metadata based data screening and error handling of logical transactions to ensure only clean and valid data is loaded and maintained. Based on the validation, either the *entire logical* business Interaction or transaction will be loaded to the ODS or no data for that transaction will be loaded.

Logical

Consequences: These are 1) improved data quality and efficient processing of logical records ultimately improves customer satisfaction and 2) loading only the clean/valid logical data into the data warehouse ensures the reconciliation needs of various business groups are better supported.

Structure: The ETL transformation processes (circles in Figure 15) extracts data from *multiple source tables* in the staging environment and populates the target tables in the ODS environment. When errors are detected, the failed records are written in 'bad' files corresponding to staging tables. Transforms using metadata for cleanup also detects faulty source records which are written out and the appropriate users notified.

Figure 15. Transformation processes (illustrated as circles) during which logical and other types of error detection occur as data moves from source to the target (in this application a data warehouse)

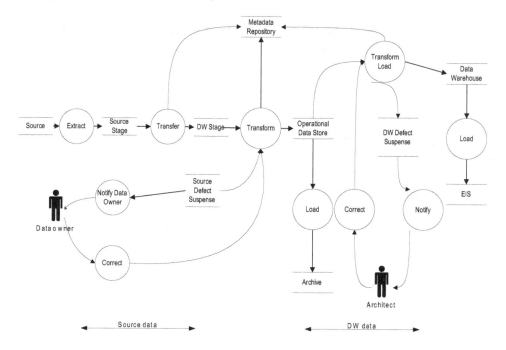

Operational IT

IT goals and dynamics: The Business user would like complete correct data related to the business Interaction. Also the source or target application data owner wants to correct errors to improve the quality of business data. This is accomplished as follows:

- *Loads:* Initial data load to ODS encompasses all records currently in the ERP system transferred to DW staging. Subsequent data loads are limited to daily entries extracted to staging tables. The record is inserted into the ODS database irrespective of whether it was an insert or an update on the ERP system.
- *Validations that cause errors:*
  - o Business validations – These validations will identify the errors in the incoming logical records of various subject areas (for example complete order record - as identified as in "Appendix B: Master Business Validations Listing")
  - o Non functional validations – These validations will include the following types of data level errors:
    - ➣ Lookup failure
    - ➣ Mandatory column missing
    - ➣ Data type mismatch

Logical view: ETL processes provide a log of rejected records and the reason for rejection so that the quality of data can be improved (This has been previously referred to as the last-mile above). The logical flow illustrated accomplishes the following:

- Utilize Individual error tables for the corresponding ODS tables to store the error records.
- Log records with errors in the Error Log Table with different types of errors as applicable for that ETL and the physical records will be written in corresponding rejection flat files.
- Log errors from quality analysis and metrics using tables (defined in section "Data Sources and Targets").
- If any record from any table (e.g. Order Line / Invoice Line/ Material Transaction/ Delivery Details) fails in validation then *the whole set of logical transactions* (for all tables, for a particular order line) will be rejected.
- Alert data owners of errors so that corrective actions can be taken.

Related Information

Similar Patterns: Reference the M-Broker pattern for error logging.
   Related Patterns:

1.   Source-to-target data movement using metadata-based loosely-coupled logic
2.   Error detection using logical transaction-based metadata
3.   Error handling and restart mechanism
4.   Data lineage for audit and regulatory compliance
5.   Dynamic authorization decorator for role-based querying of information implemented using business objects

Experience and Metrics: The use of logical transactions ensures that all related physical data is moved to the target without compromising the quality of data. When the source data is corrected, the overall quality of data improves.

Pattern Application: Error Handling and Restart Mechanism

The handling of unrecoverable logical errors using a restart mechanism based on the 1) logical transaction data analysis and process state, 2) the aborted data population, and the 3) reconciled population.

Conceptual

Strategy goal: Exception handling is determined while applying business rules against the metadata and the source data population.
   Example: The source data owner is given a chance to continue processing from the point of session failure rather than re-running from the beginning of the session.
   Problem: Improve the quality of data while minimizing operational delays and error handling resource costs. In particular, *only if an error is not recoverable* (i.e. due to functional failures for which automatic handling strategies cannot be devised) the error handling provides the user with the opportunity to correct the error without starting from scratch.
   Operational goals and analysis: Sequence and control the logical (i.e. functional) transactions by maintaining the state of sessions and their execution in tables with process control information. The solution principle here is that the process for detect-suspend-restart logic tracks the execution status of the logical transaction and provides the control mechanism.

Logical

Consequences: The ETL tools applied to process control minimizes the effort needed to minimize data inconsistency in the data warehouse. The overhead introduced by the management processes but, by recovering at the point of suspension, resources are also conserved because the entire process does not have to be re-executed.

Structure: There is a main load-and-restart mechanism.

Operational IT

IT goals and dynamics: DW Support Groups correct the error after looking into the audit history and then the appropriate module can be rerun.

Logical view: ETL Process Control is required to ensure the ETL processes are controlled in compliance with the required sequencing based on the semantics of the logical transaction. This utilizes a control table. ETL workflows manage dependencies between various logical ETL modules. Each logical module is called from the main workflow. If a particular step results in an abort, the process state is maintained and can be resumed after the data source owner has fixed the error and resubmitted the logical transaction. ETL monitoring tools provide operational monitoring supporting the recovery and restart for failed data loads.

Related Information

Known Uses: Other examples of the use of the pattern, taken from existing systems, include M-BROKER bus exceptions and audit files.

Similar Patterns: M-BROKER bus management and recovery from customer file errors.

Pattern Application: Data Lineage for Audit and Regulatory Compliance

Creation of record level logs for audit using operational metadata during loosely coupled data movement between all source and target systems within the enterprise.

Conceptual

Strategy goals: To get an accurate business status, an enterprise needs to consolidate data from multiple applications.

Example: For companies, a key concern is cost of updating information systems to comply with the *control and reporting requirements* (for example as needed for SOX). Systems which provide document management, access to financial data, or long-term storage of information must now provide auditing capabilities. In most cases this requires significant changes, or even complete replacement, of existing systems which were designed without the needed level of auditing details.

These include audits to demonstrate all source records are accounted for in the target, all the sub-transactions (perhaps completed in different source systems) that result in the business-level transaction, and also aggregation of audit reports.

Problem: Creation of audit records that trace the movement of data at the business level.

Operational goals and analysis: An audit trail mechanism is implemented using the ETL processes to log audit details for quality analysis and metrics using tables. The underlying principle for the audits is the *operational metadata* defined to be data captured during the execution of ETL functions. For example, the operational metadata keeps track of not only the number of records moved at each stage but also the logical transactions completed. This provides the traceability of logical data movement from source to target destinations. This is called *data lineage.*

Logical

Structure: The left-to-right arrows in the figure below shows the movement of data that is *captured in the operational metadata,* when following the best practice methodology and using the staging tables to consolidate and validate data from different sources:

- *Source to staging* moves full data initially, but only changed records subsequently. Transformations are applied at staging without impacting the performance at the source.
- *Staging* tables are where ETL transformations are first applied. These transformations are based on the metadata and business rules can also be applied at this point.
- *Staging to* the Operational Data Store consists of only *non-rejected* records. For updates and deletes, previous records are moved to history tables so there is an audit. A record of data transformations and operational metadata is maintained. All rejected records that do not pass field level validation are captured in error log tables with the reason for failure. (Eg. Failure to identify master record.)
- *ODS to DW or targets* – consists of ETL moving the data to its final destination.

- Finally the rejected records are logged and can be corrected and 're-started' (see the other discussions on error detection and restart patterns below) without having to re-apply all the previous transformations and staging.
- During the entire movement process data transformation statistics are written to the Audit table by calls in the Audit Routine as each ETL Load completes.

Operational IT

IT goals and dynamics: Use Cases - an Architect would like to monitor operational information, a Company would like audit reports at the business level.

Data and Integration view: The batched movement of data between the various sources and targets is controlled by processes. The implemented processes for the movement of logical transactions capture the following different data quality matrices for every ETL Process Run:

- Total number of records received from each source
- Total number of records passed validation
- Total number of records failed validation
- Total number of records rejected or in error for each source
- Total number of records loaded for each target
- Total number of records updated in each target
- Total number of records inserted in each target

This basic information is captured and now available for additional analysis at the business level – How many complete business level transactions did we have last month? What data sources contribute transaction data? What is the total number of records versus the complete logical records? And so on.

Related Information

Known Uses: Other examples of the use of the pattern, taken from existing systems include M-Broker bus exceptions and audit files.

Compliance view: The complete end-to-end logging of the movement of data though all the staging tables and the error and audit logs for each table involved provide data lineage related to the logical transactions. For example, one can now answer questions like how many sources provide order information. In addition there is a history of all the changes at the record level which provides a complete lineage of information needed for compliance to SOX, HIPA, etc.

OPERATIONAL SERVICE PATTERNS

Operational process patterns are well-articulated by ITIL V3 and more and more widely practiced by industry. The practice (now an ISO standard - ISO/IEC 20000) reflects industry experience in managing incidents and change within the installed IT infrastructure. At the heart of the ITIL processes is a shared representation of the configuration items and their association and attributes in the installed infrastructure. This is called the CMDB and is defined in ITIL as an image of the installed ICT infrastructure. ITIL operational processes – such as incident management, problem resolution, change and release management - perform more efficiently using the information about the installed system. The CMDB is also relevant to the other processes of the organization. For example the architecture process that determines enhancements by defining the impact of adding new services to existing services. This will be addressed at length, later.

INFRASTRUCTURE MONITORING PATTERNS

There is an increasing use of technologies to monitor complex IT Infrastructures. Examples include system utilization, network traffic monitoring, and application monitoring. In addition other pattern cases automate and provide increased reliability as follows.

Pattern Application: Database High Availability

Improving availability of customer-facing data accessed through portals, at the same time keeping the data most current, by redundancy employing dual data sources which are copied and configured in an active/passive manner.

Conceptual

Strategy context: Increases user confidence and loyalty when the services are always available.

Example: Customer accesses information from the Portal and the information changes frequently.

Problem: How to efficiently update a database that is being actively accessed.

Operational goals and analysis: Maintain two parallel databases where updates are preformed on the inactive database and then switched with the active database. While one copy is kept on-line the other copy is updated from the system of record in off-line mode. Once updated, the passive copy is swapped in and the active copy is swapped out, allowing the most up-to-date data to be exposed by the customer-facing application.

Consequences: Reduces the strain on the active database due to live accesses occurring while the data is being updated. Increases the possible delay in updated information becoming available through the Portal.

Structure: Figure 16.

Logical

Logical view: Figure 16. Implemented as scripts run by an agent.

Data and Integration view: Content pushed from the Application to the CMS. The CMS acts as a staging area before being pushed to the inactive database of Organization.com. After the information is written to the Organization.com database, the information is read only.

Security view: Users must be validated against the SSO.

Figure 16. Database High Availability - Business Process

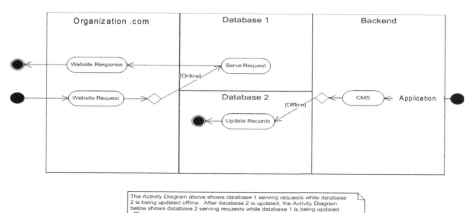

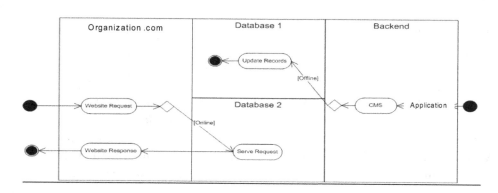

Operational IT

Deployment and Concurrency view: Two concurrent processes. Active database servers Organization.com. Inactive database receives updated information from the CMS and is updated by the Fulcrum indexing system.

Physical view: Application on DB, active and inactive database on .com servers.

Scalability and Performance view: Best used with high volume and time-consuming updates to a data source.

System Management view: The baseline data provided to disaster recovery backup group.

Related Information

Similar Patterns: Single Load Balancer[h].

Variant Patterns: Trickle-post.

Experience and Metrics: This pattern could leverage the two databases to provide fault tolerance. If the active database fails then the passive database can be switched online. This requires a sacrifice of up-to-date data for consistent data availability. The total time to sync the information is around 6 hours. Direct replication isn't done because the CMS acts as a staging step in order for business users to add hierarchy to product mappings and for indexing the information. See also Brasswell & Voegeli 2002.

INTERACTION-BASED SECURITY AND COMPLIANCE

A comprehensive Security Program includes internal controls tied to Interactions, information use, personnel and software roles and agents that are authorized to play those roles, physical and electronic operations and facilities. Security is most effective when it is an integral part of the EA management program and documentation methodology. To be effective, security must work at all physical and electronic aspects of the organization and, in addition, within all of the components. The important aspects of security are as follows:

1. *Information security governance:* An important role is identifying the Interactions that will come under governance and prioritization of those Interactions that are critical. Next all related policy is defined to meet requirements. For example, a good policy might be to start with all primary Interactions. An example of policy is to provide access to secure information only on a 'need

to know basis'. Another aspect is ensuring that security audits of the identified points take place.

2. *Operations security:* This starts with Role sets that are used in each Interaction. Where and how does the physical or electronic Interaction take place between the actual resource and the service? Who has access to the location or to the software or to the network? Are the resources mobile? For each item in this list we ensure:

    o   *Personnel resource security* – only the authorized resources have physical and electronic access based on policy. This also ensures all IT infrastructure and physical security.

    o   *Electronic information and data flow security* – only the authorized fields of the objects that are shared can be used by authorized roles for that object. This addresses security and privacy.

    o   *Systems administration and application development to ensure above.*

3. *Audit Interactions:* This is to directly show compliance.

The framework presented next summarizes a comprehensive approach to security that can be implemented between roles involved in any Interaction. (See Ramnath et al 2008, Xiao et al 2007). This can also be incrementally applied and simplified as appropriate.

Applying Goal Modeling and RED to Analysis of Security Architectures

At a high level the factors in security are 'who' the individual, 'what' the goals or tasks, 'how' the strategy, 'why' the purpose, 'where' the logical location, and 'when' or the absolute or relative time. All of these are dependent on the Interaction context or Roles and Responsibilities, Resources or Assets, and Membership of the Agent.

We begin this section by introducing some necessary terms and concepts. *Assets* are the entities to be protected. The *attacker* (a special type of agent) perpetrates the attack on the asset. There are *stakeholders* who have a vested interest in the asset and are affected if the attack is successful. Of these stakeholders, *defenders* are responsible for protecting the asset, while *performers* gain benefits from the use of the asset. *Observers* are stakeholders that do not use the asset, but will be affected by the attack, as well as impacted by the defense of the asset. A successful attack on an asset results in damage to the capabilities of the asset, a loss to stakeholders and a benefit to the attacker. We define *Risk* as the expected loss – i.e. the product of probability and loss. Finally, every attack has a cost to the attacker, as does every defense to the stakeholders. There is a *fixed cost* for defense – which is the cost of the infrastructure that needs to put in place so that defense is possible, regardless of whether the attack actually happens – as well as a *dynamic cost* – which is the cost of the response once an attack takes place. If the attack fails, there could be a loss to the attacker, on top of the cost.

Most physical spaces implement a layered security architecture characterized by multiple perimeters or layers of protection. For example, an airport might have a layer of sensors (such as cameras) along its perimeter, a drive-through check-point where identification is checked, restricted card-swipe-only entry areas, doors with mechanical locks and, finally, computing systems with userid-password based access controls. In our analysis, we place the asset within the innermost layer of security.

Security Goals

Next, we develop a set of relationships between the above defined terms as follows:

- The *Benefit* (B) of (the use of) an asset to a stakeholder is a function of the asset and the stakeholder. Thus, $B_{Stakeholder}$ = Benefit(Asset, Stakeholder). Performers gain the most benefit from an asset.
- The *damage* to an asset is a function of the attack and the asset. Thus $Damage_{Asset}$ = Damage(Attack, Asset). Different assets have different vulnerabilities, and hence different damages for the same attack.
- The *loss* to a stakeholder is a function of the damage (D) to the asset and the stakeholder himself: $L_{Stakeholder}$ = $Loss_{Stakeholder}$($Damage_{Asset}$, Stakeholder). In other words, the loss to a stakeholder is dependent on the stakeholder's perspective.
- The benefit (B) to the attacker (A) with respect to a single stakeholder is a function of the loss to that stakeholder, and the attacker. Thus: $B_{Attacker}$ = Benefit($Loss_{Stakeholder}$, Attacker). The benefit of an attacker with respect to multiple stakeholders is (at least simplistically) a summation of the benefits over all the stakeholders.
- The attacker will also have a cost (C) for the attack. In application the attack fails or is prevented there could also be a loss (L) to the attacker (such as an arrest).
- *Goals for the Adversary:* Let p = the probability of success of an attack. Then, the utility function for the attacker is: maximize ($p*Benefit_{Attacker}$ - $Cost_{Attack}$ – $(1-p)Loss_{Attacker}$). Thus, the attacker might seek to increase the probability of success, increase his benefit for the same amount of damage[i], reduce the cost of an attack, or reduce the loss in application of an unsuccessful attack. This utility function defines the goal for the attacker.

- *Goals for Stakeholders:* The stakeholder, on the other hand, seeks to maximize $(Benefit_{Asset} - p*Loss_{Stakeholder} - Cost_{Defense})$, thus, to reduce (a) the probability of a successful attack - p, and (b) the loss for the same amount of damage to the asset[j], and (c) the cost of the defense. This utility function defines the goal for the stakeholders. Note that the utility function has different coefficients (in i.e. benefits and costs) for the different stakeholders – attackers, performers and observers.[k]

RED Interactions Applied To Security

The adversary's attack may also be conceptualized as an Interaction with sub-Interactions at each layer of security, until the intended asset layer is reached. If the final Interaction (i.e. the attack) is successful, the asset is damaged, the stakeholders suffer losses, and the adversary achieves the intended benefit. Each sub-Interaction has a cost (in terms of effort and time), and the sum of these costs is the cost of the attack. However, if any of the sub-Interactions fail, the attack is unsuccessful, and the attacker suffers a loss. Figure 17 shows the attacker's Interactions and sub-Interactions.

Security activities are also RED Interactions – with clear Requirements, Execution and Delivery phases as follows:

- An attacker will typically "case the joint" in order to understand how it is being protected (Requirements), break through defenses and launch the attack (Execution) and, if successful, damage the asset (Delivery).
- A defender will respond to the attack by detecting (Requirements), resisting (Execution), successfully preventing or recovering (both Delivery steps).
- A performer will evaluate each layer of security (Requirements), do something

Figure 17. Attack Interaction and sub-Interactions

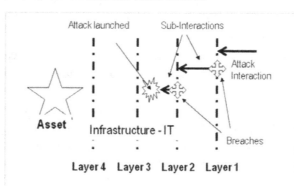

to pass the checkpoint - such as open a lock with a key (Execution) and pass through (Delivery).

In Figure 18 the asset may be considered to be at the origin. The dashed vertical lines show the layers of security. In this situation, we may plot the independent variables as follows[1].

- We show the Cost of the attack increasing with decreasing distance, since there is an incremental additional Interaction cost for each layer to be breached.
- Since a sub-Interaction must be completed at each layer, we show the Probability of an attacker penetrating to a particular layer as decreasing with decreasing distance from the asset. This probability curve is a step function, discretized by the Interaction. This intuitively matches the physical situation once a layer has been breached the attacker may freely penetrate to the layer next in line.
- For simplicity, we can consider the Loss (not shown on graph) to the attacker for an unsuccessful attack to be a constant.

Note that the Damage to the asset increases with decreasing distance – i.e. the closer to the asset the attack occurs (such as an explosion), the more the damage to. Essentially, as each sub-Interaction is successfully completed, the benefits of

Figure 18. Attack Interaction and sub-Interactions

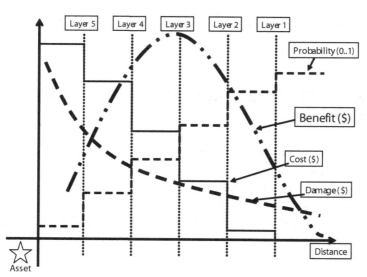

Delivery are higher.

CONCLUSION AND RESEARCH

Examples of pattern applications in this section illustrate several points. First, using patterns we can identify trends early. Redundant investments and opportunities for reuse through architecture standardization across the corporation can be identified based on frequency of occurrence. for example, as seen in the EKI cluster of mined patterns several programs are looking at providing role-based features. Another example is the need to deliver the 'last mile' of quality when moving data. The DW implementation using meta data can be used as a pattern in other bus-based architectures. Several projects are using bus-based architectures for data movement. These projects can apply successful concepts for monitoring, auditing, and error recovery using meta-data (as in DW patterns).

Another opportunity is to identify points of *weakness*. Many facades are being developed; this will result in custom implementations that will have to be later maintained. Are these facades well documented? As other projects rely on these services, what is the impact of change? Are change management procedures in place across projects? Pattern applications cases can also identify personnel *skill sets* and best practice training needed for more rapid/effective implementations. When personnel are introduced to projects, architecture-based best practice training will ensure that they are better equipped to create quality software. Identify both application and infrastructure patterns training so that individuals have a holistic perspective on the solution.

Finally an important area of research is to use patterns for change impact analysis. A starting point further research here is Aman et al 2008 and Schmidt et al. 2000.

TASKS RELATED TO BACKGROUND / SECONDARY RESEARCH

1. What patterns underlie your solution roadmap?
2. What best practices apply?
3. What academic research papers over the last few years contribute most to your understanding? Why?
4. What framework contributions could be the one of the outcomes of your project? Why?

THINGS TO THINK ABOUT

1. Discuss the relationships between an architecture pattern, model driven architecture and the CMDB.

2. Give examples of the Triage pattern application at the strategy dimension, at the business dimension, at the operational dimension and at the IT dimension.

3. A small number of patterns underlie Complex Systems, but what are the challenges in assembly? How can SOA be used to address this?

4. What does it mean to compose patterns? Support your answer by illustrating how the patterns might apply for a Lean operations.

5. What does it mean to compose services? How can two or more patterns be assembled and how would the architecture options increase? Hint - explore service orchestration. Give an example.

6. One company's network administration policies state that no connections may be initiated from a machine in the DMZ to a machine behind the DMZ on the corporate network (the reverse is allowed - that is, a machine in the corporate network can initiate the connection.) If an order placed in Oracle IStore (in the DMZ) needs to initiate an order-fulfillment Interaction in the ERP system (Oracle e-Business Suite, on the corporate network), how may we solve this problem and implement the policy?[m]

REFERENCES

Adams, J., Koushik, S., Vasudeva, G., & Galambos, G. (2001). *Patterns for E-Business*. MC Press.

Alexander, C. (1979). *The Timeless Way of Building*. Oxford Oxfordshire: Oxford University Press.

Alur, D., Crupi, J., & Malks, D. (2003). *Domain Store*. Retrieved August 18, 2006, from http://www.corej2eepatterns.com/Patterns2ndEd/DomainStore.htm.

Alur, D., Crupi, J., & Malks, D. (2003). *Data Access Object*. Retrieved August 18, 2006, from http://www.corej2eepatterns.com/Patterns2ndEd/DataAccessObject.htm.

Armour, F. J., & Kaisler, S. H. (2001 November/December). Enterprise Architecture: Agile Transition and Implementation. *IT Pro, 3*(6), 30-37.

Bontempo, C., & Zageglow, G. (September 1998). The IBM Data Warehouse Architecture. *Communications of the ACM, 41*(9).

Braswell, B., & Voegeli, R. (2002). *Database High Availability: Single Load Balancer, Section 2.3.3.* Retrieved August 18, 2006, from http://www.redbooks.ibm.com/redbooks/SG246822.html

Dirgahayu, T., Quartel, D., & Sinderen M.v. (2008). Designing Interaction Behaviour in Service-Oriented Enterprise Application Integration. In *Proceedings of the 2008 ACM Symposium on Applied Computing* (pp. 1048-1054), Fortaleza, Ceara, Brazil: ACM.

Fowler, M. (2003). *Patterns of Enterprise Application Architecture.* Boston: Addison-Wesley.

Fowler, M. (2005). *Patterns in Enterprise Software.* Retrieved August 18, 2006, from http://www.martinfowler.com/articles/enterprisePatterns.html

Fundamental Information Aggregation Concepts. (2006). Retrieved August 18, 2006, from http://www-128.ibm.com/developerworks/patterns/bi/concepts.html

Gamma, E., Helm, R., Johnson R., & Vlissides, J. (1995). *Design Patterns, Elements of Reuseable Object Oriented Software.* New York, NY: Addison Wesley.

Gartner Report. (2005). *Enterprise Architecture Patterns: Combinations That Repeat.*

Hohpe, G. & Woolf, B. (2003). *Message Channel.* Retrieved August 18, 2006, from http://www.enterpriseintegrationpatterns.com/MessageChannel.html

Hohpe, G., & Woolf, B. (2003). *Messaging.* Retrieved August 18, 2006, from http://www.enterpriseintegrationpatterns.com/Messaging.html

ITIL. (n.d.). Retrieved November 23, 2008, from http://www.itil.co.uk/

Kumar A., Raghavan P., Ramanathan J., & Ramnath R. (2008 December). Enterprise Interaction Ontology for Change Impact Analysis of Complex Systems. To appear in *Proceedings of the 2008 IEEE Asia-Pacific Services Computing Conference*, Yilan, Taiwan: IEEE Computer Society.

Keen, M., Adinolfi, O., Hemmings, S., Humphreys, A., Kanthi, H., & Nottingham, A. (2005). *Patterns: SOA with an Enterprise Service Bus in WebSphere Application Server V6.* IBM Redbooks.

Lambe, P. (2007). *Organising Knowledge: Taxonomies, Knowledge and Organisational Effectiveness* (Chandos Knowledge Management) Publisher: Chandos Publishing (Oxford) Ltd. English. # ISBN-10: 1843342278. # ISBN-13: 978-1843342274.

Manouvrier, B. & Ménard, L. (2008). *Application Integration: EAI B2B BPM and SOA*. John Wiley & Sons.

OpenAjax Alliance. (n.d.). Retrieved November 23, 2008, from http://www.openajax.org/

Powell, A. (2004). *Eclipse Modeling Framework*. Retrieved August 18, 2006, from http://www-128.ibm.com/developerworks/opensource/library/os-ecemf1/

Martin P., & Tate K. (1997). *The Project Manager Memory Jogger*. Goal/QPC.

Ramnath R., Gupta V., & Ramanathan J. (2008 August). RED-Transaction and Goal-Model Based Analysis of Layered Security of Physical Spaces. In *Proceedings of the 32nd Annual IEEE International Computer Software and Applications Conference (*pp. 679-685),Turku, Finland: IEEE Computer Society.

Schmidt, D. & Frank B. (2000). *Pattern-Oriented Software Architecture*. New York: J. Wiley & Sons.

Single Sign-On. (2006). Retrieved August 18, 2006, from http://www-128.ibm.com/developerworks/patterns/map-access.html.

Select a Business/Integration/Composite Pattern, or a Custom Design. (2006). Retrieved August 18, 2006, from http://www-128.ibm.com/developerworks/patterns/select-pattern.html

Software Product Line. (December 2008). www.sei.cmu.edu/productlines/adopting_spl.html. Accessed 12/21/2008.

Sommerlad, P. (2003). *Reverse Proxy*. Retrieved August 18, 2006, from http://www.modsecurity.org/archive/ReverseProxy-book-1.pdf

Single Sign-On (n.d.). Retrieved November 23, 2008, from http://www-128.ibm.com/developerworks/patterns/map-access.html

User Management Facade: Web Single Sign-On. (2004). Retrieved August 18, 2006, from http://www-128.ibm.com/developerworks/patterns/portal/access-sso-runtime.html

Web Single Sign-On (n.d.). Retrieved November 23, 2008, from http://www-128.ibm.com/developerworks/patterns/portal/access-sso-runtime.html

Williams, L. G., & Smith, C. U. (2002 July). PASA: a method for the performance assessment of software architectures. In *Proceedings of the 3rd International Workshop on Software and Performance* (pp. 179-189), Rome, Italy: ACM.

Xiao, K., Chen, N., Ren, S., Kwiat, K., Shen, L., Sun, X., et. al. (2007 May). A Workflow-based Non-intrusive Approach for Enhancing the Survivability of Critical Infrastructures in Cyber Environment. In *Proceedings of the 3rd International Workshop on Software Engineering for Secure Systems* (pp. 4), Washington DC: IEEE Computer Society.

ENDNOTES

[a]   A KPI, or Key Performance Indicator, is simply a metric that can be used to gauge the performance of an organization. There are standard KPI for common industrial activities.

[b]   Such as SAPs Netweaver[TM] etc.

[c]   Supply chain reference – Request - <Plan – Source – Make – Deliver>.

[d]   Need to make the distinction between secondary and sub Interaction .

[e]   The Health Insurance Portability and Accountability Act (HIPAA) was enacted by the U.S. Congress in 1996. Title I of HIPAA protects health insurance coverage for workers and their families when they change or lose their jobs. Title II of HIPAA, known as the Administrative Simplification (AS) provisions, requires the establishment of national standards for electronic health care transactions and national identifiers for providers, health insurance plans, and employers. The Administration Simplification provisions also address the security and privacy of health data. The standards are meant to improve the efficiency and effectiveness of the nation's health care system by encouraging the widespread use of electronic data interchange in the US health care system. (wikipedia).

[f]   http://en.wikipedia.org/wiki/Data_warehouse#Data_warehouse_architecture.

[g]   A rigorous introduction to patterns of enterprise integration can be found in Hohpe, Gregor et.al. *Enterprise Integration Patterns.* Boston: Addison-Wesley, 2004, which details many primitive patterns that can be used as building blocks for constructing an integration strategy. Although a message broker is only one of those primitive patterns, it is so commonly used as a starting point for more complex solutions that it deserves special attention.

[h]   Reference: http://www.redbooks.ibm.com/redbooks/SG246822.html.

[i]   For example, through propaganda.

[j]   For example, the defender might replicate the asset, or even engage in "spin" to mitigate the perception of loss.

[k]   In these characterizations the following should be noted:

[1] Note that the values plotted for the variables above are *completely* arbitrary. The point of this exercise is only to showcase a methodology. We describe later an approach for estimating these values.

[m] Move the Oracle IStore inside the DMZ and place a reverse proxy server from Apache, CISCO, etc. outside the DMZ. Then the connection between the IStore and ERP is totally behind the DMZ. Users connect through the reverse proxy which passes traffic into the IStore front end. All communication between IStore and the ERP is safely behind the firewall. Reverse proxy servers are becoming more mature and are easier to secure than trying to lock down web and application servers in the DMZ. They are lighter weight and it gives a level of indirection that shields the entire application.

[1] Loss and benefit have multiple dimensions – monetary loss, loss in privacy, loss in convenience and so on.

[2] Benefit, Loss and Cost are in the "eye of the stakeholder", i.e. they are different for each of the defenders and observers. This difference explains a common problem in security architectures – which is a differential motivation across the stakeholders to protect the asset.

[3] Benefit can be negative (i.e. a loss), such as when extensive injury to non-combatants causes a backlash against the attackers.

Section II
Co–Engineering Examples

Chapter V
Strategic Improvement of Non–Routine Services[a]

ABSTRACT

How can IT strategic planning contribute to the organization's future state?

- *Plan:* How can an IT strategic planning effort yield a business-oriented prioritized service portfolio with business benefits?
- *Act:* How is the plan deployed and executed? How does the handling of non-routine Requests provide a strategic advantage? How can hierarchical organizations address the challenge of increasingly non-routine responses that demand networked solutions?
- *Monitor:* What were the measured results?
- *Analyze:* What strategic advantages did the organization achieve towards its mission?

What is the role of EA governance?

- How was the Co-engineering method applied leading to the citizen-aligned IT strategic plan?
- How was the triage-based assignment of agents (across organizations, applications, and processes) enable more dynamic adaptation to non-routine Requests and a networking of organizations?

Figure 1. Strategy Planning and Execution

At a glance:
How can IT strategic planning contribute to the organization's future state?

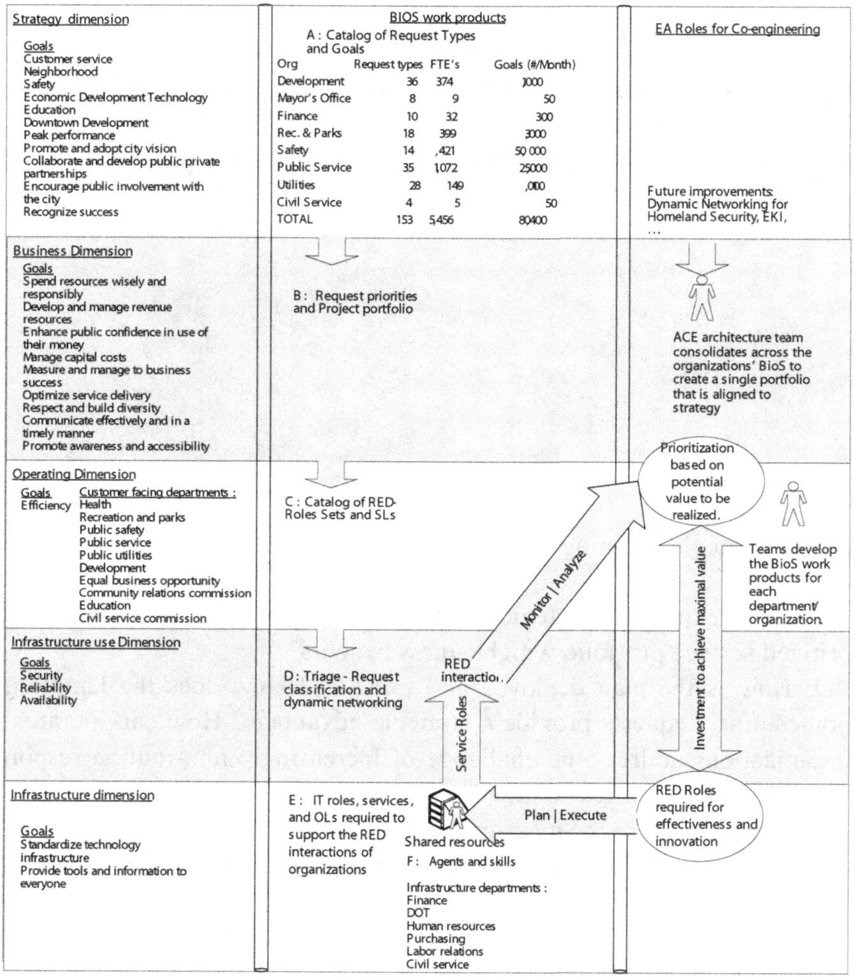

Strategy dimension	BIOS work products	EA Roles for Co-engineering

Strategy dimension

Goals
Customer service
Neighborhood
Safety
Economic Development Technology
Education
Downtown Development
Peak performance
Promote and adopt city vision
Collaborate and develop public private partnerships
Encourage public involvement with the city
Recognize success

BIOS work products
A : Catalog of Request Types and Goals

Org	Request types	FTE's	Goals (#/Month)
Development	36	374	)000
Mayor's Office	8	9	50
Finance	10	32	300
Rec. & Parks	18	399	3000
Safety	14	,421	50 000
Public Service	35	1,072	25000
Utilities	28	149	,000
Civil Service	4	5	50
TOTAL	153	5,456	80400

EA Roles for Co-engineering

Future improvements:
Dynamic Networking for Homeland Security, EKI, ...

Business Dimension

Goals
Spend resources wisely and responsibly
Develop and manage revenue resources
Enhance public confidence in use of their money
Manage capital costs
Measure and manage to business success
Optimize service delivery
Respect and build diversity
Communicate effectively and in a timely manner
Promote awareness and accessibility

B : Request priorities and Project portfolio

ACE architecture team consolidates across the organizations' BioS to create a single portfolio that is aligned to strategy

Operating Dimension

Goals
Efficiency

Customer facing departments :
Health
Recreation and parks
Public safety
Public service
Public utilities
Development
Equal business opportunity
Community relations commission
Education
Civil service commission

C : Catalog of RED-Roles Sets and SLs

Monitor | Analyze

Prioritization based on potential value to be realized.

Teams develop the BioS work products for each department/ organization.

Infrastructure use Dimension

Goals
Security
Reliability
Availability

D : Triage - Request classification and dynamic networking

RED interaction.

Service Roles

Investment to achieve maximal value

Infrastructure dimension

Goals
Standardize technology infrastructure
Provide tools and information to everyone

E : IT roles, services, and OLs required to support the RED interactions of organizations

Shared resources

F : Agents and skills

Infrastructure departments :
Finance
DOT
Human resources
Purchasing
Labor relations
Civil service

Plan | Execute

RED Roles required for effectiveness and innovation

Historically, strategic planning for the CIO has meant discerning the business's strategy and then trying to achieve it. Today ... the CIO's role cannot be reactive... The CIO has the capability to see where the basis for competition will be. That is not to say that CIOs should write their IT strategy independently and then attempt to force the business strategy to match it. Rather, the point is that both the business plan and the IT plan should be written collaboratively by the entire executive team, including the CIO.[b]

In the following sub-sections we cover how the ACE framework advances these ideas by a strategic planning and execution process. That is, how do we develop a strategic plan that defines and achieves a future state that can be fundamentally enabled by IT?

The illustrative Strategic Planning and Co-engineering of BioS is based on a major US City. The insights here are, at the same time, applicable to all types of private and public organizations that provide services.

THE BUSINESS CHALLENGE

Organizations like the City are pressured to be more and more service oriented with fewer resources. The City has an expanding service area, fluctuating revenue, and a growing population that combine to place stress on existing response systems. The Mayor has instituted a "covenant" that includes a guiding principle that technology will be a key tool to achieve city objectives and improving service responses. To this end, the City consolidated its IT operations under Department of Technology (DoT) and began implementing a series of IT improvements. Looking to the future, the DoT wished to develop a plan more strategically aligned to the City departments - that is DoT's customer.

IT-ENABLED STRATEGIC PLANNING AND EXECUTION

In this section we will illustrate the Co-engineering cycle starting with the Plan and Act step leading to the Monitor and Analyze steps in the next section.

Plan

Different City departments and teams submitted many requests to the CARs (customer account representatives that interfaced between DoT and the other organizations). The reduction of response time or the need for a new IT service was very often identified. Given the budget constraints, however, it was impossible for DoT to meet all the requirements. To ensure the projects undertaken were of maximum impact both to the external customers in the environment and to the business. We applied the Co-engineering rules to consolidate and prioritize.

Questionnaire for Gathering Organization 'Biographies' or BioS: The Since the basic goal of an IT strategic plan is to develop a precise roadmap that takes the City from as-is to to-be with a prioritized set of projects, we begin with consolidating individual departmental BioS. This begins with a questionnaire illustrated in Figure 2 that collects the information to assemble the ACE structure and work products A-F introduced earlier. We call this the BioS questionnaire. The questionnaire details are in the Appendix. The information solicited includes Request type, RED Interaction, Role Set, and desired goals. Missing Roles are also identified. The resulting work products intuitively form the 'biography' of each organization consolidated to prioritize improvements across all departments. The resulting BioS information is a precise starting representation of the overall organization and its nested organizations.

ACE Structure and Work Products: The resulting overall ACE structure is illustrated in Figure 1. The leftmost column of Figure 1 provides an overview of the high-level goals captured. The next column also identifies the work products developed, starting with the Request Types and the target goals at the highest level. They are also used in day-to-day operations. That is planning and execution use the same work products.

Application of Co-engineering principles: The sample BioS entries Figure 2 (columns two and three) illustrate how the service Requests were prioritized. Starting with the questionnaire (i.e. a spreadsheet) entries that contribute to A-F work products are created. The process requires the application of principles. For example, employing the first two Co-engineering principles, the ACE architecture team used the aggregated value of a Request type to relate it to its strategic competitive and business yield goals.

Figure 2. Example relating the business, information use, operations, and strategy perspectives of Request Types. Missing software in infrastructure is also identified.

Strategy	Business	Operation		Triage	Infrastructure use			
Request type and goal	Priority and Value to business	Request volume per month	FTE	Assigned to	Require- ments	Execu- tion	Delivery	Missing Roles
Routine: Pay- ment status > satisfaction	Medium	50	1	Accounts payable	Clerk checks		Posted status info	On-line ac- cess to status Doc manag'mt.
Non Routine: Obtain/expand water service Hydrant usage > safety	Very high	700	6	Sales office	Staff works from platt drawings supplied by developer			Automatic- permits Request capture And doc manag'mt.

The next Co-engineering principle 3 allowed us to relate missing Roles to operational performance. That is, if a complete Role Set was not available or was performing poorly, the interaction's yield will be low. As we shall see next by ordering the missing Roles according to potential maximum impact to overall performance gives us the project portfolio for investments. The other important aspect from the strategic planning perspective was to look at the Roles and agents and their availability and capability to fill roles and meet SL performance objectives. Note a Request type with high value, high volume and high benefits will show a greater return on investment. Thus improvements for the non-routine service - improve/expand water service - has a higher priority because of the request volume and the number of FTEs whose productivity will be impacted. At the same time investments can be justified for lower volume Requests if the same Role requirements are shared with several other Request types, some of which have high value.

Thus, from a *strategic goals* perspective, the primary Request types and their RED interactions were prioritized for improvement as follows:

1. High competitive value to the business
2. High Request volume
3. Lower than desired throughput
4. High queue times
5. Use of shared services with other REDs
6. Identify the possible sub-interactions of the high-priority interactions and assign these a higher priority

From a *business goals* perspective, the rules for identifying maximum return on investment were applied as follows:

- List all the missing Roles and related projects and prioritize by maximum impact to business value to one or more interactions. This gives us the maximum service level impact through the investment in operating level Role improvements and the maximum potential business value.

ACT

The above planning process lead to the prioritization of 1) 311 - a one-stop approach to handling all incoming requests into the City, 2) Human Resource Management System, and 3) Geographical Information System (GIS) services. The underlying insights achieved during analysis are interesting and discussed next.

Analysis and Prioritization: A 311 system is a central, one-stop-shop for requesting non-emergency City services (such as bulk trash pickup), reporting non-emergency information (such as potholes, water leaks, and dead animals) and receiving information – such as open routes to Fourth of July fireworks displays. In the eGovernment literature 311-like systems are also expected to play a role within public safety, as follows:

- By alleviating loads on the emergency response system (i.e. 9-1-1) through offloading non-emergency calls.
- By enabling advancing community policing, by serving as a location-based database for reporting and identifying incident hotspots, and thereby facilitating the targeting of responses.
- By being available as an established, accepted, and standardized resource for information dissemination to the public.

Thus, 311 is an application of the Triaging pattern.

Many departments identified the need for 311 since they believed that high-value non-routine Requests needed IT support in many different ways and with different priorities. Some of the ways in which they identified the missing Roles are shown below:

- Case management
- Status reporting to customer
- Order coordination and management with other departments
- Project management
- Document management
- Consolidation of call-centers

As shown the needed 311 Role was given a variety of different 'names'. Once clarified and 'taken in sum' these requirements lead to the highest prioritization of the 311 in the strategic planning effort and resulted in project investment.

At the start of the engagement, there was discussion about implementing a 'single interface' to the City; however the justification for this – the benefits and the costs - were not clear. The RED interaction analysis gave a precise justification in terms of *value to the business* and through identifying across departments where all the positive value would be of a shared service for non-routine Requests.

Underlying IT Requirements: The real underlying requirement was to provide a way to *triage* the incoming requests and manage the non-routine Interactions. These requests were falling outside the scope of their installed enterprise order management systems and help desks. While these systems were handling *routine* Requests and requirements well, they were insufficient for the *non-routine* types.

In this application, examples of such non-routine Requests include neighborhood development, events like Independence Day, or economic development tasks. What these Requests had in common was the considerable coordination effort is expended to navigate across the 'silo' organizations and enterprise systems in order to respond (Teisman, G. & Klijn 2002).

Strategic Requirements for Networking: Non-routine Requests demand *networked* solutions and require managers to weave strong hierarchies into effective networks. While we know that the innovative delivery of non-routine services is the future, it is also true that managers in government do not have a tradition of dynamic on-demand cross-silo collaboration, and have not developed the necessary competencies, simply because the need for such activity has not existed previously during their professional lifetimes.

In carrying out the 311 project there were a series of challenges to be addressed. For example, in deploying the 311 system, the presence of department boundaries makes an integrated service response difficult. Of the 17 City departments that service Requests, it is estimated that about 30% of the Requests are of a complex, non-routine nature, often requiring interactions with up to three other departments. Currently, interdepartmental response processes are all handled in an ad-hoc fashion with manual procedures (like phone calls) and hand-offs (via email). In these instances, the absence of an efficient means of coordinating across boundaries results in slow and sometimes incomplete responses to citizens. What is needed is a strategic catalyst and an enterprise architecture foundation on which to build network capability.

Finally, an external catalyst for 311 is crises-management planning since all levels are being required to develop crisis management plans and capabilities and as they do so they are beginning to at least talk about the networks required. This collaboration has momentum since cities are receiving federal and state funds to establish networks[c].

Strategic Actions: The City acted on the strategic requirement by implementing a one-stop approach to the placement of orders for city services. The 311 Project entailed centralizing the city's entire call center structure into one common call center that can be contacted through the use of one number (311). This centralized call center utilizes a common supporting type of software which is the repository for Requests for city services as well as the performance management of those Requested services. The City decided to develop its own supporting software and manage this project with its internal resources.

Monitoring and Analyze

The 311 software logs incoming requests, assignments to different departments, and maintains status. Over time it has become a very rich source of citizen and stakeholder information. This data was analyzed approximately two years after the initial installation, as discussed next.

The 311 system analysis and evaluation project had two tasks 1) to evaluate the system as-is and 2) to evaluate the impact of 311 on crises-management at the City of . Part of the funding for the 311 Project was obtained from the Department of Justice via a grant. As a requirement of the Federal grant, an impact evaluation on crises-management also had to be conducted. The criteria for impact assessment were as follows.

Assessment Criteria for Direct Impact: Three areas of direct 311 impact on crises management were identified using COPS03-1[d] as a guide. These are listed below, in order of importance:

- Workload reduction of public-safety-related departments and divisions: The impact of 311 in enabling departments and divisions in the first line of support with respect to safety (Department of Public Safety, Department of Health) to improve their performance. This is the expected result of improved through-put.
- Information clearing-house: The ability for 311 to serve as an information clearing-house, i.e. as a unified contact and information dissemination point to assist in the management of crises. This is the expected result of information sharing.
- Community Policing: The ability of 311 to provide data to pinpoint trends (such as trends in crime, or population demographics), detection of unanticipated events (such as the prototypical Baltimore example of the detection of a West Nile virus outbreak from increasing reports of bird deaths), and the ability to identify correlations among trends (such as the correlation of vacant homes to crime) is important in order to anticipate crises. This is the expected result of traceability.

Assessment Criteria for Future Impact: In addition to evaluating the direct impact of 311, we believed that a very important benefit of 311 would be as an integrative capability for creating effective informal networks within the City. We decided to investigate this integrative capability through the specific lens of emergency and crisis management. Essentially, we sought to evaluate whether and how a 311 system, its stakeholders, and its supporting services architecture would serve as a catalyst for creating network competencies for delivering critical, non-routine services. As described non-routine response requires emergent improvisation by dynamically created 'adhocracies' (Mendonca 2007) Thus, we were looking for how 311 may catalyze competencies such as:

- Activation: i.e. enlisting participation in networks.
- Framing: Influencing the operating rules, prevailing values, and norms while altering the
- Perceptions of the participants, in response to emergent phenomena.
- Mobilizing: Developing a view of the strategic whole and an ability to develop and achieve a set of common objectives based on this whole. And,
- Synthesizing: Creating the environment for interaction among network participants by blending perceptions (Agranoff & McGuire 2001). Instead of legal authority as the factor that binds actors, we wished to see if managers now rely on trust when managing across silos.

Tool used: Both structured interviews and collected data were used in our evaluation. We used information collected by 311 in terms of addresses mapped to GIS coordinates for each Request. We correlated these records with either existing data available through Census Tract or publicly available demographic data indexed by zip code.

The interviews consisted of questions asked in a setting intended to encourage discussion rather than precise answers. Certain questions were repeated in order to elicit a broader range of answers.

All departments were asked the following questions:

- *Have you heard of the City's tat 311 system? In a few words, could you describe it to us?*
- *What is your evaluation of 311?*
- *How are your Dept.'s processes and roles integrated with 311?*
- *Give examples of how 311 data has benefited or could have benefited your organization?*
- *What additional features should exist or what additional data can be collected in 311 to assist in the execution and improvement of your processes?*
- *What change management or cultural aspects have needed addressing because of 311?*
- *How has 311 been integrated into your department's systems, especially its work-order system?*
- *How have you incorporated 311 into your Crisis Management and Disaster Recovery plans?*
- *What other benefits do you see from 311?*

- *What integration issues do you see with 311 and existing systems in your organization?*
- *Has your knowledge about the operations and capabilities of other departments increased over the past year? In what manner?*
- *In what manner, other than 311, does your Dept. get citizen Requests for service? How many such Requests do you get?*

The Department of Public Safety was asked the following specific questions:

- *Has there been a reduction in 911 overtime or budget during this past year?*
- *Has there been an increased ability for 911 operators to take on additional calls because there are less non-emergency calls?*

The Departments interviewed were Public Safety, Health, Public Service, Public Utilities, Community Relations, Recreation and Parks, and Department of Development. We summarize below the direct, indirect, and potential impact analysis results.

Evaluation of Direct Impact: Overall the evaluation concluded that the City of has established a successful 311 program, and that the 311 call-center is now an established asset of the City. The 311 system has successfully transitioned from a technology project in the DoT to a service-delivery asset managed by the business – specifically the Department of Public Service (DPS).

Evaluation of Indirect Impact: The City has begun to make progress in integrating 311 more deeply into the City's day-to-day business processes, and making it a key source of data in measuring and managing the City's performance in service delivery to its citizens. In particular, DPS and DoT are working towards:

1. Safety related cost and workload reduction: Leveraging 311 to reduce costs and personnel workloads in City departments that have a direct responsibility for public safety: Residents are being encouraged to route non-emergency calls to 311. Additional service Request types have been added to *suitably characterize* these calls within 311, so they may be tracked appropriately.
2. Information clearing house: 311 is being utilized as clearing-house for resident-relevant information. Processes have been established to be able to rapidly update the 311 knowledge-base and also to quickly get new information to 311 operators at short notice.
3. Maintaining high-level support for 311: Continuing to inform the Mayor and key stakeholders of the City (such as City Council) of new 311 opportunities

and ensuring sufficient DoT representation in all strategic and any City-wide or cross-Departmental operational planning and execution.

4. Raising awareness among users and stakeholders: Marketing it both with residents and internally within the City. The goal is to make sure 311 stays front and center of stakeholders' consciousness, and being able to confirm 311 penetration by incorporating systematic feedback mechanisms into the awareness raising process.

5. Integrating 311 into internal departmental business processes: The work-order systems used by departments and divisions are being integrated with 311. A range of integration architectures must be designed to deal with the different paradigms by which work is allocated in different departments. A next step will be to integrate 311 data into the performance reporting systems within each department.

6. Extending the capabilities of 311: The capabilities within the technical and organizational architecture of 311 need to be extended to deal with special needs – in particular needs of crises management: This is being done by extending the capabilities of 311 (for example, by moving to a 24x7 operation) and by adding the necessary variation points within the 311 processes and competencies and its organizational architecture to (a) deal with areas of citizen concern – such as health and safety – where specialized expertise needs to be made available and (b) develop flexibility and extensibility in the software, as well as the personnel, needed to handle the ad-hoc information intake and dissemination that will be the requirement during a crisis.

7. Integrating it with Crisis-Management Planning: Once (6) has been addressed, DoT and DPS plan to actively promote the use of 311 in crisis-management – through incorporation into the Citywide crises-management, business continuity and disaster-recovery plans.

8. Phase-out of other access to City services: As 311 became established, the diverse call-centers within the City have been merged into 311 and eliminated. Listings of several direct-access numbers from Government section of the telephone directory (the Blue Pages) have been removed and replaced by 311. The phasing-out of additional direct lines is in the planning stages.

9. Building a data warehouse: The City plans to create a data warehouse with 311 data integrated with data from other call centers. This data warehouse is an essential enabler for data-driven community policing initiatives.

10. E-Gov: In the recent E-Government initiative, 311 has been identified as a foundational component. The E-Government initiative has been prioritized by citizen-facing requirements, which will mean that 311 will become the point of support and assistance for the electronic services delivered.

More generally speaking, 311 has had a positive impact and has left a positive impression. All the personnel we interviewed were aware of it and encouraging with respect to its continued and expanded use. For example, the Department of Health expressed interest in using 311's after-hours capability to extend availability of services. 311 has helped them understand operations of other departments in cross-over areas (such as rodent control between Health and Public Service, and in cross-departmental business continuity discussions). Interviewees have also stated that 311 has helped to systematize internal processes (mainly Public Service).

Issues highlighted with 311 were generally concrete and backed by considered and thoughtful opinion. For example, Health had (a) not proceeded to transfer their after-hours call center to 311 because it was not currently available 24x7 and (b) had not transferred its normal call center operations to 311 either, because of concerns that regular 311 operators would not be able to disseminate health-related information because of their lack of medical expertise. Certain departments are still using their separate lines (such as Health and Utilities). A 311 call is transferred to these lines, but they are still active, and are directly called by service Requestors.

Assessment of 311

The general impression of 311 is good. 311 is seen overall as a success, and is now an established asset of the City. However, in order for it to successfully progress much beyond its non-emergency call center focus to become an integral part of City crises-management processes and planning, much remains to be done in the next continuous improvement cycle.

New IT Service Requirements: As mentioned above, the future impact of 311 was identified through structured interviews and the discussions generated during the sessions. The new requirements and insights gathered were as follows:

- Capability of 311 and its service architecture of being used in an ad-hoc manner: There is currently no ad-hoc capability in 311, such as support for online collaboration, and for emergent processes. Thus, new information to be disseminated is typically supplied through email to the call center coordinator to be broadcast to all call center operators.
- Use and support of 311 for continuous improvement in Departmental processes, including those implemented within the 311 system. Use of 311 metrics in continuous improvement: We were unable to discover what departmental processes existed for continuous improvement. However, 311 metrics were extensively used for continuous improvement in certain departments (Public Service and Public Utilities), but not yet in others (Health).

- Change in support of City value systems for increased inter-departmental collaboration as a result of 311: All the interviewed departments that already collaborated prior to 311 and stated that they continued to do so. Few departments reported that this had changed at a department leadership level due to 311. However, knowledge may be spreading at the operational levels within the City. For example, Department of Public Utilities reported that staff's knowledge of other departments had increased due to 311.
- Changes in relationships and linkages across departments attributable to 311: Departments that collaborated prior to 311 (such as Health, Safety and Public Service) reported a better understanding of each others' processes and constraints after 311.
- Increased internal collaboration within departments due to 311: This was reported by the Department of Public Service only.
- Changes in City and departmental operational plans after 311: The Department of Public Service was the only department reporting changes in such plans after 311.
- Use of increased visibility of intra- and interdepartmental processes for exposing and resolving accountability and coordination issues within City Government: The Department of Public Services reported increased accountability due to visibility in the assignment of City personnel to service Requests.
- An increased ability to re-purpose resources, such as call-handlers and responders – for example, 911 operators switching to 311, and City staff being made available for activities associated with emergency response: There was discussion around this topic, but no concrete action has been reported.
- Enablement of more appropriately tailored responses to crises due to 311: We were unable to evaluate this, although it was anecdotally claimed that 311 was used to tailor a response to ice storms last year.

Future Actions: These are geared toward the continual improvement of the networking capability:

- Maintain high-level support for 311: Continue to remind the Mayor and key stakeholders of the City (such as City Council) of 311. Ensure sufficient DoT representation in all strategic and any City-wide or cross-Departmental operational planning and execution.[e]
- Raise awareness: Actively continue to market it both with citizens and showcase it internally within the City, to make sure it stays front and center of stakeholders' consciousness. Note that while marketing and publicity campaigns to date have managed to a lot with very little, a big failing is that they do not appear to have incorporated systematic feedback mechanisms into the process.

- Integrate 311 into the internal processes of City Departments and Divisions: Integrate 311 into internal departmental work-order systems. Note that a range of integration architectures must be designed to deal with the mismatches in paradigms of the 311 system and the work-order system. Integrate 311 data into the performance reporting systems within each department.
- Develop the necessary capabilities within the 311 technical architecture, variation points within the 311 processes, and competencies within organizational architecture to deal with the specialized areas of citizen concern – such as health, safety and neighborhood services. Develop the flexibility and extensibility needed to handle ad-hoc information intake and dissemination into 311. Establish a Disaster Recovery Plan for 311.
- Integration with Crisis-Management Planning: Once (•) has been addressed, actively look to promote the use of 311 in crisis-management, by incorporation into the City-wide crises-management, business continuity, and disaster-recovery plans.
- Data warehouse: Create a data warehouse with 311 data integrated with data from other call centers. This data warehouse is an essential enabler for data-driven community policing analysis and initiatives.

eGov and Enterprise Knowledge Infrastructure: While crises-management gives the context to building network capability, a 311 system and its associated organizations, processes and IT components serves as an adaptive foundation for capability development in several additional areas. The trends of end-to-end and circumstance-based services now impact public organizations and their eGov initiatives. 311 provide a source of time-variant intelligence based on the non-routine Requests. This provides the source of knowledge for the following types of new services:

- Ability to mine 311 for trend information (like senior citizen health or children's health) and push it to specialized portal communities
- Ability to apply more intelligent triage rules to route calls to operators with special capabilities – such as operators that speak Spanish, are medically trained, understand utility bills and so on.
- Direct connection between service delivery and 311 (such as integration with the refuse collection truck for dynamic handling of exceptions like a forgotten pickup).
- Being available as an established, accepted, and standardized resource for information dissemination to the public. Reporting available on-line.

- The ability to graphically "rubber-band" an area of interest, and access relevant 311 information, as well as related GIS-based information in additional mapping layers (such

- Collection of additional information specific to certain service Requests (e.g. The Department of Health identified the need for time, date, name, address, and jurisdiction of call, and expressed a desire to involve their epidemiologist in the identification of additional information to be collected).

- Selective incorporation of information currently provided by other call centers (specifically in areas where lay call center representatives can reliably provide correct information). These included providing directions to medical resources (while keeping in mind that most medical information should not be disseminated by lay operators).

- Integration of 311 and other data sources into a data warehouse. This data warehouse will provide integrated information for data analysis for purposes such as community policing.

- The ability to upload citizen provided information - such as felled trees after a storm - from mobile devices for prioritizing resources.

- Alleviating loads on the emergency response system (i.e. 9-1-1) through offloading non-emergency calls.

- Enabling advancing community policing, by serving as a location-based database for reporting and identifying incident hotspots, and thereby facilitating the targeting of responses.

- Reverse-311, i.e. an ability to use 311 to make automated telephone calls and send automated emails to user-selectable addresses.

- Speedup in taking customer information during the process of creating a service Request.

ROLE OF ACE ARCHITECTURE TEAM IN BUSINESS: IT STRATEGY ALIGNMENT

We have presented above the application of the ACE structure and framework for the strategic planning process and decision-making that allowed us to identify the right priorities and requirements for the City. We next focus on the rightmost column of Figure 1 to discuss the important role of EA governance, specifically ACE Co-engineering, within the organization.

Historically, centralized decision-making has been the typical organizational pattern within public organization for several reasons:

- Ensures fairness of treatment for both service recipients and employees
- Creates clear chains of accountability
- Minimizes the exposure of successful service delivery to political forces that typically affects only the top layers of management

In response to criticisms that centralized hierarchies are stultified and inefficient, public organizations have become more decentralization and are separating large multi-service bureaucracies into loosely coupled units called federations. Most recently, the boundaries of some public sector organizations have become more porous as service delivery is becoming the responsibility of a network of organizations – government agencies, private firms, non-profit organizations – bound together by contracts, grants, and a commitment to addressing relevant policy problems. Large metropolitan municipal governments with wide-ranging service responsibilities are thus typically conglomerations of all three of these organizational patterns: hierarchies, federations and networks (AgranSoff and McGuire, 2003; Klijn, 1996; Nohria, 1992; O'Toole and Meier, 2000).[f]

Role of EA Governance

Viewed from an IT point of view, due to the in-the-large perspective, the ACE governance team has unique roles to play in developing new opportunities for the organization. A fundamental role is in aligning IT to business needs for networking. As shown above, solution analysis techniques are applied in a focused way to achieve strategic cross-organization and enterprise-level goals. Another role is the strategic positioning of the whole organization.

For example, the concern addressed in the example is "How well do existing enterprise systems enable networking of Agents?" Existing IT systems in public institutions are designed to enable hierarchical public enterprises and are not built to adapt to each Request. The presence of organizational and IT 'silos' makes coordination and information sharing difficult (Malone and Crowston, 2001). The information flow is essential as public enterprises are increasingly more dynamic and often turbulent. Emergencies erupt. Political coalitions supporting particular services crumble. Vendor support gets discontinued. New features are slowed by legacy issues. Resources for specific efforts quickly diminish (Salmela and Spil, 2002; Thietart and Forgues, 1995).[g]

As events like these unfold, systems that are based on stable models also become very ineffective. Because large metropolitan municipal governments are conglomerations of various organizational patterns, EA must address dynamic Organization-IT alignment for effective performance.

Sense-and-Respond Planning-and-Execution: In accordance with the starting step of the ACE continual improvement framework introduced in the previous Chapter 3, the enterprise architecture teams were established to bring focus on the future. Each of the teams was composed of business analysts (customer account representatives or CARs in this case), system architects, departmental directors, and team leaders spanning the spectrum of in-the-large and in-the-small expertise.

The strategic IT planning-and-execution process followed is also illustrated in Figure 1. The arrows in the middle column reflect the initial step of creating the ACE representation and work products leading to a continual improvement cycle of services in the rightmost column. Thus the planning starts with 'sensing' the external request types in the Strategy dimension.

In the context of Figure 1 the response details of a specific externally-driven Interaction execution are given in Figure 3. These details were derived from the BioS questionnaire for each departmental. The 'BoS' goals were provided by the departmental experts and the 'i' perspective was provided by the CAR interface between the DOT and the department. Thus IT strategic planning is driven by the business organizations and nested units. The *critical relationship* with the Dot customer is maintained by the critical CAR role.

EA Work Products A-F

Each ACE domain team first created the department or organization-specific work products (see details illustrated in Figure 3 for the 'complaints' Request type). For each type of Interaction, as-is BioS work products with metrics are gathered from existing sources (strategic plan, response times, help desk reports, time cards, etc.). The result is the Service catalog of external Request types and BioS targets for each type to reflect both the *plan* and execution *for each RED interaction.* Using the RED interactions, supporting catalogs and service work products were also developed.

Note: Here we are actually applying some of the ITIL patterns to business operations rather than IT. This is one reason, to avoid confusion, that our vocabulary is based on the ontology in Chapter 2 that is independent of the type of organization to which the methodology is applied. In other words, the methodology applies equally well to IT and non-IT organizations for the management of variation.

A: Catalog of primary Request types and Strategy Goals: As with many organizations, the city had already defined its strategy, primary Request types handled by its departments, and targets. With each type there were numbers and target goals which were stated as $\triangle$ improvements. Here the $\triangle$ could be a positive or negative number. For example, 'weed abatement target' was a negative number that implied a reduction. The catalog of Request types is identified in the strategy dimension of

Figure 3. At-a-glance templates and sample work products A-E

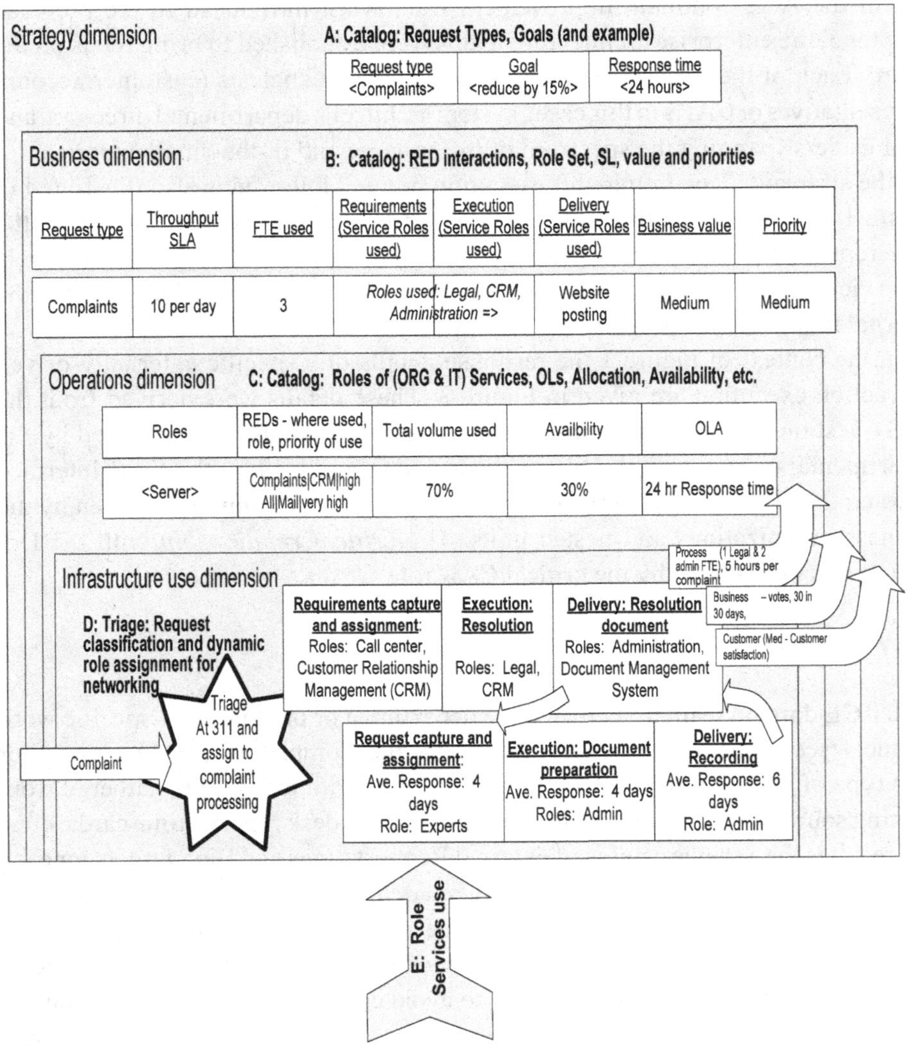

Figure 3. Strategic goals—e.g. neighborhood, citizen satisfaction—were used to set the targets and prioritize across Requests.

B: Catalog of RED Interactions, Role Sets, SLs and Business Priorities and Goals: This planning step creates the logical RED structures that relate the Request types (identified above) initiated in the customer environment to the responding Roles and performance within provider's organization (i.e. department) within the City. Note that these basic structures can be further associated. For example, a public safely interaction might trigger a health interaction. The known potential associations are also assembled into a structure as shown in Figure 3. Illustrated here is the Request type (i.e. complaint), the RED milestone specifics with the Roles Set identified (i.e. Call center, CRM, etc.), the sub-RED specifics, and the performance contribution at each milestone to the respective stakeholders (e.g. use of infrastructure services, indicated by the leftmost arrow; and Business SLAs met as 30 complaints in 30 days). Within each department this step identified different enhancements for existing agents and also new agent needs that were explicitly captured and related to the Request types and the value to business.

C: Catalog of Roles and Services, Availability, OLs: Using the output of step 2 (Figure 1), the next step was to take the perspective of each Role and determine which interactions it services by specifically identifying the REDs. For example, taking the perspective of the CRM service, it is uses in the complaint interaction but it also used in many other interactions like payment notifications.

D: Triage - Request classification for role assignment/networking and Infrastructure use metrics: Since the responses are driven by the incoming Requests, these were carefully classified. Triage rules were defined to bind the requirements to the needed roles of each interaction to the available entity services to meet OLs. These rules enable the efficient dynamic networking.

E and F: The needed Roles and Agents with the skills form the remaining two work products and will be explored at length in the next section.

With these work products completed, the ACE structure is now fully defined. Note that this structure can be defined at a level of details necessary for the project and incrementally improved over time. This can also be enhanced with additional associations as needed between the Request types, the REDs, the Roles Sets, and the Agents. For the City portfolio development additional associations, beyond Request prioritization were not needed. However, as we shall see, the initial work products can be further enhanced to implement other initiatives like chargeback and capacity management.

CONCLUSION AND RESEARCH

Strategic Benefits: In a fundamental sense, IT can play two major roles in a business process:

- Improve efficiency
- Innovatively help us rethink Interactions and the Resources needed

In the case of 311, the actual benefit of IT strategic planning was to provide a shared IT service Role - 311 - that in turn provided many advantages:

- A way to handle non-routine Requests with Interactions that were not handled by existing enterprise systems
- A way to dynamically network different organizations together to execute an Interaction
- A way to acquire citizen and community information that can be mined for innovation that enhances future services
- A way to structure organizations for chargeback, capacity management, and making decisions like in-sourcing/outsourcing/back sourcing and so on

ACE Framework: From a methodological perspective, ACE is a strategic framework for viewing the enterprise and its internal value-chains in a holistic fashion – across the BioS dimensions. By identifying the competitive goals with respect to each Request type we can apply the framework to relate the RED Interaction milestones and their goal achievement using Role sets. From a DoT strategic planning perspective, the missing Roles were important and prioritized. Thus the application of this within the City identified and prioritized a strategic gap. Not surprisingly, this was the 311 triage. However, it is also interesting to note that this gap was identified in many different ways with a different vocabulary by the different departments. The underlying ontology allowed us to identify these gaps as one and the same. In its current deployment the 311 met the stakeholder goals within each dimension.

The on-going benefit of the method was also demonstrated – the ability to build upon the 311 for continual improvement. The resulting identified requirements have potential benefits not only in the dynamic networking of agents – departments, teams and so on, but also to meet future goals and expectations of the citizens. We have also shown how the Co-Engineering principles helped constrain the solutions and achieve better decision making.

Research in organizational patterns: Our example illustrated the achievement of a networked organization through the principled IT application. In addition to more field research, the following complex organizational research issues can now also be addressed.

What are the organizational policies that can be supported within an EA to achieve the following?

- Balance of power through the division, distribution, or separation of powers within a national or international political system. This can be achieved with a variety of different policies for voting, vetoing, forming coalitions and so on.

- Maximize process throughput through automatically identifying and addressing the capacity and quality problems with a Role Set through alternative strategies. This will require the development of polices to achieve Lean by Triage policies that will eliminate need for dedicated resources and buffers, identifying root cause, and by managing the Input and Output flow across Interactions.
- Management of costs through automated guidance for identifying redundant Roles and efforts that can be shared, reducing the integration complexity, and identifying opportunities for outsourcing.

The ACE framework and related research needs to be developed further to gain a deeper understanding of customers, collaborators, and business rules (Kost 2004). Further research issues are also identified in Chapter 10. The student is encouraged to read ahead.

TASKS RELATED TO WORK PRODUCT C

1. Further develop the ACE structure and details of Work Product C (begin D if possible).
2. What are the key performance indicators associated with the Interactions?
3. How can the Interactions be improved?
4. Document and present to the sponsor the strategic implications of the selected project.

THINGS TO THINK ABOUT

1. How does Triage ensure Lean thinking and networking? What Co-engineering principles apply? Explain in detail.
2. How can one learn from the illustrated field experience to better automate systems for monitoring and analysis of performance? What comparable vendor products are in the market? What are their pros and cons?
3. Explain the claim "The underlying ontology allowed us to identify these gaps as one and the same."
4. How can the work product approach, illustrate here for the City operations, apply within the DoT organization to achieve a product line type approach to services development?

REFERENCES

Agranoff, R., & McGuire, M. (2001). Big Questions in Public Network Management Research. *Journal of Public Administration Theory and Research, 11*(3), 295–326.

Ambite, J. L., Giuliano, G., Gordon, P., Decker, S., Harth, A., Jassar, K., et. al. (2004). Argos: An Ontology and Web Service Composition Infrastructure for Goods Movement Analysis. *In Proceedings of the 2004 Annual National Conference on Digital Government Research* (pp. 1-2). Seattle, WA: Digital Government Society of North America.

Arens, Y., & Rosenbloom, P. (2002 February). *Responding to the Unexpected.* National Science Foundation Workshop. New York, NY: USC/Information Sciences Institute.

Bovens, M., & Zouridis, S. (2002). From Street-Level to System-Level Bureaucracies. *Public Administration Review, 62*(2), 174-184.

Child, J. (1972). Organizations, Structure, Environment, and Performance: The Role of Strategic Choice. *Sociology, 6*(1), 1-22.

Clegg, S., & Hardy, C. (1999). *Studying Organization: Theory and Method.* Thousand Oaks: Sage.

Conklin, J., & Weil, W. (1997). *Wicked Problems: Naming the Pain in Organizations.* Retrieved August 18, 2006, from http://www.3m.com/meetingnetwork/readingroom/gdss_wicked.html

Donaldson, L. (1999). The Normal Science of Structural Contingency Theory. *Studying Organization: Theory and Method,* (pp. 51-70).

Desai, A. (May 2005). Special *Issue: Adaptive Complex Systems. Communications of the ACM, 49*(5).

Drazin, R., & Van de Van, A. (1985). Alternative Forms of Fit in Contingency Theory. *Administrative Science Quarterly, 30*(4), 514-539.

Kost, J. (2004). Analyze Government Transactions to Make Them Citizen-Centric. *Gartner Report.* G00123516, Gartner Research.

Fountain, J. (2001). *Building the Virtual State: Information Technology and Institutional Change.* Washington, DC: Brookings Institution.

Grin, J., & Hoppe, R. (2000). Cultural Bias and Framing Wicked Problems. In H. Wagenaar (ed.) *Government Institutions: Effects, Changes and Normative Foundations* (pp. 179-199), Doderecht: Kluwer Academic Publishers.

Groenlund, A. (1998 January). Public Computer Systems – A New Focus for Information Systems Research. *Information Policy*, *6*(1), 47-65.

Gupta V., Mukri F., Ramanathan J., Ramnath R., & Yackovich K. (2009 January). CitiScapes: Architecture for eGovernment Effectiveness. To appear in the *42nd Hawaii International Conference on Systems Sciences*, Waikoloa, HI: IEEE Computer Society.

Ho, A. (2002 July/August). Reinventing Local Government and the E-government Initiative. *Public Administration Review*, *62*(4), 434-444.

Holowczak, D., Soon, A. C., Artigas, F. J., & Atlurit, V. (2001) Customized Geospatial Workflows for E-Government Services. In *Proceedings of the 9th ACM International Symposium on Advances in Geographic Information Systems* (pp. 64-69), Atlanta, GA: ACM.

Klijn, E. (1996). Analyzing and Managing Policy Processes in Complex Networks. *Administration and Society*, *28*(1), 90-119.

Kling, R., Kraemer, K. L, Allen, J. P., Bakos, Y., Gurbaxani, Y., & Elliott, M. (2001). Transforming Coordination: The Promise and Problems of Information Technology in Coordination. In G. Olson, T. Malone, & J. B. Smith (Eds.), *The Interdisciplinary Study of Coordination*. Mahwah, NJ: Lawrence Erlbaum Associates.

Landsbergen, D. (1993). *Digital Telecommunications Standards: A Problem of Procedures and Values, Informatization and the Public Sector.*

Landsbergen, D., & Wolken, G. (2001). Realizing the Promise: Government Information Systems and the Fourth Generation of Information Technology. *Public Administration Review*, *61*(2), 206-220.

Longstaff, P. H. (2005 February). *Security, Resilience, and Communication in Unpredictable Environments Such as Terrorism, Natural Disasters and Complex Technology*. Program on Information Resources Policy, Harvard University and the Center for Information Policy Research, Cambridge, Massachusetts, Retrieved November 23, 2008, from http://www.pirp.harvard.edu/publications/pdf-blurb. asp?id=606

Mendonca, D., Jefferson, T., & Harrald, J. (2007 March). Collaborative Adhocracies and Mix-and-Match Technologies in Emergency Management. *Communications of the ACM*, *50*(3), 44-49.

Moon, M. J. (2002 July/August). The Evolution of E-government among municipalities, Rhetoric or Reality. *Public Administration Review, 62*(4), 424-433.

Morçöl, G. (2002). *A New Mind for Policy Analysis*. New York: Praeger.

Nohria, N. (1992). Is a Network Perspective a Useful Way of Studying Organizations? In N. Nohria & R. G. Eccles (Ed.), *Networks and Organizations: Structure, Form and Fit* (pp. 1-22). Boston: Harvard Business School Press.

O'Toole, L., & Meier, K. (2000). Networks, Hierarchies, and Management: Modeling the nonlinearities. In C. Heinrich & L. Lynn (Eds.), *Governance and Performance: New Perspectives* (pp. 263-291). Washington, DC: Georgetown University Press.

Page, S. (2003). Entrepreneurial Strategies for Managing Interagency Collaboration. *Journal of Public Administration Research and Theory, 13*(3), 311-340.

Punia, D. K., & Saxena, K. B. C. (2004 March). E-government Services and Policy Track: Managing Inter-organizational Workflows in eGovernment Services. In *Proceedings of the 6th International Conference on Electronic Commerce* (pp. 500-505). Delft, The Netherlands: ACM.

Ramanathan, J., Ramnath, R., & Desai, A. (2008). Adaptive IT Architecture as a Catalyst for Network Capability in Government. In Saha, P. (Ed.). *Advances in Government Enterprise Architecture, editor*. Idea Group Publishing.

Ramnath, R. & Landsbergen, D. (2005 May). IT-Enabled Sense-and-Respond Strategies in Complex Public Organizations, *Communications of the ACM, 48*(5), 58-64.

Responder Knowledge Base. (2004 April). National Technology Emergency Plan for Emergency Response to Catastrophic Terrorism, MIPT (National Memorial Institute for the Prevention of Terrorism), Retrieved November 23, 2008, from http://www.rkb.mipt.org

Saha, P. (ed.). (2008). *Edited Advances in Government Enterprise Architecture*. Idea Group Inc. Publisher: Information Science Reference.

Sawyer, S., Tapia, A., Pesheck, L., & Davenport, J. (2004 March). Mobility and the first Response. *Communications of the ACM, 47*(3), 62-65.

Salmela, H., & Spil, T. A. M. (2002 November). Dynamic and Emergent Information Systems Strategy Formulation and Implementation. *International Journal of Information Management, 22*(6), 441-460.

Schwartz, P. (2003). *Inevitable Surprises: Thinking Ahead in a Time of Turbulence*. New York: Gotham Books.

Schneider, B. (2000). *Secrets and Lies: Digital Security in a Networked World.* New York: John Wiley & Sons, Inc.

Simon, H. (1960). *The New Science of Management Decision.* New York: Harper & Row.

Thiétart, R. A., & Forgues B. (1995). Chaos Theory and Organization. *Organization Science, 6*(1), 19-31.

Teisman, G., & Klijn E. H. (2002). Partnership Arrangements: Governmental Rhetoric or Governance Scheme? *Public Administration Review, 62*(2), 197-205.

Wildavsky, A. (1979). *The Art and Craft of Policy Analysis.* London: Macmillan.

ENDNOTES

[a] This chapter is based on a previous chapter written for IGI book on eGov and CACM 2005. The book "Advances in Government Enterprise Architecture" is a seminal publication in the emerging and evolving discipline of enterprise architecture (EA). Presenting current developments, issues, and trends in EA, this critical resource provides IT managers, government CIOs, researchers, educators, and professionals with insights into the impact of effective EA on IT governance, IT portfolio management, and IT outsourcing, creating a must-have holding for academic libraries and organizational information centers. ISBN: 978-1-60566-068-4 Hard Cover Publisher: Information Science Reference Pub Date: November 2008 Pages: 456.

[b] Mistakes: Strategic Planning Don'ts (and Dos), June 01, 2002 — CIO, http://www.cio.com/article/31106/Mistakes_Strategic_Planning_Don_ts_and_Dos_ says Darrell Rigby, a director at consultancy Bain & Co. in Boston.

[c] A good place to read more about emergency initiates is http://www.usa.gov/Government/State_Local/Disasters.shtml.

[d] COPS03-1: http://www.cops.usdoj.gov/txt/fact_sheets/e01060007.txt

[e] Perhaps 311 data could be made available to candidates during mayoral campaigns.

[f] Also from Ramanathan et al 2008.

[g] Also from Ramanathan et al 2008.

Chapter VI
Co–Engineering Business Need and IT Services

ABSTRACT

Vertical traceability along the internal value chain illustrated in Figure 1 below allows us to establish a charge back system for the use of IT services. In addition the fine-grain Interaction approach to implementing chargeback also encourages the discipline needed for other initiatives like capacity management, audit procedures, and aligning of IT investments with business needs. How to achieve this alignment is the subject of this chapter.

Why is a good chargeback model important for the effective organization?

- How is the chargeback model developed based on the BioS work products?
- How are chargeback and capacity management related?
- Why is a good chargeback model closely tied to retaining flexibility, effectiveness, service-level management, and a tool for customer-oriented management and visibility?

Today's enterprise must maintain a diverse portfolio of IT applications to support critical business Interactions and drive the processes responsible for the day-to-day operations and management of internal and external business services. At the same time there is a need to manage the total cost of ownership, reduce overall

Figure 1. ACE structure and associated capacity work products

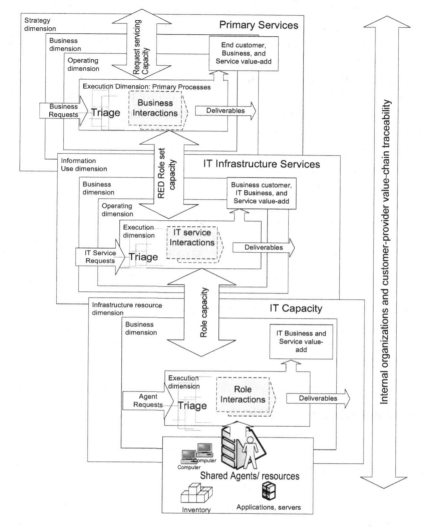

complexity of the IT assets, and properly align and control capacity. The ability to do so is directly related to several factors:

- Aligning infrastructure Agent capacity to business need,
- Charging for IT services based on the services delivered, and
- Expanding service capacity based on demonstrated need.

In addition, financial management has become an item of highest priority within organizations due to recent events like the bursting of the high-tech bubble, global economic slowdown, and scandals. This has also resulted in mandatory compliance requirements due to the Sarbanes-Oxley (USA), Basel II (Europe), and AS8015 (Australia). As a result IT expenditures are increasingly scrutinized.

One result of all this is that the justifying, directing, and controlling IT expenditure through 'chargeback' to customer organizations within the enterprise is becoming increasingly important. Another result is the understanding that chargeback is a key governance mechanism for an adaptive organization as it allows the IT infrastructure roles and their capacity to evolve more directly to meet business priorities.

Finally, service chargeback mechanisms have the ability to influence the behavior of service consumers but these mechanisms also have the capability to increase understanding between consumers and providers and enable more effective joint decision making. Ross (Ross 99) explores the impact IT chargeback has from a sample of large organizations that have established chargeback practices. The findings suggest that chargeback is, at least to some degree, a useful tool for strengthening the IT-Business relationship because it increases and promotes mutual understanding and problem solving. A cornerstone of the co-engineering approach is to build relationships that allow this style of valuable communication and joint decision making possible and the article shows that chargeback is one such mechanisms that can be used to build up a solid foundation for collaborative engineering practices.

THE BUSINESS CHALLENGE

An example of a typical *as-is* chargeback policy for the use of capacity and internal services has three aspects as follows.

Allocation of Capacity: During the budgeting process each customer organization within the enterprise is allocated certain percentages of Agent capacity. In the as-is scenarios this is typically based on based on history rather than actual use in most cases because the traceability is missing within the organization. This is often because the needed reporting and monitoring is not in plane or too cumbersome. For example, a department might be allocated ten months of a specific Agent / programmer, even if the projected and actual use might be two months.

Cost Identification: Typical sources of costs utilized for the chargeback within the organization include:

- The hours of each billable employee and resource. In the as-is this input is determined using time-card history from the previous year and spread across user organizations, as indicated by the data.
- The enterprise-wide *shared* service costs such as project management office, GIS services, customer service center, and other non-billable items. This also includes the data center facility, unspecified debt service, miscellaneous security services, and overhead such as program and fiscal offices. These are all often used for calculating the *overhead* to the IT resources hourly rate.

Cost Distribution: All costs are allocated and recovered based on the spread of IT personnel resources across the other organizational units. These costs are distributed across each of the other customer organizations by the aforementioned percentages. The resulting problem is that the time card project numbers often do not accurately reflect the services rendered, and the overhead costs often reflect expenditures due to some customer organizations, but not all.

Organizational Challenges: Several organizational issues can be illustrated with this chargeback policy:

- It is dependent upon accuracy of time-keeping related to a specific project as opposed to service. And since a project might require many services, these prices charged do not reflect the costs.
- Shared resources such as programmers and servers can serve many roles, and based on availability they should be able to be reassigned to priority tasks. If actual named resources are assigned to organizations and this limits the ability to reassign the available and unused capacity.
- Maintaining the optimal capacity to deliver business services is challenging to identify in the face of fluctuating demand.
- Actual cost of provisioning of each service from the customer's perspective is not clear.
- High overhead costs applied uniformly to all customers are related to recovery of cost but not the services used. That is some organizations might be using very little IT but still get burdened with the overhead.
- Organizations not certain they are getting the services for which they were budgeted.
- Budgeting process is complex and tracking IT expenditures and revenues at a fine grain is difficult.

To-be ACE Structure and Chargeback: Achieving this future state requires a full understanding of the use of services. This is based on the recognition that there are three nested ACE structures and organizations Figure 1, each treated as a 'business':

- The primary services
- The IT support services
- The IT capacity for services

This results in the internal customer provider value chain and ACE structure (Figure 1). Additionally, the figure shows the BIOS work products needed to align the use of services, the capacity, and the costs across the organizations.

Chargeback and Capacity Management While Retaining Flexibility: Maintaining the *infrastructure capacity* and *charging for services* used are dual aspects of the same problem. Here we are referring to the traceability between capacity of Role sets needed for Interactions and the actual charges for times utilized of underlying Agents. Idle capacity is expensive to maintain and at the same time the organization needs to be prepared for the critical fluctuations due to unforeseen events.

The ability to be flexible is greatly enhanced by the delayed binding and reassignment of shared Agent services to Roles. This is achieved by having the capability to dynamically issue Requests for Agents to fill Roles in Role sets needed to Execute a RED Interaction.

We illustrate the application of the related methods, after examining the business challenges and best practices in some detail.

BACKGROUND AND BEST PRACTICES

Co-Engineering Principle 6: IT Service capacity and chargeback alignment (Val IT)
IT-enabled investments will be managed as a portfolio of investments.
IT-enabled investments will include the full scope of activities that are required to achieve business value.
IT-enabled investments will be managed through their full economic life cycle.
Value delivery practices will recognize that there are different categories of investments that will be evaluated and managed differently.
Value delivery practices will define and monitor key metrics and will respond quickly to any changes or deviations.
Value delivery practices will engage all stakeholders and assign appropriate accountability for the delivery of capabilities and the realization of business benefits.
Value delivery practices will be continually monitored, evaluated and improved.

Managing the IT Portfolio: In order to understand the techniques for managing the IT portfolio, is useful to start with 'IT Val' - a suite of documents that provide a framework for the governance of IT investments, produced by the IT Governance Institute (ITGI)[a]. It is a formal statement of principles and processes for IT portfolio management. Val IT provides a governance framework that consists of guiding principles and processes conforming to those principles. The major processes are 1) Value Governance, 2) Portfolio Management, and 3) Investment Management. We include these as *Co-engineering principle 6* in the highlight and next look at aspects of determining value of IT Infrastructure investment by relating it to service Interactions that create business value.

Relating Demand and Capacity: Recall the Co-engineering principle 2 allowed us to relate infrastructure costs to the total value to business. Specifically, the ability of an organization to increase in value basically depends on its infrastructure capacity to provide services to meet customer demand. This in turn requires infrastructure capacity. However, maintaining excess capacity will, according to Co-engineering principle 2, reduce the yield. To increase value, the infrastructure must be effective – no wasted or idle resources within the infrastructure. Thus, to maximize the value of the organization, it is necessary to align different capacities as follows (see Figure 1):

1. *Request servicing capacity* refers to the business services an organization that delivers to the customer and the future demand as identified by a market segment or demographic,

2. *Operational Interactions and operational capacity* of Role sets that support Requests (as in 1 above). An example is the number of on-line order Interactions that must be sustained by the underlying Role set (warehousing, inventory, IT resources, etc.).

3. *Infrastructure service capacity* refers to the Role set demand (as in 2 above) that must be met by a single Role. That is, the capacity of disk arrays or of Bob the maintenance engineer to sustain and support of some level of operational Interactions. Note that the infrastructure capacity is the collective capacity of the Role sets. That is, all the Agents in the Role set must be available.

This alignment relationships is captured in Co-engineering principle 7. To illustrate the Co-engineering principle 7, consider the following analogy with an alignment needed from a manufacturing perspective: Product Line → Manufacturing Processes → Tools. Clearly all three aspects of capacity management are related to one another. Figure 2 shows how each facet of capacity works together and correlates it with the desired state of the stakeholders. The desired states can be achieved through Co-engineering principles as illustrated. The relationship

Co-engineering Principle 7: Traceability between cost identification, allocation, and recovery allows us to apply Co-engineering principle 2 to align costs to recovery.

An effective chargeback model helps control infrastructure costs and increases the capacity at the same time. The related traceability needed is as follows.

Identification of sources of costs that:
--Allows infrastructure services to be priced based on sources of costs
--Enables organizations to understand and control their service expenses
Allocation of capacity:
--Enables precise forecasting thereby easing the budgeting process
--Allows organizations to assess value of services and own performance
Cost recovery base on service capacity used:
--Strongly influences organization behavior
--Improves financial discipline in both customer and infrastructure organizations
Within an organization, the chargeback must often meet additional goals. For example, within a public organization, this is stated as - only charge what it costs, neither loose nor earn, and charge to each fund only what is estimated to that fund.

Figure 2. Relationship between business, service and resource capacity

	To-be state is identified as	To-be state can be more quantified through[b]	Primary growth limiting factor	Justification
Business Capacity	Optimal Business Strategy	Porter's Model for competitiveness	Service Capacity	Increase Penetration
Service Capacity	Process Optimality	RED Interaction metrics, CMM | Lean for process maturity and efficiency	Roles set Capacity	Increase Revenue
Infrastructure Capacity	Optimal Utilization	State of the Art of Technology for automation	Capability of individual Agents	Increase Margin

between to-be states, as-is states, and the most significant growth-limiting factor is also illustrated.

Business Service Interaction Capacity

It should be evident from Figure 2 that capacity management requires alignment from top down as well as from the bottom up. Technological breakthroughs cause a reduction in the limiting factors influencing infrastructure capacity and hence may bring about an opportunity for service, and potentially business capacity growth.

Similarly, the desire to change business capacity may warrant re-optimizing service and resource capacity to grow or shrink with the change in business capacity.

At this point it is important to emphasize that these two forces are near opposites of one another – technological improvements influence at the bottom and their effects *can* be pushed up through proper application if there is a need to increase capacity while capacity changes originate from the top *demand* a cascading effect through the bottom. Hence the first source of change is generally an opportunity while the later is best thought of as a business survival challenge.

The ACE structure and framework aligns business capacity with service and infrastructure. The goal is primarily to serve as a general reference model for capacity management as it applies to technology and IT professionals that strive to align service and resource capacity with an understood level of business capacity and its change. We will frame our discussion in the context of a top-down scenario where the business capacity has been identified by strategists and the lower layers must be aligned to support it over time. This serves as the rationale for chargeback that is quite common in enterprises and addresses the general desire for low cost and low risk IT investment. The bottom-up case is also important, particularly to promote innovations that drive business strategy. Additionally, once new technology has impacted business strategy or altered capacity demands, this framework can still serve to re-align.

We next provide an analysis of current best practices and provide continuous improvement recommendations that will allow an organization to institute a to-be chargeback policy and capacity management.

According to ITIL and COBIT, the related processes and responsibilities are as follows:

- Business Relationship Management responsible for:
  o Request Management
  o Service Catalog Development
  o Service Level Communication
- Asset and Configuration Management
- Capacity Management

We first explore the specific chargeback and then capacity management practices. In the later sections we will present the Co-engineering method for alignment of these dual aspects using the ACE representation in Figure 1 as a basis.

Chargeback Policies

Developing a chargeback model for full cost recovery, organization visibility, satisfaction with the IT services and price, and continuous improvement is hard. According to Gartner, only twenty five percent of the companies that have started the process will achieve success in the short term. However a majority of the companies are embarking on this and want to achieve the goals in the longer term[c]. It is also important for any organization to embark on a chargeback best practice to improve customer satisfaction.

A *chargeback policy* allows an organization to take a "systems perspective" by identifying and managing behaviors that need to be encouraged. It can facilitate:

- Matching of services to business need.
- Force organization to control demands (e.g. storage) to control expenses.
- Decreases costs and highlight areas of service provision that are not cost effective
- Disciplines organizations that nothing is "free"
- Better ensures alignment with enterprise goals.
- Pinpoints areas of innovation.

Industry Experience: Chargeback is difficult to get right! The following provides some context for DoT. According to Meta Group (META 2005):

- Through '05 – over 45% of DoTs will significantly refine their cost recovery mechanisms; less than 25% will succeed.
- "Full IT Chargeback" will be unrealistic for more than 90% of IT groups.
- By 2008, significant automation, configuration & asset management, and ERP advancements will lead to improvements to identify, allocate, and recover IT costs.
- 15% have defined IT products/services to which costs should be aggregated/ bundled (no service model).
- 10% have correct inventory and configuration information to facilitate cost identification and tracking.
- 5% know the true cost of maintaining their operations environment.
- 2.5% have defined IT processes to which activity based costs for IT employees may be related.

We next present the Co-engineering of IT Service Capacity, Availability, and Chargeback to meet Business use and goals.

USING ACE STRUCTURE WORK PRODUCTS FOR CHARGEBACK AND CAPACITY MANAGEMENT

Conceptually speaking, the IT department has a certain specific and limited capacity to provide services. Therefore to continue to be effective, it is important that costs are incurred only for services that meet user and business requirements. It is also important that the costs are correctly ascribed so that they can be recovered. This is achieved by the application of the ACE framework in this section based on the precise *allocation-use* associations of the ACE structure and Work Products. It is also important to note that *capacity use and chargeback* are both computed along this association. In a fundamental sense this underlies all the customer-provider Interactions. That is, provider Agents make capacity available to the customer for a certain charge. Within a business there is no free ride!

Allocate-Use: Specifically we illustrate in Figure 3 the relevant dimensions of the nested ACE structure of Figure 1. Here the work products and attributes allow us to align the organizations based on the allocate-use association along the internal value-add chain. The work products (presented to the right of the structure in Figure 3 with typical 'templates') give more details and attributes that ensure that the allocate–use associations are traceable across dimensions as follows:

- The *Request catalog* for primary business Interactions predicts future goals and priorities.
- Associated *RED Interactions* identify *Roles sets* that originate the *IT Request types* and related volumes, governing needed allocations, and SLAs to achieve the business capacity for each *business Request type*.
- Associated *IT Requests, RED Interactions* and their *Role sets* in turn identify the IT Roles and their allocations needed for business Interactions.
- Commonly used *IT Role sets* can be treated as an *utility* in which case the requests are implicit (e.g. the use of the enterprise mail or document management system) or a *service* with a *service rate*.
- *Role sets* needed for different *IT Request types* in turn identify the associated IT *Agents* that have to have enough capacity to be allocated.

Dynamic Allocation-Use Association: Note that the use of *Agents* in service Roles to deliver on *IT Requests* and, in turn, the use of *IT Requests* to deliver on Role sets for specific *business Requests* is maintained by a two-level chart of accounts[d]. This is needed to monitor 1) the Agents and the amount of each service Role provided by shared Agents, and 2) the use of that Role in each associated business Interaction. This method allows for *dynamic allocation and use associations*. That is, an Agent does not have to be dedicated to a particular organization.

Figure 3. Use of ACE structure Work Products for Alignment and Traceability. This surfaces the capacity used - charge relationships along the internal value chain illustrated in Figure 1.

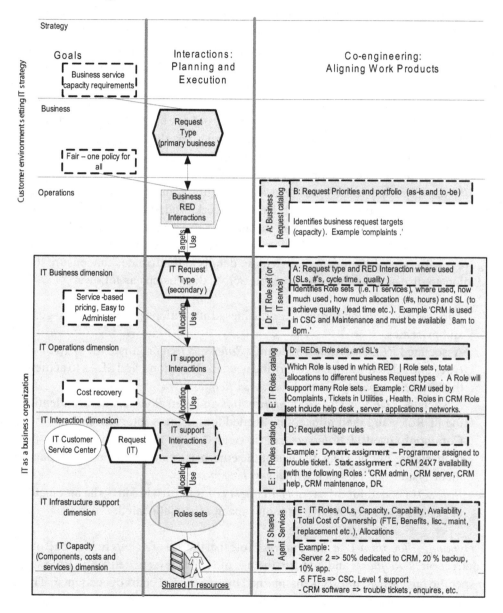

Instead based on the IT Request type that characterizes the services to be provided by a Role set enabling the business Interaction, we can assign Agents dynamically during triage. Further, the indirect traceability chain: *Business* (Request type ⇨ Interaction ⇨ Role set) ⇨ *IT* (Request ⇨ Interaction ⇨ Role set ⇨ Roles ⇨ Agents) is resolved through dynamic Requests and Role *assignments* and we are simply left with the chain as executed *Business* (Request type) ⇨ *IT* (Request ⇨ Agents). That is, Role sets and Roles are simply logical place holders that allow us to implement a virtual organization. This final assignment and use of Agents should be captured in the chart of accounts that is set up.

Capacity and Chargeback: The capacity-chargeback computations occur along the allocation-use associations. To provide full transparency for the chargeback to the business customer we again start with the business Interactions that use Role sets that generate explicit or implicit IT Requests. In turn these requests result in IT Interactions within the IT organization. These interactions are enabled by Role sets that are filled by specific Agents with certain capacities that come at certain costs. The use of these Agents is recorded. The charges for use is designed to cover the costs of maintaining that capacity for current *and future* business needs.

This bottom-up view is given in the following examples (and is a more detailed view of Figure 3) with explanations, work products and alignment examples, and benefits. The numbers in these examples are hypothetical.

Implementation of Traceability

Next the question to be answered is "what are the immediate steps that can be taken?"

Figure 4. Detailed attributes of capacity-chargeback associations

Dimension	Benefits of Traceability along the allocate-use association
IT Agent and Infrastructure: capability, capacity, allocated, costs and operating levels.	Identifies the capacity and capability of shared Agents to provide services and all related costs.
	Identifies costs consistently and collect costs in a standardized chart of accounts.
	Predicts the money required to run IT Services for a given period.
	Ensures that actual spend can be compared with predicted spend at any point.
	Reduce the risk of overspending.
	Ensures that revenues are available to cover predicted spend.

continued on the following page

Figure 4. (continued)

Example 1. Associating Work Products F&E: Agent details to IT Roles								
Usage and Capacity → / IT Human Agents ⅃	IT Service Capabilities	Available Capacity	Allocated Hours	Per unit cost	Basis...	Agent use in Role Sets of IT Request types (% Costs).		
						Web Support	Help Desk	311
MM	Help desk	1,352	1000	$50	Hrs/day	20%$	50%$	20%$
JS	Application, Help desk	1,352	200	$80	Hrs/day	0	50%$	50%$
GG	CAR, Application	1,352	500	$89	Hrs/day	20%	0	0

Usage and Capacity → / IT Agents ⅃	IT Service Capabilities	Available Capacity	Allocated Capacity	Per unit Cost	Basis...	Roles used by the Role Sets of IT Request types (% Costs).		
						Web support	Help Desk	311
Production	Mail	20,000	40%	$80	Units/day...	0	0	0
Server	Storage, Applications	xx-petabytes	80%	$80	Bytes, Lisc., Maint, power.	30%$	5%$	4%$
Help desk app.	Customer support	n.a.		$90	Lisc., Maint, Useful life. ...	0	100%$	0
Total IT service cost (add all the IT Agents contributing to the Role set)						X $	Y $	Z $

Dimension	Benefits of Traceability along the allocate-use association
IT Role sets used to service business Request types.	Allows each customer-facing Request type and service to be composed of a number of 'internal' IT-oriented services. That is, provides the ability to bundle infrastructure details and associate it to user facing IT requests, related to either delivery and support.
	Logical Role sets allows underlying Agent services to be bundled as utility computing or as a composite service. Additionally, these can identify automation targets or service candidates for in/out sourcing.
	The SLs for the business Interaction identifies the OLs to be met by the Role set.
	Allows the allocation of an Agent's capacity across Roles. Further the cost of an Agent can be recovered from the IT Requests for each of the business Interactions based usage. The services can be rolled up into a cost based and justified based on Interaction's business value.
	IT Request type classification allows routine services (e.g. utility services and fixed cost services) to be borne by existing users based on Interaction volumes. Variable non-routine services are charged by service-based pricing.
	(The template in Example 2 identifies the Roles used in business Request types for Community Relations and Parks and Recreation. It also identifies missing Roles needed for Request types.)

continued on the following page

Figure 4. (continued)

Example 2. Associating Work Products E & C: IT Role set to IT Requests & Primary REDs							
Organization allocation →		**Community Relations Organization**			**Parks and Recreation Organization**		
IT Request type ↓	**Available?**	**Request types**	**Throughput**	**FTE**	**Request types**	**Throughput**	**FTE**
Payment engine	Yes	Not used		0	Permits Special events	100	20
Order management	Yes	Not used		5	Park Maint. Servicing		100
Application service (Platinum)	Yes	Not used			Not used		
Web posting	No	Resolution	20	5	Status	300	50
eMail utility	Yes	All		20	All		150
Desktop support	Yes	Move, add, change	1		Move, add, change	6	
Case tracking (311)	Yes						
GIS based services	No	All	20	4	All	50	10
Disaster recovery				5			120
Dimension	*Benefits of Traceability along the allocate-use association*						
IT Request types	IT Request type catalog – the customer's view of services provided.						
	The Role sets for Support and Delivery Interactions can be assigned Agents at triage. This dynamic assignment supports virtualization. Dedicated resources can be pre-determined.						
	The service level of the response Interaction is linked to the underlying Agents' capacity and availability.						
	By tying the IT requests to the business REDs Interactions, we can charge based on spreading the costs across all uses within all business Interactions.						
	Charging requires the ability to predict usage.						
	Example 3 illustrates how an IT Role set and costs are allocated across business organizations.						

continued on the following page

Figure 4. (continued)

Example 3. Associating Work Products C to A: Allocating IT Requests to Business Request types								
IT Request Type ±	**Allocation Method**	**Total costs ($)**	**Total FTE business users**	**Unit Price per year**	**IT Infrastructure Roles/ Resources used**	**Costs**	**Business Organizations and Interactions**	
Desktop support	T&M				TCP/IP		All	
Email	Shared Utility (% of total FTE users)	240,000	2,000	120	Server	200,000	All except safety	
					Upgrade	20,000		
					System admin	20,000		
Email platinum					24x7 plus back up trail and electronic records management		Safety	
Application development	T&M				Development only		All	
					Maintenance			
					Backup and recovery			
Web posting	Shared utility (% by FTE)	100,000	50	…	Server		Only X, Y, Z	
					Communications			
					Application dev.			
Payment engine	Shared utility (% by FTE)				License		Only X, Y,Z	
					Upgrades			
					Backup and recovery			
Dimension	*Benefits of Traceability along the allocate-use association*							
IT RED Interactions	IT operations are around service support and service delivery Interactions.							
	RED metrics provides actual use of IT service and this is used to update the availability of each Role (example 1). This also updates quality of infrastructure; actual capacity used; Request types and volumes serviced.							
	Identifies future interaction requirements. (Details in Example 4)							

continued on the following page

Figure 4. (continued)

Dimension	Benefits of Traceability along the allocate-use association
IT Business	Costs actual dollars required to deliver a particular asset, product, or service.
	Pricing is on the SLA needed for the Interactions. Prices actual dollars required to deliver a particular asset, product, or service plus an additional dollar amount to cover difficult-to-quantify costs or investments.
	Account for the money spent in providing IT Services and provide visibility to the customer.
	Track actual costs against budget.
	Calculate the cost of providing IT Services to both internal and external customers.
	Perform cost-benefit or Return-on-Investment analyses.
	Identify the cost of changes.
	Recover the costs of the IT Services from the customers of the service.
	Operate the IT organization as a business unit if required.
	Influence internal user and customer behavior to better meet strategic needs.
	Considers all interactions and throughput and prioritizes areas of need.
Strategy impact on IT services	Predict factors that impact capacity, availability, and pricing.
	Request trends and targets to define true demand for IT services.
	Increase visibility for IT to identify and meet SLA.

Example 4. Associating IT Request types to RED Interactions

Community Relations					Parks and Recreation				
Request type, Priority and RED Interaction			**Through-put (goal)**	**FTE**	**Request type, Priority and interaction**			**Through-put (goal)**	**FTE**
High: Request: Complaints			50 (50)	5	High: Request: Permits (Golf, Fitness,…)			100 (250)	4
R: Request	E: Case tracking	D: Web posting			R: Permit applic.	E: Payment engine	D: Web posting		
IT services: Case tracking					IT services: permits, payment IT services missing: web posting with GIS.				
High: Request: Community meeting			20 (70)	5	Med: Request: Park maint.			500 (500)	110
R: Request	E: Case tracking	D: Web posting			R: Routine	E: Work order system	D: Delivery Completed		
IT services: Case tracking					IT services: Work order system				

Within the typical organization, existing practices in use today can well identify the costs (see example 1). The relationship between these costs and the allocation to the organizations for cost recovery is known to be challenging throughout industry. Consequently, as mentioned earlier, costs are often simply shared and recovered as overhead attached to IT human resources and allocated across organizations.

Using the IT costs and capacity, the immediate recommendation to improve traceability is to implement a three-step process 1) identify the IT service catalog from a customer perspective, 2) bundle services as Role sets and allocate all known underlying human and other IT infrastructure costs to the delivered IT Requests, and 3) allocate IT services to the organizations based on the allocation method appropriate to the IT service. Thus the details are:

1. *Capacity dimension:* Define an initial IT Roles catalog, easily identified bottom-up by looking at existing Agents, capacity, and costs.
2. *IT service dimension:* Allocate all existing Agents/resources to the different Role sets they can support. Use BioS questionnaire-based information to get the customers' view of the service – i.e. web support rather that web server, web admin, disaster recovery and so on.
3. *IT service use dimension:* Allocate the IT Role sets across organizations and their Request types by an allocation method (such as % utility based on FTEs, time and material, etc.).

Why three steps and not two? That is, why use the logical Role sets concept? A simpler two-step method can be considered. For example, instead of allocating the IT infrastructure Agents to Role sets and then allocating the Role sets to business Interactions across organizations, we can directly allocate the gathered costs to the customer organizations based on the FTE. However, there are several issues (e.g. fairness) related to this:

•   Certain IT components are used by different IT services but not all the IT services are used by a customer organization. Those organizations that do not use any of an underlying IT component will still have a higher overhead due to some IT that is not being used. For example, consider a database cost. Certain organizations – like community services - might not use a database at all.
•   Customer perception is harder to manage if costs are ascribed to IT components that are not visible from the customer's perspective. For example, web support is easily understood by the customer, but a charge for some underlying middle-ware upgrade is not.

- It becomes harder to tie IT Request types to customer Request types and value. This important tie helps us justify investments in IT.

The suggested three-step method illustrated above ties known Agent costs to the actual customer facing IT Request types and services which are then used by the organizations. The movement to a service-use based costing also immediately reduces the current overhead ascribed to specific resources (like human resources) and also improves the perception of the IT organization.

The customer-facing IT Request catalog and the different allocation methods related to the use of the services are also illustrated in example 2 above. We can now make the following observations:

- As the IT Request Catalog gets more customer-oriented, the customer has visibility into what they are getting for their money. CARs (customer account representatives) should now be able to communicate and explain what each service contains by using the Role set.
- CARs play a critical role in any improvement to the perception of IT. CARs have to take greater responsibility by maintaining organizational BioS and improving its quality of information.
- CARs should also be able to identify new service innovations needed in conjunction with the organizations.
- IT should not lose its ability to invest in IT advancements and benefit different organizations. It is critical that IT retain the ability to provide innovation.
- Having addressed cost identification, allocation, and allocation methods the recovery is straightforward.
- Cost is recovered based on the IT service usage.
- The following year's allocation is based on this year's actual usage or actual useage averaged over a few years.

We next note, using example in Figure 4 above, that the success of IT begins with the customers' business processes and enabling those effectiveness and innovation needs. Also any innovation with IT will be cost effective only if it improves the business process Interaction rates or reduces the number of FTEs for that process. Note that for a 'thriving' business process, an increase in the Interaction rates usually also means increased business value. Next we show how to collect complete top-down information with the BioS – Business Information use Operations Strategy – template and example 4 above.

As illustrated, each organization ('community relations' and 'parks and recreation' in the example) completes many different request types (e.g. 'complaints', 'community meetings', 'permits', and 'maintenance') with REDs. Each RED Interaction completes a request using some IT services as indicated. These are provided by the IT organizations. Note that missing services are also identified and uses for strategic planning as discussed earlier. Finally an IT Request is implemented using underlying IT infrastructure Agents (including humans, network, and software applications) that have limited capacities and costs related to increasing capacity.

Example 4 also shows how IT Requests are used by organizations and to achieve their business process performance. This also provides information on how to value-price an IT service as a service or as a utility shared across the number of FTEs and Organizations. For example, the payment engine is not shared, so the full cost is borne by one organization. On the other hand, the cost of a shared order management service can be spread across two organizations. The price charged for a service, as an example, can be on the percentage of FTEs in a user organization and the overall number of FTEs.

ORGANIZATIONAL CO-ENGINEERING

ACE governance: Organizationally, to achieve this traceability, IT must also allocate the budget and administrative capability to operate the selected allocation methods. This also includes a chargeback committee that is in place and working well within the ACE governance group. Processes and an escalation path are in place for handling exceptions. Finally, benchmarking is done to ensure that IT service costs are in line across organizations and externally to comparable enterprises. While the traceability is difficult to institute, accounts are transparent and organizations can readily access any level of detail. The work products illustrated ensure that the association between cost and service level is clear and understood by both the customers and IT service providers. Using this, the IT organization also achieves traceability to all capacity and service costs. The institutionalization of complete traceability requires organizational engineering.

Basis for rates and costs to be established (as a first step each year for budget preparation). Institute a formalized process to prepare an annual technology plan for each customer organization. Use the as-is BioS as part of the strategic planning to drive a service-based strategy. The key elements are:

- Reevaluate the primary business interactions enabled by IT and identify missing opportunities for effectiveness and innovation.
- Staffing of the fiscal section for budgeting, procurement, contracts, and legislation.
- Formulation and tracking of contracts and technical procurement activities, review, and approval of invoices.

- Establishment of a uniform process for contract renewals that is linked with the organization wide budget planning and development process.
- Organizations should implement a formal process for developing a technology plan with each of its customers (CAR responsibility using BioS).
- Develop a monthly financial condition report.

Role of Customer Account Representatives: The ACE architecture governance should ensure success by expanding the role of CARs. The CARs define and improve the interface to the customer organizations by using BioS work products for documenting each organization's service needs and developing a management strategy. This requires CARs with adequate customer and technical skills. Also clarify the role of the CAR and provide training to support their ability to serve as true CARs. CARs and project managers should be more actively involved with understanding and managing the services and associated budgets for their respective organizations (using BioS). Use of BioS by CARs as a standardized tool for understanding the customer organization's business process, required IT services, and the business value of those services to develop an service level management strategy and chargeback.

Managing Cost and Capacity: The next challenge is to avoid a bottomless pit of resources and identify capacity and availability accurately to improve the use of existing resources. The general goal of capacity management is to allow IT architects to align their capacity concerns, at the resource or service level, with the capacity concerns of the business. From this perspective there are two factors to address in order to be successful, namely cost and risk. The need for cost reduction is fairly obvious. Without concern for it the much simpler strategy of massively over-provisioning works well, but is not an option.

Hence costs must be balanced with risk because it determines to what degree the business is willing to constrain capacity with respect to the overall goal of cost reduction and service expectations. From the cost perspective there are two avenues for improvement rooted in both resource and service capacity management activities. These are resource utilization and process improvement, respectively. Addressing risk, or building resilience into a capacity management strategy, means to place limits on the amount of optimization that should be done to a resource or process to allow for some degrees of freedom in the event there are changes in the business environment. Hence, the goal of a capacity management framework can be expressed in the following two points:

- Optimize all resource and process capacity so they can exactly satisfy the current capacity demands of the business customers. In other words, make them lean, specific, and precise to maximize utilization.

- Determine the expectations of the internal business customers with regard to sources of business capacity variance and introduce under-utilization to account for it.

By building up a solid foundation for IT services chargeback in the previous section, the first step is relatively simple. The traceability associations have been identified in such a way that they are related directly through the business services to the business customers. With this in place the resource capacity can be determined by aligning them with historical trends for business services[e] and incorporating future expectations communicated to the CARs.

The second step requires a deeper understanding of the business customers' tolerance for service degradation in the case of radical unforeseen changes in the business environment. The CAR should work with business customers to identify possible scenarios, such as new advertising campaigns, take-over situations, or disastrous events, in order to elicit forces the business may be subject to in the future. Then, using the customer-facing chargeback work products as a mechanism for communication, the CARs can work with business customers to find an appropriate and cost-effective level of tolerance for service capacity. Once again, because the traceability associations back to the resource capacity have been identified in the chargeback work products, the IT organization can use these tolerances to make capacity decisions across their customer base on a continuous basis. Since this process deals with risks and unknowns it difficult to fully systematize, but the ACE work products establish the solid customer facing artifacts that are *required* for this kind of detailed and precise communication.

CONCLUSION AND RESEARCH

As can be seen with Figure 4 which consolidates the individual sub-organizational BioS into a consolidated organizational view, we can now:

- Predict demand based on business capacity goals.
- Implement more equitable cost allocation since we know who uses what services.
- Assign clear responsibility to monitor customer satisfaction and strategy.
- Enable consolidation into a portfolio with value-based priorities and cross-cutting improvements.
- Target areas of improvement and innovation as organizational throughput improvement and new products and services.
- Operationalize best practices such as ITIL.

Thus, we have shown that the short-term chargeback model, the service catalog, and the long-term strategies are closely related. The long-term improvements can be achieved through continual improvement implemented though the maintenance of the portfolio and the monitoring of performance.

The "ACE" chargeback and capacity aligns the Business-IT service functions into a holistic model to provide total traceability. The alignment ensures we are measuring what matters! That is, is the customer willing to pay for a particular service, directly or indirectly.

We wish to emphasize that the degree of success is related to "Maturity Level" of the organization. It allows IT to be aligned with customers through the annual budgeting process, developing a service catalog, and improving service level and business agreements. In the long run this provides a framework for a fully integrated, real time, automated governance process for an adaptive continually improving enterprise. Several challenges have also been identified:

- IT accounting and charging are often new disciplines in IT services and there is limited understanding of leading practice in cost modeling and charging mechanisms which could lead to over-complex or ineffective systems.
- IT accounting relies on planning information provided by other processes both within and outside of IT services management which may not be routinely available, delaying the project.
- Staff combining accountancy and IT experience are rare, so many activities may need to be shared with staff from outside IT Services who may not have this as their priority.
- The IT strategies and objectives of an organization may not be well formulated and documented and prediction of capacity requirement not accurate.
- Senior business managers may not recognize the benefits of IT accounting and charging and may resent the administrative overheads and the limitations on workload.
- The IT accounting and charging processes are so elaborate that the cost of the system exceeds the value of the information produced.
- The monitoring tools providing resource usage information are inaccurate, irrelevant, or cost too much to develop and maintain.

TASKS FOR ALIGNMENT OF WORK PRODUCTS A-F

1. Develop a charge model in the context of your project based on the process outlined in this chapter. Depending on the nature of the project you've selected you may need to consider slightly different aspects. For example if you are

working on a service innovation or improvement project you need to think about your business customer and other services, possibly outside the scope of your work, that they might need in the overall organizational setting. If you are working on deploying a best practice standard (like ITIL) or an internal governance initiative consider the details and requirements it dictates and determine what constraints it imposes on chargeback policies. If you are working on a product innovation project, you are looking at the ACE structure of market segments encompassing the organization and the incoming customer requests.

2. Consider how you might address any capacity related issues in the context of your project. Discuss how you would work with your sponsor and business customers within the organization to identify and address unknown environmental changes that could impact organizational performance. How will you handle situations where multiple stakeholders cannot agree on the service requirements or controls that need to be in place to satisfy them? Will you be able to cater to individually or will your decisions have an effect on multiple parties? How will you make the decision making process systemic? (It may be worthwhile to have a team member research some well known decision theoretic techniques, like the Analytic Hierarch Process, and discuss how they may or may not be able to assist you).

THINGS TO THINK ABOUT

1. There are countless ways to implement a chargeback strategy, some of the simplest being to charge a flat subscription fee at periodic intervals or dividing a total cost equally among a set of users. Make up a few different chargeback models, from a flat fee to per-use strategies, and a try to come up with a decision matrix showing each model against generic characteristics that make them more or less attractive. Your characteristics might be drawn from a range of concerns like organizational setting, behaviors to encourage, complexity of what is being charged for, or complexity of the model itself.

2. How does chargeback relate to product pricing? Generalize the chargeback considerations to apply to customers and market segments that the organization caters to. How do these considerations apply to service pricing to external customers? Base this on a few current papers on product marketing.

3. How does the use-allocation relationship relate to green computing? Base this on a current paper.

4. Encouraging changes in behavior is typically credited as the reason for using a chargeback policy above all else. Do you agree (and justify your argument)?

5.   Does implementing a chargeback policy for IT services change the way IT is viewed? Consider a range of stakeholders in an organization, from strategic to tactical, when answering.

6.   Capacity management is relevant when over-provisioning has a significant cost. Technological advances are constantly changing what factors contribute to this cost – what are some of the biggest challenges today and how do you think that might change over the next decade.

7.   Name other types of management that requires alignment along the allocation-use associations?

8.   In what ways can an organization be thought of as a fractal? How can this be leveraged by IT? List at least five ways.

REFERENCES

Gallegos, F., Senft, S., Daniel, P., & Gonzales, C. (2004). *Information Technology Control and Audit.* Boca Raton: Auerbach Publications.

ITIL Version 3. (n.d). Retrieved November 23, 2008, from http://www.ogc.gov.uk/

META Practice (May 2003). IT Cost Recovery: How Do We Take It?.

Ross, J. W., Vitale, M. R., & Beath, C. (1999 June). The Untapped Potential of IT Chargeback. *MIS Quarterly, 23*(2), 215-237.

Val IT Overview. (n.d.). Retrieved November 23, 2008, from http://www.isaca.org/Content/ContentGroups/Val_IT1/Val_IT.htm

ENDNOTES

[a]   Val IT is tightly integrated with COBIT Version 4, also from the Information Systems Audit and Control Association (a.k.a. ISACA). The Framework document explains the difference between COBIT and Val IT as follows: Val IT extends and complements COBIT, which provides a comprehensive control framework for IT governance. Specifically, Val IT focuses on the investment decision (are we doing the right things?) and the realization of benefits (are we getting the benefits?), while COBIT focuses on the execution (are we doing them the right way, and are we getting them done well?)

[b]   There are certainly other techniques other than the ones identified but they suffice as representative examples.

[c]   Gartner reference.

[d]   For a quick overview refer to chart of accounts - wiki.

[e]   Methods and tools for this style of capacity planning and optimization have been studied and developed extensively in Systems Engineering, Computer Science, and a number of other fields. A full discussion of these techniques is well beyond the scope of this book, but both ITIL and SEI's Architecture Tradeoff Analysis Method are good initial sources to refer to for a basic discussion of traditional optimization techniques as they can be applied to IT service management or software architecture.

Chapter VII
Co–Engineering IT Services for Lean Operations

ABSTRACT

How do we conduct successfully the design and analysis for a service improvement project?

- How do we construct the ACE structure to identify and quantify the numerous many-to-many relationships and service-based Interactions between processes, organizations, applications, and enabling IT components?
- How do we apply Lean Co-engineering principles to analyze, prioritize, and target opportunities based on impact to the overall performance of the complex system?
- How do we derive the requirements for deployment and configuration of existing enterprise systems and resources?
- How do we develop a roadmap for improvement and the related business justification?

The ACE structure is not only used to create BioS goals and work products, but also to perform the analysis needed to prioritize improvement projects and their tasks. We next show how the structure is used to define tasks and priorities to deploy in the context of existing enterprise systems and emerging technologies to reduce

Figure 1. ACE structure deployment using the ticketing of Requests, metrics capture within the CRM, and organizational changes in the physical world

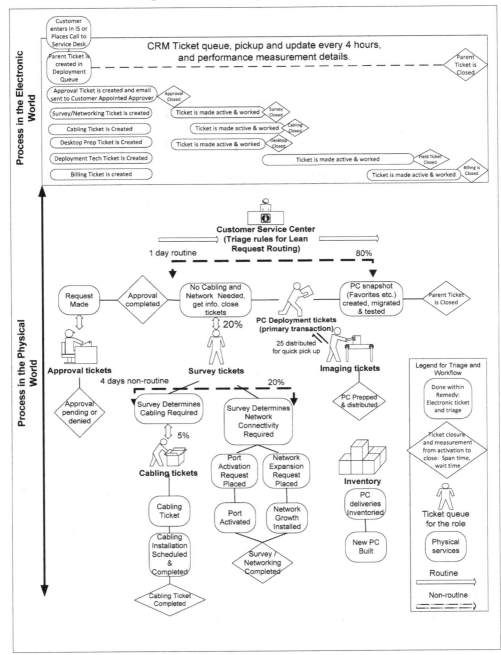

the time to install new PCs from *seventeen days to one day*. The related goals are met by quantifying the Interactions between global Lean and local Autonomic goals to achieve continuous improvement. Finally, we show here how a complex system 'improves' operationally through enhancements in a Role set that includes both Agents in the physical world and in the Electronic world. for related approaches to this also see Brittenham et al 2007[a].

We use the PC (personal computer) Build and Install service to illustrate methods for the improvement of underlying Interactions within a typical complex organization. This application was selected because it has the complex characteristics, yet it is representative and straightforward to understand. The techniques are widely applicable for the improvement of IT services and Primary services.

THE BUSINESS CHALLENGE

The IT organization of a health-care provider with a billion plus in operating revenue had as a goal the reduction of the PC build and install process from seventeen days to one day. Separate IT teams have been created over time to provide the following services: service desk, Request management, inventory management, approvals, billing, deployment, assembly, inventory, and imaging/engineering. While some of these resources are shared with other processes, each of these teams plays a role in the deployment of a PC. Roughly, eight fulltime equivalents (FTE), of the 240 fulltime employees in Information Systems, are dedicated to the PC process.

Over a hundred Requests (also *tickets*) of Request type PCs install or fix are received each month. Since the PCs serve numerous different purposes in the hospital – from use at a nurse's station to equipment monitoring - many *variations* are deployed. There are also many different types of software to be installed. Finally, there are multiple enterprise software systems in place – a customer relationship management (CRM) system is used for managing the Customer Service Center (CSC, defined as in ITIL) tickets, an asset management data base, a work order system for technicians, and a PC imaging system are all utilized. As is typical, these systems are *not integrated* and do not share ticket data or workflow status. About thirty five personnel and eight FTE are involved in this process.

A flow for the PC build and install process, or just PC install, can be seen in Figure 2. As with most service organizations, there were several challenges. The *variation* in Request s and related processing needs had caused the existing process to evolve over time to execute the worst-case scenario each time. Examples of this included waiting for approvals for small purchases or traveling to the site to survey it for proper wiring due to lack of site documentation.

How do we justify improvements and create the roadmap for the complex environment, given tight budget constraints? The case study and project objectives were to address this as follows:

- Provide a specific roadmap to improve service quality and reduce the time to deploy.
- Develop a repeatable and scalable methodology for Co-engineering business, organizations, and IT services for other service improvement programs[b].
- Enable continuous improvement through a monitoring and management framework.
- Integrate and leverage existing best practices (such as Lean, ITIL) and technology (such as CMDB and autonomic systems) as appropriate, and finally
- Clearly identify the benefits to the business in terms of opportunities for effectiveness and innovation.

BACKGROUND AND BEST PRACTICES

We first overview background research in academia and industry that addresses the service improvement challenge. In general we find much of the research in process improvement and aligning business and IT services remains disciplinary focused. Several have identified the need for *interdisciplinary* research and have referred to this emerging discipline as *Services Science* (IBM Services Science 2008)[c]. We examine the most relevant concepts next.

Best Practices for Process Efficiency: At its core the efficiency of a process is related to effective use of underlying resources and how they create the work products. A very relevant best-practice for efficient resource use is Lean (George 2002). Its principles are widely applied, and the common starting point for implementation is a value-stream representation.

The principles are applied to an *as-is process flow graph* representation with:

- Physical *work centers as nodes* performing transformations.
- Routings of Requests (e.g. tickets, work orders, incidents etc.) *as transitions*.
- Associated with each transition and node, the *value-add* and *non-value add* time that is defined from the *customers'* perspective. The non-value-add time includes the cause - for example Request s are queued waiting for data re-entry.

To-be process transitions and times are developed by the Lean Principle[d] as follows:

- Define the re-engineered process considering the Takt time objectives of produced components and sub-components from the customers' perception.
- Systematically eliminate wasted time to achieve the to-be.
- Enable decentralized multifunctional teams at work centers to make improvements locally and achieve a global impact.

Next analysis is conducted and actions are taken to achieve Lean Production Principles follows:

- Elimination of wasted time
- Zero defects
- Pull instead of push to apply resources only to customer perceived value
- Multifunctional teams to provide flexibility in using resources and knowledge
- Decentralized responsibilities to allow local adaptation to the environment
- Information to support the task at hand
- Continuous Improvement based on performance measurement

Electronic and Physical business processes management: In a physical Lean shop floor process management system, every operation and process becomes flexible. The actual process transformation step using resources for the customer creates a *demand* (pull) to produce only the amount consumed by that customer Request.

The potential of logical electronic workflows above the physical layer (e.g. above the shop floor, the physical resources of a clinic) is making the flow itself more dynamic. Every customer related Interaction needs resources - information, materials, assets and so on. This Interaction, in turn, creates a 'pull' for pre-requisite inputs so the output can be produced, and so on. This pull is determined dynamically at triage to facilitate the delayed routing and assignment of resources. Further the Interactions needed for the particular Request are also discovered. Thus the flexibility of electronic processes can be leveraged to implement lean, and leaner, operations in the physical world. We next highlight some key characteristics of electronic business process management.

Building on Chapter 2, we can organize RED Interactions and their Role sets – or electronic work centers - into a Lean BPM that creates value through processes that systematically minimize all forms of waste *at the work level*. Unlike business re-engineering and enterprise application integration (EAI), which is primarily targeted towards macro-level processes, the BPM approach is targeted to improving and automating workflow and individual work tasks and decision-making. It is analogous to streamlining work processes at the shop floor level.

The flexibility of IT manifests itself in many ways – the just-in-time assignment to retain effective use of shared resources, the dynamic Interaction sequencing and changes, and 'shipping' of electronic work packages globally and so on. In other words, the flexibility of electronic BPM can be put to work to better manage the physical world and resources in order to reduce waste. Applying Co-engineering principle 4, the Lean electronic process uses IT to reduce rework, errors, wasted time, transit time as well as improve the utilization of resources. Designed thus, the Lean organization is flexible enough to efficiently respond to *each non-routine* Request.

CREATING AN ACE STRUCTURE

Co-engineering begins with an ACE structure which is used to manage the underlying Agents and Interactions to meet goals. For example, a successful customer-driven Lean ACE structure pulls into use and dynamically integrates all other supporting internal processes and roles within the organization. This type of business process integration also results in visibility and offers significant opportunity for return as companies transform their business processes and back-end systems to create an integrated user experience. Often this requires services to be defined or granular services to be provided by back-end systems (such as order entry, supply, demand fulfillment). It also requires the internal worker, customer, and the supplier to perform different roles within Interactions. We illustrate all this with conceptual ACE structure deployed using the CRM changes, organization changes, and integration patterns.

Goals

While the initial stated scope of the project was to improve the primary PC Install Interaction, a quick exploration suggests that the larger context is important in formulating strategy goals:

- *IT Service Support context:* The PC Interaction was actually representative of many other Request types that the IT organization was dealing with. These include the move, add, and change of all items within the installed IT infrastructure. Note changes also include repair. The same IT resources (processes, personnel, enterprise software such as CRM, databases) that service the PC Requests are also shared with other incoming Request types. Therefore, making the PC process efficient could have a positive impact on other Requests as well.

- *External trends and related context*: Underlying technology and services are evolving rapidly. Supplier products and services are also beginning to provide more and more of the core IT services. Examples include the on-line ordering of specifically configured PCs, site monitoring, and configuration management technologies. One should therefore begin to ask the question of whether the services provided for these types of Requests also entailed knowledge and enabling IT that were critical to retain within the organization and needed to be developed as a capability. If not, the service could be outsourced.

These contextual aspects affect the PC install process and must be considered within the CIOs office and the ACE governance.

Since we are first developing the ACE structure for the *IT organization,* as in Figure 2, this requires us to clearly articulate the BioS goals that allow us to deliver to all the stakeholders. At the strategy dimension these are the stakeholders that are the end-users and the business customers of IT. At a high level the Figure 2 illustrates:

- Traceable relationships between the business goals, strategy goals, and the 'PC install' Request type and (as-is) service level performance in rows 1 and 2.
- Relationship of the 'PC install' Interaction types and their Role set performance in column 2, row 3 to the Request type performance.
- Metrics relating the Agents, Roles and their operating level performance to the value created at the Interaction instances as in column 2, row 3.
- *Continual improvement* actions in a column 3 that observe and improve other actions by identifying:
    o The relative Interaction priorities based on value to business.
    o The relative investments available for effectiveness and innovation.
    o The intersection of poor performing Roles and the highest priority Interactions that rely on them, as the next target.

Within this ACE structure, the external context also determines the strategy goals in column 1 of the ACE structure. Co-engineering principle 1 predominantly underlies the articulation of these goals. The next set of goals in the business dimension traceable to 'competitive pricing' is given in column 1. Take for example, 'competitive pricing' is an issue that requires the IT organization cannot take more to install a PC than it would take a vendor and supplier. As a matter of fact all the traceable relationships between hard goals and in column 1 are given. The

Figure 2. ACE structure representation of goals, Interactions, and Agents for continuous improvement

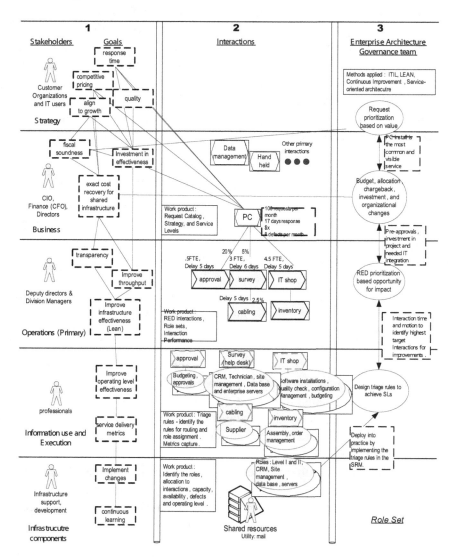

prescriptive 'competitive pricing' target goal might be set to do better than vendors by taking advantage of the volume pricing of parts. However this goal might take many service improvement program iterations, each of which focuses on specific Interactions.

More generally, a variety of traceable hard goals and soft goals have to be addressed, each to some degree and in a continual fashion, by service improvement programs. In each iteration changes are implemented in traceable actions and checked to see what the next increment of improvements should be. Focusing on achieving these traceable goals, the links relate the measurable aspects of Interactions to the IT system and Role sets as illustrated in Figure 1. We discuss the relationships between the goals across dimensions before proceeding to the actions in column 2:

- *Business goals:* Other than achieving universal goals like fiscal soundness, what are the other measurable goals that provide the business context for actions? What goals govern the priorities across Interactions based on the value to the business? Can further investments be made available for improving the response effectiveness to targeted Interactions? Should the focus of these investments be in innovation areas or on achieving effectiveness? For example, is there funding to purchase a site monitoring system? That is, by expanding the scope of the project and improving more types of Interactions with a new technology, can we achieve adequate business value to warrant investment? And, for the purposes of analysis, these goals can be stated in terms of relative weights assigned to prioritize REDs. Also certain constraints - for example the investment focus on effectiveness is greater than innovation for the next planning period – need to be identified. Co-engineering principle 2 underlies the articulation of these goals.

- *Infrastructure-use and execution goals:* Do the Role set metrics and OLs positively relate to business goals of improving high-priority Interactions and SLs? What infrastructure and information is needed but missing for the workers to achieve metrics during service Interaction execution? For example, can we justify training to improve the Interaction metrics that will increase the effectiveness goals of a high-priority Interaction?

- *Operational goals:* What changes have to be made to the enabling infrastructure roles to conserve resources and improve the service throughput of an Interaction type? Is there enough transparency to understand how the services can be streamlined? The goals would be to define and meet the SL and price requirements. Co-engineering principle 5 to reduce costs, eliminate Interactions, etc. applies.

- *Strategy goals:* For each Request type, other than the obvious customer satisfaction factors, like the response time and ability to work with minimum disruption, what are the real benefits of the organization (internal IT in this case) to the customer? Are the customer Request s projected to increase? For the PC install example, suppliers like Dell provide the ability to configure, order, and ship PCs. Is the internal IT providing more flexibility in configuration, lower costs, or installation of special software as competitive value? How much is this worth to the customer and will it increase the business value of the organization?

Not only are the goals interrelated as illustrated, they are also related to Request metrics (the PC Install metrics) and achieved through action performance - in turn achieved through improving the infrastructure. Thus, setting the appropriate goals and targets for each Request type is critical to developing a roadmap for improving actions. Once this is done the next step is developing column 2 of the ACE architecture framework. This will require us to employ the Lean and ITIL methods.

Interactions

As-is Value Stream Mapping: To get an understanding of the existing actions and to identify the non-value-add time, we complete an as-is mapping shown in Figure 2. The Request s came in through different ways (web forms, word of mouth, help desk etc.) and were not always ticketed at the Customer Service Center as required by ITIL. This often caused confusion since some orders were handled outside the system.

ACE Structure - AS-IS Work Product Details for PC Install

Strategy Dimension: Request Strategy Catalog (Work Product A)

PC installation is a primary Request type and an entry in the organizations' customer facing Request catalog. For this Request type we must identify the strategy-related goals. For example - to alignment of response to organizational growth, the expected increase in number of Requests, and the configuration deliverable options. Also we must identify any pricing and competitive constraints. In this case an important goal is to keep the price to the customer below what can be purchased from the websites of suppliers. Other value to the customer - for example the installation of custom software - is also identified for this service.

Also we must mine external Request types for variation and identify new Request types that lead to opportunity. This suggests understanding more about the customer and providing ways for the customer to participate in and influence actions to create maximum value for the customer and for the business. Opportunities for

Figure 3. As-is high-level flow for PC Build and Install process illustrating non-value add (e.g. budget approval) steps

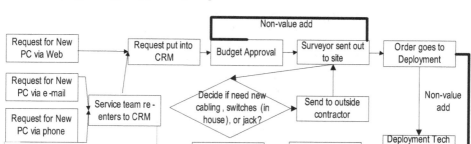

innovation include outsourcing the routine PC installs, investing in the capability to handle non-routine services and offer it as a service capability to other parts of the enterprise, or using the PC process as a vehicle to streamline internal operations to a highly competitive point and for all services.

Operations Dimension: RED Interactions and Sub-Interactions Structure, SLs (Work Product C)

Next identify the primary Interaction(s) related to each Request type and the iteratively identify all sub Interaction pairs that might be employed. Organize the Interactions and sub-Interactions to meet the processing needs from the customer's value-add perspective. In the example, there is one primary PC Deployment Interaction. Not all the sub-Interactions add value. For example, Survey and Cabling do not (as they reflect a deficiency in the infrastructure). Hence the times taken for these Interactions are non-value-add times. We would therefore like to execute these Interactions only of absolutely necessary.

As shown in Figure 4, we create an acyclic graph with the associations between the nodes reflecting the Request flow rates. The workflow routings are based on this structure and determined during triage at the Customer Service Center based on the requirements of the incoming request structure as we will see later.

Thus we can now note that routine Requests require only the primary Interaction (i.e. PC Install) and therefore this path is taken 80% of the time according to data in Figure 4. Thus, this high volume Interaction Request has highest priority for improvement. Note also that as in Figure 4, the PC main Interaction uses sub-Interactions only if needed for non-routine Requests. This is indicated by different *associations* and the *% Requests* along that association.

Figure 4. To-be ACE virtual structure with RED Interactions (and Role sets) as nodes and routine/ non-routine routings as associations

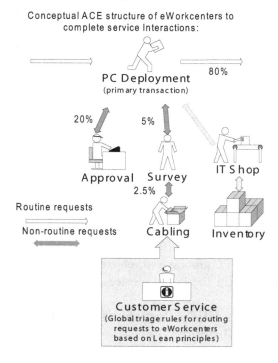

Next as-is metrics are associated with each RED - in this case *Requirements, Execution of Install, Delivery and billing.* Figure 5 illustrates the time attributes of the top ACE structure and Interaction node - the primary customer facing PC Interaction. The information includes the as-is TAKT times for routine and non-routine Requests of each type, the resources used, and wait times. The ACE structure is next augmented with TAKT times and Request percentages that flow to each Interaction. TAKT is determined with the value-add time of the main Interaction to deliver customer value. We also *apportion* the TAKT times for sub Interactions. Missing as-is TAKT times are supplied with observations. For example we found out how long a survey takes. Together with the number of times each Interaction is executed, we have a baseline for identifying areas for targeting improvements.

Infrastructure-Use and Execution Dimension: Role Sets and OLs (Work Product E)

Next we define Role improvements to meet OLs needed for each Interaction and sub-Interaction. For the primary PC install Interaction this is given in Figure 5.

Figure 5. Data for Primary PC Interaction - Queue times (gray columns), as-is TAKT time and totals for routine and non-routine Request s. Time unit is a day with eight working hours.

# Requests		PC Install (primary RED transaction):					As-is	
		Requirements	Queue Time	Execution	Queue Time	Delivery	Resource time (days)	Wasted time
		Days	wait, travel	Days	wait, travel	Days		
Type of requests ↓	100	R1: Requirements and triage (Service desk)		E1: Install (level 1)		D1: Billing	26.67	90.63
routine requests times	80	2.50	40.00	15.00	10.00	2.50	20.00	50.00
non-routine requests that need sub-transactions	20	1.04	40.00	5.00	0.63	0.63	6.67	40.63
TAKT time (for one routine request)	1	0.03	0.50	0.19	0.13	0.03	0.25	0.63
TAKT time (for one non-routine request)	1	0.05	2.00	0.25	0.03	0.03	0.33	2.03

This describes IT and organization services and the desired local improvements as well as the migration tasks to go from as-is to to-be.

Business Dimension: Request Priorities and Project Portfolio

The business constraint on improvement was that no new resources would be available. This service was indeed of highest value to the business. However, given the economic conditions, the service improvement project had to pay for itself.

The to-be Co-engineering analysis leading to business decisions and the Prioritized Project Portfolio Work Product is given in the next section.

We found that of the hundred plus Requests handled each month most are queued for a considerable time. We documented the 'hand-offs', actually Requests and *RED Interactions,* between organizations to produce sub-deliverables. We found that all sub-Interactions were always executed, even for simple Requests, to complete the primary service. For example, an 'approval' hand-off for a Request occurred even for standard 'routine' Requests thus causing unnecessary delays. More generally,

Figure 5. Role set enabling the primary PC Interaction with organization and IT services. The underlying agent improvements and migration tasks to go from as-is to to-be are also indicated.

←Role set Service Examples and Engineering to Improve Interaction Throughput →		
Enabling IT services and improvements	**Org. services and improvements**	**Migration tasks to go from as-is to to-be process**
Service desk tickets for survey, install, and billing	Identify the skill set for routine installs	How will customers enter the system in the future? Interim IT issues?
Confirm site specifics	Develop scripts for the service desk to perform the triage	Must get full, accurate requirements from customer, customer sign - off
Triage: Level 1: PC Install Queue. Level II: To create routing if needed	Single point of entry for Requests through service desk	Move the ticket to level II if anything unusual is detected
Asset info update		Triage rules to separate those Requests that need site survey, approvals or other Interactions
Invoice & reconcile		

since all the Interactions were executed all the time for all kinds of Requests, unnecessary wait was introduced for those that were routine.

To identify the sources of wasted time, we first completed a process map with all tasks and then marked the value and non-value added steps as indicated in Figure 3. Clearly this is an example of a process that has evolved and become more complex to handle the most difficult cases, leading to inefficiencies for simple, and in reality, common cases. For example a surveyor does not always have to be sent.

The time and motion study gave us the process steps that did not always add value as illustrated in Figure 3. Using this understanding we proceed to show how the Interactions of interest in the ACE structure were identified and populated with baseline metrics. We also show how the work products are defined using the structure.

TO-BE CO-ENGINEERING ACROSS DIMENSIONS AND WORK PRODUCT B

Moving to column 3 in Figure 1, we next show:

- How performance traceability is used to provide perspective on actions in column 2

- How to-be steps can be defined to meet goals in column 1
- Decisions that improve performance within and across each dimension

Business dimension: Prioritization of Interactions for improvement: As noted earlier there are many Request types that are part of the service catalog (application services, providing hand held devices etc.). These Requests are prioritized based on value to the business (e.g. PCs before handhelds or vice versa), applying Co-engineering Principle 1:

- High customer value
- Competitive value to the business
- High Request volume
- Poor throughput
- High queue times
- Identify the sub-Interactions of these Interactions and assign the same priority as the primary Interaction

The resulting priorities set the context for improvement of all primary Interactions, sub-Interactions, and infrastructure improvement. In this case, the PC Interaction was prioritized with respect to all other services offered by the IT organization since it impacted all customer processes and, further, growth was expected.

To-Be SLs

For each Interaction the as-is metrics (Figure 5) includes the wasted time (travel time, approval time, and so on). Also a Request is often queued at an Interaction until it is ready to execute due to the lack of availability of *all required agents*. All these types of wait times contribute to the as-is SL and also identify opportunities for improvement.

Using this context of ACE structure and as-is performance we can now identify a more precise to-be SL for an Interaction. This is done by noting that both the as-is and to-be Request SL performance is based on the 'E' span time of the RED Interaction. In turn, this span time is dependent on the sub-Interactions of the ACE Interaction structure. Specifically, we identified the numbers of routine and non-routine Requests per month as in Figure 4. We can then see that 80% of the routine Requests needed only the first PC Interaction executed *and nothing else*. For the remaining 20% non-routine we next identified what fraction needed specific sub Interactions and the related time metrics. We note that this requires triage rules that will be covered next.

Propagation analysis (see section later in this chapter) is also be used to obtain accumulated performance across all routine Request s or all non-routine Requests. This is based on the ACE structure and the number of Requests routed to each Interaction. From this the cumulative wasted times for the Site Survey and the Budget Approval were obtained and compared to show which Interactions had the greatest amount of wasted time is. For the example we obtained:

- The greatest opportunity for improvement is to eliminate the wasted time due to approvals. This is 303 days.
- The opportunity through accurate site information can be addressed though a technology such as a CMDB. However, the potential improvement is only 44 days.

Next let us look at RED prioritization based on effectiveness. Approvals have higher priority. Thus addressing approvals before introducing technology for site monitoring makes sense. Of course in a mixed mode system, you now also have to look at how approvals are conducted and this might indeed involve the use of technology to eliminate wasted time.

RED SLs: Achievable target SLs were also defined. For the *routine Requests* the as-is SL was 17 days but the potential was 1 day by eliminating the non-value add queue time! However this potential could *not be reached for the non-routine* Requests because of the additional sub Interactions (e.g. cabling) needed for execution! This is because Requests classified as non-routine will actually need additional sub-Interactions and consequently additional time. Thus, it is important that any SL identify the Request types and attributes for which that SL applies.

Since 80% of the routine Requests are processed by the PC Install Interaction its performance improvement has higher priority than the remaining Interactions that are non-routine and executed 20% of the time. On the other hand, within the same medical center, the 80% of non-routine Request s (i.e. patients triaged with emergency conditions) will be of higher business value and thus priority. Even external competitive pressures (such as vendor pricing of installed PCs) might set priorities and performance targets. For example, if the internal costing is above the vendor pricing, a strategic question to consider is why this is so and whether to address the important organizational reasons for it.

Opportunities for SL Innovation and Effectiveness

For the prioritized primary RED Interactions and the ACE structure, what sub-Interactions can be eliminated, shared as a service, out sourced, in sourced, and/or made more efficient through IT automation?

To answer this for the PC Install Interaction, the as-is for routine Requests was about 17 days. The to-be SL was determined by identifying how much of the non-value added wait can be eliminated and how much was the value-added TAKT. Wasted time can be eliminated by:

- Eliminating one or more sub-Interactions – in this case approval, for most cases, and keeping a batch of pre-imaged PCs (see Figure 4) for pick up at convenient locations.
- Adding more resources to reduce wait time.
- Increase training of agents so they can do multiple tasks when at the site.
- Eliminating the need for a survey by investing in a site management system and CMDB.
- Standardizing Requests – in this case eliminating special configurations and exploiting the standardization to outsource to a vendor.

Operational process innovation: Another approach is to evaluate changes in the ACE structure.

- Interaction interoperability: Identify technology to eliminate one or more services, or combine services. For example, a Request entered at the website could update the CRM automatically and generate a sub-Request to the PC vendor.
- Data sharing between Interactions: If a service is performed manually or if information that is created needs to be retained for later use, flag it as a candidate for IT automation or interoperability. For example, a CMDB service was identified to provide up-to-date information on the site and status of communications.
- Improve synchronization and real-time communication: An example of this is that a cross-trained deployment agent does not have to travel to the central IT building if the work orders can be downloaded to a mobile device and small batches of PCs can be maintained at all the main locations.

Budgeting, allocation, chargeback, and investment: Budgets and roles are allocated to ongoing operations and adjusted based on actual use. The actual charges are based on the time that an agent services an Interaction. From an improvement perspective specific investment in the improvement of an agent is based on its use in REDs and their priority in the overall organization. Higher priorities are based on:

- Customer value add: For example reducing inventory is not immediately perceptible to the customer but PC install is.
- Business value-add: For the example, this is determined from an IT perspective. When looking at a primary organization, the actual value of Interaction to the business is often determined by the margin.

Request Triage Rules: Work Product D

To deploy the improvements in response time achievable by dynamic triage, we must now route Requests more effectively. Table 1 shows the further classification of a Request type to enable this.

To-Be Roles and OLs: Work Product E

The RED priorities defined by the business stakeholders are next used to target resources for improvement. That is for those REDs in the intersection of high-value and low-effectiveness, identify the individual low-performing Agents. The objective of this action is to improve the performance of those agents first.

More generally, note that all human and system services need to be managed from the Role set perspective, separately from the infrastructure perspective. Stated another way, rarely is a service useful in isolation. The Role set is the composition

Table 1.

Request type classification and Routings to Role sets						
Request Classification			**Routing to complete Interactions**			
Request type	**Quantity**	**Configuration**	**PC Install Interaction**	**Site survey Interaction**	**Approval Interaction**	**Assembly & Image Interaction**
Routine	Less than 10	Standard	Required	Known	Not required (i.e. net new)	Standard image
Not routine	Less than 10	Standard	Required	Unknown- Cabling not required	Not required (i.e. net new)	Standard image
Not routine	Less than 10	Standard	Required	Unknown- Cabling required	Required	Standard image
Not routine	More than 10	Not Standard	Required	Unknown- Cabling not required	Required	Standard image

of services needed to deliver value. Migration tasks to evolve an Interaction from as-is to to-be (e.g. scripts, interoperability implementations, skills training) are all identified locally for each Role set so that the requirements are precisely directed at improvements to the Interaction performance.

To do this we note that a shared agent may be used in more than one Role set as shown in the infrastructure dimension of Figure 1. For example, an enterprise database agent in the infrastructure might provide capacity to multiple business Interactions thus impacting the service quality of several REDs. Also the same server may play the role of a CRM data base host for the triage Role set and a different role of the email server for all other Role sets.

We can now prioritize again across Interactions by comparing the cost of Role set operating level improvements to the potential business value resulting from the improvement of Interaction service levels. Also, if applicable, justify the improvement to the underlying agents by looking at the positive impact of the agent OLs to more than one Interaction.

In the PC example, the priority for automating a service with an underlying CMDB was less than for an organizational improvement. Specifically, by reducing the wait and introducing pre-approved Requests, we found we could can shave off more wasted time for 80% of the routine Requests than by implementing a CMDB that provides a service that identifies whether the site IT wired or not for 20% of the Requests.

Shared Self-managed agents: We thus need to identify and consolidate all the shared agent roles in each Role set along with the as-is OLs and to-be $\triangle$s. Consolidation will often result in different levels and priorities derived from different Role sets. These have to be reconciled by the agent as follows.

The $\triangle$OLs from different Role sets are ordered in importance based on the originating Interaction priority. If the agent has conflicting $\triangle$OLs, the agent negotiates with the Role set manager. For example, the OL requirement to reduce costs by having the site surveyor also implement the needed changes might not be possible as it means hiring more expensive resources that will increase the cost of the service. Whether this increased cost is acceptable can only be determined within the Role sets and the overall Interaction value.

If the cost for an agent to meet the $\triangle$OL is high, see if the cost can be shared across additional Role sets. However, also note the Role set manager can look for alternative services and sub-Interactions through in-sourcing or out-sourcing that will reduce the cost of delivering a service. For example, the PC assembly step can be subcontracted to a PC vendor. Implement the To-be $\triangle$OLs for the highest priority Interactions and enter the cycle of continual incremental performance improvement of the deployed ACE structure.

Figure 6. ACE Interaction names (and key for Figure 10) and metrics data

Input	ID	Req	Queue	Exec	Queue	Del
PC Install Transaction	Tran.1	0.03	0.50	0.19	0.13	0.03
Site Survey Transaction	Tran.2	0.05	2.00	0.13	0.03	0.03
Cabling Transaction	Tran.3	0.05	4.00	0.25	0.03	0.03
Budget Approval Transaction	Tran.4	0.03	15.00	0.06	0.03	0.03
Inventory Transaction	Tran.5	0.03	0.13	0.13	0.03	0.03

MONITORING AND ANALYSIS

ACE provides the conceptual structure for analysis and monitoring. While the monitoring can be completed in real-time with current technologies, it does not have to be automated to be useful. For example observed values and queue metrics from the CRM etc. can be manually collected and used as illustrated in Figure 6 and Figure 7. Figure 6 identifies the different Interaction in the PC process along with the R,E,D and queue times. The individual transaction times along with the % of times a particular Interaction is executed by a routine or non-routine Request leads to the ACE spreadsheet-based 'dashboard' in Figure 7. The model illustrates a simulation of the cumulative metrics based on the ACE structure (illustrated here as RED fragments and associations) and the number of Request s routed to each transaction. The simulation results in quantitative inputs for decision-making – for example the cumulative wasted time for the Site Survey (2) and the Budget Approval (4). These are encircled in red. A comparison immediately shows where the greater amount of wasted time is.

In the next section we show how this type of analysis leads to the roadmap for deploying the ACE structure that becomes the basis for ongoing adaptation.

PROJECT PORTFOLIO AND ROADMAP: WORK PRODUCT B

Co-Engineering Interactions - Priority 1

Shared Service Knowledge: As a baseline, we suggest ITIL foundation training[e] for those directly and indirectly associated with the CSC to get everyone using shared knowledge and vocabulary, making overall communications more effective.

Implement Customer Service Center, Triage and metrics: The next step is to implement a single point for ticketing all Request s and a triage process which will take all new PC Request s to determine which are routine or non-routine at the first point of customer contact. Doing this allows us to utilize or eliminate a number of RED Interactions or sub Interactions within the overall new PC deployment

Figure 7. RED Interaction metrics in Figure 6 along with the % flow of routine and non-routine Request s to each Interaction in the ACE structure obtains the aggregated value-add and non-value add results

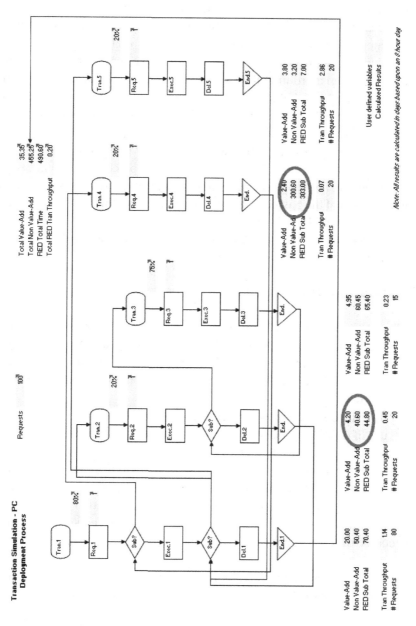

process. Note that Request classification happens at the CSC and based on that, ticket routings are created. An example of the ticketing within the CRM and the Request classification scheme and triage is given in Figure 8. Putting this in place also allows metrics to be captured for continuous improvement.

Survey Redesign: In the as-is every install site is surveyed prior to the imaging and deployment of the new PC. In order to eliminate inefficiency, survey should work in conjunction with the newly defined order triage system; the survey process can be removed from all routine Request s in order to save time and FTE hours, as well as increase the overall efficiency. By removing site surveyors from all routine orders we would reduce the time for every deployment by three to four days, and lessen the need for these resources.

Budget Approval: Currently all new PC orders have to go through the budget approval process. This occurs after an order has been placed and can occasionally take up to a month. The length of time that the budget approval takes depends on how often the CFO of the business group has a budget meeting. For routine Request s this Interaction should be eliminated.

Inventory redesign: Move from spreadsheets to an inventory data base that is accurate and has auto notify features for replenishment.

Co-Engineering Interactions - Priority 2

Our analysis showed that while priority 1 tasks will have more immediate impact on improving RED performance times, Priority 2 tasks will ultimately allow greater efficiencies not only for the new PC install but also for other equipment and other processes across IS. The suggestions in this segment indicate longer-term strategies to be followed.

EKI: While the CSC provides an integrated front-end, there are several problems due to the use of multiple systems. First, there is very little accurate customer feedback due to the use of multiple systems. If the customer wants to see where their Request is in the process, they cannot because their reference number is only valid within the system that they placed their order. A separate system is used to track the orders. Another issue is the time it takes to retype information into each system. While this may take only minutes for a single order, it will save a significant amount over the course of a year. The new integrated system has are several objectives:

- Provide a more visual interface for placing orders, help with capturing complete requirements, and allow the customer to sign off and automatically create the ticket.
- Provide a way to route the Request ticket for any additional approval information.

- Automatically check the site and create a provisioning Request if there are any deficiencies.
- Triages to the most appropriate Interaction.
- Update the underlying configuration management database based on changes to the site and assets.
- Provides the customer with an accurate status.

A first step towards this would be to develop and implement a logically unified system. This system would integrate the roles of CRM, IT Shop, Site Management, Asset Management, and Order Management. Additionally, this new system should have a friendlier user-interface at the order point. The customer should be able to see the product that they are ordering rather than simply picking from a list. After the customer completes their order they will receive an email confirming their order with a reference number. This confirmation will help to eliminate discrepancies between what the customer orders and what they want. Also, their reference number will now allow them to look up where their order is in the process at any time.

CMDB: We also propose that a comprehensive Configuration Management Database system be put in place for managing the assets, status, and locations. For example, this system would keep track of all network assets, whether that is network jacks, switches, or cabling, and where it is located and who is using it. With the implementation of a CMDB network administrators would be able to assess an up to the minute status of their network, and would be able to order needed supplies preemptively rather than reactively.

A full-function CMDB is not immediately feasible. For example, analysis showed that the time saving due to a CMDB would be less than fifty hours per month whereas the saving due to the streamlining of approvals would be four or five times as much. Additionally, the cost of the CMDB would be substantial requiring it to be justified over several projects. However, CMBD remains a very important goal for improved overall services. The economic impact and the investments for this solution are difficult to measure with the information we have to date. Naturally, there is the immediate savings of the time spent re-entering data into the different systems. However, the greatest impact from this solution lies in the improved customer satisfaction and efficiency.

There are several longer-term issues that came to light towards the end of the project. Some initial strategic issues are identified based on Lean Interaction analysis thus far but need further study.

Customer account management: Communications with the different customer departments is the key to successful internal re-engineering. This allows the prioritization of Interaction improvements to meet requirements. Also the precise Interaction metrics can be used for good communications.

Efficiency of the organization: Suppliers might soon become available to install PCs at lower costs (perhaps even at $50 per PC). Then we must consider if the IT organization can eventually reach internal efficiencies that go beyond the supplier prices? This would require implementing many Lean principles (the start of which is in the priority 1 Tasks listed above).

Outsourcing/ in-sourcing: In the longer run, what should be outsourced and what should be in-sourced? The related trade-off analysis is often difficult. The Interaction analysis method provides a precise way to proceed. The Interaction-based approach helps treat processes in a simpler and modular way to make these changes possible. In addition, it surfaces certain strategy decisions that need to be surfaced to identify Interactions that should be outsourced versus others that should be in-sourced.

PC refresh: An approach under consideration was to eliminate the Request ing process and instead budget for a batch refresh of many PCs. Given that about a thousand PCs are to be refreshed every four months, what is the overall impact to existing resources that would have to handle existing support needs?

Service catalog and SLs: The identification and classification of all customer Request s determines needed Interactions and determines the service catalog elements with the SLs and underlying OLs. An advantage is that the service catalog and its implementation starting at the CSC and metrics capture are now straightforward.

Moving to a Lean Organization: Making a change is always difficult and much of it typically occurs intuitively rather than deliberately. A lot of time is spent in meetings and discussions that may not succeed in surfacing the right trade-off issues up front. For example, technologists believe their tools will handle the challenges while other managers believe their re-engineered processes will address the problems better. An analytic approach to surfacing service improvement opportunities can cut out a lot of debate.

Finally, for an internal IT organization, Lean methods provide a way to prioritize the aspects of operations that need improvement to remain competitive. It provides a tool to guide the many talented individuals to greater levels of group efficiency. Furthermore, the principles of Lean can be taught in workshops prior to a re-engineering effort and individuals themselves can begin to apply the methods to improve and measure Interactions both from a global and from a local perspective.

CONCLUSION AND RESEARCH

The focus here is on the customer-driven improvement of services enabled by distributed heterogeneous Agents Interacting to deliver services. The ACE structure and representation here is applied towards Business-IT performance alignment scheme and serves as a basis for more precise analysis techniques that can take as-is metrics and predict the overall system behavior and target to-be improvements.

Specifically we have illustrated that the simple introduction of new technology, such as a site monitoring system, alone will often have little impact on productivity until greater inefficiencies, due to the poor synchronization of all needed services, are addressed. All associated services, local and distributed, must be addressed to achieve an overall return on investment.

Here we also think of agents as locally managed and *autonomous* – that is all decisions for 'how' improvements are made, are local. The ACE structure provides the context for more global context analysis by targeting the 'what'. This allows the local empowered improvement and for the reduction of complexity within systems. Also the prioritization of the local improvement is in the global context. At the same time, the context for the local improvements is still traced precisely to BioS goals. (See Cutlip et al 2007).

Workflow automation provides the technology for the delivery of eWorkCenters at the shop floor level has been piloted (Aparicio et. al. 1997, Apariciao et. al. 1998l). More recently BPEL standards have emerged to make workflows easier to implement over the Internet (Zhile and Zhenhua 2006). Together these types of efforts provide ways to manage Agents and monitor performance electronically. However, much research needs to be done to achieve cost effective deployment of workflows. For example, few precise and analytic methods exist to leverage technology and address requirements for operational improvement simultaneously in the physical, electronic, and shared-service worlds.

We have shown how the ACE framework is a starting point and theory for *management of Complex systems to high-level objectives.* Based on ACE we can identify areas of future research. For example, it would be useful to expand model-driven concepts to integrate development, deployment, and monitoring. This should begin with assessing state-of-the-art environments such as Eclipse. The objective would be to develop ACE-based instrumentation, runtime support for eWorkcenter monitoring, and the evolution of Agents during their life cycles. This would include not just the creation of service functions but also their non-functional monitoring to achieve objectives like minimized escalation of defects though self-management, early detection and self-healing, and so on. The environment would be for visualizing overall system behavior and applying policies interactively to adapt overall behavior.

More generally lean thinking applies to services in general (Schuh and Hieber 2008). We will explore these types of concepts further in Chapter 10.

TASKS FOR ROADMAP FOR TO-BE ACE STRUCTURE

1. How do your project results deploy within the context of the existing organizations and enterprise systems?
2. How do you justify your claims of efficiency or innovation? What measures?
3. Develop a Road Map with tasks, costs, and schedule. Justify your costs.

THINGS TO THINK ABOUT

1. What tools and methods can be provided to manage any complex system to high level objectives? Base this on the use cases implicit in this chapter, the Co-engineering rules introduced throughout this book, and the precise methods that can be implemented to achieve measurable goals.
2. What can we learn from the field and available vendor products to develop features and tools that are easier to use and apply? Start with a specific product used in operation? Base this on background research with vendor software. Try to frame the problem in a specific context, stating your assumptions and justifying your answer in that context.
3. While the monitoring can be completed in real-time with current technologies, it does not have to be automated to be useful. For example observed values and queue metrics from a CRM can be collected and synthesized for decision making. However, with automated monitoring, it becomes possible to populate a dashboard that can be used for close to real-time decision-making. How would the ACE structure provide for monitoring and analysis? What does such a dashboard look like? How does your answer compare to "dashboard" type products that are available in the marketplace today? Use specific examples.
4. ACE governance principles provide the Agents with the context of global rules that apply to self-management. As mentioned earlier, the OLs derived from the different Role set requirements taken together are the individual Agent's objectives. For example, a server has to meet the performance requirements of the email and CRM response times. The resolution of conflicting requirements is implemented locally by Agents to achieve a more stable system. In a real-world scenario of your choice, illustrate how Agents might apply principles to resolve conflicting requirements.
5. In what way is a complex system recursive? What are the fractal dimensions? Research and write about how this way of looking at systems might help reduce costs.

REFERENCES

Aparicio M., Barry J., Durniak T., Gilman, C., Lam H., & Ramnath, R. (1997). Integration of Design and Manufacturing in a Virtual Enterprise using Enterprise Rules, Intelligent Agents, STEP and Workflow. In *Proceedings of the 1997 SPIE International Symposium on Intelligent Systems and Advanced Manufacturing* (pp. 160-171), Pittsburgh, Pennsylvania: SPIE.

Aparicio Barry, J., , M., Durniak, T., Herman, P., Karuturi, J., Woods, C., et. al. (1998 November). NIIIP-SMART: An Investigation of Distributed Object Approaches to Support MES Development and Deployment in a Virtual Enterprise. In *Proceedings of the 2nd International Enterprise Distributed Object Computing Workshop* (pp. 366-377), La Jolla, CA: IEEE Computer Society.

Brittenham, P., Cutlip, R.R., Draper, C., Miller, B. A., Choudhary, S., & Perazolo, M. (2007 June). IT Service Management Architecture and Autonomic Computing. *IBM Systems Journal, 46*(3), 565-582.

Distributed Object Workshop. (1998). EDOC '98. La Jolla, San Diego, CA.

IBM Service Science. (n.d.). Retrieved September 1, 2008, from http://www.research.ibm.com/ssme/reading.shtml.

George, M., (2002). *Lean Six Sigma.* New York: McGraw-Hill.

Schuh, G., Lenders, M., & Hieber, S. (2008 July). Lean Innovation: Introducing Value Systems to Product Development. In *Proceedings of the Portland International Conference on Management of Engineering & Technology* (pp. 1129-1136), Cape Town, South Africa: PICMET.

Zhile, Z., & Zhenhua, D. (2006). Building Business Processes or Assembling Service Components: Reuse Services with BPEL4WS and SCA. In *Proceedings of the European Conference on Web Services* (pp. 138-147), Washington DC: IEEE Computer Society.

ENDNOTES

[a] The autonomic-computing-reference-architecture (ACRA)[19] conceptual view consists of three parts: a set of architectural elements for constructing autonomic systems, patterns for using these elements in a system context, and interface and data interchange specifications that facilitate integration.

[b]   Service Improvement Program, or SIP, is an ITIL term referring to the process of identifying and implementing corrective actions when a problem impacting service quality is identified.

[c]   The concept of Services Sciences has been championed by IBM and is rising in acceptance. At the time of writing, IBM has compiled a nice list of introductory material for those interesting in learning what Services Science is all about (http://www.research.ibm.com/ssme/reading.shtml).

[d]   This principle assures us that wasted time can be systematically eliminated by using only those resources needed for the customer's Request , resulting in better use of resources and lower costs.

[e]   This is a first level of ITIL certification.

Chapter VIII
Management, Monitoring, and Mining of Service Knowledge

ABSTRACT

There is consensus that *explicit* knowledge is information. In addition there is *tacit knowledge* that exists in the human minds. Tacit knowledge is applied unconsciously. It is a result of people \ Agents Interactions with each other and the environment. While explicit knowledge in the form of skills and competencies is normally acquired through training and Interaction, tacit knowledge is difficult to articulate. It is something that often cannot be expressed (Polyani 1966, Polyani 1996). Here we present various ways in which the creation and use of tacit knowledge can be assisted to become part of the Enterprise Knowledge Infrastructure to enable the BioS goals of the complex system.

How does knowledge management benefit the organization?

- How is knowledge used in the delivery of services and to reduce Interaction costs?
- What are the different aids to knowledge management?
- How can knowledge be captured?
- What processes and electronic tools enable the evolution of practice knowledge?

Figure 1. Knowledge management goals for service delivery - providers perspective

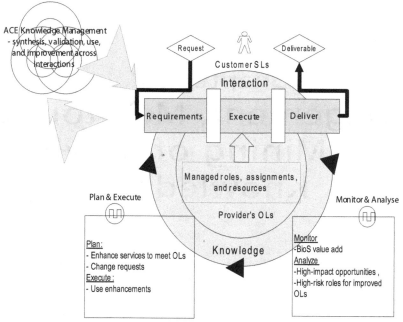

Knowledge is a "fluid mix of framed experience, values, contextual information, and expert insight that provides a framework for evaluating and incorporating new experiences and information. It originates and is applied in the minds of knower. In organizations, it often becomes embedded not only in documents or repositories but also in organizational routines, processes, practices, and norms" (Davenport 1998). The business challenge for service-oriented organizations is to provide an environment within which knowledge is actively discovered, captured, shared, vetted, and delivered to improve the service. Since Knowledge is an asset, to what extent should investments be made in its management?

Knowledge discovery related to services is the process of discovering interesting, non-trivial patterns in information that help deliver more effectively. The discovery process targets Interactions and knowledge applied by Roles. Knowledge is often discovered by generating information from data *while practicing*. This type of *reflective knowledge* (Schon 1979) can be obtained by monitoring Interactions and by *abstracting or mining* non-trivial patterns (rules or associations for example) from the information. The discovery process can also be done using numerous methods and aids - visualization, data mining, statistics, neural networks, mathematical modeling and simulation, or even organizational processes. See Despres and Chauval 2000 for an overview.

Triage to Mine Organizational Knowledge: The CSC is the heart of any customer-focused service organization since here Requests are logged and prioritized, rules are applied for classification, initial assignments made, knowledge applied, and status monitored.

Triage knowledge is applied in the form of rules applied to Requests that come in through a single point of contact for the customer. These rules are often based on organizational knowledge and applied to provide the dynamic Interaction networking capability as we have seen with the 311 example in the previous chapter. Thus, the CSCs is a good place to capture and mine knowledge applied to provide services. The Interactions initiated by the CSCs also generate performance information which can be synthesized and mined for additional knowledge.

Nested Triages: The pattern underlying CSC is triage or broker. Thus the CSC | triage is a useful organization structure that can be repeatedly applied not just for larger organizations but also for smaller teams and groups relying on shared high-cost resources that take in many Requests from their own specific environment. These points of networking often begin to capture Requests, unusual requirements, frequently asked questions, etc. as well as the knowledge needed to service them.

Often a service organization with a CSC contains nested organizations each with their own CSCs. Sometimes this structure is implicit, but it nevertheless exists. For example, within the hospital enterprise, an emergency triage CSC uses specialist administrative desks and CSCs as well as IT CSC. The IT CSC in turn communicates with a technology CSC for support with equipment failure. The incoming Requests for *different* CSCs within an organization could thus be different – including the Requests for medical assistance, Requests for equipment repair, Requests for application program services or for product maintenance. Thus, the different CSCs become the 'customer face' for all the service providers (either for external or internal customers).

Lean concept: As mentioned before, triage allows for the delayed binding of resources to Interactions - a lean concept. We will show here that triage execution performance is useful for insights on the knowledge required for Lean operations. Another way of viewing triage is the dynamic mapping of resources to Requests that originate within the customer environment. It is no surprise that some type of triage | CSC project usually surfaces as strategic and core to enterprise integration. Integration at the CSC also initiates a cluster of other secondary projects needed to achieve integrated back end information sources and an efficient organization.

ACE Knowledge Management: The are two aspects to knowledge management illustrated in Figure 1 - 1) global ACE Knowledge Management that optimizes across interactions and 2) local Interaction Knowledge applied in an autonomous manner during Interactions. The former concerns itself with the creation of new knowledge that fine tunes the triages to become more and more effective and new operational knowledge that ensures that the resource assignments are effective. The latter is based on the view of an Interaction as an an autonomic structure with the 'Request' and 'Deliverable' forming the 'Sensor' and 'Effector' of the Interaction. Local knowledge is applied to complete the tasks within the Interaction. We refer to all these types of knowledge collectively as ACE Knowledge.

The creation and use of ACE knowledge in Figure 1 is best understood when an Interaction is viewed in full detail from the provider's perspective as in the complementary Figure 2. This illustrates the ACE knowledge management with the internal knowledge-enabled value chain that underlies effective triages. Thus the many on-going Interactions of an ACE form a system of autonomic structures, with the knowledge management providing the global information context for these independent structures to make improvements locally. We will also use this abstraction to study the underlying layers of knowledge that support the successful delivery at the CSCs.

ACE Knowledge Management views Interactions as a source of knowledge. Thus the Interaction performance is mined from the BioS perspectives illustrated in Figure 2. Specifically, there are different types of knowledge to be discovered and managed. Some of these are discussed next:

- *Strategy knowledge:* That identifies externally-driven trends by monitoring Requests and Deliverables. Looking to the future, more and more we want

Figure 2. BioS Knowledge management perspectives across Interactions and their internal associations

to acquire this knowledge by moving closer and closer to the customer point of use. Technology can be used to monitor events and circumstances of use. For example advanced insights are also mined from the Internet by analyzing blogs and other patterns of consumer behavior.

A specific example of moving closer to the customer is opinion mining (Liu 2007). One of the types of information on the Web is the opinions expressed in the user-generated content, e.g. customer reviews of products, forum posts, and blogs. Of particular interest here is the problem of determining the semantic orientations (positive, negative or neutral) of opinions expressed[a]. Another example is the tracking of user information implemented in enterprise portals.

Such portals act as the front-end integrators of a variety of services like one stop service, self-service, human resource services, and so on. Customer satisfaction with the services, preferences for services and so on can be captured by tracing the different paths that different users might take through the site. A final example illustrates how advanced knowledge about weather events that impact customers can also result in more effective service delivery. Here an insurance company can keep track of weather events and a GIS-based synthesis of impacted customers. This will allow Agents to better plan on how to respond quickly to claims.

- *Business knowledge*: that defines goals and priorities by gaining insights based on current Interactions and their performance. More useful predictive knowledge includes insights on maximizing business value and new business models. Sources of valuable information include enterprise data warehouses and CMS-based front-ends that support and monitor multiple communities of users. In all such cases the front-end is connected to back-office application components and services.

- *Operational knowledge*: that ensures the Interactions are properly resourced and knowledge is applied in the most effective way possible. Of value here is also the knowledge that can lead to Agent innovations that increase throughput, quality, and new services.

- *IT Knowledge:* that supplies the most effective resources to support and deliver the IT services. The skills of resources and the service knowledge identify opportunities for both effectiveness and new ways of doing things.

In the following sections we will cover these different layers of ACE knowledge management followed by automated monitoring methods that often provides the context for mining new knowledge.

ENABLING STRATEGY WITH CUSTOMER KNOWLEDGE

We begin with an example of knowledge mining that contributes to organization strategy. The type of knowledge is customer focused and can be mined from portals, enterprise data warehouses, and other user interfaces. Specifically we examine eGov portals. City portals which initially started with just providing information to the citizens have progressed over the past few years to provide more and more services to the citizens, the current challenge being the integration and quick access to all these services and information. The following are the stages of progression for city portals (Belkin 1992, Center for Digital Government 2007, HM Government 2005):

- *Stage 1: Information presentation of static material* such as publications and information about the services provided by the agency. This information is seen as "packaged" by the agency, with only limited possibilities to interact with the Web site.
- *Stage 2: Interaction that provides information* such as searching in agency databases, ordering publications, downloading and ordering forms, relating agency services, and subscribing to newsletters from the agency.
- *Stage 3: Transaction picking up and leaving personal information* related to the services provided by the agency. This includes initiating and following agency-specific services.
- *Stage 4: Integration addresses the integration of services between government agencies* through the realization of a one-stop government that, regardless of organizational boundaries, provides services at one point of entry, even where several agencies are involved.
- *Stage 5: Life Events addresses the citizen events* to live, work, and raise a family. It also motivates features like Personalization, Customization (with options like using Personnas).

At the same time technology is also being applied for managing customer-to-organization, organization-to-resource, and organization-to-suppliers Interactions. Here new trends are emerging (DiMaio 2007, DiMaio 2007b) due to technologies like web services. For example - "The first-stop shop for almost anything on the Internet is a search engine, a personal home page, or a preferred home page that matches the consumer's needs and interests. This type of home page is likely to be provided, not by the government organization, but by an Internet player (such as Google, Yahoo or MSN), a media company (such as CNN or The New York Times), a telecom operator (especially for mobile devices), an investment firm, a parent association or a golf club.[b]" This affects the way we might look at portal enhancements.

As eGov implementations move from a simple website to an integrated portal and front-end to a complex of services (Figure 3) many challenges arise:

- Complexity due to the number of objects and different associations
- Complexity due to mapping between the layers of services
- Services desired by different communities of users vary widely.
- More and more types of services are being delivered.
- Many underlying competencies and component services (often in the thousands, see IPSV 2006).

Figure 3. Examples of the layers of knowledge related to Customer service use, Business prioritization, Triage and Agents based on a City example

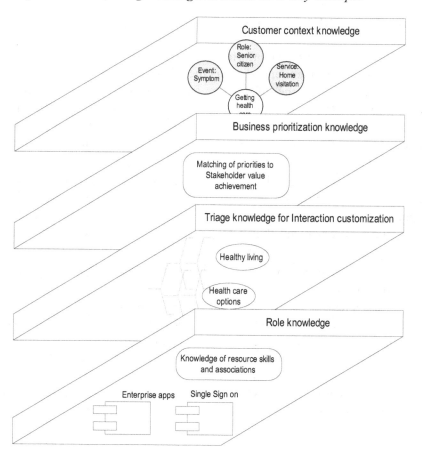

- Mapping between the layers that changes often as new services get added more and more frequently.

The underlying consequences are not only the complexity of associating mapping but also the complexity of dynamic changes based on *evolving* knowledge. For example, citizens' health care needs might become more specialized as 'Health needs for Senior Citizens' and 'Health needs for School Children.' This knowledge actually might be mined based on an understanding of the demographics of the portal visitors and their underlying needs. This requires new ways of viewing existing services to be supported (McClure 2007).

Thus underlying back-office services have to also be suitably addressed. Existing information components are typically not designed to be useable and available for use from multiple entry points. Thus, it is often difficult to provide services that are user-centered. To provide greater flexibility, we need ways to mine user needs – for example, what was the original service Request via which the user ended up here? Can we make the service easier to find? Award winning websites (City of Tampa, City of Aurora) have the following types of characteristics:

- *Identification of roles:* The information and services provided are organized in a structured manner depending on the role of the user interacting with the system. For example, the information and services are organized according to user groups like residents, visitors, business, government etc. This ensures that the portal presents citizens with a view of the information that is most relevant rather than providing them with a great deal of information that had little value.
- *Identification of context:* The context in which a particular user interacts with the system is captured in order to project those services which were most applicable in that context. For example, instead of viewing healthcare as a government department, the portals included healthcare as a service which different user groups of residents might be interested in.
- *Using right levels of abstraction:* When interacting with the portal for accessing a particular service, the citizen should not be bothered with having to find out whether the service is a private or public and which department is offering that service. Thus, the right level of abstraction is needed which hides the unnecessary details. This is achieved by providing a citizen-centric view as opposed to a government-centric view of the information and services.
- *Providing information in multiple ways:* The same information could also be obtained from multiple views which ensures that all the relevant information is available irrespective of the path that the user takes. For example, 'Animal

Care' could be accessible to the residents as information or an e-service, but it could also be accessed as part of the 'Neighborhood Services'.

- *Focus on giving more than what is currently needed but not more than what's necessary:* This increases user satisfaction by going a step beyond what the citizen currently requests and giving him what he might need next. For example, when accessing the portal as a 'visitor' to the city, the user is given information to plan for a move into the city (like housing, services like gas, water, electricity etc.). However, the information is organized in such a manner that additional details are provided only if the user is interested.
- *Making most needed information most easily accessible:* The news and current events or FAQs on topics that would mostly be of interest to the citizens should be accessible most easily. For example, the Tampa City portal includes 'Today in Tampa' a section on daily events of interest like exhibitions, association meets, news etc that the citizens could participate in. This has the potential to be extended in a crisis situation like an epidemic by providing information on vaccinations and preventive measures for handling the crisis effectively.
- *Encouraging participation of citizens:* The citizens are encouraged to voice their opinions on complaints or issues they face in their daily lives. For example, the Singapore website encourages citizen feedback on issues and their solutions through REACH (reaching everyone for active citizenry at home) by maintaining blogs and discussion boards where they share their experiences and opinions and uses that as a feedback for the government.

The conceptual models presented next helps guide the implementation in a typical CMS and leverage knowledge. The objective is to meet the goals of citizen satisfaction. The concept is the that uses views of underlying taxonomies, rules to understand the needs of the citizens and the goals of the government, and uses triage rules as a means of aligning both of them.

Conceptual Model for Portals: Figure 3 helps us conceptualize the main layers of knowledge needed for delivery of services and ways in which this can be mined using the attributes of monitored events. The layers and *associations* between them are further discussed in Figure 4.

The typical implementation vehicle for portals is CMS. Many specific abstractions - like taxonomies, site maps and folder hierarchies - in the typical CMS both organize and deal with the complexity. However, they typically do not have *service matching knowledge* concepts that allow the user to navigate between the layers and apply 'triage' rules in an automated fashion to 'pull' services that match their needs. To elaborate on this we first define the base terminology is defined as follows.

Figure 4. Types of Knowledge within a Portal

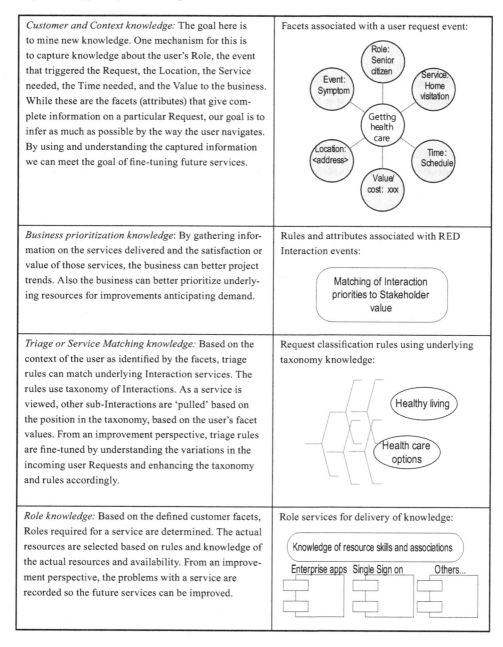

Customer and Context knowledge: The goal here is to mine new knowledge. One mechanism for this is to capture knowledge about the user's Role, the event that triggered the Request, the Location, the Service needed, the Time needed, and the Value to the business. While these are the facets (attributes) that give complete information on a particular Request, our goal is to infer as much as possible by the way the user navigates. By using and understanding the captured information we can meet the goal of fine-tuning future services.	Facets associated with a user request event:
Business prioritization knowledge: By gathering information on the services delivered and the satisfaction or value of those services, the business can better project trends. Also the business can better prioritize underlying resources for improvements anticipating demand.	Rules and attributes associated with RED Interaction events:
Triage or Service Matching knowledge: Based on the context of the user as identified by the facets, triage rules can match underlying Interaction services. The rules use taxonomy of Interactions. As a service is viewed, other sub-Interactions are 'pulled' based on the position in the taxonomy, based on the user's facet values. From an improvement perspective, triage rules are fine-tuned by understanding the variations in the incoming user Requests and enhancing the taxonomy and rules accordingly.	Request classification rules using underlying taxonomy knowledge:
Role knowledge: Based on the defined customer facets, Roles required for a service are determined. The actual resources are selected based on rules and knowledge of the actual resources and availability. From an improvement perspective, the problems with a service are recorded so the future services can be improved.	Role services for delivery of knowledge:

Information Object: This is a collection of attributes that logically defines an entity. Attributes include those that are normally considered "data" along with "metadata".

Object: For purposes of simplicity, this term is used to refer to information objects, aggregates of information objects, services, or process interfaces. Objects are used to simplify the users Interactions. For example, instead of typing in a subject, which is prone to error, selecting an object that already exists in the system enforces reuse of the existing information, avoids duplication, and specifies a relationship between the two objects. Another example is a query is automatically constructed to find any news release objects related to a given object. More sophisticated implementations use logic and ontology languages such as RDF and OWL (RDF) which can be used to express relationships between objects and facilitate flexible queries and searches, as well as inference.

View: One or more views are defined on each object to dictate the appearance of the object in a given space. From here, we can define an item as an object with a specific associated view, and define a Collaboration Space as a logical collection of items. Each object ideally is unique in an underlying information system, but an object can have multiple points of Interaction by appearing in multiple Collaboration Spaces.

Facets: To characterize the collection of objects in a space, we borrow ideas from faceted classification (Lambe 2007). In faceted classification, information is organized based on a collection of categories, called facets, each of which has a group of associated values that describe the information. Each space is characterized by facets:

- *User focus*, which corresponds to the user group that the space is aimed toward.
- *Service focus*, which corresponds to the interest area that the items in the space relate to.

Additional facets may apply to certain spaces, including geographic locations and accessibility alternatives (as illustrated in Figure 4).

Collaboration Space: is a higher-level abstraction with a *service focus*. It is a starting concept for design that allows us to connect the conceptual services to implementation services in a content management system, according to the taxonomy. It is grounded in an object-oriented model of content management. At the same time, it also allows us to organize CMS objects into larger display-independent abstractions for re-use that allows us to share specific information and services, and has several additional advantages that will be discussed later.

The service focus corresponds to the objectives of participating in the collaboration. To characterize the range of services for Collaboration Spaces, we turn to work in taxonomies for eGovernment (Lambe 2007, HM Government 2005). The taxonomies define the areas of concern for users interacting with governments, and so they work well for defining the possible interest areas of Collaboration Spaces.

With the Collaboration Spaces themselves, we need to include users and roles in the conceptual model. The *user model* specifies that users may be members of zero, one, or more groups. The *role model* bears similarities to models further discussed in (Tolone et. al 2005, Nita Rotaru and Li 2004, and Butler and Coleman 2003); each combination of an item and a user (or group) has a role. The role describes the user's (or group's) relation to the item. These roles can be used to determine access and permissions; for example, one user's role in relation to one news release object may be "author" or "editor" or simply "reader", and the appropriate access permissions can be associated with these roles (Hiller and Belanger 2001).

Collaboration spaces can become virtual spaces where Interactions can take place between organizations (Daws and Eglene 2004). For example, the "Health Space" can facilitate early exchange of information about unusual cases between the City's health department and other organizations, like the local hospitals. The potential for this type of integration between organizations needs to be researched further (Mukri et. al. 2009).

ENABLING OPERATIONS WITH IT KNOWLEDGE MANAGEMENT

There is a growing realization of the importance of knowledge management[c] within the CSC for IT support. This is because there is a vast body of coordination and system knowledge that comes into play while delivering services especially at the CSC and subsequent IT functions. Some related observations follow.

IT departments manage, monitor, and deliver, with increasing quality, on all customer-to-IT, IT-to-IT, and IT-to-Supplier Interactions. These Interactions could arise due to any of the following - Incidents, Problems and Questions, interfaces to Change Requests, Maintenance Contracts, Software Licenses, Service Level Management, Configuration Management, Availability Management, Financial Management for IT Services, and IT Service Continuity Management. This is as defined in ITIL (Vam Bon et. al 2004). The CSC service desk is at the heart of supporting IT services. The CSC for the IT organization is also similar to the 311.

The first step and the critical starting point for eventually building an effective CSC is the handling of *incident management*. Getting it right is important as it interfaces with the customer This chapter provides the solution steps for incorporating effective knowledge creation and use to continuously improve the performance of the CSC for incident management. The objective of Knowledge Management is to improve both employee productivity and service quality (see Figure 5). Thus, as illustrated, there is a direct cause-and-effect linkage over time between investment in Knowledge Management and customer satisfaction.

Knowledge is a shared organizational resource. There are four relevant dimensions to the enterprise architecture that allows us to define the goals of a Knowledge Management (KM) System in more detail. These are 1) the strategy and business customer, 2) the operations for the incidents, 3) IT organization, and 4) the enabling knowledge system. As illustrated in Figure 5, the measurement of KM use (e.g. number of units used) allows us to determine how successful the Knowledge Management effort is. For example we wish to demonstrate that management is critical to achieving organizational performance objectives such as improved request quality and throughput, customer satisfaction and business growth. It requires that the acquisition and dissemination of service practice knowledge be systematically managed. Experience with KM steps such as acquisition of knowledge as an asset, the development of delivery channels, and the process flows during incident management are as follows.

Figure 5. The ACE Structure and Goals for knowledge management

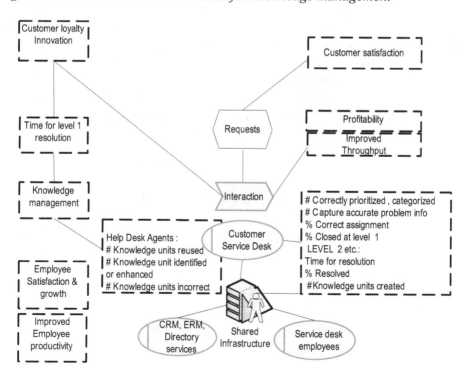

Time for payoff for KM: The time to acquire knowledge will be initially high and will obscure initial gains. However, as knowledge is created and shared performance improvements will be more dramatic. (See the best practice example below.) The best approach to reduce the time is to ensure this is to have a quality knowledge management team that is committed to success.

Time to acquire Is-Is Not Knowledge: For resolving *routine* incidents (e.g. with resolutions like password reset, reboot) the Is-Is Not[d] process is fairly straightforward as illustrated in Figure 6. But for non-routine incidents that arise in complex ways and from an existing configuration context of thousands of components, identifying the cause and providing a fix can become extremely difficult. Furthermore, the maintenance of such knowledge with changing vendor information is challenging.

This is also where the greater payoff might lie. The approach is to develop a single template scheme which can be shared by all experts to record their knowledge and changes to the knowledge, so that fixes can happen more quickly and by less skilled resources. This is also one use of the CMDB. Getting this right is critical not only for rapid acquisition of knowledge, but also the overall implementation of other ITIL processes. This challenge is usually underestimated.

Multiple knowledge viewpoints: An incident triaged at the help desk, might get triaged again by level 2 roles, and so on. Furthermore, the *classification knowledge* for level 1 will be different from level 2 networking, level 2 applications, and so on. Generally speaking, the triage rules will vary based on the level and function. However, the *triage pattern* – is the same. By taking the approach that each level x triage function acts in a fairly independent empowered way, but implements the same pattern with different knowledge makes the task of deployment and management much easier. (We note that this composition of patterns is an example of the fractal enterprise.) An example of what to expect with a knowledge management system in place is based on a simulation study using real data from a fortune 500 company in the hospitality industry (Gonzalez 2003).

Figure 6. An example of a classification resulting from Is and Is-not decision-making

A knowledge management system (illustrated in Figure 7) requires us to carefully identify:

- Types of knowledge to be managed within the incident process - *knowledge for Request classification, knowledge for correct assignment, and the knowledge for correct resolution etc.*
- Roles and responsibilities for knowledge management, and
- Knowledge system configuration specifications. (Here we use the term knowledge system to mean both configured software and procedures that are executed by defined roles and organizations.).

Figure 7 presents the integration of the knowledge management within the incident process. The customer request starts the incident process with a Request. Knowledge use must help close the request within level 1, if at all possible. Knowledge is also used to triage to level 2 when a request cannot be resolved at level 1. New knowledge must be acquired whenever missing or incorrect.

As illustrated in Figure 6, the performances across the dimensions are related. We begin with the *time to resolve* an incident as a critical measure from the customer's

Table 1. Gonzalez (2003)

Variables	Agent-centric system (average)	Knowledge management-centric system (average)
Throughput (calls/time period)	2733	3371 (23% Improved Throughput)
Time in system critical calls (minutes)	416.73	329.74 (20% Savings in Labor)
Time in system high priority calls (minutes)	503.07	240.54 (52% Reduction in High Priority Efforts)
Time in system medium priority calls (minutes)	547.07	193.99 (64% Decrease in Medium Priority Efforts)
Time in system low priority calls (minutes)	360.94	152.06 (57% Decrease in Low Priority Efforts)
Number of problem calls in technicians' queue	88	6 (93% Significant reduction of fixes in tech job queues)
Number of problem calls in second level' queue	103	25 (75% Significant reduction of "Expert Level" queues)
Number of problem calls in third level' queue	83	88 (6% Increase in lower level fixes)

Figure 7. Relating Knowledge Management to Strategy, Operations, IT use, and IT support

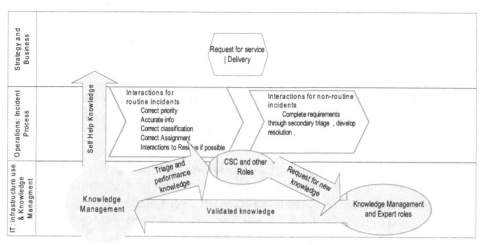

perspective. This performance is in turn traceable to other 'incident' Interaction measures. For example, # correctly assigned. This needed knowledge is measured in the operations dimension as 'increased incident Interaction throughput'. Finally the knowledge system manages the creation and delivery of knowledge and underlying information without any breakage as shown in Figure 6.

Types of Knowledge

To manage knowledge better and create a knowledge system we begin with the different types of knowledge that must come into play:

1. *Triage knowledge* is used to 1) classify the incident for resolution and 2) make level 2 assignments for triage. Each of these is explained below.
2. *Classification knowledge* takes the incoming incident and categorizes (i.e. identifies software, hardware, etc.), identifies item (i.e. what is the service item?), identifies the incident type (i.e. can't see patients), and begins resolution (i.e. refresh button). See Figure 6 for an example. In order for us to improve the knowledge, we must also identify the incident as follows: <known error with fix>, <service request>, <known error without a fix (problem)>, <known with fix to apply at next levels>, <unkown>, <other>.
3. *Role assignment knowledge* based on expertise needed to resolve the incident at level 2. This is used if a resolution does not exist or if it does not work.

4. *Resolution knowledge* for fixing the problem begins with the existing configu-
    ration to isolate and pinpoint the cause and combine it with vendor provided
    knowledge to fix the problem. This knowledge can be in one of two forms.
    a. Which is well understood and can be documented with Is-Is Not templates
        for isolating and fixing the problem. (See Appendix for Details.)
    b. For resolving the incident is not yet captured as an Is-Is Not procedure and
        requires a knowledge management process and access to expertise.
5. *Policies and procedures* apply during the incident process (for example, call
    the customer if the elapsed time is more than 24 hrs.).

Knowledge Management (KM) Roles

The knowledge management process for mining tacit knowledge during practice and
creating explicit Is-Is Not resolution knowledge is implemented by the knowledge
management role in conjunction with the expert roles as indicated below. (*Note:*
The expert roles are not necessarily the same as the level 2 roles.)

The knowledge management roles are responsible for processing knowledge
tickets. This includes:

*   Examining the related incident ticket(s).
*   Identifying defective classification or resolution knowledge.
*   Creating sub tickets for the expert roles to create or improve the knowledge.
*   Validate and format the knowledge submitted by other.
*   Identify gaps and create needed training.
*   Maintain the classification knowledge and keep it current in the help desk
    software.
*   Maintain the knowledge ticket metrics and the relationship to performance
    (such as the balanced score card).

The *expert roles* and responsibilities are as follows:

*   There is an identified expert for each component / feature in the classification
    matrix.
*   They provide expertise to create and validate resolution knowledge in specific
    topic areas.
*   They receive knowledge (sub) tickets routed to them for additional processing
    by the knowledge management role.
*   Once completed they route the knowledge (sub) tickets back to the knowledge
    management role.

Knowledge System

Each type of knowledge identified above is *supported* by the Knowledge System (Tiwana 2002) including organization processes and software systems) as follows:

- *Triage knowledge management:* is the proper configuration of the knowledge management component of the help desk software. The detailed form of this knowledge is given under the Functional System Requirements. The *Is-Is Not template* used for continued classification leading to further resolution using explicit knowledge for fixing the incident is provided in the *Appendix.*
- *Resolution knowledge acquisition:* uses supporting knowledge ticket types and knowledge roles to create explicit resolution knowledge from tacit knowledge. Functional System Requirements provided in detail later describe how the knowledge management steps are integrated with the incident process. This also identifies the system integration needed to provide seamless access to underlying information. Thus, the Knowledge Management system implementation is provided as 1) incident process policies, 2) system configuration requirements, and 3) knowledge management roles and process steps also supported by the configuration of the underlying systems. The next sub-sections give details.
- *Policies and procedures:* These are supported by process specific help and training information. For each step in the incident process, specific help information must be easy to assess. Examples of policies include send email massage to customer every 24hrs with a status approved for customer viewing; seek expert help after an initial attempt to resolve the incident. The details are in the Incident Management Process included in the Functional System Requirements.

Triage Knowledge Management

The form of triage knowledge is given in Table 2. When completed for the organization, this matrix is configured in the knowledge management component of the help desk software.

Note that the triage matrix for the Help Desk reflects agreement within the level 1 team. Similar *but not identical* triage knowledge will exist for level 2, level 3 teams. The help desk software should be able to use different matrices to provide different guidance to the different functional groups.

Table 2. Classification matrix

Classification Matrix							
Request Type	**Category**	**Item**	**Services**	**Incident types**	**Resolution procedure**	**Role and assignment policy**	**Role access**
Known errors with a fix	Options: • Software components • Hardware components • Network components • OS components	Features provided by the component – e.g. data management	Catalog of services provided for each system category – e.g. backup, recovery, etc.	E.g. corrupt file, routine backup failed.	Is-Is Not questions to identify, isolate the incident so that the right fix(s) can be applied. It begins with identifying the category, feature, service and incident type as in this matrix.	Level 2 etc. role assigned based on suitability to resolve the incident, if level 1 cannot resolve it.	Options for roles this resolution procedure is visible to: • Customer • CSC • Level 1 • Etc.
Service request	Same as above	Same as above	Same as above	Same as above	Same as above	Same as above.	Same as above
Unknown errors (an incident for which no fix exists and knowledge must be created)	Same as above	Same as above	Same as above	Same as above	Same as above	Knowledge Management Role assigned knowledge ticket when no knowledge exists. Sub tickets may be created for the expert roles by the Knowledge Management Role.	Same as above
Known error w/o a fix	Same as above	Same as above	Same as above	Same as above	Same as above	Same as above	Same as above
Other long-term requests	Same as above	Same as above	Same as above	Same as above	Same as above	Same as above	Same as above

Knowledge System Requirements (Integrated with Incident Management)

The details of the knowledge system requirements for the incident process steps are identified in Table 3, using the same step numbering scheme as in the Incident Process provided in Appendix.

Knowledge Management Process and Roles

The KM process is distinct and has its own objectives as identified in Table 4.

Organizational Aspects - Knowledge Management Team, Roles, and Skills

The organizational environment to support KM is also critical to achieving the desired performance (Cameron & Quinn 1999). The KM team consists of roles involved in the knowledge management process. As introduced earlier, these are: 1) Knowledge management (KM) and 2) Experts. While the expert roles can be played by individuals with also other responsibilities, it is recommended, that at least initially, one to two individuals should be dedicated to the KM role.

The knowledge management team is crucial to the continuous improvement of the incident process; hence it must be staffed with some of the best promising talent. The role of the team is also to keep the metrics for the help desk at all the dimensions identified in Figure 4. Finally, the knowledge management team is the glue that relates the level 1 and level 2 (and higher) functions. The team should view one of its responsibilities as advocating process improvements across the functions. Specifically the skill requirements for the KM role include:

- Customer perspective and experience working the help desk
- Technical skill in modeling and representing complex systems (using for example Unified Modeling Language)
- Ability to create and edit technical materials
- A working knowledge of ITIL

The skill requirements for the expert roles include:

- Customer perspective and experience working the help desk
- Skill in modeling and representing complex systems (using for example Unified Modeling Language)

Table 3.

Step Definition	Knowledge System Requirements
Incident Acceptance & Record Initial Information (Critical Point)	None
Verify correct Asset Information	None
Generate an exception report for Asset Group.	None
Determine if the contact is associated with an existing Incident	None
Classify the Incident	• During resolution, the classification guides the user. For example, the categories are presented first, the features next and so on. Search based navigation should be possible to speed up the process. • An Is Is-Not resolution procedure asks a sequence of questions that resolves the incident. Each incident may require *multiple* resolution procedures to be tried out. These attempts have to be recorded with the incident so that they can be analyzed for effectiveness later. • An incident request is considered classified only if all the columns and attributes in the matrix are identified (except for the role) and type unknown is not selected. • If incident is of type unknown or other long term requests, the ticket type 'knowledge' is created by any help desk user and assigned to the Knowledge Manager Role. The knowledge ticket is associated with one or more incident tickets as needed. • A knowledge ticket type can be created at any point and to it can be attached references to existing tickets for which adequate resolution knowledge did not exist. That is, during the course of a resolution, additional ticket(s) can be created of type knowledge. • Features should be available to select and bundle tickets, relate them to a knowledge ticket. • Integration Requirements: • The persons playing roles will be fed from CRM roles (e.g. job number).
Prioritize the Incident	• A ticket maybe bundled with other tickets related to the same incident or to multiple incidents. • The priority of a root ticket can be different from the children and vice versa. • The policy by which priorities are assigned is visible as help. • Priorities can be changed, but record for internal processing.
Verify existence of specific Service Level Agreement	Integration requirements: The SLAs for each customer are visible.
Determine if the contact is a Service Request (Critical Point)	

continued on the following page

Table 3. (continued)

Determine if the contact is a Problem (Critical Point)	
Determine if there is a Fix or Workaround	Use classification to retrieve appropriate Is-Is Not resolution options.
Apply the Fix	Update the Incident Ticket with all knowledge found and tried.
Is the Incident & Recovery completed?	If the incident is not resolved it means explicit knowledge does not exist, and a knowledge ticket must be created.
Continue KB search	If the incident is not resolved it means explicit knowledge does not exist, and a knowledge ticket must be created.
Continue to Investigate, Diagnose & Research the Incident	--
Escalate the incident (Functional)	• On-call and Escalation policies and processes available as help. • Configure the CSC Triage roles as identified in the Classification Matrix. • The role assignment for escalation is obtained based on the way the incident is classified thus far. This is also in the classification matrix.
Monitor & Track the Incident Self monitoring	• If tickets and sub-tickets are escalated to another level by a user, it should still be visible to the original CSC user. • Monitor knowledge type tickets. Monitor the ticket even if it is re-assigned. Monitor (sub) tickets associated with the main ticket. • Customer self monitoring requires the status to be presented with only the information approved for customer dissemination visible. • Fields in the incident can be edited with comments approved for customer view.
Resolution Confirmation with the Customer	More examples of Policies that must be edited as help: In the event that you cannot make contact with the customer you are permitted to close the ticket after two (2) business days. Ensure that you properly document your customer contact experience in the Incident Ticket. Close the ticket by proceeding to Step (A17) Ticket Closure.
Document new knowledge	All the exploration conducted in resolving an ticket is maintained with the ticket in a complete fashion.
Incident Ticket Closure	Closing an Incident Ticket should be taken seriously. In this step: • Confirm and update the true cause of the problem. This could result in a secondary and more accurate Incident Classification that's driven by the actual resolution. • Survey the customer for service satisfaction • Verify that all information needed to properly track Incident trends is present in the Incident Ticket. An incident ticket can be closed even though it maybe associated with one or more knowledge tickets. However, the incident will remain associated with the knowledge ticket which is creating the new knowledge related to the incident.

Table 4.

Identify missing knowledge	This could occur in any one of several steps in the Incident Process, as documented. The result of this step is the creation of a knowledge ticket that is assigned to the knowledge management role.
Create resolution knowledge	The following Roles for Knowledge Management will be configured: • Knowledge Management Role responsible for knowledge tickets • Experts, one for each feature e.g. scheduled backup, reports. The tickets of type 'Knowledge' can be routed between these roles as needed. Standard escalation features apply. The knowledge management and experts have queued knowledge tickets with associated incidents that can be viewed as they are being resolved. The roles can continue viewing the incident tickets even after they are closed. The knowledge manager role can work on the creation of new resolution knowledge the moment a knowledge ticket is received. But only once an incident is resolved at the customer site is the knowledge considered validated. Take the resolved incident information (that was once identified as type unknown) and create or update the Is-Is Not information. Create sub tickets for expert roles as needed to complete and validate the knowledge. It should be possible to have one or more knowledge tickets and sub tickets associated with one or more incidents. The knowledge ticket and related incident tickets are processed, collaborating with the CSC team as needed. Examine the current and closed incident tickets classified as unknown errors, related to each Knowledge ticket. Examine the classification and resolution information used to identify if this could be done more efficiently.
Document expertise	Provide resolution knowledge or other expertise needed as defined in the sub-ticket of type knowledge. Route back to the knowledge management role.
Represent knowledge	When the experts provide the needed input the tickets are all routed back to the knowledge management role that completes the final edit of the Is-Is Not template, configures the knowledge management system, and tests the use of the new resolution procedure. Representation of new knowledge has to be thoughtfully accomplished. For example, what is the best way to evolve the classification matrix so that we have fewer errors? What is the best way to design a resolution? What other resolutions might have to be enhanced, unified, or replaced?
Knowledge Validation and closure	Update the classification knowledge and resolution knowledge maintained in the knowledge management component by the Knowledge Management Role. Test access to that knowledge and fix any problems.

- Deep technical expertise in specific areas
- a process orientation in solving problems

KM Performance

The KM team is charged with monitoring and continuously improving the performance of the Help Desk, from a customer's perspective. This requires individuals in the team to think about group productivity rather than their own productivity. This is not traditionally the way engineers think, as their focus in solving technical problems. It is therefore recommended that engineers be rotated as experts support-ing the help desk. The KM roles should be viewed as a reward for performance and filled on a rotational basis. This will help the KM team promulgate a combination 'customer and technical focus' within the organization. As such it is recommended that this team meet on a weekly basis and on a semi-social basis (say over pizza or tai chi) in order to 1) look for new areas of knowledge acquisition and 2) imple-ment improvements in the incident process, classification, training, etc. based on metrics collected.

CMDB and IS-IS-Not Template

Finally the role of the Is-Is Not template in creating knowledge about the installed IT infrastructure and agents is important to consider. In the larger context, these questions asked during the incident process illustrate one way in which the IT infrastructure is viewed and is an extension of the classification matrix. After the initial classification, the more detailed questioning needed for resolution is con-tained in this template[e].

More generally, the CMDB is a shared repository of configuration items and their use in the enterprise architecture. To be useful, its eventual function is to hold the knowledge needed for the ITIL service life-cycle processes needed to function properly. An overview (in UML) of objects and relationships required for knowledge management is illustrated in Figure 7 below. It is quickly apparent that while the classification matrix configured in the help desk knowledge component will deal with some of the requirements, the extended requirements will require the CMDB, including the identification of all the assets, SLAs, Services, features, and their interrelationships. The classification matrix is just a view of this. Knowledge Management will eventually encompass all these relationships.

MONITORING THE BIOS VALUE AND RESEARCH

Finally, we look at the insights that we can get from monitoring the installed IT infrastructure. Figure 9 illustrates the four types of entities that we assume in any enterprise system – business goals, process Interactions, service components, and infrastructure components. Progressing from the top to bottom their roles in the enterprise are as follows:

1. *BioS goals* reflect the interests of stakeholders. There can be many goals and stakeholders.

2.   *Interactions* that execute and in turn 'deliver' on business goals. Interactions are abstractions that represent the performance milestones of end-to-end business processes and sub-processes 'executed' to fulfill business-requests.

3.   *Service Roles and Components* that are Agents that 'run on' the infrastructure and whose space and processing speed needs are thus provisioned by the infrastructure; or else the service components 'provide' services to other service components.

4.   *Infrastructure components* that are primarily the physical machines, routers, and essential operating software. We will also place human agent in this category.

Figure 9 is just another more precise view of Figure 2 that highlights the attributes that we want to monitor. The attributes associated with each entity are identified in Figure 8. For a service component, these S-S attributes are also of two types - intrinsic and extrinsic S-S attributes. The intrinsic S-S attributes are determined by the characteristics of the software component. For example, like those determined by running a database service component in a test infrastructure machine environ-

Figure 8. Integrated knowledge management and incident management

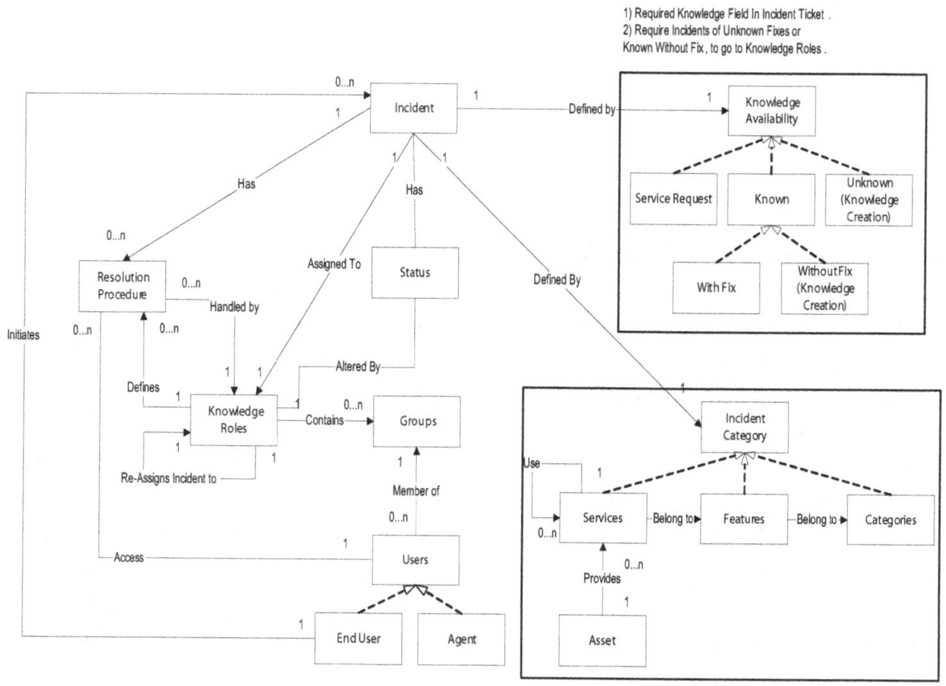

Figure 9. Service ontology

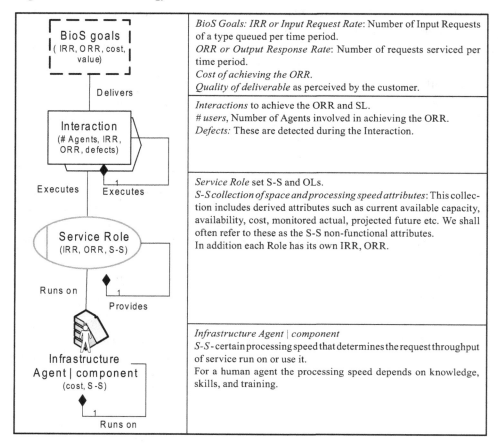

BioS goals (IRR, ORR, cost, value)	*BioS Goals: IRR or Input Request Rate*: Number of Input Requests of a type queued per time period. *ORR or Output Response Rate*: Number of requests serviced per time period. *Cost of achieving the ORR*. *Quality of deliverable* as perceived by the customer.
Delivers **Interaction** (# Agents, IRR, ORR, defects)	*Interactions* to achieve the ORR and SL. *# users*, Number of Agents involved in achieving the ORR. *Defects:* These are detected during the Interaction.
Executes Executes **Service Role** (IRR, ORR, S-S)	*Service Role* set S-S and OLs. *S-S collection of space and processing speed attributes*: This collection includes derived attributes such as current available capacity, availability, cost, monitored actual, projected future etc. We shall often refer to these as the S-S non-functional attributes. In addition each Role has its own IRR, ORR.
Runs on Provides **Infrastructure Agent	component** (cost, S-S) Runs on	*Infrastructure Agent	component* *S-S*- certain processing speed that determines the request throughput of service run on or use it. For a human agent the processing speed depends on knowledge, skills, and training.

ment, on benchmarks and in isolation. Extrinsic attributes are those S-S attributes that are affected by business requests from other entities along associations that we will explore later. We will henceforth use the function C, as in $C_x(S\text{-}S)$, to reflect the intrinsic and extrinsic S-S values of component X's. Each entity identified above also has specific attributes as illustrated in Figure 9.

What do S-S attributes convey differently for infrastructure components and service components? To answer this let us first think of service component X that runs on an infrastructure component or machine. In its essence the hardware has a certain available space and is able to process at a certain speed. However, the machine can accommodate a component such as a data base only if the machine's available S-S is greater than the data base own needs or $C_{database}(S\text{-}S)$. The needed data base S-S also increases with the number of requests serviced from different process transactions. To accommodate this increase the hardware must in turn have the extra needed S-S available. That is more generally, the software has a certain fluctuating C_x(S-S) footprint due to extrinsic circumstances that it needs from the hardware. The process transaction entity and its attributes introduced next allow us to compute the needed extrinsic S-S values due to external requests.

Interaction attributes include #Users, IRR, and ORR. Here IRRs are incoming business requests distinguished from the request throughput ORR by the fact that the former is initiated and queued by the customer while the latter is the actual number processed (and could include many internally generated requests serviced by the lower level entities). Finally, Business goal attributes include IRR and ORR costs.

Note: In addition to the essential attributes identified above there are additional attributes that reflect target and actual values for costs, resource costs of S-S for processing a request, and so on.

We can now also introduce specific *Service Levels* (SL) and *Operating Levels* (SL). The SL of a process transaction is reflected by its request throughput - ORR. As we shall see, this is provisioned by the service components and their S-S attributes at certain ORR Operating Levels (OLs) to achieve process transaction and business RR targets.

Available Tools and Gaps

Many different types of tools are available to monitor attribute values related to the service ontology defined in Figure 9. These are summarized in Table 5.

CONCLUSION AND RESEARCH IN KNOWLEDGE MINING

The tools/methods identified above allow us to monitor each individual layer. However, they do not allow us to relate the use of Agents vertically to goals. For example, we cannot easily relate the capacity of an Infrastructure component to the Business Interaction capacity that it facilitates. This requires a capability to trace requests across the layers. We refer to this as *vertical traceability*. With this ability we can begin to align capacity and S-S attributes more closely to fluctuating IRRs at the business layer. However, this vertical traceability is missing. One approach is to dynamically propagate the identity of the initiating Request to retain full traceability (Sandip 2007). Another is to apply data mining strategies (with some starting points in Belkin & Croft 1992, Bonaceto & Craig 2002, Ding et al. 2008).

Finally, if this vertical traceability is made available, organizations can be armed with predictive knowledge that will allow them to manage by objectives.

Specifically, the requirements in this area can be divided into 1) dynamic vertical traceability monitoring, 2) knowledge mining, and 3) predictive capability. These categories are explored further in Table 6.

Assuming that we can capture all the information needed to build the relationships above, what types of knowledge can we mine? What 'dashboard tools' can we build? To answer these questions, we note that with the underlying ACE ontology presented above and the resulting vertical traceability; we can develop run-time tools that form the basis of a Co-engineering environment. This type of research should lead to:

- Monitor Interactions between business users and IT assets in order to acquire SL requirements without needing human intervention.

Table 5.

Entity type	Functions available and vertical traceability gaps	Examples of applicable methods, commercial and open source tools
Business, Information use, Operations, and Strategy goals *IRR, ORR, Cost, Quality*	Business applications maintain Request information. With these requests, there is information on value provided to the customers and business. The business value is mainly indicated by the revenue. Gap: Many Interactions may be needed to deliver on a single Request. Within current systems it is however difficult to associate all the Interactions that deliver on the Request and associated value. The dynamics of how multiple organizations can impact each other is difficult to obtain. Specifically, how do different ORR rates of sub-Interactions impact the ORR of the original request?	Enterprise data warehousing, CRM, CSC (Customer Request Logs), and so on. Systems dynamics tools like Vensim[f] could be used to create simulations of Request cycle times for Request types and define throughput of the requests (ORRs for IRRs).
Interactions *Request type, IRR, ORR*	Interactions volumes (IRR) for each type of Request can be estimated by analyzing the results from the software applications and assets used in the current Interaction context. Gap: Current Interaction context. That is, how much of the underlying Roles and capacities were used in the current Interaction and sub-Interactions? This is difficult to estimate completely since the Interactions make use of shared resources. Thus the Roles and capacities for a particular type of Interaction are difficult to isolate.	There is a gap in available technologies.
Service Roles *Agents SS,, Knowledge needed*	The tools here monitor the performance and help apply knowledge in serving the Interactions in the operations layer. Many tools here actually have features to identify the IRR and ORR. Gap: The gap is in identifying the ORR related to a specific Interaction.	There is a gap in available technologies. Knowledge mining to improve Agent performance within an Interaction.

Table 5. (continued)

| Infrastructure *Infrastructure used, capacity* | The tools/methods in this layer monitor the specific IT infrastructure components to give us the current state (SS) of the system.
Dynamic operations monitoring tools are focused on monitoring the live system while it is in execution and providing that information to the user to improve the performance of the system. For example, tools like HPs SiteScope help in monitoring the performance of distributed IT infrastructure assets. It is a web based software that provides a centralized view of the entire infrastructure in real time. The highlight is that you can gain the real-time information you need to verify operations, stay apprised of problems and quickly address bottlenecks in your system. For example, if a database server is not running and this leads to bottlenecks in the system when the application server starts issuing requests to the database server, the deviation in the performance of the database server can be identified proactively (during reduced availability itself as opposed to when the server completely shuts down) Thus the problem can be diagnosed and corrected early resulting in performance improvement. This database also serves as the primary point of accountability for the life-cycle management of information technology assets throughout the organization.
Gap: Maximizing the performance and lifetime value of complex assets can be done by improving return on assets, decrease cost and risk, increase productivity and improve asset related decision making. This helps you closely align your assets with your overall business strategy. However, the ability to relate capacity to the individual Requests and the originating business Interactions is missing. This is needed to have precise accountability between the capacity and its point of use. | Component monitoring tools. These are tools (like the funnel analyzer[g], database monitoring[h], web server monitoring, etc.) and methods in the layers of IT infrastructure and operations. InsightETE[i] provides solutions for measuring and troubleshooting IT system performance by monitoring flow of information to and from IT users. It measures availability and response in real time and helps track service levels and reduce outages.
Another example is IBM's Asset management solution called Maximo™ Consists of six key management modules — asset, work, service, contract, materials and procurement management |

Table 6.

| Knowledge mining | With operations monitoring, logs from the different layers of operations of the system can be analyzed to gain useful insights into the system. To achieve vertical traceability, the logs can be used statically. For example, these logs can be analyzed using tools like Starlight which gives a conceptual \| visual understanding of relationships across the layers.
Gaps: The weakness that remains is the fine granularity of traceability to truly understand how increments in the higher dimensions will place incremental demand on the lower layers. | An example is Starlight. Other specific types of tools also exist for particular type of logs, for example web logs can be analyzed using tools like web funnel analyzer which gives more insights into user behavior in the web system. |
| Predictive methods | While system dynamics and simulation tools can help in analyzing to-be performance based on future needs, there are few principles that relate current value to future value of services.
For example, how will increased availability/capacity actually increase the value of the Interaction?
Gaps: The theory of service value is missing. For example, we really do not know why retaining certain architecture options will increase the value of future Interactions. These sorts of questions need to be answered for improved EA governance. | Analysis methods that justify investment based on increased future value are relevant. |

- Identify service improvements that meet OLs and better relate to stakeholder Goals.
- Integrate business and system simulation tools to better pin-point Interactions needing improvement to meet Goals.
- Identify achievable OL performance in the context of the target environment and architecture.
- Provide trade-offs and costs associated with improving different Roles and Role sets.
- Quantify the impact of a new services to be deployed into an existing environment.
- Extend simulation capability to considerations of capacity, availability, and security.

TASKS FOR ACE STRUCTURE AND CONTINUAL IMPROVEMENT

1. Identify the roles of knowledge management within your service innovation and project.
2. Define the processes to accomplish this.

THINGS TO THINK ABOUT

1. In what ways can autonomic Agents use internal knowledge to reduce the time for level 1, 2, and 3 incident resolutions? Illustrate with specific examples.
2. The on-going maintenance of the vendor knowledge needed for level 1 and level 2 resolutions is very time-consuming. To address this, we can start with vendor product information can be received through feeds. In addition, local installed asset status and configuration knowledge must all be organized for guiding and assisting in the incident resolution. Is there a case for collaborating to jointly develop and manage a knowledge base for all help desks. Is this feasible? Is there a business case for an open-source knowledge base solution that is used industry?
3. How does your answer to 2 motivate a standards?

REFERENCES

Agarwala, S., Alegre, F., Schwan K., & Mehalingham, J. (2007 June). E2EProf: Automated End-to-End Performance Management for Enterprise Systems. In *Proceedings of the 37th Annual IEEE/IFIP International Conference on Dependable Systems and Networks* (pp. 749-758), Washington DC, IEEE Computer Society.

Belkin, N.J. & Croft, B. (1992 December). Information Filtering and Information Retrieval: Two Sides of the Same Coin. *Communications of the ACM, 35*(12), 29-38.

Bonaceto, C. & Burns, K. (2005 November). *Using Cognitive Engineering to Improve Systems Engineering.* The MITRE Corporation, Retrieved November 23, 2008, from http://www.mitre.org/work/tech_papers/tech_papers_05/05_1361/

Bon, J., Pieper, M., & Annelies V. (2005). *Foundations of IT Service Management Based on ITIL.* Van Haren Publishing.

Butler, T., & Coleman, D. (2003 September). *Models of Collaboration.* Retrieved November 23, 2008, from http://www.collaborate.com/publication/newsletter/publications_newsletter_september03.html

Cameron, K. S., & Quinn, R. E. (1999). *Diagnosing and Changing Organizational Culture.* Boston: Addison-Wesley.

City of Tampa, Florida. (n.d.). Retrieved February 24, 2008, from http://www.tampagov.net/

City of Aurora, Colorado. (n.d.). Retrieved February 24, 2008, from http://www.auroragov.org/

Davenport, T. H., & Prusak, L. (1998). *Working Knowledge: How Organizations Manage What They Know.* Boston, MA: Harvard Business School Press.

Dawes, S., & Eglene, O. (2004). New Models of Collaboration for Delivering Government Services: A Dynamic Model Drawn from Multi-national Research. In *Proceedings of the 2004 Annual National Conference on Digital Government Research* (pp. 1-11), Seattle, WA: Digital Government Society of North America.

DiMaio, A. (2007 September). *Government and Web 2.0: The Emerging Midoffice.* Gartner Report G00151283, Gartner Research.

DiMaio, A. (2007 March). *What Does Web 2.0 Mean to Government?* Gartner Report G00146261, Gartner Research.

Ding, Xiaowen. Liu, Bing. Yu, Philip S. (2008). Web Search and Web Data Mining archive. Proceedings of the international conference on Web search and web data mining table of contents Palo Alto, California, USA SESSION: Social search table of contents Pages 231-240 Year of Publication: 2008 ISBN:978-1-59593-927-9 Sponsors ACM: Association for Computing Machinery.

Despres, C., & Chauvel, D. (2000). *Knowledge Horizons.* Oxford: Butterworth-Heinemann.

Engage: Creating e-Government that supports Commerce, Collaboration, Community and Commonwealth. (2007). Center for Digital Government, e.Republic Inc.

Fayyad, U., Piatetsky-Shapiro, M., Smyth, P., & Uthurusamy, R. (1996). *Advances in Knowledge Discovery and Data Mining.* Menlo Park: AAAI Press.

Gonzalez, L. M., Giachetti, R. E., & Ramirez, G. (2005 August). Knowledge Management-centric Help Desk: Specification and Performance Evaluation. *Decision Support Systems, 40*(2), 389-405.

Gupta V., Mukri F., Ramanathan J., Ramnath R., & Yackovich K. (2009 January). CitiScapes: Architecture for eGovernment Effectiveness. To appear in the *42nd Hawaii International Conference on Systems Sciences*, Waikoloa, HI: IEEE Computer Society.

HM Government. (2005). *Transformational Government Enabled by Technology.* Norwich, UK: TSO.

Hiller, J.S. & Belanger, F. (2001). *Privacy Strategies for Electronic Government.* The Pricewaterhouse Coopers Endowment for the Business of Government Report, Retrieved November 23, 2008, from http://www.endowment.pwcglobal.com/pdfs/HillerReport.pdf.

IPSV Board. (2006). *Integrated Public Sector Vocabulary, Version 2.00.* Retrieved November 23, 2008, from http://www.esd.org.uk/standards/ipsv/

Lambe, P. (2007). Organising Knowledge: Taxonomies, Knowledge and Organisational Effectiveness. Oxford: Chandos Publishing

Liu, B. (2006) *Web Data Mining, Exploring Hyperlinks, Contents, and Usage Data.* ISBN 3-540-37881-2.

McClure, D. (2007 September). *Government Transformation: Getting Joined-Up Governance Right.* Gartner Report G00151641, Gartner Research.

Mitra, A., & Amar, G. (2008). *Knowledge Reuse and Agile Processes: Catalysts for Innovation.* Information Science Reference.

Nita-Rotaru, C., & Li, N. A. (2004 September). Framework for Role-Based Access Control in Group Communication Systems. In *Proceedings of the 2004 International Workshop on Security in Parallel and Distributed Systems*, San Francisco, CA.

Polanyi, M. (1958). *Personal Knowledge: Towards a Post-critical Philosophy.* Chicago: University of Chicago Press.

Polanyi, (1966). *The Tacit Dimension.* New York, NY: Doubleday.

ReadWriteWeb. (2008). Retrieved November 23, 2008, from http://www.readwrite-web.com/archives/e-government_meets_web_20.php

Tolone, W., Ahn, G., Pai, T., & Hong, S. (2005 March). Access Control in Collaborative Systems. *ACM Computing Surveys, 37*(1), 29–41.

Tiwana, A. (2002). *The Knowledge Management Toolkit.* Englewood Cliffs: Prentice Hall.

ENDNOTES

[a]   This problem has many applications, e.g., opinion mining, summarization and search. Most existing techniques utilize a list of *opinion (bearing) words* (also called *opinion* lexicon) for the purpose. Opinion words are words that express desirable (e.g., great, amazing, etc.) or undesirable (e.g., bad, poor, etc) states. These approaches, however, all have some major shortcomings. In this paper, we propose a *holistic lexicon-based approach* to solving the problem by exploiting external evidences and linguistic conventions of natural language expressions. This approach allows the system to handle opinion words that are context dependent, which cause major difficulties for existing algorithms. It also deals with many special words, phrases and language constructs which have impacts on opinions based on their linguistic patterns. It also has an effective function for aggregating multiple conflicting opinion words in a sentence. A system, called Opinion Observer, based on the proposed technique has been implemented. Experimental results using a benchmark product review data set and some additional reviews show that the proposed technique is highly effective. It outperforms existing methods significantly (Liu 2007).

[b]   http://www.readwriteweb.com/archives/e-government_meets_web_20.php

[c]   Help Desk Institute: http://www.thinkhdi.com/

[d]   Is-Is Not template by MicroSoft™ guides the CSC personnel though a decision tree that allows them to classify the incident.

e   Microsoft's Is-Is Not template also provided in the Appendix.

f   http://www.vensim.com/software.html

g   http://linux.wareseeker.com/Internet/funnel-web-analyzer-5.0.zip/319940

h   http://www.uptimesoftware.com/

i   Insightete: http://www.insightete.com/

Chapter IX
Relating IT to Service Innovation

ABSTRACT

We explore how different types of opportunities for Interaction improvement - innovation, effectiveness, and resilience can be identified. We use the evolution in new media to illustrate:

- How can we systematically explore the opportunities?
- What are examples of innovation applied to new media?
- What is the larger role for IT in enabling new models for the business?

Our goal here is to explore how an understanding of Interactions also helps identify opportunities for innovation and resilience. Previously we have already covered examples of IT use in Interaction effectiveness though Lean and Knowledge Management. Our focus here is on identifying opportunities through a systematic understanding of Innovation.

First we present some recent definitions and background (Larson & Brahmakulam 2001) related to innovation:

Innovation is a locally-driven process that succeeds where organizational conditions foster the transformation of knowledge into products, processes, systems, and services. The local part of this is very important . . . it's only when local expertise,

Figure 1. The competitive forces on a newspaper company due to traditional and emerging value-chains defining the strategy context

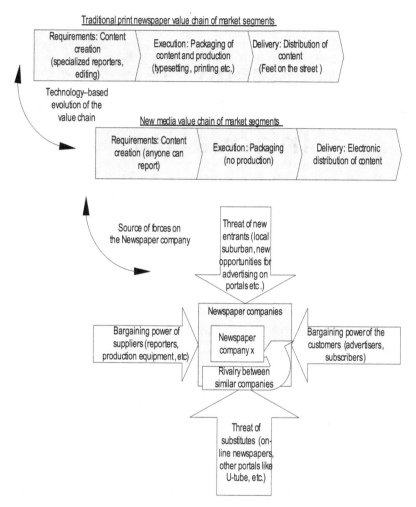

and knowledge of local needs, local conditions, and local resources, can be brought to the picture, that innovation will truly happen.

The first link in the innovation chain involves transforming what may be predominantly theoretical knowledge into a practical application, whether in terms of a product or a process[a]. The tangible outputs include both a technology that can be transferred to industry and the knowledge capital (know-how) embodied in scien-

tists and engineers who are responsible for technology breakthroughs; both can disseminate through the economy.

A common view that was also expressed at this 2001 National Science Foundation sponsored workshop was that work at the seams - i.e., work that cuts across traditional disciplinary lines and across university-industry lines - was where the unexpected could be expected to happen, with the result being innovation. The reason seemed to be that solutions not obvious in one realm might be perfectly obvious in another and that these sorts of Interactions enhanced the prospects that such solutions could be made obvious.

This view lends its self to a better understanding of potential innovations by focusing on Interactions and agents as we will see here.

BEST PRACTICES IN INNOVATION

Around the turn of the millennium and with the opportunity for innovation in eBusiness, most organizations sought to define their own unique advantage. At about the same time Christiansen (Christensen 1996) introduced the Theory of Innovation with the following basics:

- Successful innovation is based on the actual circumstances of use and not usually on a demographic of the market.
- Disruptive innovation targets un-served, under-served and over-served markets.
- Successful innovations must align with the resources, processes and values of the enterprise.
- Methods based on an understanding of the Innovation Stages and Activities and Portfolio Thinking.

It was also found that the actual innovation varies from industry to industry. Broadly speaking there are different types of innovations:

- Disruptive change in the market
- Sustaining target in the same market
- Incremental improvement of the product or process
- Architectural change in the composition
- Modular substitutes

An example of technology-based a disruptive innovation is the Digital Versatile Disc (DVD) which replaced the VHS/Beta magnetic video tape. The more compact DVD technology was able to deliver more content, play longer and with higher quality. In this case the disruption was successful as the market was underserved. We have also studied an example of sustaining the target with continual improvement. That is, the City 311 system which brought new services to a captive market of residents. Additionally the city also achieved transparency of operations, and, hence, continuous improvement and collaboration across Departmental silos applying 'Crossing the Chasm' principles (Moore 2002) to under-served *reference departments*. Thus the City also illustrates that the pre-dominant role and value of IT is in enabling primary processes.

Drawing upon examples like this, our focus here is in understanding how to increase the business value of IT through systematic *methods of enterprise architecture* management and portfolio thinking. We begin with a systematic way to look for innovations that enhance Interactions using Porter's *ten drivers* as a basis (Porter 1985)[b]. We will also show to IT facilitate innovation and resilience through methods and new levels of insight through an enterprise-wide view of Interactions and enterprise architecture management.

Targeting Interaction Vulnerabilities: Targeting and protecting against vulnerabilities like disaster and threat scenarios require us to examine the *resiliency* of the Interaction chains and RED milestones. For example, the capacity management example of Chapter II shows how we can now look at Request-RED-Role Set-Deliverable associations to understand the impact of a threat like Katrina on server resources needed to process insurance claims. This requires an understanding of potential impact if Role set services become unavailable and identifying alternate assignments to the Role set. Vulnerable Interactions can also be identified and prioritized (e.g. based on high value and volume) and alternate *Role Set assignment strategies* developed. If a Role is unable to be performed, alternate or additional capabilities can thus be assigned quickly if this is anticipated. This may often involve the re-purposing of existing infrastructures and related policies. For example during normal triage and circumstances, an Interaction is assigned alternate resources only if this is pre-approved. However during triage and emergency circumstances, other assignment policies for larger good come into play. The emerging field of Resilience explores these issues as they relate to the supply chain and other related areas (Christopher & Peck 2004, Hamel & Valikangas 2003).

Combining Interactions to Develop New Business Models: While the jury is still out on new Internet business models, companies have successfully moved into leadership positions in specific markets using technology. Many brokerage firms offer traditional services such as the ability for clients to view their own records and get personalized advice over the web. Others like Fidelity Investments and

Charles Schwab provide additional complementary services. For example Charles Schwab provides the performance information necessary to make investment decisions. This in fact disintermediates the stockbroker. It is also interesting to note that these features have been developed based on over two decades of technology experience (Looney & Chatterjee 2002; Prasarnphanich and Gillenson 2003, Hart & Milstein 1999).

Economies of scale: This requires us to look for ways in which Interactions can be scaled. This plays into IT strengths as it can facilitate more Interactions with shared resources and even improve competitive positioning by executing more Interactions leading to an increase in the potential market share for a Request type. The recent emergence of cloud computing has contributed to IBM's strategy (Economist 2008).

Learning and knowledge delivery: Look for ways in which IT can be used to improve resources and knowledge needed for performance. This can be achieved by improving the training, automating and reducing the level of expertise needed, better more current work instructions, or context-based knowledge. A related emerging trend is in monitoring fielded systems and components. Not only does this apply to products with embedded IT components, such as a car with health check technologies – but also processes like customer service where new knowledge can be captured to improve customer satisfaction. Finally, IT can better monitor IT itself thus increasing an understanding of the enterprise and through relating Strategy, Operations, Financials, Resources, and Goals. See Tiwana 2002.

Capacity utilization: Look for ways in which more high value, high priority Request types can be supported with the sharing of existing capacity. This can include providing the capacity to potential customers in other organizations. For example Amazon.com provides some services that were developed for Amazon. com use.[c] Note that an IT implementation can keep options open with the delayed binding of Role sets to agents. With strategies like this an organization has significant capability to enable and apply dynamic rules to use capacity.

Sense and optimize request-to-delivery processing: Identify related Interactions (Porter's linkages among activities) that can be integrated to handle customer requirements and new opportunities. This can take several forms. For example, by sensing preferred or emerging Request types (e.g. sensing preferred custom products) or new Interactions types (customization features) we can detect trends early.

Optimize Request-to-Delivery Processing: Firms have implemented customizable 'alert' systems that provide investors with the ability to be notified in real time via email of events particular to securities of specific interest (such as Charles Schwab described in Looney & Chatterjee 2002).

Leverage relationships among organizations: Look for customers and competitions that support complementary Interactions in the marketplace. Look for ways in which new capabilities can be assembled to support new Request types. Here services of existing organizations within the extended enterprise can come together to offer new services through new Interactions. For example, the collation of Role sets allows us to define services that are needed and future alternatives. To illustrate, the laptop manufacturer negotiates contracts that can be exercised by using capacity from alternate providers when the demand is high. A more complete example of this is given in the next section of this chapter.

Degree of vertical integration: Reduce costs Interaction by owning or streamlining the customer-provider chain. For example, Role sets determine Interaction needs, but, as long as the Role is becoming a commodity there are many cost advantages to outsourcing. This type of analysis leads to an identification of many synergies with other organizations. The potential for e-business is more apparent in upstream in the business-to-business value chain (Coltman 2002). For example, Dell has successfully implemented the movement of products away from detailed designs to basic commodities through a supply chain. Dell's on-line catalogue-fronted IT competencies enable quick response though low-cost fulfillment based system characterized by direct customer Interactions and made-to-order manufacturing Interactions. Lowering procurement costs is also an example of using the company value chain to set priorities for improvement.

Timing of market entry: Monitor the Request catalog of competitors to identify the strategy for internal innovation and investments. The organization focus on the request catalog and metrics concretizes the methods for business intelligence mining and strategy definition. One can now contemplate the use of technology to gather more circumstance-based information. For example, RFID tags can identify the correlation between events, seasons and product types purchased at a convenience store. Because shelf space is scarce, this type of information is critical in stocking to maximize purchase. Related concepts in Roth 2008.

Organization's policy of cost or differentiation: Monitor the Request catalog (in particular the potential offerings) of competitors to identify the competitive strategy for each. This requires an understanding of the maximum value of the service to the customer, an understanding of the costs of the Interactions needed, and an understanding of the implications of product and market life cycles. Also relevant are principles of diffusion. (Rogers 1976).

Geographic location: As mentioned before, Requests originating from the customer's environment can be used to provide significant information related to the circumstance captured using GPS position, IP address, local context, proximity, and so on. This allows the response Interactions to be customized to location by using virtual or local service capabilities. As a specific example, consider the placement of advertisements based on the location of the user, previous sites visited, and queries.

Institutional and other factors: Look for ways to improve the cost of Interactions with respect to regulation, union activity, taxes, etc. For example, compliance requirements can be turned to an advantage providing enterprise-wide visibility. Finally, policy making government organizations might also influence the actual Interactions and forces (e.g. trade restrictions).

THE BUSINESS CHALLENGE

A specific example of the way in which Interactions influence each other is explored further is the traditional print media companies – such as regional newspapers – that are by and large at the crossroads. A particularly disturbing trend is that print media companies are losing revenue to the Internet (Forbes, Time Inside Business, Business Week Online). With the advent of the internet and new media, many related market segments in areas such as print media, video games, television, radio, and particularly advertising and marketing (which seeks to gain from the advantages of two-way dialogue with consumers) are rapidly evolving. For example, content production can be by individuals and distribution can be though U-tube, thus disrupting the traditional value chain (content production, packaging, distribution) of newspaper companies. The advertising industry has capitalized on the proliferation of new media by new technologies for interactive advertising (Arie 1997, Boczkowski 2004).

To understand the larger context within which Interactions change we re-draw and re-associate both the traditional and the more disruptive new media Interaction context and value chains in this industry at the top of the Figure 1. The traditional RED Interaction chain of content *creation → packaging → distribution* is deployed by a specialized infrastructure of agents – reporters, production equipment and feet on the street. This is now being replaced. The RED Interaction in New Media is now being supported by a new Role set of individuals, inexpensive equipment, and the Internet. In the context of this dynamic we can also next identify the forces on the traditional print media companies.

Strategy definition: From the newspaper company's perspective (illustrated at the very center), strategy takes into consideration the forces that result from the trends identified above. The five forces framework identifies and illustrated the threats and opportunities for the Newspaper company shown at the center as follows: 1) threat of new entrants – electronic media, delivery on portable devices, 2) threat of substitutes – again electronic media and devices, 3) bargaining power of the suppliers – typesetting companies, 4) bargaining power of customers – advertisers, individuals who want to report, 5) rivalry within the market segment – other local suburban news competing for the same advertisement revenue.

However in the surrounding context we note that several market value chains (segments) might be in evolution causing new forces as illustrated in Figure 1. To understand this we identify the actual impact of the five forces by looking in detail the market Interactions and the underlying capabilities (supporting Infrastructure Interactions) and factors that complete the 'New Media request-to-delivery Interaction' in Figure 2 (Capra 2002, Al Gore 2005, The Paper Trade 2005, Stopping the Presses 2005, The Future of New York Times 2005).

Noting the role of IT, from the perspective of the customer, the rapid evolution of technology can even be considered a *sixth force*[d] in this case. The rationale for this is technology is enabling the traditional Role sets to be rapidly replaced with alternative less expensive agents and infrastructures in this case. To make some of these observations more concrete, we look at the implications of IT trends and the effect of these trends on Interactions within the extended print media enterprise. We next explore the technology dimension in detail.

Figure 2. The Primary Content Interaction and the Infrastructure Interactions

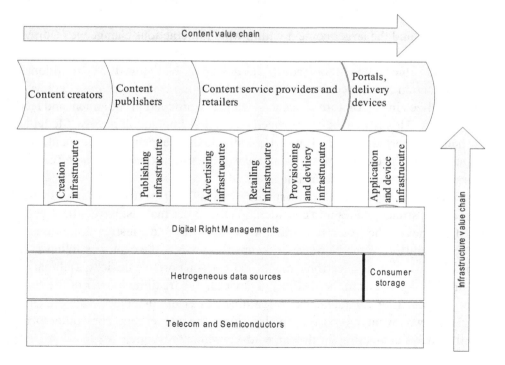

IT TRENDS AND IMPACT TO ENTERPRISE INTERACTIONS

There are increasing efficiencies potentially due to emerging IT technology and through resulting coordination, accurate information delivery, and Business-Intelligence gathering. Emerging IT technologies in this case includes a wide range – Mobile devices, ePaper, Service-Oriented Architectures, Web 2.0 collaboration technologies, Workflow, Web 3.0 semantic technologies – OWL/RDF, visualization capabilities, location-awareness RFID, GPS/GIS, Cellular, Wireless, and Intelligent Networked Sensors! But more interesting and important to *print media strategy* are the innovations in *'digital media'* that these technologies facilitate.

Digital media: We define "digital media" as those companies that engage in or enable the creation, publishing, distribution and consumption of content - audio, video, images, and games stored in digital form. Consumption of Media - commercial and non commercial - includes a range such as Teenage populations, Restaurants, Magazine Publishers, Portals etc. There is a trend to access richer content and increased range of utility access. Content business is very time sensitive. For example, there is competition for revenue between Theaters, Blockbuster, and Cable with a movie release date. For each the credo is 'earlier the better'. In this market segment, there are two major value chains 1) the content and 2) the infrastructure as in Figure 2.

Each market segment and the related value chain is introduced below followed by the potential infrastructure applications. For each we also present relevant challenges and possible solutions in content delivery.

Content Value Chain

1. *Content Creation* - These businesses (Composers, Screen writers, Performers, Artists, Engravers, Music Copyists, etc.) invest time to develop new skills, new equipment (Hard and/or Software). They are looking for more opportunities to have creations remunerated, lessen dependence on producers and benefit from the widening of market presence (e.g. via internet).
2. *Publishing | Packaging* - These businesses (Film/TV/Music studios, Publishers, Sony – film, Brill – TV, Random House, Sony, NY Times, HBO) are experiencing a loss of control to creators and an increased range of requirements (product types / variations) that must be pushed to the consumers. They have the potential for control of more value chain elements and thus increase opportunities for revenue. They are creating new platforms - Content repositories, Studio Libraries (like Turner Classic Movies). They are exploring possibilities of providing universal access to content. They are the managers and owners

of content, and often production and distribution facilities. With the accelerating transition to digital they have more opportunities to distribute content; e-commerce, data assets; consumer application sales. Radical reduction of piracy is critical to their success. Click and mortar companies (like Nike, Budwiser etc.) are also publishers of content – in this case advertisements of their products.

There is a synergistic relationship between content publishers and companies with a click-and-mortar presence, as they drive each others' revenue. The mutual goal is to increase audience. For example, less than 5% of ad revenue goes online but 33% of people's time is spent online. All of the revenue for is from add-supported products. Creating environments that can be monetized through advertising.

3. *Content service providers and retailers* - These companies include aggregators and broadcasters (Radio / TV Stations, CBS, New York Times, Clear Channel, Netflix) that provide more ways to offer content.

4. *Portals and delivery devices* - These companies provide a gateway to media services (Amazon, e-Music, Google). There is a need to negotiate rights, advertisement-revenue with content service providers and retailers. They can mine customer intelligence to offer more services than possible today. They have opportunities to bundle search services with actual content offers. Portals are massive technology purchasing machines Google etc. See above.

Advertising Infrastructure Applications of Technology

The placement of advertising to reach consumers on the Internet is increasing rapidly. Once related scenario discussed here is the placement of advertisements within the content publishing portals. Advertising networks (for example, AddMeld. com, Burst Media, Pop-up Network) match the inventory of ads that come from their own sites and publishers at large to the specific characteristics of the portal communities. Advertising networks sell the advertisement and compensate. Ad networks are valued because they help reach niche markets (through the long tail[c]) which are hard to reach through direct sales which does not scale. The amount of unsold ad inventory is large. The biggest challenge that they face is the loss of audience to smaller size blogs, startups etc.

Market factors: Current technology is inadequate and the technology practice is to address integrated service challenges through acquisitions resulting in a portfolio of online products - search, email, social networking, online classifieds, and content. Major players have also made big investments on the ad side. They have bought ad networks, exchanges, ad serving companies. In general this market buys a lot from technology startups and buys a lot from database companies. For example, AOL bought Truvio, Singing Fish[f]. Integration tends to be a big part of expense for a system. Cost of switching from one product to another is extremely low. Acquisitions depend on the "edge".

Benefit of using technology: Improved ways to match consumer behavior with ad profiles in publisher databases through federated search is a useful IT service. It is still challenging and time consuming to have integrated searches. For example, typical practice is to import and combine data within a system. Any large content site that pulls from multiple sources (like Ask.com) could use new technologies such as ontology-based querying of large scale databases.

Provisioning and Delivery Infrastructure Applications of Technology

The connectivity providers (network service providers, Cable, and IP based content providers like CNN; Satellite companies, two-way-IP based service providers like Earthlink) have investments in infrastructure (servers, satellites etc.) but have no link to end-user devices. They are concerned with service provisioning and infrastructure upgrades. These companies track their assets across multiple company databases. They don't want to be just a 'fat pipe' and a commodity. They are looking for opportunities to bundle infrastructure services with higher-level services. For example, increase customers use in a region for video on demand (VOD). VOD is primary competitive advantage. They would like to release content other ways, but cannot. *New opportunities might lie in VOD long-tail – niche content.* It might not be competitive for one cable operator to do this. But if industry as a whole had an infrastructure through standards to provide long-tail market - could be possibility (reference Digital Media Project). They are prevented by regulation from content going outside set-top box[g].

Benefit of using technology: One example here is the ability to answer questions to discover whether the local infrastructure would support new services. For example, what devices in a region and network upgrade path limit connectivity/bandwidth required by customer users' types? This type of data would be maintained in a CMDB and CRM. Another example is the performance monitoring and analysis of pathways. This is especially true for DOCSIS 3.0 - on channel bonding - how to manage, upgrade, configuration? Relevant Standards bodies: Digital Lifestyle Networking Alliance – services into and around the home. A recent example of such a complex system management effort funded by NSF is GENI[h].

Portal and Device Infrastructure Applications of Technology

Portals (Ask.com, Google, AOL, social networking sites, etc.) and Consumer Appliance Players (Motorola, Scientific Atlantic bought by Cisco) are in this market, our focus is on the former.

Benefit of using technology: Portals like Ask.com pull data from multiple sources to match specific customer profiles and questions. This includes looking at social networking analysis, directionality, temporal, geospatial attributes for better publishing and advertising.

Digital Rights Management: Rights Societies

DRM solution providers: Provider of Rights Management Systems and integrators (SAP, Rightsline, BearingPoint) that integrate Sales and Marketing to content solutions to track and monitor use for royalties. While standards sometimes implies loss of levies opportunities of new services also arise by broadening the base geographically. A rights intermediary and standards developer in this area is ASCAP[i], HFA.

Benefit of using technology: Ability to reason about access to content based on security policy and the specific context of the access.

RESEARCH IN ACE INNOVATION AND RESILIENCE

More generally, section 9.2 presented the evolution in the New Media market segments and section 9.3 presented the enabling IT trends and product implementations as illustrated in Figure 2. Here we explore how the ACE framework presents an approach for understanding such complex systems of Interactions in different scales.

Note that all these Interactions in different scales are locally applied by agents. Interactions completed by individual Agents contribute value within by overall framework of Stakeholders (also Agents) as in Figure 3. The Agents work locally but when their individual contributions are aggregated and viewed from the perspective of Stakeholders, we can begin to understand the potential global impact across the business and economic dimensions of the enterprise. Thu to understand the competitive forces, we can look at the Interaction value contribution and competitiveness of an Agent, the aggregated Interaction value and competitiveness of a group of agents (i.e. a business), and the Interaction value and competitiveness' of a group of group of Agents (a market segment), and so on. More specifically, Porter's framework allows us to look at the competitive strategy of a service in a

Figure 3. Fractal Dimensions of the Service Enterprise

	Scope	Agent roles	Scale of Interaction	Service delivered	Performance	Disciplines etc.
Environment (Business-social interaction dimensions)	Groups of groups of agents as in market segments of orgs	Origin of requests and satisfaction – customer agents (and stakeholders)	Interaction refers to a sequence of activities by groups of groups of agents– as in the value chain: device producers => distributors => health care clinics. Here an activity is a market segment.	Satisfactory use of the deliverables in the customer's environment	Improved direct/ indirect value-add to customer's primary Interactions.	Public policy, Economics, Law (Sarbanes-Oxley, HIPAA).
Business	Groups of agents as in a business with orgs	Response strategy for each type of request and value to business – executive agents	Interaction refers to a sequence of activities by orgs– as primary value chain: as in customer center=>inbound logistics => assembly => outbound logistics	Sustainability, competitiveness, survivability, and growth.	Improved business-value add by each org and for each request type.	Business, MIS. (COBIT, Balanced ScoreCard).
Operations	Group of agents (also called org or organization).	Execution strategy for each type of request and resource optimization – operational agents	Interaction refers to a sequence of tasks (i.e. activity) that provides resources for Interactioning a specific request: as in resources for device assembly for a customer.	Response time, throughput, cost, and continuous improvement.	Improved efficiency by each org and for each request type.	Systems engineering (Lean, ISO)
Execution	Agent that is active applying knowledge, or passive as in the example of a tool.	Interaction execution – resource agents	Interaction refers to a sequence of instructions and knowledge applied that adds value to the product and complete the task.	For each request, actual value added to the service and to interaction stakeholders	Improved product/ service value add for each request and by each resource.	Systems engineering (Six Sigma).
Environment of IT (Enterprise Knowledge Infrastructure Dimensions)	Group of agents	IT service requirements identified and criteria for satisfaction established – business-IT liaison agents	Interaction can refer to activities by orgs in the business dimension or in the operating dimension or a sequence of instructions in the execution dimension.	Enterprise Knowledge Infrastructure.	Enterprise-wide visibility – both horizontally and vertically	Business-social computing (enterprise integration)
Business of IT	Groups of agents	IT service response strategy to customer and cost effective IT operations – business-IT agents	Interaction refers to the primary value chain of IT orgs as in: customer help desk. request resolution, request delivery.	Reliability, cost effectiveness and competitiveness.	Improve direct value-add to primary Interactions.	Enterprise architecture (Zachman, Togaf, etc.)
Operations of IT	Group of agents	Delivery of a particular type of customer service request:– business-IT operational agents	Interaction refers to resources for specific requests– problem resolution, enhancement etc.	Response time, throughput, cost, and continuous improvement.	Meet service level (SLs) for executing IT services.	IT operations (ITIL, Six Sigma).
Execution of IT services	Agents – active as in human and automated resources passive as in IT components	Task execution – IT resource agents	Interaction refers coordination needed to deliver IT services to the business agent.	Information and workflow services.	Meet IT service OL.	Computing technologies (service-oriented architectures)

relatively universal manner across the enterprise to gain an understanding of trends and potential areas of innovation. Here we have also shown how the IT dimensions influence the business and strategy execution by Agents and Groups of Agents (i.e. organizations). Additionally, the strategy layers of the business influence other Agents that consume services within different markers (groups of groups of Agents).

Sampson's article critiques the commonly held stance that technology is becoming so powerful it will unilaterally tear down all sorts of industrial barriers and displace the role of the large organization (Sampson 2003). To do this he introduces a bit of economic theory based on the notions and interrelations of transaction and organizational costs and concludes that there is neither any reason to believe that IT will have such a dramatic impact nor any way to predict exactly what impact will have at the current time.

On the other hand, research in complex systems has lead to an improved understanding of resilience along the supply chain (Levy 1994, Mackenzie 2002). At its core is a better understanding of the inter-connectedness along the customer-provider Interactions of the supply chain. Thus from an enterprise architect's perspective complexity theory and the recursive relationships within the extended enterprise allow us to better understand how IT solutions can alter transaction costs, the costs of collaborative interactions, and at the same time change organizational costs, the costs of structuring these collaborations. This view not only allows us to look systematically into innovation and development issues but also into breakages and the need for resilience.

Resilience is defined as the organizations' ability to withstand significant and potential economic or systemic impact to its operations. In the case of the print newspaper company, it became critical to look at the very challenges of survival and dealing with immediate and longer-term forces during the *strategy* definition process. Looking at an isolated Interaction improvement – such as improving the portal Interactions to become more engaged with the local community was no longer adequate. As the discussion above illustrates, a more global understanding of shifts in Interaction trends due to technology shifts within the market value chain is critical to survival. Resilience must therefore take a broader perspective in general, and definitely so in the case of the print media company.

At the same time innovation benefits from a more macro perspective as well. What types of IT Interactions positively impact agents in higher dimensions? As we get better at mining related knowledge and leveraging the EKI we can begin to identify social structures and phenomenon like trust, mutual commitments, and so on. These factors will increasingly play a role in IT's ultimate utility and related innovation.

TASKS FOR ACE STRUCTURE AND INNOVATION

1. What future innovations could benefit the organization?
2. What are the tradeoffs - costs and benefits from the perspective of BioS stakeholders?
3. Identify how the potential innovations influence the strategy of the organization.

THINGS TO THINK ABOUT

1. Elaborate further on the opportunities for innovation that present themselves to the print media companies.
2. What operational and organizational impediments exist? How can these be overcome?
3. In what ways does IT enable the fractal enterprise? What are the advantages and disadvantages? Illustrate your argument with a detailed example in a specific domain.

REFERENCES

Arie, G. (1997). *The Living Company: Habits for Survival in a Turbulent Business Environment*. Massachusetts: Harvard Business School Press.

Battram, A. (2001). *Navigating Complexity*. London: Industrial Society.

Boczkowski, P. J. (2004). *Digitizing the News*. Massachusetts: The MIT Press.

Bower, J.L. & Christensen, C.M. (1995 January/February). Disruptive Technologies: Catching the Wave. *Harvard Business Review, 73*(1), 43-53.

The Future of the New York Times. (2005 January). BusinessWeek Online, Retrieved November 23, 2008, from http://www.businessweek.com/magazine/content/05_03/b3916001_mz001.htm.

Capra, F. (2002). *The Hidden Connection*. NY: Random House.

Christensen, C. M., & Bower, J. L. (1996 March). Customer Power, Strategic Investment, and the Failure of Leading Firms. *Strategic Management Journal, 17*(3), 197-218.

Christopher, M., & Peck, H. (2004). *The Five Principles of Supply Chain Resilience*, Logistics Europe.

Coltman, T., Devinney, T. M., Latukefu, A. S., & Midgley, D.F. (2002 August). Keeping e-business in Perspective. *Communications of the ACM, 45*(8), 69-73.

Digital Media Project. (n.d). Retrieved November 23, 2008, from http://www. chiariglione.org/project/

Economist.. (October 2008). *Where the Could Meets the Ground*. The Economist Online. Retrieved November 23, 2008, from http://www.economist.com/research/articlesbysubject/displaystory.cfm?subjectid=348909&story_id=12411920

Stopping The Presses. (2005 February 22). Forbes Online. Retrieved November 23, 2008, from http://www.forbes.com/2005/02/22/cx_pm_0222news.html

Fiksel, J. (2006). Sustainability and Resilience: Toward a Systems Approach. *Sustainability: Science, Practice, & Policy, 2*(2), 14–21.

Fiksel, J. (2003). Designing Resilient, Sustainable Systems. *Environmental Science & Technology, 37*(23), 5330-5339.

GENI: Global Environment for Network Innovations. (n.d.). Retrieved November 23, 2008, from http://www.geni.net/

Hamel, G. & Valikangas, L. (2003 September). The Quest for Resilience. *Harvard Business Review*, (pp. 52-63).

Hart, S., & Milstein, M. (1999 Fall). Global Sustainability and the Creative Destruction of Industries. *Sloan Management Review, 41*(1), 23-33.

Hollnagel, E., Woods, D., & Leveson, N. (Ed.). (2006). *Resilience Engineering: Concepts and Precepts*. Aldershot: Ashgate.

Kaufmann, A., & Todtling, F. (2001). Science-industry interaction in the process of innovation: the importance of boundary-crossing between systems. *Research Policy, Elsevier, 30*(5), 791-804, May. [Downloadable!] (restricted)

Larson, E. V., & Brahmakulam, I. T. (2001). *Building a New Foundation for Innovation: Results of a Workshop for the National Science Foundation*. Retrieved November 23, 2008, from: http://www.rand.org/pubs/monograph_reports/MR1534/MR1534.chap3.pdf

Levy, D. (1994). Chaos Theory and Strategy Theory, Application and Managerial Implications. *Strategic Management Journal, 15*, 167-178.

Looney, C. A., & Chatterjee, D. (2002 August). Web-enabled Transformation of the Brokerage Industry. *Communications of the ACM, 45*(8), 75-81.

Mackenzie, D. (2002 February). The Science of Surprise: Can Complexity Theory Help Us Understand the Real Consequences of a Convoluted Event like September 11. *Discover, 23*(2).

Mobile Computing Opportunities and Challenges. (2003 December). *Communications of the ACM, 46*(12).

Moore, G. (2002). *Crossing the Chasm.* New York: Harper Business.

Nord, W., & Tucker, S. (1987). *Implementing Routine and Radical Innovations.* Lexington: Lexington Books.

Ottino, J. (2003 February). Complex Systems. *AIChE Journal, 49*(2), 292-299.

Prasarnphanich, P., & Gillenson, M. L. (2003 December). The Hybrid Clicks and Bricks Business Model. *Communications of the ACM, 46*(12), 178-185.

Porter, M. (1985). *Competitive Advantage.* New York: Free Press.

Pettit, T., Fiksel, J., & Croxton K. (2008). Ensuring Supply Chain Resilience: Development of a Conceptual Framework. To appear in *Journal of Business Logistics.*

Rogers, E. M. (1976 March). New Product Adoption and Diffusion. *Journal of Consumer Research, 2*(4), 290-301.

Roth, A. E. (2008 March). What Have We Learned from Market Design? Hahn Lecture, *Economic Journal, 118*, 285-310.

Tiwana, A. (2002). *The Knowledge Management Toolkit* (2nd ed.). Englewood Cliffs: Prentice Hall.

Starr, R., Newfrock, J., & Delurey, M. (2002). *Enterprise Resilience: Managing Risk in the Networked Economy.* strategy+business, Issue 30, Retrieved November 23, 2008 from http://www.strategy-business.com/press/16635507/8375

Sampson, G. (2003 November). The Myth of Diminishing Firms. *Communications of the ACM, 46*(11), 25-28.

Stromberg, S., & Carlson, J. M. (2006). Robustness and Fragility in Immunosenescence. *PLoS Computational Biology, 2*(11), 1475-1481.

The Paper Trade. (2005 July). Time Inside Business.

The Digital Media Manifesto. (n.d.). Retrieved November 23, 2008, from http://www.chiariglione.org/manifesto/

Time Magazine (2005 August 8). Al Gore: Business Man.

Walker, B., Holling, C. S., Carpenter, S. R., & Kinzig, A. (2004). Resilience, Adaptability and Transformability in Social–ecological Systems. *Ecology and Society, 9*(2), 5.

Zhou, T., Carlson, J. M., & Doyle, J. (2005). Evolutionary Dynamics and Highly Optimized Tolerance. *Journal of Theoretical Biology, 236*(4), 438-447.

ENDNOTES

[a] This report summarizes the results of a National Science Foundation workshop, Partnerships: Building a New Foundation for Innovation, held June 18–19, 2001, in Arlington, Virginia. The workshop and this report were sponsored by the National Science Foundation's Partnerships for Innovation program and were conducted within RAND's Science and Technology Policy Institute. The PFI's focus on the seams was a feature of the program that most workshop participants seemed to find quite laudable. A recent study by Kaufmann and Todtling concludes that "[c]rossing the border to science, in particular, increases the diversity of firms' innovation partners and respective innovation stimuli which, in turn, improves the capability of firms to introduce more advanced innovations." See Kaufmann and Todtling (2001).

[b] Also see http://www.12manage.com/methods_porter_value_chain.html

[c] http://en.wikipedia.org/wiki/Amazon_SimpleDB

[d] Orthogonal to Porter's five forces introduced in Chapter 2.

[e] http://en.wikipedia.org/wiki/The_Long_Tail

[f] http://www.truveo.com/

[g] Regulations apply - 1394, HDMI. IP is not an allowed digital output. Fore example Cablelabs.com has PHILA license agreement, CHILA license agreement.

[h] http://www.geni.net/

[i] http://www.ascap.com/index.html

Chapter X
Research Topics in Complex Systems

ABSTRACT

The Adaptive Complex Enterprise framework presented provides a basis for integrating many related areas of research into a services discipline. We have shown the framework is widely applicable to any kind of organization. Here our focus is on the articulation of further research needed for the IT-enabled business innovation, resilience and effectiveness. At a high level, see Figure 1, the related research topics are 1) ACE Co-engineering Theory which covers the development of context-based methods for the conceptualization, prioritization, and implementation of service-oriented solutions; 2) Knowledge Infrastructure for delivery of services, 3) Integrated Development Environment for service life-cycle management and continuous improvement of highly distributed complex systems, and 4) Transformation and Innovation Practice.

While it is true that technology research in emerging trends like bio-info-nano integration will increase in importance, there is also a fundamental realization that the management of complexity will itself become a critical area of research. This is especially true since other related IT trends like virtualization, miniaturization, and distribution will also increase the complexity of deployed systems. Here we will explore the underlying challenges.

Industry relevance: To leverage IT for enterprise transformation, we need to be able to reason about highly complex systems and maximize their performance to meet business and process Goals. The overall objective is to streamline the way by which value is delivered by technology both 1) within service-oriented primary

Figure 1. ACE research topics and relationships for complex systems

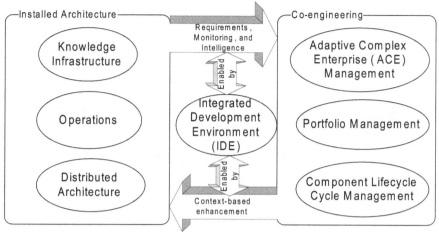

processes and 2) internal secondary IT and related processes that enable primary processes. In addition opportunities for new business process services and their enablement must be also identified and deployed without impeding the on-going services. This requires a conceptualization that enables us to make good engineering decisions about improving performance in the context of existing systems.

To begin an understanding, we turn to Figure 2 that puts into perspective the evolution in IT-related disciplines. As illustrated, IT has been evolving from making it easier to program (in the 80's and 90's) to making it easier for technology to adapt to the changing business processes (2000s). Consequently, the research issues are no longer just on the creational aspects of technology, but have shifted also to the service life-cycle management aspects. This shift is illustrated by increasing interest in the 'Co-engineering' areas on the right of Figure 1.

Adaptation is achieved through the alignment of service-oriented components as determined by the portfolio to meet the ACE needs for achieving the BioS goals. At the same time in Figure 1, there is a need to acquire knowledge (based on requirements, monitoring, and mining) from the distributed architecture and operational Agent Interactions. The information is synthesized to inform ACE decision making and the next generation of enhancements. Thus the role of the Interactive Development Environment (IDE) has evolved in recent years to the management of complex systems and the life-cycles of their constituent services. We cover each of these research areas next.

Figure 2. Evolution of research in IDE from creational aspects to life-cycle and continual improvement aspects

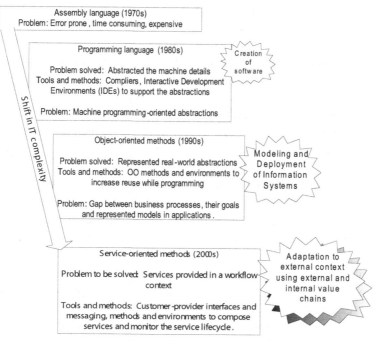

CO-ENGINEERING

The research is to develop the theory of Agent Interactions and resulting value-creation within any goal-directed complex system. The Co-engineering theory, based on a widely-applicable ontology, provides a framework for knowledge formalization and sharing across disciplines that also increases opportunities for better management. Since the Interactions of Agents are managed to deliver value to *Business-IT use-Operations-Strategy* as they provide services, the ontology forms the basis for methods that provide the right information for decision-making. Research topics here are as follows.

ACE Management

ACE ontology and Services Science: The objective of the ACE Framework is to begin with an Ontology[a] for customer-provider Interaction that allows us to understand in a deeper way and organize the numerous dynamic many-to-many relationships between processes, organizations, applications, and assets for business purposes. The ACE ontology proposed here is minimal and focuses on points of variation. It organizes the extended enterprise into a complex of external and internal value-chains of adaptive integrated planning-execution Interactions. The result is the representation for work products, inter-disciplinary analysis, and consequent engineering of services delivery. Important features of this conceptualization are to:

- Frame the value of the *to-be* solution for all the stakeholders of the complex system when adapting the as-is actions to achieve the next to-be state.
- Provide a structure for the integration and application of interdisciplinary selected complementary best practices, tools, and methods in a consistent way so that both the architecting and operating – that is, the *life-cycle* aspects - of the complex systems and services are addressed.

While this provides a solid basis for applying and related existing best practices as we have shown in this book, the ACE framework must be more widely research to develop 1) empirically-based principles and theory, and 2) tools and methods for the adaptive business and technology Co-engineering. See other approaches in Akerman & Tyree 2006. The reader is also encouraged to peruse recent special issues Services Science 2007, Services Orientation 2008.

Complex System of Autonomous Agents: How does a complex organization react and adapt to external goals? According to contingency theory, differentiation and integration in complex organization changes with external forces (Lawrence and Lorsch 1967)[b]. How do Roles interact and work collaboratively to achieve system Goals? What types of requirements for effective self-correcting components can be derived from the ACE context? What tools and methods can help us better manage the operational behavior of a complex system, given service and operating levels? What principles identify the achievable service levels and relationships to operating levels through realistic definitions that reflect available Roles and resources?

Policy Languages: The behavioral adaptation of a complex system requires the development of a policy language that can state declaratively the needed changes that must occur within the system. This will allow us to effect changes though computer assisted environments that implement the details though rules and directives to the Agents. Related research issues are - How can we design policy languages that precisely represent and relate externally-driven system Goals to Interaction changes and vice versa (a starting point is in Dakshi et al 2007)? Can we better determine the achievable operating levels given a particular binding? How can we develop 'critics' that can monitor autonomic Agents, their Role performance and their ability to adapt? How can we formalize the SL-to-OL mappings to explore issues like derivation of OLs from SLs, the "satisficing" of SL by OL, and the resolution of conflicting OL directives on a resource (Aib et. al 2006). How can we determine the achievable OL of a Role set? Of a Role?

Enterprise Modeling Research: What precise notations and semantics allow us to create work products that help represent and Co-engineer the Interaction behaviors within complex systems? Does the modeling represent the correct and complete set of abstractions to allow us to reason about both technology and organization-level problems and help us achieve the Goals? How can we model the layers of the Business-IT behaviors and develop methods to align this with improved value to stakeholders? How does this relate to existing modeling environments? How do we characterize, model, measure, and manage the performance of service life-cycles in complex systems?

Enterprise Architecture Patterns: How does the ACE theory along with architecture patterns help us move enterprise integration from an art (resulting in unpredictable project cycles, hard-to-maintain code, high costs, and risks of outsourcing) closer to an engineering discipline? That is instead of treating each enterprise project as a 'one-off', how can the conceptual framework allow us to develop complex systems by assembling patterns, recursively? How does this work with existing frameworks and patterns? How can we leverage the recursive ACE structure to define standardized enterprise work products that make it easier to train and deploy quality services. (Wang 2003).

Scaling through Composition: What are the patterns that allow us to compose and scale methods to support services within a larger complex of services? In computer science 'design pattern' has come to mean the design-oriented problem-solving template, applicable in specific contexts, for assembling objects into a solution (Gamma 95, Alexander 77). For example, a pattern begins with a business problem, context, solution principle, performance, structure, deployment, variants, known uses, dynamics, and implementation. An ACE pattern template, in addition, includes 1) measurements of the effectiveness of the final solution execution with the BioS goals, 2) accumulated benchmarks across solutions, and 3) a Web Services based pattern configuration environment. Thus, we use the word pattern to refer to the problem solving and also the dynamic behavior during the life-cycle of the eventual solution. Since patterns apply in a precisely defined context and solve a specific type of problem, patterns provide an enhanced vocabulary, a basis for relating patterns, and a resulting ontology for ACE.

Eventually the goal would be to develop a theory of adaption for artificial systems.

Portfolio Management

What general principles and systematic techniques relate the specific ACE Interaction structures and performance to BioS value? We would like to understand how the Interaction networks relate to the achievement of goals. For example, the response time of Interactions is important to an agility goal but the method of resource use of the same Interactions also impacts the somewhat different Lean goal. We wish to better understand and quantify the relationships between such goals. By using the underlying principles, we can apply algorithms to better understand trade-offs that relate the service Interactions, service life cycle considerations, and service goals. The result would be in visualization at a conceptual level - using techniques such as 'heat maps' (as in Business Components) - that aid decision making.

Component Life-Cycle Management

What knowledge (based on monitoring, behavior mining, and simulation) will help develop a better understanding of where to prioritize local improvements and what impact to expect globally. For example where can we change the workflow to achieve better behavior though automated Agents? Can rapidly identify the change of resource capacity and binding to Roles for improving performance? What are the policies that govern Interactions and Role set services to achieve overall service levels? How can these policies be rapidly deployed? How does this relate to the underlying CMDB?

INSTALLED ARCHITECTURE

The enterprise portal and related web services are fast becoming an interface for all kinds of Interactions - self-service, business events, collaboration between Agents involved in delivering a service and so on. This is especially true within the service-oriented businesses, where the non-routine processing of requests requires a greater degree of social Interaction and knowledge in order to achieve an effective response.

As systems like CMS, CRM and ERP become the EKI front-ends to a variety of back-end components within the organization they are also required to enable Socio-technical Interactions and address the challenges of knowledge capture and delivery. They have to be designed to evolve in the way business-technical-social Interactions evolve. They also become the interface to more traditional services provided by enterprise data management back-end systems. These are typically considered 'closed' as their inherent models do not permit the evolution of practices through sharing within the network of practitioners.

The ACE framework supports Co-engineering of strategic front-end and enabling back-end transformations. Within organizations the strategic *front-end evolution* is reflected by trends like self-service, flexible collaborative Interactions, end-to-end support, crisis management, emergency response, and circumstance-based mining of user patterns. Performance-based analysis schemes like the 'competitive model' and 'balanced scorecard' direct the Co-engineering roadmap to meet strategy targets. The *back-end evolution* is towards efficiency and resilience leveraging frameworks like ITIL, Lean, TOGAF, Quality, and software development methods. Thus, at a high level the front-end evolution is towards Collaboratories and the back-end evolution is towards Lean and Quality services. Understanding this evolution also provides the context for innovation. For example, the evolution of an organization towards a more adaptive complex one often begins with enterprise integration projects for the Customer Service Center. Many front-end and back-end challenges underlie this, thus providing a fertile ground for field research and practice as follows.

Knowledge Infrastructure

New approaches are emerging. For example, OpenSocial helps sites share their social data with the web. Applications that use the OpenSocial APIs can be embedded within a social network itself, or access a site's social data from anywhere on the web. See also Opensocial 2008. Another example covered here is the Customer Support Service Center where the knowledge of known problems would reduce the time to handle new incidents.

Self-service: As the customers seek more customized products, the role of self-service has increased in importance. These services range from accessing status (as in postal tracking) to product configuration at the website. How are these services composed and used from the users' perspectives?

Collaboration: Another starting point is the concept of 'Collaboratory' which has been defined to be a place where scientists and researchers work together to solve complex interdisciplinary problems, despite geographic and organizational boundaries[d]. Many processes encompass a wide range of technical, social, and procedural activities (see some examples in GAO reports 2004, 2005, 2006). Information is collected, combined, analyzed, derived, discussed, and distributed. It is not just an infrastructure for dissemination but also for integration from multiple content sources and web services. Related research topics include the following.

Communities of Practice: As mentioned earlier, socio-technical Interactions also result in the Enterprise Knowledge Infrastructure (EKI, Maier 2005) phenomenon in which local knowledge emerges during practice. This can range from customer knowledge to response knowledge. Due to this, new types of requirements are often encountered as part of enterprise portal initiatives to provide an integrated interface to different communities of users.

Knowledge Structures: What are useful underlying methods (ontologies, mining techniques, etc.) to understand and configure the services of the evolving complex system so that 1) services can be specific to communities and 2) collaboration around service life cycle can capture and use new knowledge. For example, how do we know that a website works well for new purposes? How can we mine the intent from posts and blogs to better understand the communities being serviced? What are the abstractions to better to mine business intelligence and use this to support stakeholders? How can we identify and support new contexts in which the user may want to access existing services? Overviews are in Mazzola, G. and R. Poli 200, Fayyad et al 1996 and Han 1995.

Monitoring: What are ways of monitoring community performance and the value of Interactions to support the evolution of knowledge? How can we show that performance improves through more relevant knowledge? Can we use IT to better support this evolution? An example of support for a practice community is the professional development for teachers, knowledge creation, and assessment of skills. Are Interaction patterns of high performers the same as others? What are the measures of sustainability of a website or community? What is the resource and service consumption during Interactions? Can this be used to predict the needs of users?

Pull System: How can we use the mined knowledge for more effective support. For example, can we improve using 'pull' rules to automate the accessibility to better underlying services and content? An example is the use of ontology principles like facets that help go beyond the standard search with views tailored to a community of users. What rapid deployment frameworks and patterns help organize significant amounts of content and deliver value leveraging the advanced functionality of content management systems? How can we enable end users to do more?

Visualization, GIS etc.: What are ways of visualization community and performance information from the perspective of stakeholders? How can we integrate web services and GIS within collaboration spaces to provide customized services? What new ways of knowledge capture and dissemination can be accomplished through web 2.0 features?

Mobility: What new types of business processes are made possible through remote access and mobility?

Security and Assurance: What are the needs of inter-organization collaboration? How can we integrate content from multiple sites? What are the related issues like copyright and Role-based security? What are the standards that apply and how, especially when going across organizations? A good starting point is Bertino et al 2009.[c]

Operations

Application Research: Evolve ACE framework and related patterns through field research. This is achieved by showing exactly how the conceptualization and

Work Products improve complex system performance in specific domains. More case studies are needed to provide insights. What are prototypical Interactions in a domain? How can they be mined to help us identify and automatically synthesize actual Interactions within the existing environment? How can we draw upon Business Component research and Interaction performance to provide automatic maps for different types of decision-making? What solution patterns tie service Goals to technology deployment? What can we learn through applications and empirical results that will guide the refinement of theory? What principles relate service life cycle aspects such as architecture, development, operations, capacity, security analysis, economics, retirement, and audit.

Empirical Research: What empirical evidence can be obtained to support the identified principles for achieving specific Co-engineering of BioS Goals?

- *Business Intelligence research:* What intelligence mining opportunities exist with Interaction performance to provide traceability between business Goals and Interactions? What layered sensing and monitoring frameworks provide information for decision making? What is the nature of the underlying federation and reference architecture? What layers and components is this made of? What policies of information management apply and how can these be supported?
- *Policy research:* Validation of management policies relating SLs to Agent OLs through an in-depth exploration of different Business-IT scenarios such as capacity management, charge-back, and disaster recovery with the objective of identifying policies which are successful for ACE (See Efstratiou et. al for a starting point in policy driven adaptation of mobile computing).

Innovation Research: Applications of technology to areas of innovation within the primary Interactions to improve competitive positioning. For example, the sensing of patient movement and workflows for improved efficiency within the hospital emergency rooms.

Pattern Mining Research: EA pattern mining to identify the occurrence patterns in the field and to understand the gaps that must be addressed by existing patterns and the actual solution requirements. Of particular interest here is the composition of patterns for more rapid and predictable software development.

Distributed Architecture

Given the trend is towards mobility and distribution, what framework can help in better defining solutions? In efforts to build development and experimental tools for mobile and pervasive applications, it is useful to characterize potential applications using a common vocabulary, so that we can engage in discussions about their architectural, middleware service and development tool requirements. Here we categorize mobile, pervasive applications based on application-specific characteristics independent of underlying architectures or other software or hardware involved in the operation of the system. We also characterize a mobile and pervasive application as an application integrated with its physical environment and/or aware of its location. Note that an application running on a mobile device is not necessarily a mobile application under this characterization. In the remainder of this section we present our method (published in Dombroviak and Ramnath 2007) for developing the taxonomy, the taxonomy itself and possible uses.

Method: To develop the taxonomy, we looked at 14 sample applications from a range of domains, drawn from projects undertaken by us and from the research literature To establish a representative set of applications, we first embarked on a survey of pervasive computing literature. We identified several areas of research including middleware, device communication and discovery and pervasive computing challenges such as security and power management. Additionally, we found many papers describing applications of pervasive computing technologies in the following broad domains: business, medicine, scientific research and entertainment. We selected representative applications from each of these domains and eliminated similar applications. This gave us a set of example applications. Using these applications, we identified a set of relevant characteristics of the applications and associated them with the applications. To show the taxonomy is consistent and complete, we charted the associated characteristics for each application to visually demonstrate the similarity of the categorizations of similar applications as well as the differences between the categorizations of different applications. We determined the taxonomy is useful by providing counterexamples to show that the characteristics are independent from one another.

Characteristics: In this section we identify and describe the characteristics. Note that some characteristics, such as time constraints, have sub-categories. Finally, for each category, we provide examples of how each characteristic impacts the application architecture.

Transitionality: The degree to which use of the application occurs in varied environments. The transitionality could range from having to operate in just one environment to having to transition between many varied environments. More transitionality indicates the need for or the existence of multiple architectures with varied devices and hardware.

Time Constraints: Whether the application has real-time constraints or is delay-tolerant. Applications can either accept some delay in output or require a real-time response. Real-time requirements usually indicate the need for greater and more reliable bandwidth than delay-tolerant applications

Goal: We describe the goal as the type of benefit to be achieved from the application. The goal may simply be entertainment. The goal may also be increased access to information or improved performance. The goal can affect, amongst others, the security, reliability and quality aspects of the architecture.

Collaboration: The degree to which multiple agents participate in a single instance of the application. An agent may be a person or a device located in either a static or mobile location. We define the degree of collaboration as the extent to which the context of agents must be shared, and can be affected and manipulated by the other agents.

Lifetime: The length of time an instance of the application runs. An application may run from a few seconds to several days or for years. The longevity of an instance of the application impacts power requirements and what degree of persistence is required in the infrastructure.

Centricity: A data-centric application primarily collects data. An action-centric application also performs actions in response to the environment. The centricity of an application affects requirements for storage, in-network computation, and communication.

The next 4 categories are all related to location awareness – which is the knowledge by an object of its location. As detailed in [16] there is a rich taxonomy of location awareness. This taxonomy is not a simple one that can be represented as points on a continuum of location awareness, hence we have chosen to list these location-related categories as separate categories.

Absolute Location Awareness: In this taxonomy absolute location is a position in a coordinate system, frequently the geographic coordinate system. Applications that require knowledge of absolute location typically use methods such as GPS or signal triangulation. Applications may require varying degrees of precision in absolute location information.

Space Awareness: Awareness of location as described by a presence in a particular space. The space may be a building, a room inside it, etc.

Proximity Awareness: The self-awareness of an object's proximity to another object. Proximity awareness generally indicates a need for methods such as sensors.

Transition Awareness: The degree to which an application's behavior depends on knowledge of transitions between spaces. Note that while transitions can be extracted using any of the methods used to determine location, a transition is a location-based event.

Event Awareness: Awareness of events in the application's environment. Event awareness requires sensing capabilities in the system. Higher-level events may be extracted from the occurrence of other events.

Object Awareness: Awareness of other objects in the system and their state. Awareness of the other objects includes their location and attributes of the objects such as their identification, type, owners, changes to the objects, capabilities and simple attributes such as color.

Operational Awareness: The degree to which an application's behavior depends on awareness of system history, such as the context of a workflow.

As mentioned previously, the characteristics in this taxonomy may be used to compare and contrast applications in terms of their requirements as well as middleware frameworks, in terms of their services provided. A very robust middleware would provide many of the services represented by these characteristics. For example, for collaboration, a middleware must provide APIs for sharing and manipulating context. To implement transitionality, a middleware might provide APIs for detecting changes in the environment, locating available services in a new environment as well as handling loss of access to services in the previous environment. Event awareness may require sensing services to detect changes in the environment.

We are currently using the taxonomy as a foundation for building an application simulator framework for this class of applications. Such a framework is aimed at allowing users to quickly develop simulations using parameterized services that correspond to each of the elements in the taxonomy.

Edge-to-Enterprise and RFID-based Applications: A lot has also been said about how RFID tags and other smart sensors embedded into devices can benefit enterprise operations. Pervasive computing goes beyond simple sensing. It integrates intelligence and actuation into the devices and allows the devices to react to events. Not only do pervasive computing enable us to track inventory, but it also has the capability to detect the state of deployed products, gather and communicate to sort and orient inventory according to the content, and detect new conditions that are critical to improved service. Pervasive computing systems can not only monitor resource usage in an enterprise and provide clues to long-term planning, but they can also provide real-time control of resources. Apart from the various challenges in designing the pervasive computing systems itself such as resource constraint devices, mobility and loss prone wireless channels, there are also many challenges involved in applying pervasive computing technology to enterprises:

- How can one seamlessly integrate existing enterprise software with pervasive middleware services? (As an example consider a person or object location / tracking service that is integrated with enterprise software such as Lotus.)
- What type of enterprise and system architecture, for example with autonomous agents, will strike the balance between local capabilities, communicating to enterprise systems, and acting on global directives?

- How can we ensure autonomous agents with accurate information for quick responses, capability improvements, and innovations without the overhead of long-planning and execution cycles?
- What changes are required to currently existing enterprise resource planning software to incorporate pervasive computing systems?
- How can one efficiently store and mine the vast amount of data to facilitate planning?
- What are the techniques for monitoring such complex architectures to reason about the health of enterprise pervasive computing?
- How can one ensure data security?
- How can we reason about variations in the environment and leverage the dynamic assembly for needed service capability?

INTEGRATED DEVELOPMENT ENVIRONMENT

At the heart of the evolution of the service-enterprise is the IDE that will help manage the complex system to meet business objectives. This requires us to rethink and elevate the environment for supporting the entire services lifecycle. We can leverage open environments (like Eclipse model-based tool-integration workbench) to increase the quality and manageability of complex systems, especially in the non-functional areas. In the long-term the workbench must assist in developing components with emergent behaviors to achieve solution Goals. In the short term we must simplify many factors including the distributed nature of service architecture, design, development, testing, operations, and continual improvement. Some of the related technology research topics are as follows.

Model-driven ACE environments: We would like to move to a model-driven environment for complex systems. Such systems would provide traceability at the right points and levels for effective decision-making by BioS stakeholders. The underlying ontology should strike the right balance between a top-down control versus bottom-up evolution to allows us to derive insights and move to new Goal desired states. Such a system should also allow us to define and implement policies with rules that relate desired changes in Goals to Interaction service levels and operating level performance changes in underlying workflow, data and resource services.

From a technical perspective this also requires an understanding of how autonomic concepts can reduce management complexity. Not only must we identify the principles and patterns for localization of complexity into autonomic components but also address the global directives and policies. Within an adaptive environment, all this begins with a cycle starting with the monitoring of autonomic Agent behavior knowledge to identify behaviors of Agent clusters leading to understanding and improvement.

There is a need for vendor-agnostic foundational tools for the rapid assessment of possible scenarios and an integration platform for a suite of tools. The basis for will come from expanding current model-driven programming concepts to an enterprise and business computing tool set as illustrated in Figure 1. What modeling abstractions, like ACE, help with more effective development of services and compositions in the context of the deployed system characteristics?

Integrated Real-time Monitoring: Develop Open Standardized Application Monitoring Interfaces (that can be integrated with heterogeneous products) for ACE Visualization and for knowledge-based decision making that can be installed in an evolutionary way with existing technologies. This includes the *development and real-time monitoring environments* that are extensions to commercial products and the use of standards (like OASIS standards for Web Services).

Use of existing frameworks: How can we leverage today's enterprise systems that are evolving to become enterprise frameworks and offer development environments to build upon underlying services (SAP[f])? While such frameworks enable the development of new services on proprietary systems, what challenges remain when considering heterogeneous components and composite services? How can we populate the more abstract models suited for decision-making using real-time monitoring tools[g] and the use of standards[h]? How can we provide integrated monitoring of deployed IT services? Many tools exist for individual platforms and applications. How do we synthesize this information into more abstract models and use visualization for effective decision-making?

Reverse engineer legacy-rich environments: What can we learn from production flow analysis, material flow analysis, part family formation, design of manufacturing cells, facility layout design to support facility planning and extend to complex systems involving varied processes involving Goals, stakeholders, information, resources and assets?

Virtualization: Vendor products are rapidly evolving to support virtualization and autonomic concepts to implement this using dynamic provisioning. How do complex system patterns leverage this evolving trend and address non-functional aspects?

WS* components: Existing specifications for Web services describe the indivisible units of Interactions. It has become clear that taking the next step in the development of Web services will require the ability to compose and describe the relationships between lower-level services. How do we enable new Interactions with Web services linked to support new usage patterns using standards like OASIS?

Real-time interface: Develop Open Standardized Application Monitoring Interfaces (that can be integrated with heterogeneous products) for Interaction performance visualization. What ontology underlies the organization of enterprise architectures so that we can organize work products and use semantic technologies retrieve them as needed during the service lifecycle. The Business-IT aligned ACE scheme serves as a basis for analysis techniques that can take as-is metrics and predict the overall system behavior and target to-be improvements. The environment would also be for developing and modifying policies interactively. Validation in real environments that use RFID and wireless sensor deployments, monitoring, and telecommunications software is important for further understanding.

When fully implemented, ACE will provide the context for self-managing autonomous system components that reduce the cost of management of complex systems by adapting to achieve desired behaviors. This is conceptualized as different types of Interactions and monitoring technology that yield insight into the successes and failures in the evolution of services and knowledge. We are exploring the use of an ACE based ontology and technologies like the semantic wiki and web.

With these motivations we suggest the development of Process-based integration of engineering tools as a starting point[j]. In addition it is important to integrate frameworks for a simulation environment for mobile and pervasive computing applications with the goal of gaining an understanding of pervasive software and to provide a framework for reasoning about it. A roadmap is to begin with integration issues related to platform, presentation, data, control, and process using Eclipse as the platform basis, jBPM as process component[j], domain tools, GUI Frameworks (Standard Widget Toolkit [Eclipse], JFace[k]), and Eclipse API and Plug-in manifests for control[l].

TRANSFORMATION AND INNOVATION PRACTICE RESEARCH AND CHALLENGES

One of the most basic observations made in Engineering 2020 that we would like to echo is that much innovation occurs when working on Industry sponsored challenges. Most of the applied research reported here was conducted through long-term collaboration with Industry. Such long-term projects are infrequent in research institutions, especially in the field of computer science. Further the nature of many of the results here are such that they have required an immersion in Industry-facing challenges so that the appropriate solution experiences could be abstracted and consolidated with academic methods. For more of this type of research to be feasible, a re-examination of the roles of typical research institution is insightful. We begin such a process especially for Engineering disciplines below, using the techniques presented within this book.

Environmental context and trends: As global forces change the environment for organizations it also seriously impacts the environment within which academic organizations and units (colleges, schools, departments, centers, teams) must succeed in the future. For example, in the U.S. there is a reduction of funding available to academic Engineering departments; outsourcing of commodity skills have resulted in important shifts in workforce needs and graduate demand; and opportunistic commercial training and educational businesses encroach on the traditional academic roles of mining, developing, and freely disseminating knowledge. Since the changes impacting businesses are accelerating, these forces too might significantly affect dormant academic institutions.

How will the academic engineering departments (especially in computer science) stay competitive in such circumstances and provide a supportive environment for the future workforce and economic growth? These types of questions have been posed and researched in several recent reports[m] such as the 'The Engineer of 2020' and the Millenium Project's 'Engineering for a Changing World' (Duderstadt 2008). To summarize the key concepts of the latter: "The purpose of this study is to pull together the principal findings and recommendations of the various reports concerning the profession of engineering, the technology and innovation needs of the nation, and the role played by human and intellectual capital, into an analysis of the changing nature of engineering practice, research, and education. More specifically, it considers the implications for engineering from several perspectives:

1. As a discipline (similar to physics or mathematics), possibly taking its place among the "liberal arts" characterizing a 21st-century technology-driven society.
2. As a profession, addressing both the urgent needs and grand challenges facing our society.
3. As a knowledge base supporting innovation, entrepreneurship, and value creation in a knowledge economy.
4. As a diverse educational system characterized by the quality, rigor, and diversity necessary to produce the engineers and engineering research critical to prosperity, security, and social well being.

More generally, it addresses the question of what our nation should seek as both the nature and objectives of engineering in the 21st century, recognizing that these must change significantly to address rapidly changing needs and priorities. In a sense, this report asks questions very similar to those posed a century ago by noted educator Abraham Flexner, when he examined implications of the changing nature of medical practice for medical education. His premise, "If the sick are to reap the full benefit of recent progress in medicine, a more uniformly arduous and expensive medical education is demanded", drove a major transformation in medical *practice, research, and education.* Today the emergence of a global, knowledge-driven economy based upon technological innovation is likely to demand a similarly profound transformation of engineering *practice, research, and education.*"

In particular we look at why the *mining of practice knowledge* in collaboration with industry and through practice by academics is critical to the creation of new knowledge, innovation, and education in complex systems and services science (Bitner & Brown 2006). Here we apply the ACE framework at a high level to identify some of the actions that must be taken by the interested stakeholders.

Strategy dimension: In the face of the environmental trends, academic leadership often poses the question "What should be the focus of our energies in academic programs and research areas?" In today's world, this is no longer the complete question. By adding the needed emphasis *"...that are most relevant to local and national needs?"* the focus expands from a narrow to a broader view that includes the innovation needs of industry. Academic units that are historically vigilant in assessing publications and grants primarily through peer review must now also sense the *external* context.

In addition to the more traditional purer technology and disciplinary answers to the question of relevance, academic institutions must now also sense and respond to needs of the workforce more effectively. They must now become sensitive to the interdependencies along the value chain consisting of local and national, public and private organizations, and the academic units that are the providers of knowledge. To develop a value-providing strategy, the interactions between all of these organizations must be understood.

Using IT, as an example, we note that the businesses in the United States are now expending 60 to 80 percent of their *internal IT* budget on maintenance. Further, the costs of many business processes executed in the U.S. are often too high to stay competitive. Outsourcing is often seen as a way to reduce costs and free up some of the IT budget held captive in maintenance. This is changing the job market for computer science students in many ways. For example, the official curriculum rarely addresses the challenging aspects of managing IT operations and complex systems, illustrating specific needed skills that are not addressed.

Meanwhile the explosion in the service and system integration business continues to create more and more one-off solutions within a time-and-materials mentality. With a few exceptions, most useful frameworks and methods often become part of the proprietary toolkit of consultants. Not only does this perpetuate the maintenance challenges, it prevents academic involvement and strategically useful research and knowledge creation through practice. Consequently, important challenges of IT remain unaddressed and projects continue to fail to deliver a return. Finally, U.S. is at the apex of the consumption pyramid and juggernaut that creates demand for the global supply chain. In the case of IT, the wake of the resulting outsourcing also helps create competence in other countries. Many are now positioned with the knowledge needed to potentially outstrip their U.S. counterparts. This scenario is also being repeated in other areas like component manufacturing and the pharmaceutical industry.

In other countries, U.S. outsourcing has helped spawned a large number of companies often with a huge impact on the economies, changing the total landscape of cities. Compliance (e.g. ability to meet federal requirements, ISO standards), process quality assurance, and service orientation is becoming part of the culture within some of these more successful organizations. And sometimes this is occurring more quickly than the western and U.S. counterparts. Even within academic institutions, in Asian countries, the leadership is looking at the next level of challenges – ways to provide true value and stay competitive with respect to other emerging rivals within Asia itself. Research investments are often in leapfrog technology that is expected to altogether avoid the problems (pollution clean-up costs etc.) resulting from the engineering and infrastructure choices pursued by the West. Finally, their environment provides opportunities for innovation through the exploration of new markets at the bottom of the consumer pyramid, typically not known to the West. While all this creates a formidable challenge it could also be an opportunity for an improved world order.

Figure 3. Typical forces on a typical academic unit that must be sensed in order to develop a responsive academic strategy

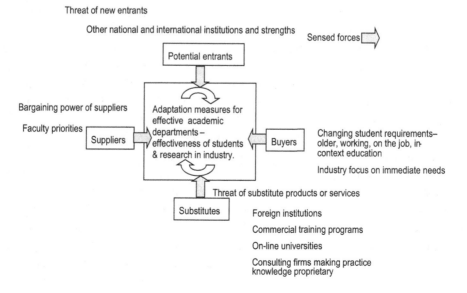

To understand the forces on academic units (departments, colleges, centers etc) we use the competitive forces model of Figure 3. To be successful, the forces (identified by the arrows) need to be sensed both by the academic organizations and their individual academic units.

Academic units interested in stepping up to address the challenges are confronted with today's inadequate knowledge and performance measures. Existing performance criteria (used for example by the National Research Council and U.S. News and World Report) for academic rankings are based heavily on the assessments of peers[n], publications, grants, and other aspects such as resources. While these are very useful measures of ranking, *additional performance questions* are needed to sense innovation areas for each region, industry, and academic discipline.

A more complete set of strategic questions must now be posed and answered as illustrated in Figure 3, based on Porter's framework. Even some externally-oriented industry questions can now be articulated from the strategic perspective of an academic unit as illustrated in Table 1.

Business and operation dimensions: The answer to the properly formulated questions senses the environment to which the academic unit can now *respond and adapt.* The adaptation objective is to align research, practice, and teaching programs to address the critical trends. For example, a faculty member seeking to sense industry challenges through immersion for a five years (i.e. typical cycle-time of a couple of challenging projects) can now do so without penalty. Another response could be to set up effective industry – university collaborations. Such collaborative centers can provide real-life complex test-beds for more relevant research and practice. A more complete set of responses is illustrated in Figure 4.

The benefits to the students entering the workforce are clear. It will allow departments to anticipate the future with appropriate curriculum developments rather than follow the pack. For example, instead of just comparing with other similar institutions, a unit can now also begin to identify new research areas and carve out a niche. In addition, an externally-driven strategy is significantly less risky since by meeting requirements, revenues are more likely to increase. Investments can be then better targeted to achieve external results. However, all this requires decisive actions such as adjusting revenue flow to successful units and to units that will meet future emerging needs. By execution of the priorities, other objectives (e.g. improved rankings, better student placement, and national recognition) can also be better met.

Performance Measures for Continual improvement: The academic unit should also have a built-in SR (Sense and Respond) framework for improvement – a) Sense and measure *external* forces on the department, then prioritize internal response, b) Respond and measure the execution by external customer satisfaction and market

Table 1.

Buyer attributes – student
Does the student have skills to meet immediate business needs or does the business have to invest a significant amount in on-the-job learning? Or is the particular set of skills a commodity? What are the trends in the student population? Are more and more students holding part time jobs? How can these students compete with their peers in other countries that are completely supported and thus more dedicated during the learning process? Should we provide more education in the job context? Which industries are hiring our students? Is this what the students thought they were trained for? For example, are students more likely to work for internal IT departments than IT technology companies? Are the recruiters from targeted institutions coming here? What are they giving as reasons? What are graduating students working on in one year, three years, five years and ten years?

Buyer attributes - practice in industry
How is the practice of a discipline changing? For example, new IT needs are now increasingly generated by uncertain external conditions rather than precisely defined internal considerations. Some recent examples of external conditions affecting business process solutions are growth by mergers and acquisitions, rapidly changing competitive scene with new business models made possible by the Internet, and outsourcing. Even innovations and products are increasingly required to work with pre-existing external components and blend seamlessly into the customers' business processes. Add to this compliance requirement for assurance, privacy, etc. and we have significant complexity. Successful software engineers must manage this complexity and enable the use of IT as a tool to transform the business. Are we training these types of students, according to the changing needs of industry? Is faculty aware of the latest practice methodologies to make their teaching and research more relevant? Are there external sources that are verifying this? How long does it take faculty to react to changes in trends? (For example, does it take ten years to introduce curriculum changes such as an SQL lab after the introduction of the technology? Or, does it take one or two years?)

Buyer attributes – medium and long-term research relevance to industry
Are we exploring the right issues at the boundaries of disciplines that come together in solutions where new challenges first arise? Would industry also agree with these issues? Are there national funding trends supporting this? Can we better influence those funding trends? If we are focusing research on fine-tuning within existing disciplinary boundaries, are we making an order of magnitude impact? Or is industry further ahead of academia in specific areas? With outsourcing for example, even the nature of research topics required to keep U.S. businesses competitive is changing.

Supplier attributes – rewarding performance
Is the applied research group of a unit having measurable impact on businesses? Does our measurement system for faculty facilitate the additional effort needed to establish short-term and long-term industry relevance and changes to the curriculum? Can industry performance and academic performance be better related to allow faculty and industry personnel to move easily between academia and industry? Are there positions, such as Clinical or Practice Faculty, which can promote deeper industry-university interchange? Are the positions defined to attract high-caliber individuals with academic and industry experience and on par with tenure track positions?

needs met, c) Cycle. The SR cycle forces continuous improvement and adaptation. It is an active, systemic approach, fine-tuned by measured attributes.

Understandably, due to the difficulties involved, data identified in the table above is hard to get. But, a start must be made - a few data points being better than none. Whatever the findings for the individual unit, each SR academic units will take root only if some fundamental changes occur in the academic community:

Figure 4. Adaptive Responses by the Academic Units

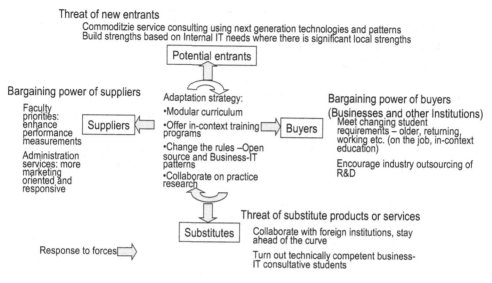

1. Commitment of the ranking agencies to include additional criteria based on the innovation and value to industry. Same with premier funding agencies.

2. Commitment of the academic administration and leadership to provide an environment that fosters relevant faculty as well as team performance through appropriately revised performance measurements and incentives. For example, the value of curriculum development and related innovations should be better reflected.

3. Commitment of academic and industry leaders to foster extended sabbaticals of both industry professionals and faculty in different environments to benefit from project experience and academic theory leading to better formulated research and innovation. This will require strategies to evaluate and equate academic and industry performance within the tenure system as well as the industry merit system.

4. Commitment of each academic unit to maintain an externally-oriented frame-work of attributes and measurements (with feedback from students, alumni, industry) to guide strategy and execution.

5. Commitment by industry to participate actively in advisory boards, provide funded field opportunities for enriching student and faculty and graduate students experience on real-world problems, collaboration on research, and, thus, providing effective feedback and guidance to academia.

6.   Commitment by academia to develop new interdisciplinary capabilities to respond to new situations with a modular organization and curriculum architecture. This includes providing industry professionals with the ability of coming back to the universities for advanced degrees where suitable credit is given for project expereince.

The creation of SR units will initially require effort and more alignment and sharing between individuals. This may be difficult for faculty used to considerable autonomy. Once in place, however, it will result in continuous adaptation to the industry environment. Academic institutions will begin to better fine-tune the skills and innovation needed to stay at the apex of the global value chain and compete successfully. Of course, any course of action pursued in the U.S. must take include collaboration with the global counterparts for the full benefit.

Academic Engineering Center: The Millenium Project (Duderstadt 2008) describes perhaps the best model for a comprehensive approach to creating an "academic engineering center" spanning the full spectrum of engineering education, research, and professional practice as the *academic medical center*. These organizations exploit the synergies of combining medical education, research, and practice. In additions they provide educational programs ranging from undergraduate ("pre-med") programs to graduate and post-graduate training in the health professions to graduate research degrees (M.S. and Ph.D.) to advanced postdoctoral and clinical training. Their research activities range from the most fundamental investigations in genomics and proteomics to translational research with strong clinical applications. Their service activities are similarly broad, from operating large health maintenance organizations to providing medical care at the most sophisticated level to public health policy and civic education. By gathering all of these activities under the umbrella of the academic medical center, one achieves enormous synergies both intellectually (connecting fundamental research with translational research and clinical practice), but also financial management (supporting education and scholarship in part from clinical income). More generally, such an organization takes advantage of the American research university's core competency in building academic programs characterized by an unusual combination of quality, breadth, and capacity in order to achieve maximum impact on society.

TASKS FOR ACE RESEARCH REPORT

1.   Complete your project research report containing - problem, background research and solution.
2.   Make the final presentation to your project sponsor.

3. Apply the five forces to yourself as an individual. Viewing yourself as a consultant, articulate your strategy to be professionally competitive.
4. What are the research issues you have identified?

REFERENCES

Academies, N. (2003). *The Impact of Academic Research on Industrial Performance.* Washington: National Academies Press.

Aib, I., Salle, M., Bartolini, C., Boulmakoul, A., Boutaba, R., & Pujolle, G. (2006 April). Business-Aware Policy-Based Management. In *Proceedings of the First IEEE/IFIP.*

Akerman, A., & Tyree, J. (2006). Using Ontology to Support Development of Software Architectures. *IBM Systems Journal, 45*(4), 813-826.

Author, A. (2004). *The Engineer of 2020.* Washington: National Academies Press.

Bertino, E., Martino, L., Paci, F., & Squicciarini, A. (April 2009). *Security for Web Services and Service-oriented Architectures.* Publisher: Springer.

Dakshi, A., Calo S. B, Lee, K. W., & Lobo, J. (2007 May). Issues in Designing a Policy Language for Distributed Management of IT Infrastructures. In *Proceedings of the Tenth IFIP/IEEE International Symposium on Integrated Network Management* (pp. 30-39), Munich, Germany: IEEE.

Dombroviak, K., & Ramnath, R. (2007 March). A Taxonomy of Mobile and Pervasive Applications. In *Proceedings of the 2007 ACM symposium on Applied Computing* (pp. 1609-1615), Seoul, Korea: ACM.

Duderstadt. J. J. (2008). *Engineering for a Changing World: A Roadmap to the Future of Engineering Practice, Research, and Education.* The Millennium Project, Retrieved November 23, 2008, from http://milproj.dc.umich.edu/publications/EngFlex_report/.

Efstratiou, C., Friday, A., Davies, N., & Cheverst, K. (2002). Utilising the event calculus for policy driven adaptation on mobile systems. *3rd International Workshop on Policies for Distributed Systems and Networks.*

Fayyad, U. M., Piatetsky-Shapiro, G., & Smyth, Padhraic. (1996). From Data Mining to Knowledge Discovery: An Overview. In *Advances in Knowledge Discovery and Data Mining* (pp. 1 – 34), Menlo Park, CA: American Association for Artificial Intelligence.

Friedman, T. (2005). *The World Is Flat: A Brief History of the Twenty-First Century.* New York: Farrar, Straus and Giroux.

GAO-04-321 Report. (2004 May). *Cybersecurity for Critical Infrastructure Protection.* Retrieved November 23, 2008, from http:// www.gao.gov/cgi-bin/getrpt?GAO-04-321

GAO-04-678 Report. (2004 May). *Defense Acquisitions: Knowledge of Software Suppliers Needed to Manage Risks.* Retrieved November 23, 2008, from http:// www.gao.gov/cgi-bin/getrpt?GAO-04-678

GAO-05-434 Report. (2005 May). *Critical Infrastructure Protection: DHS Faces Challenges in Fulfilling Cybersecurity Responsibilities.* Retrieved November 23, 2008, from www.gao.gov/new.items/d05434.pdf

GAO-06-392 Report. (2006 March*). Information Assurance: National IA Partnership Offers Benefits, but Faces Considerable Challenges.* Retrieved November 23, 2008, from http://www.gao.gov/cgi-bin/getrpt?GAO-06-392

Han, J. (1995). Mining Knowledge at Multiple Concept Levels. In *Proceedings of the Fourth International Conference on Information and Knowledge Management* (pp. 19-24), Baltimore, MA: ACM.

Lawrence, P. R., & Lorsch, J. W. (1967 June). Differentiation and Integration in Complex Organizations. *Administrative Science Quarterly, 12*(1), 1-47.

Mazzola, G., & Poli, R. (2000). Semiotic Aspects of Generalized Bases of Data. *In Proceedings of the 9th European-Japanese Conference on Information Modelling and Knowledge Bases*, Hachimantai, Iwate, Japan, IOS Press.

Maier, R., Hädrich, T., & Peinl, R. (2005). *Enterprise Knowledge Infrastructures.* Berlin: Springer.

Open Social. (n.d.). Retrieved November 23, 2008, from http://opensocial.org

International Workshop on Business-Driven IT Management (pp. 55-62), Vancouver, Canada: IEEE Computer Society.

Schon, D. A. (1983). *The Reflective Practioner: How Professionals Think in Action.* New York: Basic Books.

Sheppard, S., & Sullivan, W. (2007). *Educating Engineers: Theory, Practice, and Imagination.* Jossey Bass Wiley.

Service Orientation. (2007 November). *IEEE Computer, 40*(11).

Services Science. (2006 July). *Communications of the ACM, 49*(7).

Services Science Management and Engineering. (n.d.). Retrieved November 23, 2008, from http://www.research.ibm.com/ssme/

Wang, Y., Verbowski, C., Dunagan, J., Chen, Y., Wang, H. J., Yuan, C., et. al. (2003 October). Strider: A Black-box, State-based Approach to Change and Configuration Management and Support. In *Proceedings of the 17th Large Installation Systems Administration Conference* (pp. 159-172), San Diego, CA: USENIX Association.

ENDNOTES

[a] 'Ontologies' and related studies have begun to enjoy currency in various sectors of artificial intelligence, and particularly in (i) the representation of knowledge; (ii) theory of databases; (iii) natural language processing; and (iv) automatic translation. In short, those who most frequently talk about ontology are researchers in the acquisition, integration, sharing and reutilization of knowledge. Ontology comes into play as a viable strategy with which, for example, to construct robust domain models. An ontologically grounded knowledge of the objects of the domain should make their codification simpler, more transparent and more natural. Indeed, ontology can give greater robustness to models by furnishing criteria and categories with which to organize and construct them; and it is also able to provide contexts in which different models can be embedded and re-categorized to acquire greater reciprocal transparency. This piece is based on two talks I gave in the spring of 2005 -- one at the O'Reilly ETech conference in March, entitled "Ontology Is Overrated", and one at the IMCExpo in April entitled "Folksonomies & Tags: The rise of user-developed classification." The written version is a heavily edited concatenation of those two talks. Accessed Dec 2008. Clay Shirky http://www.shirky.com/

[b] Contingency theories generally assert that there is no single best way to lead or structure an organization because the most appropriate ways at any given time are dependent on internal and external environmental factors. In this article Lawrence and Lorsch provide some empirical evidence for their structural contingency theory which illustrates that overall organization performance is correlated to the ability of the individual units of the organization to differentiate themselves to suit the particular kinds of tasks they must accomplish, and their collective ability to integrate with each to support organizational goals. Although much work has been carried out since this article was written, it is

clear that adaptation in the face of increasingly rapid environmental changes is still difficult to achieve in practice and has lead us to explore the interaction patterns and guidelines that can make the process more understandable.

c Sparx http://www.sparxsystems.com.au/ provides an environment for creating UML 2.1, TOGAF, Zachman, OMG SysML (OMG Systems Modeling Language), ICONIX, BPMN, MindMapping, WebModeling, WSDL (for web services), and Schemas for XML. I is also integrated with environments like Visio, Eclipse and so on.

d One example http://www.nsf.gov/statistics/#collab. Another is GENI.

e More information on Center site: http://projects.cerias.purdue.edu/ocrproj/index.html.

f http://www.sap.com/platform/netweaver/index.epx

g Like Tivoli©, InsiteETE©, and Openperspective©.

h Like OASIS standards for Web Services.

i Related work includes Eclipse Process Framework, tools like Tivoli™, Tripwire™, InsightETE™, HP Openview™, and AC policy management tools.

j http://www.jboss.com/products/jbpm

k http://wiki.eclipse.org/index.php/JFace

l http://www.eclipse.org/articles/Article-Plug-in-architecture/plugin_architecture.html

m According to the National Academy of Engineering 2005 report, …"Current trends in research investment and workforce development are early warning that the United States could fall behind other nations, both in its capacity for technological innovation and in the size, quality, and capability of its technical workforce. Unless, the United States maintains its resident capacity for technological innovation and its ability to attract the best and the brightest talent from abroad, the economic benefits of advances will not accrue to Americans."

n Some of the criteria used include peer assessment; graduation and retention rate; faculty resources (for example, class size); student selectivity (for example, average admission test scores of incoming students); financial resources; alumni giving; and, only for national universities and liberal arts colleges, graduation rate performance. The indicators include both input measures, which reflect the quality of students, faculty, and other resources used in education, and outcome measures, which capture the results of the education an individual receives.

Appendix

ACE Continual Improvement Framework Overview

Step 1: Establish the governance, teams, and responsibilities: Team members include ACE in-the-large governance with portfolio responsibilities and in-the-small teams with specific Interaction improvement responsibilities. Together the teams carry out the following steps.

Step 2: Create ACE Structure and model: Use the enterprise modeling notation and patterns to create represent the as-is ACE structure of the business, related BioS goals, Interactions, and Roles. For each Request-Interaction type, create as-is (work products A-F) with metrics attributes gathered from existing sources (strategic plan, response times, help desk reports, project time cards, and financial reports).

Step 3: Co-Engineering loop:
Plan: Apply Co-engineering principles and analysis to identify the to-be enhancements for Interactions, infrastructure Roles, and the related attributes.
Execute: Develop, deploy, and execute the service improvements.
Monitor: Collect metrics (such as cycle time, throughput, and resource use) and use traceability to synthesize as performance attributes of the ACE Goals. Use ACE to see if the desired Interaction improvements are achieved to impact BioS goals.
Analyze: Define project details to reflect the specifics of the next increment of Interaction improvements. Based on cost and value to the business, prioritize across Interactions to develop a roadmap for achieving to-be BioS goals. Maintain the ACE structure as the traceability and rationale for the portfolio of services and portfolio of the related projects.

CREATING THE ACE STRUCTURE FOR CONTINUOUS IMPROVEMENT

The strategy for service improvement is in context based on the Co-engineering BioS. That is we improve Business through supporting an Information infrastructure that enables Operations to deliver on Strategy. The steps to develop these overall relationships are given next. These steps are based on the questions that follow and the filled templates for each organization and sub-organization.

Develop Organizations' BioS profiles. Fill BioS template by answering questions that document the business, information services, operational services, and service strategy of the customer Organizations. This methodology also allows us to follow the Gartner approach of categorizing the core ingredients of IT strategy under 1) Business, 2) Application, 2) Infrastructure, 4) Architecture, 5) People and 6) Financial when developing a "Common Requirements Vision". Teams (with account managers, in-the-large and in-the-small architects involved) complete the template from existing documents (e.g. using the existing Strategic Plan, Organizational charts, and enterprise documents, etc.). Review the BioS with the organizations.

Develop strategic plan. Develop the ACE structure associating the existing and missing services to the goals with as-is performance attributes as identified in the BioS. Co-engineer to develop the to-be attributes of Interactions and consolidate as needed to develop the Organization's strategy as a portfolio of projects for addressing customer's prioritized request servicing needs.

BUSINESS

Performance:

What measures do you regularly report to the Finance Organization for presentations? How does you and your team internally evaluate the performance of your Organization? Can you provide two or three of your key performance measures? What are your annual performance *improvement* targets? How difficult is it to implement performance measures?

Resources:

In which of your priority services or products do you see resource (budget, human) shortfalls (See Strategy Section below)? How many employees do you have? About how many employees do you plan to need in three years? Five years?

INFORMATION and INFRASTRUCUTRE (Team level questions)

Available and missing systems: (To be filled in before the interview process.)

What systems do you use? What software systems are missing? --What are the three most critical sources or pieces of information needed for your Organization to function? -List features or information that you would like to see put on the City's Website and/or intranet to help you achieve your mission. --Identify useful ways to present information to your customers (like

---

GIS). Interoperability needs? --Can you give examples of information-reporting requirements that take time away from focusing on your mission? Who requires this information? --Do you readily have the information to write effective funding proposals or to make the case to extend existing funding? --What three to five pieces of information are you frequently asked to provide on short notice? Who usually requests this information and why? --Do your employees do multiple tasks that require them to use multiple systems or multiple sources of information? What kinds of tasks are these?

Ongoing IT projects: List. **Infrastructure Services:** What other critical infrastructure do you rely on?

IT Feedback: Value of IT?--Has the quality IT services increased, decreased or remained the same over the last, one, three, and five years? -Does the existing Charge-Back Model help you understand what benefits and value you are receiving from IT? How do you interface and plan with ORGANIZATION for upgrades and new initiatives of your Dept.? Name three things that Information Technology is doing well for your Organization? Name three areas in which Information Technology needs to improve?

OPERATIONS (Team level questions)

Requests, Interactions and Priorities: (Some of this can be obtained from the strategy document.) What types of requests do you handle? What are the volumes of each? What resources are dedicated to each type of request? Provide the average time and throughput for each type of request. Identify three highest priority requests. What are the top three information issues in delivering or developing those priority services or products? What do you see as the three to five types of requests that take up the most time in your Organization? Is there any additional information that would significantly help speed up the most time-consuming jobs?

Use of information for process service transactions: What systems do you use to capture the requirements, execute and deliver on each type of request? Is there any additional information that would significantly help you produce or deliver you most critical products or services? Do any of those time-consuming jobs interfere with your ability to produce or deliver your most critical products or services?

STRATEGY (Manager level questions)

Goals: How do you define the mission of your Organization? How does that mission advance the strategic priorities and overall mission of the Organization? What are three specific strategies or priorities and corresponding "strategic activities" for this year for your Organization? How do you view your role? How do you further the goals?

Customers and Products (and Services): Who do you consider your "customers" (citizens, industries and other City Organizations) and what goods or services do you provide for them? What are the three to five services or products that are the priority for your agency at this time? Are these goods or services bundled with, or part of goods and services of any other Organization? Which ones?

Forces – Competition, Substitutes, Compliance: Is there private, public or internal competition for these goods and services? If so, who is it? What environmental (political, legal, economic, regulatory) factors affect the way you operate or do business? Are there any boundaries, regulations, or management constraints or desires on how your Organization operates? What trends do you see in your customer base or environment that are likely to affect your Organization?

Strength, Weakness: How would you characterize your Organization – growing, containing cost, becoming more competitive, transforming etc.? What is your plan to provide more services with fewer resources? How do you intend to become more agile and adaptive to customer needs? What are the three to five internal strengths of your Organization? What are the three to five internal weaknesses of your Organization?

Suppliers: Who do you consider your "suppliers" (all of citizens, industries, other Government agencies, and other City Organizations) and what goods and services do you get from them?

IT Strategy Planning: Do you do a formal justification analysis when requesting funds for continuing or new programs? What information goes into the costs and the performance measures used in this justification? How do you plan for capital needs? What is your process for long term (3-5 year) strategic planning? Is this process documented? **Other:** Please list any additional comments you have.

Organization:. Manager/Director(s): Organization Account Manager: Contributors:	
Business dimension:	
Revenue:	
Budget:	
Resources:	
Performance:	
Other sources:	

Assessment Questions   Score*
(*1.0 = not started to 5.0 = perfection (Source: Gartner))

1   People

    1   Human Resources: We have the right skills and teams in place?

    2   Organization: Our organizational structure is the most appropriate to deliver our services?

    3   Client Relationships: A strong relationship of trust and respect exists with IT?

Information and infrastructure dimension:		Avail.?
IT services		
Vendor services:		
Other dept. services:		

Other Facilities and Assets:		
IT Status and Feedback:		
Projects on-going:		
Feedback:		

Assessment Questions   Score

2   Financial

    1   IT Governance: We have clarity about who makes decisions?

    2   Performance Metrics: Scorecards measure and report performance against the critical success factors?

    3   Budgets   Quality of budget process and charges for services?

3   1   Information Management: Timely information is available and of the right quality?   _____

4   1   Application Strategy:

    2   Business Application Systems: All major systems support the business strategy explicitly?

        _____

    3   Personal Productivity: The right tools are in the place to get the job done?   _____

5   Infrastructure

    1   Service Management: Internal IT processes conform to a recognized quality framework - for example, ITIL?   _____

    2   Technology Environment: Reliable and cost-effective? _____

    3   Asset Management: Our IT resources are well managed?   _____

Operations dimension:

Request type (pri-oritized)	Through-put (avg. # per month)	FTE	Requirements using:	Execution using:	Delivery using:
Teams/Sub-units					

6: Innovation: New opportunities identified and implemented?

Strategy dimension:

Goals:	
Customers:	
Products | Services:	

Forces: Competition, Substitutes, Customer and Supplier Trends:	
Assessment Questions Score*	
6 Business and IT Strategies	
1 Business Strategy: We are clear about the business strategy? _____	
2 IT Strategy: Our IT strategy is clear to all, and the value contribution is recognized. _____	
Strengths | weakness:	
Compliance:	
IT Strategy Planning:	
Other comments:	
IT Assessment: of Architecture	
1 Architecture Framework: We have a well-defined and stable architectural plan. _____	
2 Progress Achieved: We are getting progressively closer to our desired architecture each year? _____	
Total Assessment Questions Score:	

The above questionnaire leads to complete interaction detail as follows:

Strategy	Business	Operation		Triage	Infrastructure use			
Request type and goal	Priority and Value to business	Request volume per month	FTE	Assigned to	Require-ments	Execu-tion	Delivery	Missing Roles
Routine: Payment status > satisfaction	Medium	50	1	Accounts payable	Clerk checks		Posted status info	On-line access to status Doc manag'mt.
Non Routine: Obtain/ex-pand water service Hydrant usage > safety	Very high	700	6	Sales office	Staff works from platt drawings supplied by developer			Automatic-permits Request capture And doc manag'mt.

and also leads to the following work products and associations between them:

A: Request strategy catalog consisting of Request types, deliverables, and strategy goals: These identify the business customer-facing items in a service catalog and goals.

C: RED, Roles Sets, and SLs: for each Request type, the as-is/to-be Interaction service levels, the RED metrics, and the Role Sets and Roles needed to achieve the service.

E: Roles and OLs: A catalog of Roles and OLs needed across all REDs.

F: Agents and Skills: These define what is available to fill Roles as resources.

From these individual catalogs we can create the following work products leading to a set of priorities and rules:

B: Request Priorities and Project Portfolio: This defines the relative value of each Request type to the business which is the basis for focusing improvement resources to achieve to-be service levels. The gaps between the to-be and as-is along with the relative value of fixing the Interactions and underlying Agents forms the project portfolio. The project portfolio consolidates across Interactions based on the costs, value, and scope of Agent improvements.

C: Request Triage rules for incoming Request classification and resource assignment.

Request Triage Rules						
Request Classification			Routing to complete Interactions based on Interaction, Process and Product Characteristics.			
Request type	Quantity	Configuration	PC Install Interaction	Site survey Interaction	Approval Interaction	Assembly & Image Interaction
Routine	Less than 10	Standard	Required	Known	Not required (i.e. net new)	Standard image
Not routine	Less than 10	Standard	Required	Unknown-Cabling not required	Not required (i.e. net new)	Standard image
Not routine	Less than 10	Standard	Required	Unknown-Cabling required	Required	Standard image
Not routine	More than 10	Not Standard	Required	Unknown-Cabling not required	Required	Standard image

EA DOCUMENTATION

The overall objective of the next EA template is to capture experience and create related knowledge for re-use. The governance processes to facilitate this must be implemented as identified in Chapter 3. As mentioned earlier, this template can apply to a continuum of needs:

- For the documentation of a *specific project*
- For the documentation of a *domain-specific case*, that is a specific application of a very generic pattern (e.g. broker) applied to a solve a range of problems in a particular domain (e.g. triage applied to operations).
- For the documentation of a widely applicable pattern of *problem solving* (e.g. broker pattern).

Template fields for EA Business, Information use, Operations, and Strategy Goals:

Strategy Dimension: Competitive perspective

Example: A real world business challenge demonstrating the existence of the problem and a need for the new service or service enhancement.

Context goals: The business situations and goals to which the service may contribute value. What is the fundamental customer satisfaction goal and competitive reason for this service? What is the primary Interaction that will use this service? What are the other Interactions that could use this service?

Business Dimension: Business growth and sustaining perspective

Problem: The business problem addressed in terms of the impediment to the value contribution of the Interaction. Any other relevant details.

Consequences: The benefits the enhanced service provides and any potential liabilities.

Business Performance goals: Value due to the enhanced service? Cost-benefit discussion (e.g. hardware software, investments versus payback). Have all software licenses been paid for?

Operations Dimension: High-level functional flow

Structure: A conceptual specification of the functional and structural aspects underlying the service Interaction. A typical representation is a high level business process flow or package diagrams (for example in SSL). Does the diagram provide a conceptual overview of the system (or proposed solution)? Are all external entities (systems

---

and actors) that interact directly with the system captured in the diagram? Are all the boundaries of the candidate system understood? Does the work product capture the information exchanged between the candidate system and the external entities? Have all relevant interface details been captured? (e.g. input/output, format, frequency) Has the document been reviewed with business users and external system owners (end users and/or domain experts) to verify the system's external Interactions?

Solution: The fundamental solution principles or patterns underlying the service. Were any guiding principles used to arrive at architectural decisions? Examples include identifying a Reference Architecture, Reference Implementation, or Architectural patterns (MVC, n-tier, etc.), design principles, industry standard frameworks/packages.

Analysis: Examples of impact such as side-effects, impact to existing systems, interoperability requirements etc. How did the classic tradeoffs impact the architectural decisions? Examples of classic tradeoffs are: throughput vs. response time, availability vs. backup window, disaster recovery vs. cost.

Operational Performance Goals: Service level requirements such as increased throughput, high availability, reduced resource needs, etc.

Known Uses: Other examples of the underlying pattern in existing systems.

IT Use Dimension: Execution (User/Worker) dimension: Use Cases

Dynamics: Typical scenarios describing the runtime behavior from the business-user perspective. Identify any collaboration and knowledge management use cases. Has the user interface design been documented? For example, with prototype, screen shots, etc. Do the Interaction s between the user and the system meet the users' expectations? Navigation - Have the main flow of navigating between screens/pages/windows/etc. been captured and documented? Window Layouts - Is there a common/consistent "look and feel" from one screen/window/page/etc. to the next? Has the project followed User Interface Guidelines that are applicable to this system? Does the system define types of accessibility, such as Internet, VPN, wireless, PDAs, clients, etc.?

Infrastructure Roles and Goals: *End user goals and metrics:* Usability experience, service-level considerations such as response time.

Role services provided to: All the Roles played by the implemented application/service? What are the services provided by this application/ component (or Agent) to other components that are in deployment? For example, what are the services provided by a directory component and where is it used? For example a SSO might be used in many different ways and in many places. A change to this service Role will impact these.

Services used: Are additional enterprise services used by the proposed application captured? For example, e-mail, authentication, backup and recovery, disaster recovery (DR), system management, security, etc

IT Architecture and Goals: Coding and Testing View: This is what the programmer sees and typically uses design patterns as needed. Are all the key business and supporting classes documented? Are all the static relationships between these key classes identified? For example, relationships such as: association, aggregation, inheritance, etc. Are there test scripts for the major stories and scenarios? Were the test scripts for the major stories and scenarios successfully executed? Are the positive and negative values for each scenario documented? Have you documented the test results? Are separate development, test, and production environments in place?

Has change management software to administer and maintain version control been implemented and is it being used? Is segregation of duties being maintained throughout the change life cycle? For example, source code must be accessible to only the responsible development staff; developers must not have update access to the production environment, including libraries and data; migration of code to production must be the responsibility of non-developer support areas, etc. Is access to source code for internally developed or commercially purchased software limited to those personnel responsible for distribution, maintenance, and management of the software?

Logical View: Document the BB services and relationships, including libraries, application programs, databases, etc. A typical representation is package diagrams. Have all the major architectural components of the system that have or can influence the architecture decisions been captured in the logical architecture? Does the logical architecture capture components such as data repositories used by the system, etc.? Is it possible to trace the major transactional flows in the system using the logical architecture diagram? Are all technology areas and impacted solutions depicted in the logical end-to-end diagram? Does the solution use the enterprise BBs standards such as the directory solution? Are the exceptions recorded?

Data and Integration View: In the logical data model, have all business groupings been identified? (e.g., persons, places, items, concepts and events related to the business needs of the application). Have all the relationships between business groupings been documented? Do the relationships between business groupings show cardinality? Do all the business groupings identified have a name and attributes? Have all the attributes that could serve as unique identifiers been captured? Does the supporting text capture definitions for all business groupings and attributes? Is a standard glossary used where available?

Does the logical architecture capture the mode of information flow between the architecture components and the external systems? Are all the messaging that takes place in order to send or receive information through a common interface been documented? (Bus, data source, XML standards etc...)

Physical View: Aspects of deployment such as servers, routers, workstations, firewalls. Does the diagram representing the physical architecture of the system include the hardware, software and network connectivity, etc.? Does the solution support the TCP / IP standard stack? Are the protocols required by the solution documented? Will the solution use local attached storage; network attached storage, or frame-based storage?

Deployment View: This is how the packaged code will be deployed and managed in operation. This includes a mapping from the logical view to the physical view. A typical representation is using deployment packages. Is there a documented code migration process? How is a code fix produced? How is code promoted into production? How is code demoted from production? Does it map the standard code migration process or are there any deviations?

Has a Deployment Plan been created? Does the deployment plan contain installation steps for all components? Does the deployment plan contain tests to verify that the installation was successful? Does the deployment plan contain tests to verify that the installed system functions properly? Does the deployment plan indicate a back out procedure (i.e., the full scope of back out such as application code, networks, hardware. software, etc.) to back out the changes both immediately (upon installation) and at a later date (after the system has been in production for a number of hours/days)? Does the System Deployment plan cover installation of all system dependent components including (but not limited to) hardware, operating systems, purchased software (from a software vendor), customization necessary for purchased software, and the application?

Have all the configuration items including software and hardware assets been identified (i.e. hardware/software versions, operating system, applications, middleware, settings, drivers, etc.)? Does this address the non-functional requirements of the system, such as availability, disaster recovery, etc.?

Does the deployment plan include training for Users, Help Desk, Operations, etc.? Does the deployment plan contain the escalation procedures?

Does the deployment model reflect the severs, networks, switches, firewalls, etc., for an end-to-end component view? Are all technology areas and impacted solutions depicted in the logical end-to-end diagram? Are single points of failure documented for the end-to-end solution? Does it include all in-scope components / devices and associated risks and mitigation plans? If the solution has a client requirement, does it support a thin or thick client? Will client software need to be loaded? If the solution uses a Java Runtime environment (JRE) which version will be used? Is this version interoperable with the enterprise infrastructure? Will the solution support the standard operating systems? Will the solution support the approved Security templates for servers?

Concurrency View: When a complex system is deployed onto one or more computational resources, this view is needed to reason about the communication and sharing of data later in the Service Level analysis section that follows. Does the model show all the physical nodes? Nodes can include: application server node, directory node, web server node, database server node, etc. Is there a detailed description of each physical node being built, including geographical location, software components, hardware (capacity, CPU, etc.), etc. Does your model represent connectivity information between nodes (i.e. WAN, LAN, Intranet, ISP's, etc)? Is there detailed information on the connections? Such as: ports, protocols, etc.

Code Management View: Configuration management, release management, backup and recovery procedures. Has a formal change management process for making changes to the application and infrastructure (i.e., operating system upgrades/patches) been implemented?

Are change Requests documented? Are change Requests approved by the user and prioritized? Are change Requests tested (e.g., users, IT application areas)? Are change Requests approved (e.g., users, IT application areas) prior to implementation to production?

Does a complete audit trail exist for changes (i.e., can trace change in production back to each key control in the process)? Have procedures for emergency access by developers to production systems been developed, implemented, and tested?

Security View: A) Authentication, authorization, directory services B) Detect, resist, and mitigate C) Logging. Are user security administration procedures in place? Are the functions of access administration and access approval segregated? Are user access Requests documented and approved by user/systems management? Is a periodic review performed to ensure access remains commensurate with job responsibilities (i.e., terminations and transfers)? Are access violations logged, reviewed, and a follow-up performed? Are Special Case IDs utilized? Were alternatives researched, and was it determined that a Special Case ID is the only viable solution? Is an ID Guardian assigned to each Special Case ID?

Have controls been incorporated into the application to help ensure the integrity of system data? Based on the value and sensitivity of the information being protected, are encryption systems and techniques being used, and do they comply with the enterprise framework? Have appropriate controls been incorporated into the application (and interface processing) to ensure the complete processing of data transferred between systems (batch or real time)? Have controls been implemented to ensure that transactions are not "lost" in transit? Are header/trailer records, or similar file integrity checks, being utilized? Are date checks, date and time stamps, and/or error messages/alerts being used? Have edit checks such as reasonableness checks and field validity, balancing routines, management oversight, etc., been incorporated? Are procedures in place to log and resolve abend/production problem/response time issues in a timely manner? Does an audit trail exist indicating who changed the data, and when (date/time stamp)? Is a periodic comparison and/or verification of the database totals to an independent source being performed to ensure data integrity? Has the application's Systems Recovery Plan, which includes supporting infrastructure components, been documented? Has the Plan been tested and updated (based on the enterprise standards)?

Is there a single authentication process for all users to access the system (there are no back doors to the system)? Is all access to backend systems and databases driven by a well defined authorization schema? Are all attempts to access business sensitive resources logged (audit trail)? Is it possible to easily track all access failures so they can be isolated and investigated?

Are intrusion detection systems in place to monitor system access? If applicable, have all firewall ports and protocols been documented (These must be documented in a secure, highly confidential manner)? Has application/data security been implemented to support user Roles and/or privileges? Have application users been granted only the access they require to perform their job responsibilities? Have infrastructure users (i.e., operating system support) been granted only the access they require to perform their job responsibilities?

Have administrative users (i.e., system administrators, database administrators, etc.) been granted only the access they require to perform their job responsibilities? Are users assigned unique user ID's for accessing the application, infrastructure, and data? Does the software that is loaded to workstations, servers, and other computing equipment comply with information security configuration resources, where enterprise has provided such a resource (e.g., Security templates - Windows 2000, UNIX, IIS, etc.)?

Is all access to backend systems and databases driven by a well defined authorization schema? Are all attempts to access business sensitive resources logged (audit trail)?

Is it possible to easily track all access failures so they can be isolated and investigated?

Are intrusion detection systems in place to monitor system access? If applicable, have all firewall ports and protocols been documented (These must be documented in a secure, highly confidential manner)?

Template fields for Operations

Operational View: The specific ways in which operational process (e.g. ITIL support processes) will be supported and how. Have incident, problem and change management processes and procedures been documented to support the solution (I.e. ITIL)? Are the key contacts indicated in the deployment plan for questions before the installation, during installation and after installation? Does the deployment plan contain the escalation procedures? Does the deployment plan include training for Users, Customer Service Center, Operations, etc.? If so, have Users, Customer Service Center, Operations, etc., accepted and signed-off on the training plan?

Has a Request for change (RFC) been Requested and approved? Has an Operations Manual been created? If you have updated an existing Operations Manual, are there any deviations? Has all your SLA performance information been documented? Is it documented in the operations manual?

If your application is responsible for a nightly/weekly/monthly flow of information, have you documented all systems, timeframes, implications involved in that flow of information in the operations manual? Have you identified/documented those components that will need to be backed up (including how often and when) in the operations manual? If your processes have procedures for re-run and/or restart capabilities, have they been documented for both manual and automated startup/restart procedures in the operations manual?

What is the system's expected availability window (i.e. how many hours per day/week is the system to be up and available for use)? Has this been documented in the operations manual and communicated? How long will it take to switch from a primary component/system to a backup component/system? Is it documented in the operations manual? Is the tolerable downtime for the system known and considered an acceptable best practice? Is it documented in the operations manual? Are system components easily upgradeable/ patchable? Have all Roles and responsibilities for vendor, application and infrastructure support areas been documented? Has the impact of failures for one or many application and infrastructure components been analyzed and mitigations documented? Have the data center facilities been documented (I.e. grid locations, power, cooling, etc.)? Has the IP addresses been documented (These must be documented in a secure, highly confidential manner)?

Infrastructure Management View: This includes Administration, Capacity Management, and Disaster Recovery. Are procedures in place for performing application, data, and infrastructure backups with the backup media being retained off-site to facilitate restoration within the recovery windows? Are the backup media rotated off-site to an approved facility? Are errors encountered in the backup process identified and resolved?

Is there a Disaster Recovery Plan (Backup, Recovery, Hot-site, Hardware replacement plan) for the system? If so, please provide the DR plan. Does the Disaster Plan cover installation of all system dependent components including (but not limited to) hardware, operating systems, purchased software (from a software vendor), customization necessary for purchased software, and the application? Does the Disaster Plan cover procedures to restore data and system specific parameters (i.e., passwords and server instance specific variables)? Can this system be installed at a hot site based upon the contents of the Disaster Recovery plan? Has the DR plan been tested? Is there a single authentication process for all users to access the system (there are no back doors to the system)? Does the DR requirements document recoverability expectations between data centers (i.e., RPO, RTO, manual, automated, etc.)? Does the DR option selected map to the Reference Architecture or is it a custom solution? Will standard or custom ITSM processes, such as change, problem, incident, configuration, etc., be used? Does the requirement specify any special requirements beyond basic server/network monitoring, such as processes, transactions, scripts, etc.?

Do the capacity requirements include growth and load for the overall number of users, maximum concurrent users, number/type of transactions, peak transactions, etc.? How does the future capacity compare with current capacity?

Scalability and Performance View: An analysis of peak capacity needed, growth rates, etc. Has the project documented the Non-Functional requirements (the "What" not the "How") of the system? For example, system availability, performance expectations, capacity requirements, disaster recovery, etc. Does the expected availability reflect business hour availability, scheduled maintenance windows, time of day, day of the week, etc.? Do the performance expectations reflect response time for key transactions?

What are the normal quantities of information (traffic) flowing through the system? What level of traffic would be considered abnormal? Have these numbers been documented (i.e. number of concurrent users, number of web site hits, number of batch jobs run, etc.)? Does the failover / redundancy include expectations for components within the data center (i.e., clustering, load balancing, etc.)? Do the scalability requirements describe how the system will handle growth?

Availability Analysis: A definition of availability and the impact on resources. Is system availability monitored to ensure high availability and overall systems availability? If so, what monitoring tools and processes are in place? Are the tools and processes that are in place able to measure system performance to provide an "early warning" of potential failures of the system and it's components? Are all key components within the system monitored and proactive management techniques in place to insure optimum service levels?

Are application errors in key components trapped and corrected automatically when practical? Is the application constructed with the appropriate instrumentation to allow for the monitoring of the performance of each component to measure the End User Response time? Who will be responsible for the repair of system components (including network, software and hardware components)? Has this been documented?

System Management – Monitoring and Analysis: Business continuity, disaster recovery, monitoring, and reporting. Does the system management requirement support the end-to-end solution?

Are impact statements documented for the technology areas used (i.e., server, network, database, web hosting, etc.?

Will the solution require system monitoring capabilities above the standard server and network environments? Are these additional monitoring capabilities documented (i.e. J2EE process monitoring, business transaction monitoring, etc.)? Do the system management tools and alerts support the end-to-end solution? Has a system management structure been documented to include layers to be monitored, tools, and any customization (i.e. network layer, server layer, application layer, etc.)?

Does the documentation describe how storage capacity was derived? Does WAN or LAN network capacity need to be added? Does the documentation describe how the network capacity was derived? Does the solution describe how code/new software will be migrated to production (i.e. test, development, staging, production, system test, unit test, performance test, alpha, beta, etc.)? Has the capacity and performance model been completed? Has the impact to the Customer Service Center and other resources been assessed?

Conformance to Corporate Standards and Guidelines: Document major exceptions from the reference implementations.

Related information

Similar Cases/Patterns: References to patterns that solve similar problems

Related Cases/Patterns: Patterns that help us refine the pattern we are describing.

Variant Cases/Patterns: A brief description of the variants or specializations of the pattern.

Potential Reference Improvements and other Applications: Potential enhancements in the current system or other areas.

Other applicable Best Practice, Standards, Technologies and References: Further information related to the pattern.

Experience: The capture of non-functional tradeoffs related to the above models.

About the Authors

Jay Ramanathan obtained her PhD in computer science from Rice University in 1977. She is currently the director of research at the National Science Funded research site called Center for Experimental Research and Computer Systems for Enterprise Transformation and Innovation (or CETI) at The Ohio State University. She is engaged in developing innovative programs of industry-focused research, practice, and education. Previously she was the founder and board member of Concentus Corporation, Columbus, Ohio and has served in the chief executive officer and chief technology officer roles. In this capacity she managed the commercialization of enterprise workflow technologies and large DARPA funded research programs. She has also served as the engagement consultant deploying solutions for business process management at over 150 companies using emerging technologies for the first time within their organizations. She has also written numerous papers and directed many doctoral students in these areas while a faculty member earlier. She is currently leveraging this industry and academic experience by researching more principled ways for the emerging discipline of services science. Particular areas of interest are adaptive complex enterprise frameworks for business-IT alignment, management and innovation. The underlying research includes both developing more analytic architecture frameworks using conceptual techniques such as patterns, complexity theory and autonomic computing as well as technologies such as middleware, mobile computing, and Web services. This also includes validating the overall effectiveness of business services within its economic ecosystem.

Rajiv Ramnath obtained his PhD in computer science from The Ohio State University in 1988. He is the director of practice at the National Science Funded research site called Center for Experimental Research and Computer Systems for Enterprise Transformation and Innovation (or CETI) at The Ohio State University. He was formerly a vice president and chief technology officer at Concentus Technology Corp. and involved in government and DARPA-funded R&D programs such as the National Information Infrastructure Integration Protocols (NIIIP) project. In this capacity he was also responsible for the development of enterprise workflow technology and its highly distributed development process. He is currently engaged in industry-facing programs of applied R&D, education, technology transfer and practice. Dr. Ramnath's expertise and research interests range from wireless sensor network and pervasive computing applications in the enterprise, to the alignment of business strategy and processes with information technology, enterprise architecture, technology management and integration and software engineering, e-Government, collaborative environments, configurable enterprise systems, workflow, and work-management systems. He has published numerous papers in these areas. He also teaches graduate and undergraduate research, technology strategy and software engineering courses at the Ohio State University.

Index

A

absolute location awareness 361
academic engineering center 372
academic medical center 372
ACE modeling 31, 79, 85, 104, 106
ACE ontology and theory 353
ACE structure 29, 35, 52, 53, 54, 55, 56, 63, 64, 70, 71, 75, 77, 79, 80, 83, 84, 86, 93, 95, 96, 115, 117, 121, 122, 125, 142, 150, 151, 152, 162, 163, 164, 165, 167, 168, 169, 172, 224, 235, 239, 241, 247, 250, 253, 255, 256, 268, 271, 272, 276, 277, 278, 282, 284, 285, 286, 287, 289, 290, 291, 294, 295, 296, 355
ACE structure-based work products 93
Adaptive Complex Enterprise (ACE) 2
allocation of capacity 248, 252
Amdahl's Law 92, 113
application research 358
application server 177
architecture views 20, 23
As-is Value Stream Mapping 280
asset management 131, 254, 273
autonomic computing 14, 17, 112

B

Balanced Scorecard 35, 40, 90, 107, 111, 112, 154, 357
BioS 1, 2, 10, 11, 12, 13, 14, 18, 20, 24, 25, 27, 28, 29, 30, 32, 33, 34, 35, 46, 52, 53, 54, 55, 56, 57, 58, 61, 64, 67, 69, 70, 71, 73, 74, 75, 77, 78, 79, 85, 87, 90, 91, 98, 100, 102, 103, 119, 120, 125, 131, 139, 140, 145, 149, 150, 163, 164, 167, 223, 224, 237, 240, 246, 262, 263, 264, 265, 266, 271, 277, 295, 299, 302, 322, 324, 347, 352, 355, 359, 363
bounded rationality 30
BPEL 135, 157, 295
business and operation dimensions 369
Business Process Lifecycle 9
business process management (BPM) 16, 17, 31, 128, 129, 130, 131, 132, 133, 134, 135, 136, 137, 138, 139, 141, 154, 157, 217, 275, 276
business service capacity 82